W9-BGS-385

Educational Media and Technology Yearbook

For further volumes:
http://www.springer.com/series/8617

Michael Orey · Stephanie A. Jones ·
Robert Maribe Branch
Editors

Educational Media and Technology Yearbook

Volume 35, 2010

In cooperation with the AECT

 Springer

Editors
Michael Orey
Department of Educational Psychology
    and Instructional Technology
University of Georgia
604 Aderhold Hall
Athens GA 30602
USA
mikeorey@uga.edu

Stephanie A. Jones
Leadership, Technology, and Human
    Development Department
Georgia Southern University
P.O. Box 8131
Statesboro GA 30460
USA
sjones@georgiasouthern.edu

Robert Maribe Branch
Department of Educational Psychology
    and Instructional Technology
University of Georgia
604 Aderhold Hall
Athens GA 30602
USA
rbranch@uga.edu

ISSN 8755-2094
ISBN 978-1-4419-1502-3   e-ISBN 978-1-4419-1516-0
DOI 10.1007/978-1-4419-1516-0
Springer New York Dordrecht Heidelberg London

Library of Congress Control Number: PCN applied for

Printed on acid-free paper

Springer is part of Springer Science+Business Media (www.springer.com)

Preface

The audience for the *Yearbook* consists of media and technology professionals in schools, higher education, and business contexts. Topics of interest to professionals practicing in these areas are broad, as the Table of Contents demonstrates. The theme unifying each of the chapters in the book is the use of technology to enable or enhance education. Forms of technology represented in this volume vary from traditional tools such as the book to the latest advancements in digital technology, while areas of education encompass widely ranging situations involving learning and teaching, which are idea technologies.

As in prior volumes, the assumptions underlying the chapters presented here are as follows:

1. Technology represents tools that act as extensions of the educator.
2. Media serve as delivery systems for educational communications.
3. Technology is *not* restricted to machines and hardware, but includes techniques and procedures derived from scientific research about ways to promote change in human performance.
4. The fundamental tenet is that educational media and technology should be used to

    a. achieve authentic learning objectives,
    b. situate learning tasks,
    c. negotiate the complexities of guided learning,
    d. facilitate the construction of knowledge,
    e. aid in the assessment/documenting of learning,
    f. support skill acquisition, and
    g. manage diversity.

The *Educational Media and Technology Yearbook* has become a standard reference in many libraries and professional collections. Examined in relation to its companion volumes of the past, it provides a valuable historical record of current ideas and developments in the field. Part I, "Trends and Issues in Learning, Design, and Technology," presents an array of chapters that develop some of the current themes listed above, in addition to others. Part II, "Trends and Issues in

Library and Information Science," concentrates on chapters of special relevance to K-12 education, library science education, school learning resources, and various types of library and media centers – school, public, and academic among others. In Part III, "Leadership Profiles," authors provide biographical sketches of the careers of instructional technology leaders. Part IV, "Organizations and Associations," and Part V, "Graduate Programs," are, respectively, directories of instructional technology-related organizations and institutions of higher learning offering degrees in related fields. Finally, Part VI, "Mediagraphy: Print and Nonprint Resources," presents an annotated listing of selected current publications related to the field.

The editors of the *Yearbook* invite media and technology professionals to submit manuscripts for consideration for publication. Contact Michael Orey (mike-orey@uga.edu) for submission guidelines.

For a number of years, we have worked together as editors, and this is the seventh year with Dr. Michael Orey as the senior editor. Within each volume of the *Educational Media and Technology Yearbook* (EMTY), we try to list all the graduate programs, journals, and organizations that are related to both Learning, Design, and Technology (LDT) and Information and Library Science (ILS). We also include a section on trends in LDT and trends in ILS, and we have a section profiling some of the leaders in the field. Beginning with the 2007 volume, we have attempted to generate a list of leading programs in the combined areas of LDT and ILS. Last year, we were able to compose an alphabetical list of 30 programs that people told us were among the best. However, this year we decided to be more systematic. Instead of following the *US News and World Report* model and have one top program list, we decided to use some of the same numbers that they use and generate a collection of top-20 lists, rather than attempt to generate a statistically significant rankings list. One thought was to rank programs according to the number of publications that were produced; however, deciding which journals to include was an issue. We decided to use 2007 and 2008 as the years to count (since at the time of writing, it is still 2009 and so we do not have a complete year). Furthermore, we decided to only count actual research reports that appeared in one of two journals, *Educational Technology Research and Development* and the *Journal of the Learning Sciences*. These two journals were primarily selected based on the general sense that they are the leading journals in the area of LDT. Noticeably absent is the area of information and library science. So, while these numbers are pretty absolute, choosing to only count these journals is somewhat arbitrary.

The other top-20 lists are based on self-report data collected as part of the program information in the *Educational Media and Technology Yearbook*. Every year, we collect general information about programs in LDT and ILS and publish this information in the *Yearbook*. This year we opted to collect some additional data. We asked the representatives of each of the institutions to enter the US dollar amount of grants and contracts, the number of PhD graduates, the number of master's graduates, and the number of other graduates from their programs. We also asked them for the number of full-time and part-time faculty. We then generated a top-20 list for some of these categories. The limitation in this case is that it is self-report data and there is no real way of verifying that the data is accurate. So, while the list of the 30 top programs last year lacked hard data, and the lists this year are based on numbers, those numbers may be just as unreliable. In the end, we have a collection of lists that we hope will be of use to our readers. Many of the universities that appeared in the top-30 list last year are here again, in addition to many others. More information about many of these universities can be found in Part V of this edition.

There are six top-20 lists in this preface. The first of these top-20 lists is based on a count of publications. We used every issue from the 2007 and 2008 volume years of the *Educational Technology Research and Development* journal and the *Journal of the Learning Sciences*. We eliminated all book reviews and letters to the editor and such others. We only used the primary academic articles of these journals. Each publication counted 1 point. If the article had two authors, then each author's institution received 0.5 points. If there were three authors, then 0.33 was spread across the institutions. Also, as an additional example, if there were three authors and two of them were from the same institution, then that institution received 0.66 points and the institution of the remaining author received 0.33. Finally, the unit receiving the points was the university. So, in the case of Indiana University where they have both a Learning Sciences and an Instructional Technology program, all of the points for IT and LS were aggregated into one variable called Indiana University. Table 1 shows our results. Nanyang Technological University came out as the top LDT program in the world. They were also in my list last year. Interestingly, the University of Wisconsin and the University of Colorado, numbers 3 and 4, were not even on last year's list. The list this year is much more international with universities from all over the world. An interesting result is that since there is not enough variance, we have a 5-way tie for sixth and a 28-way tie for twentieth. We would love to hear your feedback on this approach for the future. Are there other journals that ought to be included? Is it unfair that there are more publications in ETRD than IJLS? What about recent graduates publishing with their new institution when the work was done at their previous institution? I am certain there are many other issues, and we welcome constructive feedback.

The two primary measures of research achievement are publications and grants. While choosing ETRD and IJLS was somewhat arbitrary, the numbers are verifiable. In Table 2, we present the top-20 programs according to the dollar amount of grants and contracts for that program over the academic year 2008–2009. While Table 1 was constrained to LDT, Table 2 has both LDT and ILS programs, which resulted in UNC being number 2 in the grants and contracts list, but not appearing at all in the publication list. Next year, we will count publications in the ILS area. University of Calgary comes out as the top program in terms of grant and contracts. They nearly doubled the amount of the number 2 institution. Texas Tech, who did not show up on my list last year, comes in a strong third in the area of grants and contracts.

Tables 1 and 2 are measures of research productivity. The remaining four tables are more related to teaching than research. The first, Table 3, shows the top-20 programs in terms of the number of full-time faculty. You will notice that the list is correct under the FT category, but number 4, Université de Poitiers, has more total faculty than number 3, the University of North Carolina. We decided that full-time

Table 1 Top-20 graduate programs in the area of Learning, Design, and Technology as measured by the number of publications in *Educational Technology Research and Development* and the *Journal of the Learning Sciences*

Rank	University	Pubs	Rank	University	Pubs
1	Nanyang Technological University	4.33	20	Edith Cowan University	1
2	Arizona State University	3.66	20	Mandel Leadership Inst	1
3	University of Wisconsin	3.3	20	Miami University	1
4	University of Colorado	2.83	20	MIT	1
5	Indiana University	2.66	20	National Cheng Kung University	1
6	Sultan Qaboos University	2	20	Northern Illinois University, De Kalb	1
6	SUNY-Buffalo	2	20	Oklahoma State University	1
6	University of Georgia	2	20	Open University of the Netherlands	1
6	University of Hong Kong	2	20	Queensland University of Technology	1
6	University of New Mexico	2	20	Rutgers	1
11	UCLA	1.83	20	SUNY-Albany	1
12	Stanford	1.5	20	Tel-Aviv University	1
12	University of Illinois	1.5	20	University Central Florida	1
14	Purdue University	1.46	20	University of British Columbia	1
15	Brigham Young University	1.33	20	University of Cambridge	1
15	Florida State University	1.33	20	University of Gothenburg	1
15	Lehigh University	1.33	20	University of KwaZulu-Natal	1
18	University of Memphis	1.2	20	University of Mass-Dartmouth	1
19	Utrecht University	1.14	20	University of Michigan	1
			20	University of Missouri	1
			20	University of Nevada	1
			20	University of Pittsburgh	1
			20	University of Rochester	1
			20	University of Sydney	1
			20	University of Washington	1
			20	UC-Santa Cruz	1
			20	Universidad de La Sabana	1
			20	Wayne State University	1

faculty was more important than part time as a measure and so only generated one list for number of faculty. We just thought it would be interesting to see the total number of faculty as well. For example, it is very interesting that the number 1 university for full-time faculty, Drexel University, has a whopping total of 111 total faculty.

The next top-20 list is the number of PhD graduates. This list might be a good measure of research productivity as well as teaching productivity. It is interesting that Indiana University came out on top, yet I am unsure if this is the number of Instructional Technology or Learning Sciences or both? George Mason comes

Table 2 Top-20 LDT and ILS programs by the amount of grant and contract monies

Rank	University	Department/Program	Total in US$
1	University of Calgary	Graduate Division of Educational Research	$20,000,000
2	University of North Carolina, Chapel Hill	School of Information and Library Science	$11,502,614
3	Texas Tech University	Instructional Technology	$6,000,000
4	Harvard University	Graduate School of Education	$3,000,000
5	George Mason University	Instructional Technology Programs	$2,500,000
6	University of Houston	Curriculum and Instruction	$2,000,000
6	Utrecht University	Educational Sciences Learning in Interaction	$2,000,000
6	Arizona State University; Educational Technology program	Division of Psychology in Education	$2,000,000
6	Ewha Womans University	Educational Technology Department	$2,000,000
6	University of Bridgeport	Instructional Technology	$2,000,000
6	Drexel University	The iSchool at Drexel, College of Information Science and Technology	$2,000,000
12	Indiana University	School of Education	$1,450,000
13	The Ohio State University	Cultural Foundations, Technology, and Qualitative Inquiry	$1,200,000
14	University of Hawaii-Manoa	Department of Educational Technology	$1,097,246
15	University of Wisconsin-Madison	Curriculum and Instruction, School of Education	$1,000,000
15	California State University Monterey Bay (CSUMB)	Interdisciplinary Master in Instructional Science and Technology (MIST)	$1,000,000
15	University of Florida	School of Teaching and Learning	$1,000,000
15	University of Massachusetts, Amherst	Learning, Media and Technology Masters Program/Math Science and Learning Technology Doctoral Program	$1,000,000
15	Université de Poitiers	Ingénierie des médias pour léducation	$1,000,000
20	University of Missouri-Columbia	School of Information Science and Learning Technologies	$800,000

in second and Wayne state as number 3; some people I talked to last year mentioned these two schools as more practitioner oriented than other programs. These numbers, as research numbers, would suggest that this is not correct. Another measure that might be interesting to count is the number of graduates who have taken academic positions as opposed to practitioner-oriented positions.

Table 3 Top-20 LDT and ILS programs by the number of full-time faculty (also shown is the total faculty, which includes both full- and part-time faculty)

Rank	University	Department/Program	FT	Total
1	Drexel University	The iSchool at Drexel, College of Information Science and Technology	38	111
2	University of Missouri-Kansas City	Curriculum and Instructional Leadership	30	45
3	University of North Carolina	School of Information and Library Science	26	32
4	Université de Poitiers	Ingénierie des médias pour léducation	25	50
5	Middle East Technical University	Computer Education and Instructional Technology	20	60
5	Valdosta State University	Curriculum, Leadership, and Technology	20	30
7	Towson University	College of Education	17	22
8	Regis University	School of Education and Counseling	15	165
9	The University of Hong Kong	Faculty of Education	12	102
9	Valley City State University	School of Education and Graduate Studies	12	20
9	Utrecht University	Educational Sciences Learning in Interaction	12	19
9	Fordham University	MA Program in Public Communications in the Department of Communication and Media Studies	12	16
9	University of Georgia	Department of Educational Psychology and Instructional Technology, College of Education	12	14
14	Athabasca University	Centre for Distance Education	11	26
14	University of Bridgeport	Instructional Technology	11	25
14	Indiana University	School of Education	11	15
14	Louisiana State University	School of Library and Information Science	11	11
14	The University of Oklahoma	Instructional Psychology and Technology, Department of Educational Psychology	11	11
19	Penn State Great Valley School of Graduate Professional Studies	Education Division/Instructional Systems Program	10	25
19	California State University Monterey Bay (CSUMB)	Interdisciplinary Master in Instructional Science and Technology (MIST)	10	22
19	University of West Georgia	Department of Media and Instructional Technology	10	14

Table 3 (continued)

Rank	University	Department/Program	FT	Total
19	University of Missouri-Columbia	School of Information Science and Learning Technologies	10	12
19	Utah State University	Department of Instructional Technology and Learning Sciences, Emma Eccles Jones College of Education and Human Services	10	11

Table 4 Top-20 LDT and ILS programs by the number of PhD graduates

Rank	University	Department/Program	Grads
1	Indiana University	School of Education	16
2	George Mason University	Instructional Technology Programs	15
3	Wayne State University	Instructional Technology	11
4	Middle East Technical University	Computer Education and Instructional Technology	10
4	Texas Tech University	Instructional Technology	10
4	University of Houston	Curriculum and Instruction	10
4	Pennsylvania State University	Instructional Systems	10
4	University of Georgia	Department of Educational Psychology and Instructional Technology, College of Education	10
9	Drexel University	The iSchool at Drexel, College of Information Science and Technology	9
9	Utah State University	Department of Instructional Technology and Learning Sciences, Emma Eccles Jones College of Education and Human Services	9
11	University of Calgary	Graduate Division of Educational Research	8
12	University of Bridgeport	Instructional Technology	6
12	University of Missouri-Columbia	School of Information Science and Learning Technologies	6
12	Virginia Tech	College of Liberal Arts and Human Sciences	6
12	University of Balearic Islands	Sciences of Education	6
16	Utrecht University	Educational Sciences Learning in Interaction	5
16	The Ohio State University	Cultural Foundations, Technology, and Qualitative Inquiry	5
16	University of Louisville	College of Education and Human Development	5

Table 4   (continued)

Rank	University	Department/Program	Grads
16	Concordia University	Education – MA in Educational Technology, Diploma in Instructional Technology and PhD (Education), Specialization, Educational Technology	5
16	University of Florida	School of Teaching and Learning	5
16	Arizona State University; Educational Technology program	Division of Psychology in Education	5

Table 5   Top-20 LDT and ILS programs by the number of master's graduates

Rank	University	Department/Program	Grads
1	Drexel University	The iSchool at Drexel, College of Information Science and Technology	332
2	University of Bridgeport	Instructional Technology	294
3	University of Calgary	Graduate Division of Educational Research	235
4	Regis University	School of Education and Counseling	200
5	Towson University	College of Education	157
6	George Mason University	Instructional Technology Programs	130
7	University of North Carolina	School of Information and Library Science	115
8	Utrecht University	Educational Sciences Learning in Interaction	110
9	Nova Southeastern University – Fischler Graduate School of Education and Human Services	Programs in Instructional Technology and Distance Education (ITDE)	100
10	Azusa Pacific University	EDUCABS – Advanced Studies	90
11	Barry University	Department of Educational Computing and Technology, School of Education	75
11	University of Arizona	School of Information Resources and Library Science	75
11	University of Maryland Baltimore County (UMBC).	Department of Education	75
14	University of Missouri – Columbia	School of Information Science and Learning Technologies	72
15	The University of Rhode Island	Graduate School of Library and Information Studies	68
15	University of Colorado Denver	School of Education and Human Development	68
17	University of Central Florida	College of Education – ERTL	65
18	University of Missouri-Kansas City	Curriculum and Instructional Leadership	60
18	Louisiana State University	School of Library and Information Science	60

Table 5 (continued)

Rank	University	Department/Program	Grads
18	University of South Florida	Instructional Technology Program, Secondary Education Department, College of Education	60
18	Minot State University	Graduate School	60

Table 6 Top-20 LDT and ILS programs by the overall total number of graduates

Rank	University	Program	Num Grads
1	Drexel University	The iSchool at Drexel, College of Information Science and Technology	432
2	University of Bridgeport	Instructional Technology	417
3	University of Calgary	Graduate Division of Educational Research	254
4	Regis University	School of Education and Counseling	200
5	Valley City State University	School of Education and Graduate Studies	181
6	Towson University	College of Education	161
7	George Mason University	Instructional Technology Programs	145
8	University of North Carolina	School of Information and Library Science	140
9	Utrecht University	Educational Sciences Learning in Interaction	115
10	Nova Southeastern University – Fischler Graduate School of Education and Human Services	Programs in Instructional Technology and Distance Education (ITDE)	100
11	Azusa Pacific University	EDUCABS – Advanced Studies	90
12	University of West Georgia	Department of Media and Instructional Technology	89
13	California State University Monterey Bay (CSUMB)	Interdisciplinary Master in Instructional Science and Technology (MIST)	80
14	Barry University	Department of Educational Computing and Technology, School of Education	75
14	University of Maryland Baltimore County (UMBC)	Department of Education	75
16	University of Missouri – Columbia	School of Information Science and Learning Technologies	72
17	University of Colorado Denver	School of Education and Human Development	70
18	The University of Rhode Island	Graduate School of Library and Information Studies	68
19	Wayne State University	Instructional Technology	67
20	University of Central Arkansas	Teaching, Learning, and Technology	66

Our next top-20 list is based on the number of master's graduates. In our mind, we might consider this an indication of whether the program is more practitioner oriented than, say, the number of PhD graduates. Interestingly, George Mason comes in sixth here, whereas they were number 2 in PhD graduates. So, this differentiation may be meaningless. It is interesting to note that schools like Drexel University, University of Bridgeport, University of Calgary, and Regis University are producing 200 or more graduates per year. In Georgia (United States), Walden University and the University of Phoenix are very active; however, neither of these two schools chose to complete the form. We are not implying that the large numbers are necessarily because these programs are online, but online degree programs certainly allow many more people to further their education.

The final top-20 list is the combined degree graduate list. It is very similar to the master's list, but since the online form had entries only for PhD graduates, master's graduates, and other graduates, I thought it might be most useful to just show the total number of graduates from each of the programs who chose to update their information in our database.

We acknowledge that any kind of rankings of programs is problematic. We hope you find our lists useful. If you have suggestions, please let us know and we will try to accommodate those changes in future publications of the *Yearbook*.

Athens, GA   Michael Orey
Statesboro, GA   Stephanie A. Jones
Athens, GA   Robert Maribe Branch

Contents

Contributors

Robert Maribe Branch Learning, Design, and Technology Program, The University of Georgia, Athens, GA, USA, rbranch@uga.edu

Curtis Jay Bonk Instructional Systems Technology, Indiana University, Bloomington, IN, USA, cjbonk@indiana.edu

Abbie Brown Department of Mathematics, Science and Instructional Technology Education, East Carolina University, Greenville, NC, USA, brownab@ecu.edu

John Burton Instructional Systems Development/Educational Psychology, Virginia Tech, Blacksburg, VA, USA, jburton@vt.edu

Rajat Chadha Department of Instructional Systems Technology, School of Education, Indiana University, Bloomington, IN, USA, rajatchadha@gmail.com

Kaye B. Dotson Department of Library Science, East Carolina University, Greenville, NC, USA, dotsonl@ecu.edu

Kylie P. Dotson-Blake Department of Counselor and Adult Education, East Carolina University, Greenville, NC, USA, blakek@ecu.edu

Lesley S.J. Farmer Librarianship Program, California State University, Long Beach, CA, USA, lfarmer@csulb.edu

Theodore Frick Department of Instructional Systems Technology, School of Education, Indiana University, Bloomington, IN, USA, frick@indiana.edu

Pamela Fortner Department of Educational Psychology and Instructional Technology, The University of Georgia, Athens, GA, USA, phales@uga.edu

Tim Green Department of Elementary and Bilingual Education, California State University, Fullerton, CA, USA, timdgreen@gmail.com

Sarah Hug ATLAS Institute, Assessment and Research Center, University of Colorado at Boulder, Boulder, CO, USA, hug@colorado.edu

Diane Igoche Learning, Design, and Technology Program, The University of Georgia, Athens, GA, USA, dai011@uga.edu

Stephanie A. Jones Leadership, Technology, and Human Development Department, Georgia Southern University, Statesboro, GA, USA, sjones@GeorgiaSouthern.edu

Susan Jurow School of Education, University of Colorado at Boulder, Boulder, CO, USA, susan.jurow@colorado.edu

Beaumie Kim Learning Sciences and Technologies, National Institute of Education, Nanyang Technological University, Singapore, beaumie.kim@nie.edu.sg

James D. Klein Educational Technology, Mary Lou Fulton Graduate School of Education, Arizona State University, Tempe, AZ, USA, james.klein@asu.edu.

Min Liu Instructional Technology Program, Department of Curriculum and Instruction, University of Texas, Austin, TX, USA, mliu@utexas.edu

Liz May Learning, Design, and Technology Program, The University of Georgia, Athens, GA, USA, lizmay3@hotmail.com

Ali S. Al Musawi Instructional Learning Technologies Department, College of Education, Sultan Qaboos University, Al Khodh, Oman, asmusawi@squ.edu.om

Michael Orey Learning, Design, and Technology Program, The University of Georgia, Athens, GA, USA, mikeorey@uga.edu

Seanean Shanahan Instructional Media Services for the Los Angeles Unified School District, Los Angeles, CA, USA, sshanaha@lausd.net

Gary Shattuck Learning, Design, and Technology Program, The University of Georgia, Athens, GA, USA, shattuck.gary@newton.k12.ga.us

Seng-Chee Tan Learning Sciences and Technologies, National Institute of Education, Nanyang Technological University, Singapore, sengchee.tan@nie.edu.sg

Jinn-Wei Tsao Learning, Design, and Technology Program, The University of Georgia, Athens, GA, USA, miketsao@uga.edu

Diane L. Velasquez Graduate School of Library and Information Science, Dominican University, River Forest, IL, USA, dvelasquez@dom.edu

Ying Wang Department of Education, Northwestern College, St. Paul, MN, USA, ywang@nwc.edu

Carol Watson Eppley Institute for Parks and Public Lands, Indiana University, Bloomington, IN, USA, watsonc@indiana.edu

Jennifer Yeo Natural Science and Science Education, National Institute of Education, Nanyang Technological University, Nanyang Walk, Singapore, jennifer.yeo@nie.edu.sg

Part I
Trends and Issues in Learning, Design, and Technology

Introduction

Liz May and Michael Orey

This is the ninth edition of this book where I have served as the editor of the "Trends" section and the first where I have enlisted a coauthor. I have used a variety of strategies for organizing this part. For this year, we sent an invitation to one or more individuals from our top 10 list that was created based on the number of publications in the *Educational Technology Research and Development Journal* and the *Journal for the Learning Sciences*. Unfortunately, we were unable to get chapters from the University of Wisconsin, the State University of New York-Buffalo, the University of New Mexico, and the University of Hong Kong. We did get a chapter from each of the other 6 top 10 schools. We did this in order to try and gain a snapshot of what is going on in the general field of learning, design, and technology. However, we also have been editing this part for many years, and we have included a chapter on "Trends and Issues" that has been written every year for at least 10 years, though the authorship has evolved. This year, Abbie Brown and Tim Green have taken on the task again. What follows is our attempt to weave the chapters in this part into a coherent whole.

While giving a nod to epistemological or pedagogical causes, Shattuck's chapter focuses on school leadership as the critical factor for teachers' technology integration (or lack thereof). Designed to investigate whether or not school leaders can influence technology integration (and if so how), the study centered on eight strategic factors for getting teacher buy-in. These include vision, expectations, modeling, encouragement, sufficient resources, hiring the right people, professional development opportunities, and building community in the organization. Conducted in four middle schools in the same suburban school district in the Southeastern United States, the research consisted of a pre-survey to identify who the teachers considered a technology leader in their school, followed by interviews of the four principals,

L. May (✉)
Learning, Design, and Technology Program, The University of Georgia, Athens, GA, USA
e-mail: lizmay3@hotmail.com

M. Orey (✉)
Learning, Design, and Technology Program, The University of Georgia, Athens, GA, USA
e-mail: mikeorey@uga.edu

M. Orey et al. (eds.), *Educational Media and Technology Yearbook*,
Educational Media and Technology Yearbook 35,
DOI 10.1007/978-1-4419-1516-0_1, © Springer Science+Business Media, LLC 2010

and concluded with a focus group that included the identified school leader as a way to cross-check data gathered from the interviews. The study concluded that in schools where all eight strategic factors were in place and where the origin was the school leadership rather than merely pioneering tech users on the faculty, the rest of the teachers were more inclined toward technology integration.

If Shattuck is correct in linking school leadership to technology resistance, then Brown and Green would urge school leaders to take a second look at the free web-based tools that students are already using outside of school. Furthermore, they make a case for the use of Web 2.0, online learning, and social networking sites as a way to save money and still maintain a growth model during these challenging economic times. The bulk of this chapter, however, is a synthesis of the findings of several major annual reports about technology use and growth in business, higher education, and the K-12 sector. Even without a robust economy, they predict that instruction via technology will continue to be a winning strategy for both business and education since it affords opportunities for growth and learning at a lower cost. They urge educators to reconsider resistance to using some of the tools, especially the social networking sites, and to consider new and innovative ways to overcome the current economic challenges.

Lack of confidence has often been cited as an impediment to technology integration and is addressed in Batane's chapter. While teaches are still content experts, their students, the digital natives, are the technology experts, and this can be intimidating to some teachers. Batane's study focused on the use of the Rapid Prototyping Model since it allows opportunities for feedback and revisions along the way rather than after an entire course has been developed and field tested. Based on Elaboration Theory, he contends that Rapid Prototyping affords a *one step at a time* approach to technology integration, which can then build confidence for future forays into the digital wilderness. He further contends that getting student feedback at each stage of the lesson development takes the participation of students beyond mere course work into course design, which is a win for all. Taking small steps and getting the students involved in the process could be an important component of technology integration as the digital immigrants continue to teach the digital natives, at least for a few more years.

The digital natives are tech savvy; however, some have expressed concern that the majority of US college graduates lack proficiency in desired academic skills, and this is a cause of concern to anyone in higher education. This concern led Frick to analyze course evaluation data and its correlation with student learning achievement. This led to a plan to connect course evaluations to instructional theory in order to provide data that could lead to improvements not only in instruction and course quality but in student learning achievement as well. A survey was therefore designed around Merrill's *First Principles of Instruction*, as well as the concept of *Academic Learning Time*. The thinking was that items that were rated low would have a clear connection to what needs to be revised or improved. The study results showed that there was a strong correlation between student ratings of the course and its instructor and student mastery when *First Principles* and *ALT* were in place.

Embedding instructional design theory in student evaluations is not a bad idea; but perhaps embedding one goal inside another does not always work, as evidenced by this study of a *girls only* technology program. The girls were encouraged to use tech tools as a way to create, tell stories, and express themselves in a "technology as paintbrush" 8-week learning experience at Silver Stream Clubhouse in the Western United States. The girls did pick up some computer skills, but the paintbrush metaphor may have limited acquisition of technology fluency according to Hug and Jurow. By focusing on the product of technology and getting things to "look pretty," the authors felt that the process of technology was underemphasized. Technology expertise was valued for its ability to help the girls become adept storytellers, for example, rather than video editors. Hoping for more female representation in technology fields, the authors suggest that a program that gets girls to learn about how the tools work as well as principles of design and development may be a better way to prepare them for jobs in the digital marketplace.

Sultan Qaboos University's Musawi has written about the history, present status, and future plans of the Instructional and Learning Technologies Department in the College of Education. Since its start in 2005 the program has established a B.A. degree with four cohorts currently in attendance and its first graduating class this year. This short chapter outlines the program, catalogs the resources for students and faculty, tracks research and faculty status, and concludes with an index of areas for improvement and challenges for the future. Three particular challenges that have been targeted for improvement are the large teaching load of its faculty, the need for accreditation level quality in all courses, and the need to foster more independent learning in students. With the strong administrative support that this young program has enjoyed since its inception, these goals are not only reasonable but quite attainable.

Nanyang Technological University of Singapore is likewise interested in improving learning and focusing on the future as they shift from longstanding instructional strategies to technology-enhanced education. Not satisfied with simply pasting technology into existing pedagogical structures, Tan, Kim, and Yeo write about the importance of students' agency in knowledge construction as well as in the development of content. They contend that the application of the social constructivist learning paradigm can make technology-assisted instruction more meaningful. Two case studies are included in their research, and these serve to illustrate the need for scaffolding to help learners move from passive to active participants, as well as the need for teachers to adapt to new roles as designers and facilitators rather than as traditional instructors.

Human performance technology (HPT) is a broader discipline than instructional design (ID); however, similar to ID, it includes a systemic analysis and design of some performance problem or need. Taking a course in HPT might be a hard sell for some graduate students in IT/ID programs; however, there are several factors that could justify its inclusion in one's program of study. For one, the critical analysis of a performance problem and its underlying causes is an important component in the skill set of all graduate students. Furthermore, the sorting of problems into instructional and noninstructional *piles* is a good prerequisite skill for the novice instructional designer. For an HPT course to be successfully implemented in a graduate education, however, a connection to a real-world problem or need is best, but these situations are not always easy to come by. This chapter reports on lessons learned by the faculty at Arizona State University as they employed a performance improvement project as part of the HPT course work. It also makes a case as to why such a course may be a good elective even for those outside of the HPT program.

Understanding School Leaders' Role in Teachers' Adoption of Technology Integration Classroom Practices

Gary Shattuck

Abstract The educational technology research community documents that technology is not integrated into teachers' classroom practices other than to reinforce or augment current practices (Becker, 2001; Cuban, 2001). Adopting technology at this level is called first-order change (Ertmer, 1999); the explanation the research community reaches is that teachers' belief structure is incompatible with high-level technology integration (Cuban, 2001; Ertmer, 2005). This study explores another explanation for teachers' reluctance to adopt technology integration – school leaders. Furthermore, this study outlines strategies a school leader must adopt to leverage his or her leadership position to increase technology utilization among the faculty.

Keywords Technology integration · School leadership · Educational change · Technology leaders · Organizational change

Introduction

The purpose of this research described in this chapter is to understand school leaders' roles in teachers' adoption of technology-integrated classroom practices. Although educational leadership researchers such as Fullan (2001) and Sergiovanni (2006) agree that school leaders play a significant, if not a vital, role in the success of any instructional initiative within their school, very little literature (Staples, Pugach, and Himes, 2005) targets the school leaders' role in teachers adopting technology-integrated classroom practices. This gap in the literature is glaring, because most educational technology researchers, such as Cuban (2001), Hernandez-Ramos (2005), and Windschitl and Sahl (2002), agree technology, for the most part, has not significantly impacted teachers' classroom practices nor has

G. Shattuck (✉)
Learning, Design, and Technology Program, The University of Georgia, Athens, GA, USA
e-mail: shattuck.gary@newton.k12.ga.us

M. Orey et al. (eds.), *Educational Media and Technology Yearbook*,
Educational Media and Technology Yearbook 35,
DOI 10.1007/978-1-4419-1516-0_2, © Springer Science+Business Media, LLC 2010

it significantly transformed teachers' classroom practices. Understanding causes of why technology is not being integrated into teachers' classroom practices is complex because this research finds causes that cross academic disciplines. Furthermore, this research finds that the lack of technology integration may be caused by a misalignment between the school leaders' vision of technology integration and the teachers' vision of technology integration. It identifies five academic disciplines that impact the ability of teachers to implement technology-integrated classroom practices. In addition, it identifies eight strategies that a school must employ in order for teachers to integrate technology into their classroom practices. These five academic disciplines identified are instructional technology, educational leadership, educational laws and policies, educational and organizational change, and diffusion of innovation. The eight strategies identified are establishing vision, setting expectations, modeling expected behavior, offering encouragement, supplying sufficient technology resources, employing the right people, providing ample professional learning opportunities, and building capacity within the building. Not surprisingly, then, this research finds that integrating technology is very difficult due, in large part, to the interaction between these five academic disciplines. More importantly, however, this research discovers eight strategic factors school leaders must adopt if school leaders hope to leverage their leadership roles in order to influence teachers into adopting technology-integrated classroom practices.

Research Questions

The purpose of this study was to determine if school leaders effect teachers' attitudes toward the integration of technology into their classroom practices. This research was designed to find answers to the following questions:

1. Can school leaders influence teachers' adoption of technology integration classroom practices?
2. How do school leaders influence teachers' adoption of technology integration classroom practices?

   2.1 Who are the technology leaders within each school?

   2.2 How can a leader assist teachers in overcoming barriers that prevent the integration of technology?
   2.3 In what ways do teachers feel encouraged and/or supported when they take risks concerning integrating technology into their classroom practices?
   2.4 How do the teachers' vision for why technology should be integrated within a classroom differ from the principal's vision for why technology should be integrated within a classroom?
   2.5 Does the principal's expectations for technology integration influence teachers' integration of technology into their classroom practices?

Review of Literature

In 2001, Larry Cuban wrote a stinging rebuke of the Instructional Technology Movement in *Oversold and Underused: Computers in the Classroom.* Cuban's basic premise was that billions of dollars were spent on instructional technology in the K-12 educational realm in the 1990s and that this influx of money failed to provide promised benefits claimed by proponents of instructional technology, such as by Seymour Papert (Cuban, 2001; 2004; Ferneding, 2003). Most instructional technology researchers agreed with Cuban's basic premise (Becker, 2001; Cuban, 2001; Ertmer, 1999; Ferneding, 2003; Hernandez-Ramos, 2005). Even though there were themes most researchers agreed were root causes for this situation, such as that teachers' belief structure about teaching and learning did not support a constructivist pedagogy (Becker, 2001; Cuban, 2001; Ertmer, 1999; Hernandez-Ramos, 2005), teachers were not being supported either technologically or instructionally in their efforts to integrate technology (Becker, 2001; Cuban, 2001) and they lacked effective and sufficient professional development (Becker, 2001; Brinkerhoff, 2006; Cuban, 2001; Dwyer, 1995; Mouza, 2003). There was also disagreement as to other root causes (Becker, 2001; Cuban, 2001; Ertmer, 1999; Ferneding, 2003; Hernandez-Ramos, 2005). Each researcher had additional reasons for this lack of progress, such as from Larry Cuban's claim that structural design of schools' organization was a cause, from Howard Becker's thesis that lack of computer density within classrooms was a cause to Peggy Ertmer's premise that barriers to the change process was a cause. Herein lies the conundrum that the instructional technology community faced. The world had dramatically changed economically, socially, and politically to some degree due to a technological revolution (Friedman, 2005; Postman, 1992; Toffler, 1970), whereas education had not changed to meet this changing global landscape (Cuban, Kirkpatrick, Peck, 2001). Whatever the reasons, it had become apparent to the research community that integration of technology was a complex issue involving multiple variables from multiple disciplines including instructional technology theories, educational leadership theories, educational laws and policy theories, educational and organizational change theories, and diffusion of innovation theories. Equally important as change theories, understanding the difficulties faced by classroom teachers in implementing technology integration practices was also important.

It was also important to understand the role of educational leadership in overcoming these difficulties faced by classroom teachers in technology integration practices. Michael Fullan (2001) described the role of school leader as being vital, not only to the health of any school, but also to the success of any educational change. Research showed that for educational change to become successful, it required the involvement of educational leaders; furthermore, research showed that successful educational leaders' change depended on inclusion of teachers in the planning and implementation of change (Fullan, 2001). It was this duality of involvement that provided the framework for understanding how integration of technology may become successful. Sergiovanni (2006), in his book on school principals, pointed out that the culture of a school is actually a negotiated product between school leadership and teachers within that school. As a result, school leadership's participation in and support for educational change, such as the integration of technology within teachers' classroom practices, were keys for this educational technology innovation to be adopted in the K-12 educational environment.

Another issue impacting teachers' willingness to adopt technology-integrated classroom practices was educational laws and policies. With the *No Child Left Behind Act of 2001*, the federal government had changed the educational landscape, which in turn impacted the integration of technology (Ferneding, 2003). This law stressed accountability and high stakes testing to the exclusion of other forms of assessment. Becker and Lovitt (2003) postulated that the type of learning that took place in technology-integrated, project-based learning settings could not easily be measured by objective, multiple-choice tests. As a result of the *No Child Left Behind Act of 2001* emphasis on standardized tests and on accountability in the form of Adequate Yearly Progress, school leaders and teachers had, to some degree, abandoned efforts to adopt technology-integrated classroom practices (Cuban, 2003). As a result, the efforts to integrate technology into the nation's classrooms had become infinitely more complex. In Fig. 1 these various issues that impact a teacher's willingness to adopt technology-integrated classroom practices are illustrated.

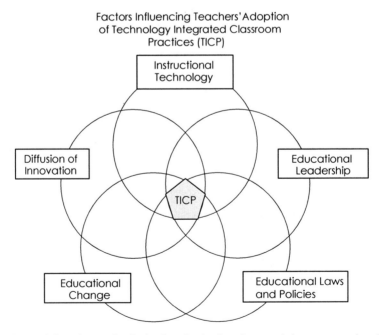

Fig. 1 Factors influencing teachers' adoption of technology-integrated classroom practices (TICP)

The final issues of educational change theories and of diffusion of innovation theories were inextricably interwoven together dealing with essentially the same phenomenon – the change process (Elmore, 2003; Fullan, 1993; Rogers, 2003). According to Michael Fullan, one of the driving forces in the educational environment was the need for continuous change. Fullan went so far as to say, "It is no exaggeration to say that dealing with change is endemic to post-modern society" (p. 3). In order to understand this changing landscape within which teachers were supposed to adopt new pedagogies, it was necessary to understand the change process and how that change process could be used with a conservative educational environment (Cuban, 2001) with a changing society (Toffler, 1970), and with a changing student (Healy, 1990; Prensky, 2006).

Theoretical Perspective

According to Crotty (1998), there were two approaches to research: "Verstehen" or understanding and "Erklären" or explaining. Understanding focused on the human or the social sciences; explaining focused on the natural sciences. Therefore, in an attempt to interpret the social nature of schooling and how this social nature encouraged or discouraged adoption of technology integration strategies by teachers, this study attempted to understand the relationship between school leaders and teachers and how this relationship impacted teachers' willingness to adopt technology-integrated classroom practices. Because this chapter deals with a study of the interaction between school leaders and teachers, Symbolic Interactionism was the theoretical perspective from which this study was conducted.

Interaction between cultural subgroups, such as between leaders within schools and teachers, was first postulated by George Herbert Mead (Blumer, 1969; Crotty, 1998) in the early part of the twentieth century and was based on the symbols of language, thus the name Symbolic Interactionism. In order to understand interaction between leaders within schools and teachers, it was best to first comprehend the theoretical perspective on which this study was based. Herbert Blumer outlined three basic premises that were the basis for the Symbolic Interactionism theoretical perspective: (1) human beings acted toward things on the basis of the meaning those things had for them; (2) the meaning of such things was derived from, or arose out of, the social interaction that one had with one's fellow humans; and (3) these meanings were handled in, and were modified through, an interpretive process used by the person in dealing with the things she or he encountered.

As a result of these three premises it became apparent that for most teachers in a K-12 school environment the meaning technology had for teachers was one of research and of administrative functions but not one of instruction. Research conducted by Becker (2001), Cuban (2001), Hernández-Ramos (2005), and Windschitl and Sahl (2002) indicated most teachers used technology only for administrative functions, for research in planning lessons, and for personal productivity, but not for instruction. Teachers did not use technology to transform their instructional practices into a constructivist framework because teachers' belief structure did not support this transformation.

Methodology

This research used a case study methodology by examining four middle schools within the same suburban school district in the Southeastern United States. The initial method used was a pre-survey to determine who the technology leaders within each school were and what were the principle issues affecting teachers' adoption of technology-integrated classroom practices. Using data collected from the pre-survey as the basis of questions, the principal at each of the four middle schools was interviewed using a semi-structured in-depth interview method. After in-depth interviews with the principals, teachers who were identified as technology leaders in the pre-survey were asked to participate in a focus group interview. By interviewing the principal and a focus group of teachers at each school, a cross-check was created to verify data from the principal and from the teachers. Focusing just on middle schools in a single school district was an attempt to minimize contextual variables extant in other settings. Even though each school was its own case study per se, the entirety of this research was a case study for that school district. Since there were four schools, each school acted as a comparison for the other three, thus allowing for triangulation of data.

Pre-survey

The pre-survey's primary purpose was to identify technology leaders within each school and specific issues concerning integration of technology within each school. In all four of the middle schools, the media specialist was selected as a technology leader for that school; in only two of the schools, however, was the principal selected as a technology leader. Reasons for this are discussed in detail later in the case studies. Furthermore, teachers were asked to identify any other school personnel considered to be technology leaders.

One of the most important findings of the pre-survey was the disparate views that teachers had concerning vision and expectations (see Tables 1 and 2). In the pre-survey I asked two questions dealing with why technology should be used within the classroom. These questions were vision questions. The first vision question asked what the teacher's vision was; the second vision question asked what the teacher thought was the principal's vision. Unexpectedly, the teachers' idea about their own vision did not necessarily align with the teachers' idea about the principals' vision. This misalignment became a significant factor

In addition to the two vision questions, another question in the pre-survey dealt with teachers' perception of what the expectations for technology utilization in the

Table 1 Comparison of percentage of teachers' perspectives concerning what their vision is and what they think the principal's vision is concerning the integration of technology

School	Perspective	Reward students	Basic skills	Prepare for future	Critical thinking	Motivation	Do not know
Adams	Personal	3	13	12	35	26	–
	Principal's	–	13	–	25	21	42
Jefferson	Personal	–	9	33	24	33	–
	Principal's	1	32	18	15	6	26
Madison	Personal	–	19	23	12	46	–
	Principal's	–	15	30	15	30	11
Washington	Personal	–	16	11	37	37	–
	Principal's	–	33	17	6	17	28

Table 2 Percentage of respondents to pre-survey when asked what their school's expectations concerning technology utilization were

School	To prepare for standardized tests	To take accelerated reader tests	To prepare for twenty-first century	No expectations
Adams	33	13	38	17
Jefferson	29	21	26	24
Madison	13	4	75	4
Washington	42	–	32	26

teachers' schools were (see Table 2). There were significant differences between schools in how teachers answered this question.

Principal Interviews

Each principal of these four middle schools was interviewed. The purpose of each interview was to understand the leadership style of each principal, to ascertain each principal's commitment to technology integration, to comprehend each principal's perception of technology, and to identify how that technology could be leveraged to better administer a school to improve student learning. All the principals' interviews lasted approximately an hour in length; all interviews were conducted during the working period after the school year was completed and the vacation period began.

Each principal professed a belief that the integration of technology was important in education, and each perceived herself or himself as supporting that endeavor. An analysis of principal interviews and of focus group interviews revealed that each principal's perception, with the exception of one, was skewed to present herself or himself and their schools in the best possible light. Each principal viewed herself or himself as being technology leaders in their school even though only two of the four principals were viewed by their faculty as being technology leaders.

Focus Group Interviews

Focus group interviews for each school were conducted after the principal was interviewed. The interviews lasted approximately 1 hour; data gathered during the interviews were instrumental in cross-checking data from principals' interviews and were instructional in understanding formal leadership's role in teachers' adoption of technology integration strategies. Out of these focus group interviews it became apparent that there were two technology leadership roles at work within a school: formal or administration's technology leadership role and informal or teachers' technology leadership role. Also apparent in the data was that each role was vitally important for a school's teachers to be willing to adopt technology-integrated classroom practices into their classroom practices. Each role served an important function in influencing teachers to adopt technology-integrated classroom practices, but the synergy that was created when both technology leadership roles were present raised the level of technology integration exponentially as will be evident when each school's case study is detailed.

Documentation Review

After principal and focus group interviews were analyzed, there were several areas of disagreement that needed further clarification. In order to resolve these areas of disagreement, a review of district-level documentation was undertaken to get a better understanding of underlying facts supporting or not supporting various perspectives. The bases for conflicts were the availability of funds to support the addition of technology resources and the willingness of school administrators to allow teachers to participate in district-level professional learning.

Case Studies

Washington Middle School

By any definition, the situation at Washington Middle School was challenging. According to the criterion of the *No Child Left Behind Act of 2001*, Washington Middle School had been in the Needs Improvement category for the past 5 years. Due to the Choice provisions of *No Child Left Behind*, Washington Middle School had to offer its students the choice to move to another middle school. In the 2006–2007 school year, 226 students chose to move, 130 to Jefferson Middle School and 96 to Adams Middle School, whereas in the 2007–2008 school year, 322 students chose to move, 160 to Adams Middle School and 162 to Madison Middle School. Demographics of Washington Middle School also represented a challenge for the school's administration. The school had a very high percentage of students in subgroups that had traditionally performed less well on standardized tests: economically disadvantaged students. When compared with the other middle schools, Washington had the highest poverty rate, with 68.8% of students qualifying for the Free and Reduced Lunch Program.

Washington Middle School was one of two middle schools in which the misalignment was severe on the pre-survey between the teachers' perception of the principal's vision concerning technology integration and the teachers' perception of their own vision concerning technology integration (see Table 1). For example, on the two questions on the pre-survey that focused on vision, 37% of Washington Middle School's teachers thought that technology should be used to teach critical thinking skills, whereas only 6% of these same teachers perceived that the principal thought technology should be used to teach critical thinking skills.

Furthermore, during the principal's interview, Mrs. Almond, the principal of Washington Middle School, stated she considered herself to be a technology leader in her school. In contrast, only 6% of her teachers who filled out the pre-survey judged her to be a technology leader. It was this misalignment between what the teachers' perceptions were and what the principal's perception was that contributed to Washington's lack of progress toward development of a focused approach to the usage of technology. While answering a question during her interview, Mrs. Almond commented that she needed to use PowerPoint more frequently at faculty meetings as a confirmation of her belief that she was a technology leader in her school. She never spoke of setting expectations for technology utilization for her teachers. She never spoke of encouraging her teachers to adopt technology integration strategies. But she spoke of herself as being technology competent saying, "When the teachers know that the principal is technology savvy enough to know how the programs are to be used (the teachers use these programs more)." On the other hand, the focus group painted a very different picture of Mrs. Almond's technology competence as well as of her leadership role in promoting the use of technology. In fact, one teacher stated that Mrs. Almond was "a computer phobic," and she refused to use email because she was concerned about getting caught writing something that she would later have to explain (Jim, language arts teacher). With an administration that was technology challenged, the focus group interview indicated that it was difficult for teachers of that school to adopt a teaching style integrating technology into their classroom strategies.

When the question was posed to Mrs. Almond of what her expectations were of teachers to use technology, she never once mentioned expectations. Instead she only talked about how she led her faculty by modeling the use of technology at faculty meetings, or at other in-service activities, and about how technology had to be coupled with assessment. Members of the focus group all agreed that the principal and other administrators had not articulated their expectations for the use of technology by teachers. Andrew, a science teacher, reinforced this point when he said, "They cannot hold the teachers accountable for something they themselves do not understand." There were obviously very differing views about the status of technology and about the utilization of technology within Washington Middle School between the principal and the teachers.

Another issue highlighting differing perceptions between principal and teachers as represented by members of the focus group was the availability of technology resources within Washington Middle School. As Becker (2001) illustrated, the more resources teachers had available to use within their classrooms, the more likely teachers were to integrate technology. Mrs. Almond, however, blamed lack of computer resources on "Central Office policies" and on "lack of funding" even though she had available, at her discretion, $37,399 from Title 1 funds and $61,506 from School Improvement funds (see Table 3). From Title 1 funds Mrs. Almond spent only 8% on technology; from School Improvement funds she spent only 16% on technology (see Table 4). For teachers filling out the pre-survey, 56% listed lack of resources as a barrier to their ability to integrate technology; yet Mrs. Almond chose not to invest in technology even though funds were available to do so.

Table 3 Availability of Title 1 funds per school

School	Total allocation ($)	Amount spent for staff salaries ($)	Amount spent at principal's discretion ($)
Adams	145,125	114,136	30,989
Jefferson	203,450	97,870	105,580
Madison	185,750	136,379	49,371
Washington	185,500	148,101	37,399

Table 4 Percentage of discretionary funds spent on technology resources

School	Amount spent at principal's discretion ($)	Amount spent on technology ($)	Percentage spent on technology
Adams	30,989	25,411	82
Jefferson	105,580	11,614	11
Madison	49,371	44,928	91
Washington	37,399	2,992	8

The reason Mrs. Almond did not spend available funds on technology can be attributed only to a lack of vision about how technology could transform education. This lack of vision conclusion was supported by results from the pre-survey when 28% of Washington Middle School teachers indicated they did not know what the principal's vision was concerning use of technology; another 33% thought the principal's vision was to teach basic skills. To further illustrate this point, Washington Middle School had one computer lab originally designed as an instructional lab for teachers to sign up to use. Mrs. Almond turned this computer lab into a remediation lab for low-achieving students, thus depriving middle- and high-achieving students access to this lab. When teachers were asked in the pre-survey if lack of access to the computer lab was a barrier to their integration of technology, 56% responded positively; yet when Mrs. Almond was asked during her interview if teachers had access to the computer lab, her answer was in the affirmative. One of the focus group participants best expressed the situation at Washington Middle School when she said,

"The best way I heard it described is that this is a rudderless ship. We just stand around, stand around, stand around; there is no port we are aiming for" (Andrew, science teacher).

Jefferson Middle School

Jefferson Middle School had fewer challenges than had the other middle schools when it came to student demographics in the sense that Jefferson had the smallest percentage of economically disadvantaged students traditionally performing less well on standardized tests. However, Jefferson had other challenges. Due to Choice provisions of *No Child Left Behind*, Jefferson Middle School experienced a sizeable 130 student in-migration from Washington Middle School in August 2007. At that time Jefferson Middle School had the largest student population of all four middle schools and was using 19 portable classrooms.

When I asked the principal of Jefferson Middle School, Joseph Callifano, if he considered himself to be a technology leader, he responded that he did. Likewise, 80% of teachers responding to the pre-survey indicated the principal was a technology leader. Mr. Callifano admitted he did not know a lot about technology but tried to use it in a variety of ways as a model for teachers to use technology.

Mr. Callifano said he encouraged teachers to use technology in their classroom practices. When I asked focus group teachers if they were encouraged to integrate technology into their classroom practices, their perspective was different from Mr. Callifano's. One of these focus group teachers responded, "When I am around my colleagues, I do (feel encouraged). I feel I get lip service from above the collegial level 'Make us look good,'" (Jonas, mathematics teacher). This "make us look good" comment was referring to how students scored on standardized tests. This sole focus on the standardized test seemed to pervade all aspects of Jefferson Middle School as will be illustrated. Mr. Callifano also said he encouraged all his teachers to use interactive whiteboards even though there were only six interactive whiteboards in his school. Mr. Callifano accomplished what he interpreted as integration of technology by mandating those teachers who had interactive whiteboards in their classrooms to make their classrooms available to other teachers so they could experience interactive technology. Considering the fact that there were only six teachers who had interactive whiteboards, and considering the fact that Jefferson Middle School had over 80 teachers, this effort seemed somewhat futile at best.

For those teachers who were interviewed during the focus group interview, this issue with the interactive whiteboards was just another example of the lack of technology resources available to the teachers and, thus, to the students. Lack of technology resources was cited by 77% of respondents to the pre-survey as a barrier to their utilization of technology. Mr. Callifano blamed a lack of resources on the lack of funds he received from the Central Office; however, a review of Central Office documentation revealed that Mr. Callifano had, at his discretion, Title 1 funds in the amount of $105,580, of which he spent only 11% to purchase technology resources (see Tables 3 and 4). Mr. Callifano admitted that lack of resources was a huge problem when he said, "If you do not have the resources (the teachers) need then (technology) becomes a frustrator."

In addition to a lack of classroom resources listed in the pre-survey, 77% of Jefferson Middle School's teachers listed the inaccessibility of the instructional computer lab as a barrier to their ability to integrate technology. Mr. Callifano refuted this assertion. From his perspective, the computer lab was open for blocks of time during the day for whole classes and for individual students all day long. The focus group participants had a different perspective from Mr. Callifano's; the reason the lab was unavailable was because it was being used full time to provide remediation to students who needed help learning basic skills. Therefore, teachers did not have access to technology within the classrooms; neither did they have access to technology in school-wide facilities like in the instructional computer lab. The reason that the lab was unavailable to whole classes and the reason that interactive whiteboards were unavailable to all but six teachers within their classrooms can be attributed only to a different vision for technology usage and to a different set of expectations for technology utilization. It appears that Mr. Callifano's vision for technology was limited to that of providing remediation in basic skills for low-achieving students. Later in his interview he admitted that regular students had access to "a computer" only once every 2 weeks in group settings.

When I asked Mr. Callifano what his expectations were for teachers integrating technology into classroom practices, he replied that his expectations were implied, "Those expectations are there, I don't really have to say anything." Valerie, one of the focus group teachers, said, "There are no expectations of technology utilization." Later Mr. Callifano admitted, "I think that it is really hard to have that expectation when I can't provide (the teachers) with the resources they need." Not only did teachers at Jefferson Middle School have a different perspective from their principal's on how technology should be used, but these teachers also recognized this different perspective. In the pre-survey, teachers were asked, "What is your vision for technology utilization?" Only 9% selected the answer "To Teach Basic Skills." On a different question, teachers were asked what they thought the principal's vision for technology utilization was; 32% selected the answer "To Teach Basic Skills." This was a wide disparity between the principal's vision and the teachers' vision (see Table 1).

During the 2007–2008 school year, Jefferson Middle School had more Title 1 funds available than had any of the four middle schools; yet only 11% was spent on technology (see Tables 3 and 4). Thus, the issue was one of vision about how technology could be used to help students succeed. The obvious conclusion was Mr. Callifano's vision for technology usage was to help low-achieving students master basic skills to increase their test scores. This vision, if used exclusively as it was being used at Jefferson Middle School, was a detriment to using technology in enriching ways for student learning by integrating technology into each teacher's pedagogy.

When discussing spending priorities at Jefferson Middle School, Mr. Callifano emphasized the point that his leadership team set all spending priorities. He said that the leadership team looked for initiatives that would benefit all teachers and students. This was his justification for not taking the measured approach, which was to buy some technology each year until all teachers had resources they needed to integrate technology into their classroom. For Mr. Callifano, it had to be an all-or-nothing proposition, but since it could not be all the first year, it remained nothing in the first year and nothing in subsequent years.

Adams Middle School

Although Adams Middle School had many of the same challenges as had the other middle schools, challenges at Adams were not as severe as those at two of the other schools. For example, student ethnic demographics were the most balanced of all the middle schools. In addition, Adams had the smallest student population of the four middle schools until the beginning of the 2007–2008 school year when Adams received 160 students from Washington Middle School as a result of Choice provisions of *No Child Left Behind*. When combining that number with the 96 students who transferred from Washington in August 2008, Adams had absorbed 256 students in the past 2 years just from transfers. Adams Middle School had been a little over 50% Free and Reduced Lunch for the past 4 years. Surprisingly, with this increased number of students, the highest in-migration increase of all the four middle schools, Adams Middle School's number of students who qualified for Free and Reduced Lunch had not changed significantly.

At Adams when I compared perceptions of the principal with those of the teachers in the focus group concerning usage of technology, there was only a slight misalignment between these two perceptions. Mrs. Buchanan, the principal of Adams Middle School, viewed herself as a technology leader within her school because she tried "to use a lot of different things," even though only 32% of teachers who responded to the pre-survey considered her to be a technology leader. Mrs. Buchanan mentioned using PowerPoint and Outlook, and mentioned publishing an electronic newsletter. She talked at length about how she was using the "Attend a Meeting" request feature in Outlook to remind teachers of faculty meetings. Throughout the entire 1-hour interview, however, Mrs. Buchanan never once mentioned modeling technology usage.

Although Mrs. Buchanan's technology expertise was obviously limited, she saw the value of technology and she promoted use of technology by teachers. She mentioned on several occasions of observing teachers integrating technology into their classroom strategies and of being amazed at how engaged students were in the lessons. As a result of seeing technology being used in classrooms, Mrs. Buchanan said, "Technology has become part of the instructional dialogue with our staff." Although technology was beginning to reach center stage at Adams Middle School, there was a certain resistance to the use of technology, or at least there was hesitancy to the use of technology, because Mrs. Buchanan at one point called technology a "plague." Furthermore, she had not articulated a clear vision about how technology should be used within the classroom as evidenced by the fact that 42% of teachers indicated in the pre-survey they did not know what the principal's vision was. This lack of clear vision was more apparent during the focus group interviews. William, an eighth-grade science teacher, expressed concern that new technology, such as data projectors, was just replacing old technology, such as overhead projectors, without changing the pedagogy of the teachers. This sentiment was echoed by a seventh-grade social studies teacher, who thought that most teachers were not correctly using technology they had been given because mounted projectors just were being used as "a glorified overhead projector."

When comparing two teachers whom Mrs. Buchanan observed teaching the exact same lesson, one with technology and one without technology, the principal came to the conclusion that students in technology-enriched classrooms were more involved in their lessons. In spite of the fact that Mrs. Buchanan experienced, firsthand, the power of technology to engage students in the student-learning process of lessons, she was still a little hesitant about technology in the classroom. For example, when asked what her expectations were for technology use in her school, Mrs. Buchanan said she did not "want to get to the point where we [have] teachers who feel like they can't do their job because the technology gets in their way." In other words, Mrs. Buchanan was not willing to commit wholeheartedly to technology.

Mrs. Buchanan realized that funding was a major obstacle to providing the level of technology resources requested by teachers. To counteract this dilemma, she committed to spending 88% of her Title 1 discretionary funds (see Tables 2 and 4) on technology purchases during the 2007–2008 school year. She bought three interactive whiteboards including a projector, three interactive slates and accompanying projectors, two laptop computers, two student response systems, and two projection carts each with a projector, sound system, and DVD player. Although all purchases were needed and would be put to good use by teachers, the sheer variety of purchases seemed to indicate a certain lack of focus as to how Mrs. Buchanan saw technology being used in the classroom.

Madison Middle School

Madison Middle School had the second highest percentage of economically disadvantaged students at 57% traditionally scoring less well on standardized tests. As a result, Madison faced more challenges than did any of the other middle schools except Washington. Furthermore, in August 2007 Madison was required to absorb more than 200 Choice students from Washington Middle School, resulting in the increase of an additional seven portable classrooms. Although Madison Middle School did not make AYP for the 2007–2008 school year, it had made AYP in previous years, meaning that Madison was not yet a Needs Improvement school. The one thing that Madison had that the other three middle schools did not have is an alignment of perspectives between administration and teachers (see Tables 1 and 2).

It is this alignment of perspectives that allowed teachers at Madison to integrate technology in a manner that engaged all students in the learning process.

When I was setting up my interview with the principal, Mrs. Lynda Duncan, she asked if her assistant principal for curriculum, Mr. James Robinson, could be included in the interview process. I agreed. This decision turned out to be extremely beneficial because Mr. Robinson had been given the responsibility of ensuring that technology was adopted by all teachers. This was my first indication that Madison Middle School's attitude about usage of technology was significantly different from what I had found at the other three middle schools. Technology had become essential to how the school functioned; technology had become the essence of the school. At the very beginning of the interview, Mrs. Duncan stated one of her goals was to make Madison Middle School more technology literate. The one way she felt she could accomplish that was to hire a new assistant principal who could model technology integration behavior. Mrs. Duncan hired a relatively young, energetic math teacher to take over as assistant principal for curriculum, who, as a teacher, regularly integrated technology into his classroom practices. This decision proved instrumental as Mrs. Duncan articulated, "So he was really the vehicle for us to model the technology from my administration stand point."

This modeling of technology started the very first day of preplanning. When teachers reported back from summer vacation in July 2007, Mrs. Duncan took them on a retreat. It was at this retreat on the first day that Mr. Robinson began modeling technology usage and began articulating the administration's expectation that every teacher use technology every day. Mr. Robinson's strategy that brought teachers onboard included using technology for three different purposes. This strategy was purposefully implemented. First, Mr. Robinson wanted to use technology to make school information more accessible and to make communication easier to use. To do this, the administration refused to use paper notifications; instead, Mr. Robinson began sending daily emails to school employees listing all the activities for each day. Teachers in the focus group credited this one simple step from Mr. Robinson as the step that got everyone to buy into using technology as a form of communication. In addition to using email to communicate, Mr. Robinson also began using the district-wide intranet to store documents accessible for teachers to use such as curriculum guides and pacing guides.

The second purpose that Mr. Robinson wanted to use technology was to make record keeping easier. In the past, teachers were not required to use electronic grade-books or to take attendance electronically. When Mr. Robinson became assistant principal, he insisted that all teachers use the electronic gradebooks and that all teachers use the electronic attendance program. To enforce this expectation, Mr. Robinson did not hand out paper-based gradebooks.

Finally, Mr. Robinson wanted to use technology instructionally. He implemented this by modeling technology integration during his weekly grade-level curriculum meetings. Teachers who participated in focus group interviews gave credit to Mr. Robinson for providing enthusiasm to use technology. Jeannie, a non-core subject teacher, said, "The Assistant Principal, Mr. Robinson, is the main reason that technology is being accepted so well in this school." The media specialist echoed this feeling, "You know when you are really excited about something; it is contagious." This strategy that Mr. Robinson devised to get teachers to begin using technology actually began before school started at the beginning of the 2007–2008 school year. In another purposeful move, the administration showed teachers during preplanning how to utilize technology for graphing students' test scores in Excel to analyze areas of weakness.

Mr. Robinson also knew this modeling of technology could not stop once preplanning was over; so when he conducted his grade-level curriculum meetings with teachers after students returned, he modeled technology. Mr. Robinson told me, "They weren't going to use the projector, they weren't going to use their slates, they weren't going to present information to their students in a digital format unless I was doing it to them." Modeling technology usage and setting clear and uncompromising expectations became some of the key elements that brought all teachers onboard.

Mrs. Duncan talked about changing the culture of her school as the reason for this transformation, "I think it is a testimony to the attitude we've got at this school and then the culture we are developing and people willing to move forward. That is the thing. I have not seen anybody resistant to change."

Another element that Mrs. Duncan realized must be addressed was lack of resources that plagued all four middle schools. She made the commitment to invest in technology so teachers could have needed resources. She bought 12 interactive slates and projectors in August 2007, and in the spring of 2008, utilizing Title 1 funds, bought an additional $38,000 worth of interactive slates and projectors (see Tables 3 and 4). This expenditure represented 91% of Madison Middle School's Title 1 allocation for that year. Mrs. Duncan expressed her vision about investing in technology when she concluded, "We are either moving ahead or moving behind; there is no standing still."

It was this vision about technology that was another key element fueling the technological transformation at Madison Middle School. Mr. Robinson succinctly articulated this visionary approach to technology, "It requires more than just a single person to set the vision; it takes everyone being on the same page, same direction." Mr. Robinson mentioned that everyone had to have a common understanding about technology usage. This common understanding was what Fullan (2001) called "shared meaning." According to Fullan, this shared meaning was essential for the kind of second-order change that Mrs. Duncan tried to implement at Madison Middle School.

Another key element to this technological transformation was professional learning. At Madison Middle School, Mr. Robinson provided most of the formal professional learning for teachers, but professional learning did not stop there. Teachers selected as technology leaders by their peers in the pre-survey provided informal professional learning on how to use technology within their curricula areas by going into classrooms to present model lessons that integrated technology for individual teachers who requested this help. The other professional learning opportunities that were available to teachers were those offered from the Central Office during the school year and during the summer. The synergy that took place at Madison Middle School paid huge dividends.

Overall Analysis

The first goal of this study is to understand if school leaders can influence teachers into adopting technology-integrated classroom practices; the second goal of this study is to understand how school leaders can influence teachers to accomplish the first goal. Data collected provide evidence that school leaders do influence teachers into adopting technology-integrated classroom practices, but, more importantly, data indicate that there are eight key strategies school leaders must use if they are to become a technology leader in their school and if they expect to influence how much technology is integrated by teachers. After analyzing the pre-survey, the principal interviews, and the focus group interviews, it becomes clear that one school has implemented all these necessary key strategies, another school has implemented most of these key strategies, and two schools have implemented only a few of these key strategies (see Table 5). The differences between these four schools can be viewed as to the degree of acceptance each principal has for the eight strategies of becoming an effective technology leader within their school. Even though these eight key strategies are equally important, the strategy first among equals is vision, for without vision a school becomes a "rudderless ship" not knowing from where it comes nor to where it is headed.

Table 5 Analysis of which schools are implementing the eight strategies

Strategy	Adams MS	Jefferson MS	Madison MS	Washington MS
Vision			Complete	
Modeling	Partial	Partial	Complete	Partial
Expectations		Partial	Complete	
Resources	Complete		Complete	
Encouragement	Complete	Partial	Partial	
Hiring			Complete	
Professional learning	Partial	Partial	Complete	Partial
Building capacity	Complete		Complete	

Strategy 1: Vision

An analysis of the pre-survey, the principals' interviews, and the focus group interviews provides insights into necessary ingredients a principal has to adopt if he or she becomes a technology leader of his or her school. Obviously, everyone has a vision, but the key to creating a successful organization is that everyone within that organization must share the same vision (Fullan, 2001; Sergiovanni, 2006). This is particularly true in education because teachers have a great deal of autonomy within their classroom; if a teacher's vision is not aligned with the principal's vision then the principal's vision will not be implemented (Fullan). The pre-survey contains two questions that deal with vision. Analysis of the pre-survey reveals that only in Madison Middle School is there alignment between the teachers' vision of technology utilization and the teachers' perception of the principal's vision of technology utilization (see Table 1).

Strategy 2: Modeling

Although all the principals talk about modeling use of technology in their schools, only the assistant principal at Madison Middle School models technology utilization every day. Teachers in the focus group credit Mr. Robinson for transforming teachers into technology users because Mr. Robinson daily models technology. At Jefferson Middle School, Mr. Callifano models technology utilization, but the difference is he does not model it every day; he models technology only on special occasions. Mrs. Almond at Washington Middle School models technology utilization by using a data projector to project a PowerPoint presentation occasionally at faculty meetings. Mrs. Buchanan at Adams Middle School does not mention modeling in her interview; but she talks about allowing some teacher leaders to model technology to the faculty. However, if only teachers are doing the modeling, the impact that modeling can have on the faculty is partially effective: the principal and the assistant principal also need to be doing the modeling. Data indicate that consistent modeling and frequent modeling are necessary to influence teachers to adopt technology integration classroom strategies.

Strategy 3: Expectations

When comparing data from the pre-survey, from principals' interviews, and from focus group interviews, a similar pattern emerges with the strategy on expectations as with the strategy on vision. When teachers are asked in the pre-survey what expectations are there in their school for teachers' utilization of technology (see Table 2) only 4% of Madison Middle School teachers answered that there are no expectations. In comparison, the percentage of teachers at the other three middle schools is much higher: at Adams Middle School 17%, at Jefferson Middle School 24%, and at Washington Middle School 26%. During interviews with these three other principals it is clear these school leaders do not explicitly tell their faculties what their expectations are. For example, in the interview with Mrs. Almond, the principal at Washington Middle School, the word "expectations" is never mentioned. Another example of lack of communicating clear expectations comes from Jefferson Middle School's Mr. Callifano, who says he never explicitly tells his faculty what his expectations are. At Adams Middle School the principal uses the word "expectations" only once during our interview.

Strategy 4: Resources

Not having enough technology resources is the one topic where there appears to be uniform agreement among all principals and among all teachers who respond to the pre-survey, and among all teachers who participate in focus group interviews. On the pre-survey, teachers in every school list lack of technology resources as the number one barrier to integrating technology. The percentage of teachers who list this answer as a barrier ranges from 56% at Washington Middle School to 78% at Madison Middle School. The only other barrier that comes close to these numbers is a lack of access to the computer lab's technology resources ranging from 56% at Washington Middle School to 77% at Jefferson Middle School. Even though every school faces the same problem of lack of resources, after I analyze spending of Title 1 funds for the 2007–2008 school year, I conclude that two of the principals, Mrs. Buchanan at Adams Middle School and Mrs. Duncan at Madison Middle School, decide to mitigate this problem by expending significant sums of their Title 1 funds on technology purchases during the summer of 2008.

Strategy 5: Encouragement

When attempting to promote technology utilization, the encouragement strategy is the companion opposite of expectations. Encouragement to promote technology utilization without explicit expectations is empty rhetoric; explicit expectations to integrate technology without encouragement are pernicious dogma. Each must occur frequently, and each must occur consistently. In three of the four schools, principals offer encouragement for creative lesson planning. At Washington Middle School the opposite is happening; teachers are not encouraged to integrate technology. Integrating technology into classroom practices is difficult enough without support from and encouragement of the school leader (Mouza, 2003). To overcome these barriers, teachers need to be encouraged and need to feel their efforts are appreciated.

Strategy 6: Human Capital

One of the most important findings in Jim Collins' (2002) *Good to Great: Why Some Companies Make the Leap . . . and Others Don't* applies to education, that of the leader hiring the right people. Collins explained who the right people are: the people who share core values of the organization and the people who do not have to be managed. Collins uses a metaphor for this hiring process; he calls it getting the right people on the bus and getting the wrong people off the bus. Of all the principal interviews that I conducted, only one of the principals expressed an interest in hiring teachers or assistant principals who have technical expertise. When Mrs. Duncan at Madison Middle School talks about the process of hiring a new assistant principal, she says she looks for three characteristics: passion, energy, and technology literacy. Accordingly, if the school leader does not get the right people on the bus, then the school leader's vision will never be implemented.

Strategy 7: Professional Learning

Since integration of technology represents change for most teachers, significant professional learning is required. After trying for 5 years in the late 1980s and in the early 1990s to transform classrooms into student-centered technology-integrated classrooms, the Apple Classroom of Tomorrow concluded that intensive, formalized professional training was necessary (Ringstaff & Yocam, 1992). Principals at Adams Middle, Jefferson Middle, and Madison Middle talk extensively about providing onsite professional learning opportunities for teachers. Mrs. Almond at Washington Middle only talks briefly about in-service training. In order to quantify this commitment to technology-focused professional learning, I analyze the number of teachers who have participated in two different programs offered by the Central Office. Jefferson Middle allows only 26 teachers to participate in technology-focused professional learning, while Washington Middle allows 29 and Adams Middle allows 32. Madison Middle is more committed by allowing 54.

Strategy 8: Building Capacity

In Fullan's (2001) book on educational change and in Sergiovanni's (2006) book on school principals, one of the most significant determinants for successful school leaders was creating a sense of community, a feeling of connectiveness, and a common purpose. Sergiovanni explained this sense of community as a group of individuals bonded together by relationships but also bound together by shared ideas and ideals. This bonding and this binding of individuals to common goals, to shared values, and to shared beliefs were what Sergiovanni called the "community of mind." By creating this community of mind within the culture of the school, the principal is creating an authentic community in which the whole is greater than the sum of its parts. Mr. Callifano at Jefferson talks about creating "shared governance," and at Adams Middle, Mrs. Buchanan hints at "creating a community of leaders," but at Madison Middle, this sense of community of mind is being created due to the leadership of Mrs. Duncan. Teacher leaders exist at all four schools promoting the utilization of technology, but only at Madison are these teachers actively modeling technology integration within other teachers' classrooms. It is these activities that are helping to create a community of mind, and, as a result, it is these activities that are helping to build capacity within Madison Middle School.

Conclusion

Implications from this research are many. At each of the four middle schools is a core group of teachers, trailblazers, and early adopters, integrating technology every day in spite of barriers. However, these early adopters are not enough to transform a school; it takes the commitment of the school leader to influence teachers' adoption of technology integration classroom practices. The real question is how. A thorough analysis of various data sets shows all eight leadership strategies need to be implemented en masse for successful technology integration.

In 2001, Larry Cuban in his landmark book *Oversold and Underused: Computers in the Classroom* declared that technology integration was being used only at the first order of change and that the promise of technology in education was destined to fail. What Cuban did not comprehend was the importance of school leaders in influencing teachers' attitudes and practices. The key, therefore, is the alignment between the principal's vision for technology integration and the teachers' vision of technology integration. This alignment is crucial. Of course, all this is dependent on the principal being not only a school leader but also a technology leader for his or her school. The path to dispelling Cuban's thesis, to achieving technology's promise, and to achieving technology integration success is the path of eight strategies leading to principal and teacher alignment, and, as a result, to student success in learning.

References

Becker, H. (2001). How are teachers using computers in instruction? Paper presented at the 2001 Meeting of the American Educational Research Association, Seattle, WA. Retrieved August 25, 2004, from http://www.crito.uci.edu/tlc/FINDINGS/special3/

Becker, H., & Lovitts, B. (2003). A project-based approach to assessing technology. In G. Haetel & B. Means (Eds.), *Evaluating educational technology*. New York: Teachers College Press.

Blumer, H. (1969). *Symbolic interactionism*. Englewood, NJ: Prentice Hall.

Brinkerhoff, J. (2006). Effects of a long-duration, professional development academy of technology skills, computer self-efficacy, and technology integration beliefs and practices. *Journal of Research on Technology in Education, 39*(1), 22–43.

Crotty, M. (1998). *The foundations of social research: Meaning and perspective in the research process*. London: Sage Publications.

Cuban, L. (2001). *Oversold and underused: Computers in the classroom*. Cambridge, MA: University of Harvard Press.

Cuban, L. (2003). Forward. In A. Sheekey (Ed.), *How to ensure ed/tech is not oversold and underused* (pp. vii–xi). Lanham, MD: The Scarecrow Press.

Cuban, L. (2004). *The blackboard and the bottom line*. Cambridge, MA: Harvard University Press.

Cuban, L., Kirkpatrick, H. & Peck, C. (2001). High access and low use of technologies in high school classrooms: Explaining an apparent paradox. *American Educational Research Journal, 38*(4), 813–834.

Dwyer, D. C. (1995). Changing the conversation about teaching, learning, and technology. Retrieved on November 18, 2006, from http://www.apple.com/education/k12/leadership/acot/library.html

Elmore, R. E. (2003). The limits of change. In M. Pierce & D. L. Stapleton (Eds.), *The 21st century principal: Current issues in leadership and policy*. Cambridge, MA: Harvard Education Press.

Ertmer, P. A. (1999). Addressing first- and second-order barriers to change: Strategies for technology integration. *Educational Technology Research and Development, 47*(4), 47–61.

Ertmer, P. A. (2005). Teacher pedagogical beliefs: The final frontier in our quest for technology integration?. *Educational Technology Research and Development, 53*(4), 25–39.

Ferneding, K. A. (2003). *Questioning technology: Electronic technologies and educational reform.* New York: Peter Lang Publishing, Inc.

Friedman, T. L. (2005). *The world is flat: A brief history of the 21st century.* New York: Farrar, Straus and Giroux.

Fullan, M. (1993). *Change forces: Probing the depth of educational reform.* New York: Falmer Press.

Fullan, M. (2001). *The new meaning of educational change* (3rd ed.). New York: Teachers College Press.

Healy, J. (1990). *Endangered minds: Why our children don't think.* New York: Simon and Schuster.

Hernández-Ramos, P. (2005). If not here, where? Understanding teachers' use of technology in Silicon Valley schools. *Journal of Research on Technology in Education, 38,* 1.

Mouza, C. (2003, Winter). Learning to teach with new technology: Implications for professional development. *Journal of Research on Technology in Education, 35*(2), 272–289.

Postman, N. (1992). *Technopoly: The surrender of culture to technology.* New York: Knopf.

Prensky, M. (2006). Listen to the natives. *Educational Leadership, 63*(4), 8–13.

Ringstaff, C., & Yocam, K. (1992). Creating an alternative context for teacher development: The ACOT teacher development centers. Retrieved on November 18, 2006, from http://www.apple.com/education/k12/leadership/acot/library.html

Rogers, E. M. (2003). *Diffusion of innovations* (5th ed.). New York: Free Press.

Sergiovanni, T. J. (2006). *The principalship: A reflective practice perspective.* Boston: Pearson Education, Inc.

Staples, A., Pugach, M. C. & Himes, D. (2005). Rethinking the technology integration challenge: Cases from three urban elementary schools. *Journal of Research on Technology in Education, 37*(3), 285–311.

Toffler, A. (1970). *Future shock.* New York: Random House, Inc.

Windschitl, M., & Sahl, K. (2002, Spring). Tracing teachers' use of technology in a laptop computer school: The interplay of teacher beliefs, social dynamics, and institutional culture. *American Educational Research Journal, 39*(1), 165–205.

Issues and Trends in Instructional Technology: Growth and Maturation of Web-Based Tools in a Challenging Climate; Social Networks Gain Educators' Attention

Abbie Brown and Tim Green

Abstract Composed of four sections – Overall Developments, Corporate Training and Development, Higher Education, and K-12 Education – this chapter synthesizes the findings of major annual reports including ASTD's *State of the Industry Report*, the *EDUCAUSE Core Data Service Fiscal Year 2007 Summary Report*, *The ECAR Study of Undergraduate Students and Information Technology*, Education Week's *Technology Counts 2009*, Project Tomorrow's *Speak Up 2009*, and the Greaves Group's *America's Digital Schools*. The authors describe the economy's impact on instructional technology and comment on the importance of Web 2.0, online learning, and increased attention paid to social networking sites for educational purposes.

Keywords Educational technology · Instructional technology · Training

We continue the tradition of reporting the issues and trends of instructional technology that have continued or arisen within the past year. This chapter is composed of four sections: Overall Developments, Corporate Training and Development, Higher Education, and K-12 Education.

Overall Developments

The U.S. economy has taken a major downturn during the time since the previous review was written (Brown & Green, 2009). Although the specifics leading to this

A. Brown (✉)
Department of Mathematics, Science and Instructional Technology Education, East Carolina University, Greenville, NC, USA
e-mail: brownab@ecu.edu

T. Green (✉)
Department of Elementary and Bilingual Education, California State University, Fullerton, CA, USA
e-mail: timdgreen@gmail.com

M. Orey et al. (eds.), *Educational Media and Technology Yearbook*,
Educational Media and Technology Yearbook 35,
DOI 10.1007/978-1-4419-1516-0_3, © Springer Science+Business Media, LLC 2010

downturn will not be discussed due to the complexity and contentious nature of the topic, we can write with some certainty that the troubled financial and housing markets are often cited as major contributing factors. As a result of the economic downturn, a rise in unemployment and a decrease in tax revenues occurred. Add to the mix an uncertainty of the impact of the policies and actions of the new U.S. presidential administration. The overall impact of these circumstances led to less robust funding for K-12, higher education. Subsequently, spending on technology in the public sectors was conservative and cautious.

Web 2.0 Continues to Mature: Social Networks Achieve Greater Popularity

We reported last year that Web 2.0 tools were reaching a maturation stage. We continue to see this as the process of including audio, video, and still images to Web-based communications becomes increasingly easier. Text-based communications including instant messaging and blog posts and responses have become more a part of everyday life as well, as has participation in social network sites such as Facebook, along with increased use of wikis and blogs. Although employers and school officials continue to voice concerns about access to such sites, social networking saw a significant gain in popularity among educators in all settings, from K-12 to business (Irons, 2008; Paradise, 2008; Salaway, 2008; Weekes, 2008; Wexler et al., 2008; Young, 2007). Salaway (2008) refers to social networking sites as "... one of those quintessential new forms that define a generation" (p. 5).

Online Learning Continues Its Growth

Online courses and programs continue to increase in popularity (Allen & Seaman, 2008). Fuel costs seem to play a role in increased online enrollment (Allen & Seaman). The economy factors into online learning's popularity as programs of interest to working adults and rising unemployment rates factor into expanding online learning opportunities (Allen & Seaman).

Corporate Training and Development

As has been done in previous issues and trends chapters of the yearbook (Bichelmeyer & Molenda, 2006; Brown & Green, 2008, 2009), we continue to track corporate application of instructional technologies primarily by referring to the American Society for Training and Development's (ASTD's) *State of the Industry Report* (Paradise, 2008). The current ASTD annual report is based on data collected from the Benchmarking Forum (BMF) organizations, ASTD BEST award winners, and responses from users of ASTD's WLP (Workforce Learning and Performance) Scorecard. The report describes the activities of organizations recognized as exemplary in their approach to workplace learning and performance as represented by the BEST award winners; larger, global organizations typically represented by BMF members; and data collected from users of ASTD's WLP Scorecard benchmarking and decision support tool.

Learning Expenditure and Employee Use

In a reversal of the previous year's report, the average direct learning expenditure increased among all organizations, from $1040 per employee in 2006 to $1103 in 2007, a gain of 6.1% (Paradise, 2008). Organizations continue to direct most of this spending to internal resources despite the prevalence of external training providers and learning specialists: 62.2% of learning costs were internal, and outsourcing continues to decrease (Paradise).

The average number of learning hours used by employees increased between 2006 and 2007, from 35.1 in 2006 to 37.4 in 2007 (Paradise). The average cost per learning hour used or received rose 2.5%, from $54 in 2006 to $56 in 2007 (Paradise). Paradise notes these gains suggest that business leaders expect professionals to incorporate a number of learning activities into their schedule; more formal learning opportunities are being offered than have been in the past.

Instructional Content

The average reuse of learning content continues to rise; in 2007 the ratio reached 44.8, meaning that every hour of content provided was used 44.8 times (Paradise, 2008). Three areas accounted for 37% of instructional content in 2007: profession or industry-specific content; management and supervision; and processes, procedures, and business practices (Paradise). The least amount of content was devoted to executive development, sales training, and interpersonal skills.

Use of Technology: E-learning Is Still on the Rise

Computer-based learning delivery continued its upward trend; the average number of e-learning hours available rose from 30.3% in 2006 to 32.6% in 2007 (Paradise, 2008). For the first time since 2003, however, self-paced online learning declined in use from 19.1% in 2006 to 18.2% in 2007, although it continues to be the most frequently provided e-learning (Paradise).

Higher Education

We examine universities' information technology (IT) use and instructional technology application primarily by referring to the *EDUCAUSE Core Data Service Fiscal Year 2007 Summary Report* (Hawkins & Rudy, 2008). Nine hundred ninety-four institutions submitted the 2007 survey; the data set was frozen in May 2008 to prepare the analysis for the summary report released in September 2007. Undergraduate trends in particular are examined by referring to *The ECAR Study of Undergraduate Students and Information Technology, 2008* (Salaway, 2008). A total of 27,316 students at ninety-eight 2-year and 4-year institutions responded to the ECAR survey. Trends in online learning are examined by referring to *Staying the Course: Online Education in the United States* (Allen & Seaman, 2008), supported by the Alfred P. Sloan Foundation and based on responses from more than 2500 colleges and universities.

Information Technology Planning and Budgeting on Campus

The *EDUCAUSE Core Data Service* report (or CDS) once again indicated a wide diversity of campus constituents who contribute to IT strategies (Hawkins & Rudy, 2008). Planning input from president's cabinet/councils, system/district offices, student committees, academic/faculty committees, and administrative committees seems to be developing into a standard practice. Furthermore, IT planning and budgeting increased substantially from past year, with a significant increase in staffing (Hawkins & Rudy). Online learning as a critically important long-term strategy remains a focal point for public institutions, but least important for baccalaureate institutions and private nonprofits (Allen & Seaman, 2007).

Campus Technology Support and Use of Technology for Instruction

The CDS notes a significant increase in wireless network connectivity along with a trend toward faster connectivity speeds. Classrooms equipped with wireless Internet connectivity increased around 8% overall (Hawkins & Rudy, 2008). Also, classrooms equipped with LCD projectors increased about 5% (Hawkins & Rudy).

Ninety-three percent of the institutions in the CDS report that they support at least one course management system (CMS, e.g., Blackboard), with 35% of the institutions reporting CMS use for all or nearly all courses – a 4% increase in ubiquitous use over the previous year (Hawkins & Rudy).

ECAR study results indicate that fewer than half the students surveyed think their instructors use IT effectively: 44% report most of their instructors use IT effectively in courses, 34.1% report instructors provide students with adequate training for the IT used in a course, and 35.2% report their instructors understand the IT skill levels of their students (Salaway, 2008). However, the same study indicates that 45.7% of respondents believe the use of IT in courses increases learning, 31.8% of respondents report greater engagement with courses that use IT, and 65.6% report that IT makes completing course activities more convenient (Salaway). Clearly there is room for improvement among instructors making use of IT, and the effort is worthwhile because students find the use of IT helpful.

According to Allen and Seaman (2008), over 3.9 million students are taking online courses, a 12% increase over the previous year's reported number. More than 20% of all U.S. higher education students took at least one online course in the fall of 2007 (Allen & Seaman). Online enrollments grew by 12.9%, which drastically exceeds the 1.2% enrollment growth in higher education overall.

Technology Support for Faculty

Offering faculty training upon request and offering training through scheduled seminars were once again the two most common methods of assisting faculty according to the EDUCAUSE Core Data Service survey (Hawkins & Rudy, 2008). Training upon request was offered by 95% of the campuses surveyed, and training through scheduled seminars was offered by 88% of those campuses (Hawkins & Rudy). A significant increase in support offered through the use of student technology assistants, activities for faculty to share innovative ideas, and special grants and awards for faculty using technology were reported by the CDS (Hawkins & Rudy).

Student Computing

Laptops are once again the preferred computer style; 80.5% of ECAR survey respondents report owning a laptop, and most freshmen at 4-year institutions have new laptops when they begin college (Salaway, 2008). Besides, 66.1% of ECAR respondents own Internet-capable cell phones, though most do not use the Internet capability; students report that high cost, slow response, and difficulty of use are barriers to making use of their cell phone's Internet features (Salaway).

Students are online for work, school, or recreation an average of 19.6 h per week (Salaway, 2008). Almost all respondents reported having high-speed access to the Internet (Salaway, 2008). Of the students responding to the ECAR survey, 85.2% report using a social networking site, most often Facebook (Salaway); 73.9% of students use graphics software to create or manipulate images, and highly interactive games are popular with almost a third of students (Salaway). Most college students consider themselves reasonably skilled in applications used for course work (e.g., the Microsoft Office suite, course management systems, and browsing the Web).

K-12 Education

The primary reports used in the identification and analysis of the issues in K-12 instructional technology were *Technology Counts 2009, Speak Up 2009,* and *America's Digital Schools. Technology Counts 2009* is the 10th annual report provided by *Education Week.* The *Speak Up 2009* report is a national survey of approximately 100,000 students, teachers, and administrators conducted by the Project Tomorrow. *America's Digital Schools* is a summary report created by the Greaves Group and the Hayes Connection on K-12 educational technology trends.

Issues regarding instructional technology use in K-12 continue to remain consistent in comparison to the issues from past reviews. With each review year, however, a new issue surfaces that gains significant attention. The major issue reported in the last year's review was the push for improvement in science, technology, engineering, and mathematics (STEM) education (Brown & Green, 2009). Significant federal monies – up to 3 billion is estimated – were allocated by Congress for STEM educational initiatives (Cavanagh, 2008; Technology Counts, 2008). The goal of the initiatives was to develop STEM programs in higher education and K-12 in order to advance student training and knowledge in these areas.

For this review, e-learning is the issue that took center stage (Davis, 2009a). Although the number (2%) of students taking part in e-learning is small in comparison to the total public school population, the number is significantly increasing. The Sloan Consortium reported that the enrollment of K-12 public school students in online courses rose 47% from 2005 (Piccianno & Seaman, 2009). The total enrollment in online courses was approximately 1 million public school students during 2008 (Piccianno & Seaman, 2009). In addition to student use of e-learning, an increase in online teacher professional development was reported (Sawchuk, 2009). A more detailed discussion of these and other issues will be done later in this section.

The Overall State of K-12 Technology

The *Technology Counts* report provides an overall snapshot of technology use by the 50 states and the District of Columbia. Data was collected by the EPS Research Center on 10 indicators covering state technology policy and practice. Due to the lack of certain data that has been available in previous years, an overall grade for the nation was not given as it was last year when the nation earned a C+. Instead, letter grades were given for two areas of technology – use of and capacity to use. Technology use was based on four policy indicators: student technology standards, student testing on technology, virtual school, and computer-based student assessment. Technology capacity focused on six measures: technology standards for teachers and administrators, course work or a test for initial professional licensure, and technology training or a technology test for professional recertification. The nation earned a B in technology use and a C+ in technology capacity for use. Nine states received A grades for technology use, while 11 received D+ grades and the District of Columbia received an F. Three states earned A grades in technology capacity for use, while seven earned D grades and five earned F grades (Hightower, 2009).

Funding

Data that outlined overall K-12 IT spending in the United States was difficult to obtain. We believe this is due to fluctuating state budgets resulting from mid-year cuts and the infusion of federal monies from the American Recovery and Reinvestment Act (ARRA). We can report that an estimated $650 million was allocated by Congress to educational technology programs such as improving broadband access to rural schools and data-management systems. Specifically, an estimated $250 million was provided to support existing statewide longitudinal data system programs to help states and districts build the capacity to accurately collect and analyze student data for decision-making purposes (Davis, 2009a). The overall exact impact ARRA monies had on IT spending in 2009 was difficult to establish as will be the long-term impact on IT spending because much of the available funds are a one-time infusion (Klein, 2009; Samuels, 2009).

As mentioned, specific uniformed data that summarized the overall magnitude of cuts made to IT spending was not readily available. The existing data was reported on a state-by-state basis, thus making it difficult to provide a definitive statement about the whole United States. Yet we can write with some certainty based on the individual state reports that the overall spending on K-12 technology was down, despite the infusion of ARRA funds. To provide some perspective on spending, we reported last year (according to Dyril, 2008) that districts' technology spending in 2007 averaged $577,100 per district for an estimated total of $4.3 billion nationwide. Coping with technology budget cuts led many districts to examine areas where cuts could be made without drastically compromising network security and hampering teaching and learning. Software licensing was an area where many districts looked to lower costs by exploring open source products (Davis, 2009a).

Teacher Technology Training, Certification, and Professional Development

During the previous two reviews (Brown & Green, 2008, 2009), we have expressed optimism that the number of states with technology standards for teachers would increase. We were especially hopeful that the updated International Society for Technology in Education technology standards (in 2008) would provide states with reason and opportunity to revaluate their own state teacher technology standards and technology requirements for licensure. Although the increase has been minimal from year to year, the good news is that there has been growth. The current number is 46 – up two from the previous review and up six from 2004. Of the 46 states with teacher technology standards, 37 have technology standards for administrators; this is an increase of two from 2008 (Bausell, 2008; Hightower, 2009). Although we would like to remain optimistic that additional states will join the states currently implementing teacher and administrator technology standards, we predict that the numbers will remain the same.

The number continues to be much lower for teachers to demonstrate technology competence for initial licensure; only 21 states require either technology course work or the passing of a test to demonstrate competency. Since the last review that number has increased by two (Hightower, 2009). This reverses what took place last year when the number decreased (Brown & Green, 2009). Ten states require course work or a test for initial licensure for administrators (Hightower), which is up one from last year. We echo the trend we predicted last year that there will be an increased integration of technology into content area courses rather than stand-alone courses. We predict the number of states requiring technology course work or the passing of a test to demonstrate competency will slightly increase, as has been the trend over the past review years.

Ten states require teachers to demonstrate ongoing competence in technology or to complete professional development related to technology before being recertified (Hightower, 2009), an increase of one from last year. The number of states requiring ongoing technology training or testing for competence for administrators is seven (an increase of one). California continues to require technology-related professional development only for principals of low-performing schools (Hightower).

A trend in teacher professional development is the increase in online offerings (Sawchuk, 2009). We see this trend continuing – especially in states that have built a virtual school infrastructure (e.g., Florida and Michigan). Thirty-three percent of teachers surveyed ($n = 29,644$) for the annual *Speak Up 2008* survey indicated that they have enrolled in an online professional development course (Sawchuk). The top three reasons cited by these teachers for taking online professional development are "fits my schedule" (56%), "ability to customize learning to fit my needs" (37%), and "I can review materials as I need them" (35%) (Online PD, 2009). Although online training has the potential to lower costs, provide flexibility for teachers, and provide standardized professional development, issues regarding quality remain.

In sum, the *Technology Counts 2009* report indicated that the states averaged a C+ grade for helping build the capacity of teachers and administrators to effectively use and integrate technology in the classroom. This continues the trend of a slight improvement over the previous year (a C grade was given in 2008). Three states (Georgia, Kentucky, and West Virginia) earned A grades – the same states that earned A grades last year. One fewer state earned an F grade; four states (Idaho, Montana, Nevada, and Utah) and the District of Columbia earned F grades. Based on past trends, we predict that the numbers we have reported will again remain relatively consistent.

Student and Teacher Access to Technology

Student Access. In last year's review, we reported that student access to instructional computing had significantly improved since 1999 (Brown & Green, 2009). At the time of writing the current review, there is no new data available that indicates a change in student access to instructional computing. Thus, we can only include what we reported last year. We reported that the ratio of students per instructional computer in the United States was on average 3.8 to 1 as compared to 5.7 to 1 in 1999 (Project Tomorrow, 2009a). Despite this decrease, state ratios varied considerably – 15 states having ratios above 3.8 to 1. Utah had the highest ratio at 5.4 to 1, while South Dakota had the lowest, with two students per instructional computer. Ninety-five percent of fourth-grade students had access to instructional computers; the percentage of eighth-grade students with access was slightly lower at 83% (Bausell, 2008). Overall, the United States earned a C grade for student access according to the *Technology Counts 2008* report (Bausell).

We predict, as we did last year, that when new data becomes available, the ratio of students per instructional computer in the United States will have slightly dropped for several reasons such as the increase in large-scale 1:1 initiatives and the decrease in cost of computers. In the 2008 review, we reported that 24% of school districts were in the process of implementing 1:1 computing programs, which was an increase of 20% since 2004 (eSchool News, 2006). According to the latest *America's Digital Schools* report, 50% (double the current percentage) of school districts reported that they will have 1:1 computing by 2011 (Greaves & Hayes, 2009). This is double the current percentage.

Student access to the Internet has drastically improved over the years as well. Almost all public K-12 schools have access to the Internet. This is up from 35% of public K-12 schools having access in 1994 (NCES, 2005. The inclusion of the Internet into the classroom has followed a similar path – in 1994 only 3% of classrooms had Internet access and by 2005 the percentage increased to 94% (Bausell, 2008). This equates to 3.7 students for every high-speed, Internet-connected computer in the United States. Utah had the highest ratio at 5.3:1, while South Dakota had the lowest at 1.9:1 (Bausell). Relatively significant access differences continue to exist when comparing urban schools to nonurban ones. The NCES reported that 88% of inner-city classrooms were equipped with Internet access in contrast to 95–98% of classrooms in nonurban schools (Bausell, 2008). Secondary schools, larger schools, and low minority enrollment schools are slightly more likely to have higher access levels (Bausell, 2008). We predict that Internet connectivity will continue to improve for K-12 schools. We are hopeful in large part because of such U.S. government programs as the rural broadband initiative.

Teacher Access. Last year we reported that data describing teacher access to technology in schools are inconsistent from year to year. Unfortunately, we must report the same for this year. A significant annual report – *Teachers Talk Tech* – from which extensive teacher use data was pulled from for the 2008 review has been discontinued. At the time of our writing, there were no other available reports outlining specific teacher access data. Thus, we infer, as we did last year, that the technology access teachers have in schools mirrors student access levels (according to *Technology Counts 2008*, students per instructional computer averaged 3.8 in the United States). Access to computing technologies is most likely higher for teachers of upper grades than of lower grades (following the same access patterns for students).

It is clear that access to technology in K-12 has significantly increased over the past decade. Although there have been no new studies since 2005 that indicate a change in student and teacher access, we believe that access to instructional computing has remained relatively consistent over the past 3 years (with a possible decrease in the number of students per instructional computer). As computing tools continue to lower in price, coupled with the number of districts reporting that they will implement 1:1 computing initiatives in the next 2–3 years, we have evidence to believe that access to computing tools by students and teachers will continue to increase.

Student Use of Technology

Last year we reported that students in grades 6–12 surveyed for *Speak Up 2008* (Project Tomorrow, 2009a) indicated that their top five schoolwork-related activities involving computers were writing assignments (74%); researching online (72%); checking assignments or grades online (58%); creating slideshows, videos, and Web pages for schoolwork (57%); and e-mailing or IM with classmates about assignments (44%). The data from the *Speak Up 2008* survey indicates similar trends for students surveyed in grades 6–12. After the top two activities of writing assignments and online research, the next five schoolwork-related activities were creating presentations and videos, communicating with others, taking online tests, accessing class information, and playing games. Last year the survey indicated that over 50% of high school students reported using e-mail, IM, and text messaging on a regular basis (Project Tomorrow, 2009a). This number increased by 27% for the 2008 survey, while the use of social networking sites to collaborate with classmates increased by 150% (Project Tomorrow, 2009b).

When looking at 8- to 18-year-olds' use of media in and out of school, a Kaiser Foundation Study conducted in 2005 reported that this group spends an average of $6\frac{1}{2}$ h a day with media. During this $6\frac{1}{2}$ h, they are actually exposed to the equivalent of $8\frac{1}{2}$ h of media. This media ranges from watching television, listening to music, to reading print-based media. The largest percentage of time is spent using digital media – such as watching live and recorded TV (almost 4 h a day), listening to music (1.75 h a day), and using a computer (1 h a day) (Rideout, Roberts, & Foehr, 2005). These results are supported by the data provided in the *Speak Up 2008* survey that indicates that approximately half of the students surveyed had access to a cell phone, approximately 65% had access to an MP3 player, and close to half had access to a laptop (Project Tomorrow, 2009b). All (grades 3–12) students surveyed overwhelmingly indicated that they wanted to be able to use mobile computing devices at school to support learning and conduct research, for reminders and alerts, to record lectures (grades 6–12), and to upload or download content from a portal (grades 6–12) (Project Tomorrow, 2009b).

Innovative and Emerging Technologies Used in K-12

The major trends from the past two reviews in this category were ubiquitous networks and computing and Web 2.0 tools. We predicted that the adoption of wireless networks in K-12 would continue to increase, allowing teachers and students to integrate various mobile devices into the classroom. There is some evidence (see Project Tomorrow, 2009b) that supports the accuracy of this prediction. We discussed that laptops would be the main type of mobile computing devices districts would purchase. There is no direct data supporting this prediction. Finally, we predicted that students would continue to lead the way in pushing the use of Web 2.0 tools in the classroom. There is strong evidence to support the accuracy of this prediction as students are continuing to use Web 2.0 for schoolwork and non-school-related activities (Project Tomorrow, 2009b; Greaves & Hayes, 2009). For the current review, we see three major innovative and emerging technology trends: online education, mobile devices, and Web 2.0 tools.

Online Education. In last year's review we wrote that online education holds a great deal of promise for K-12 education despite the challenges associated with it. We predicted that online education would continue as a key trend in K-12 education (Brown & Green, 2009). In examining available data, we can see that this prediction was realized. According to the Sloan Consortium (2009), the growth of K-12 students using online courses significantly rose (more than 1 million public school students) over the past year, which is a 47% increase from 2005.

There are various models of online education being implemented from purely virtual to blended learning where in-class learning is being supplemented with digital curriculum (Davis, 2009b). The various models provide opportunities to differentiate curriculum and meet the needs of various students. We wrote in last year's review that online learning has the potential to provide access to learning opportunities that some students might not have otherwise – such as advanced placement (AP). We believe this potential is being realized. According to *Technology Counts 2009*, student demand for AP courses has risen despite 40% of high schools not offering these courses (Davis, 2009b). Several for-profit companies have emerged to fill the void. In addition to AP courses, remediation and credit recovery are two new areas where online education is moving (Davis, 2009b).

Another trend we believe is helping drive online education is the continual development of learning management systems (LMS). We predict that LMS will continue to gain traction in K-12 education. According to the latest *America's Digital Schools* report (2009), 47% of the districts surveyed indicated that they were using an LMS. Of the students and teachers surveyed from these districts, approximately 40% of the students reported using an LMS daily (approximately 90% reported at least once-a-week use), while approximately 30% of the teachers reported once-a-day use (approximately 85% reported at least once-a-week use). Only 10% of students and teachers reported accessing an LMS daily from home. Approximately 50% of students and 60% of the teachers reported use at home at least once a week. The top three student uses were supplementation of a traditional course, credit recovery, and core curriculum access for online students. High school students were the most likely student users of an LMS, although middle school and upper elementary school students were close behind percentage-wise (Greaves & Hayes, 2009).

A major challenge we discussed last year regarding online education was teacher skill and comfort with online education. We believe this remains a challenge. However, this challenge is being addressed as the number of online professional development opportunities for teachers increases, as does the number of teachers taking online professional development. Thirty-three percent of teachers surveyed for the annual *Speak Up 2008* survey indicated that they have enrolled in an online professional development course (Sawchuk, 2009). We predict that this increase will help teachers develop some of the skill and dispositions needed to become comfortable with online education.

Mobile Devices. The popularity of mobile devices in K-12 continues as a trend. *Speak Up 2008* reported that student access to mobile devices increased dramatically in the year since their last survey (Project Tomorrow, 2009b). As a reminder of what we wrote on K-12 student technology access, approximately half of the students surveyed had access to a cell phone, approximately 65% had access to an MP3 player, and close to half had access to a laptop (Project Tomorrow, 2009b). We believe the numbers of students having access to mobile devices will continue to rise. As a result, students will continue to put pressure on schools to allow these devices as learning tools. Students will continue to expect that their teachers integrate these devices into the instructional environment.

Data outlining the most popular mobile devices purchased by schools is difficult – if not impossible – to find. Based on the number of current 1:1 initiatives in K-12 and the reporting of school districts (79% of districts according to the current *America's Digital Schools* report), we infer that laptops are the most frequently purchased mobile device by districts. Current data indicating the potential purchases of districts was not available at the time of our writing. We do predict that until the economy stabilizes and budget cuts to K-12 stop, funding on computing hardware will remain limited.

Web 2.0 Tools. As we mentioned in an early section of this chapter, Web 2.0 tools have continued to mature since the last review. These tools have become more sophisticated, and additional tools have been developed – some specifically for the K-12 environment. Students in increased numbers since the last review are using Web 2.0 tools in various ways – such as communication, collaboration, and the creation and consuming of digital media and information. We believe this trend will continue as the process of including audio, video, and still images to Web-based communications becomes increasingly easier.

A specific Web 2.0 tool category that saw a significant increase (150% increase from last year) in use by K-12 students was social networking sites such as

MySpace, Facebook, and Friendster (Project Tomorrow, 2009b). Students reported that they regularly use social networking sites to communicate and share information with peers outside of school time. Forty percent of high school students, 35% of middle school students, and 28% of third- to fifth-grade students surveyed for the most recent *Speak Up* report indicated that they update their profile regularly on a social networking site.

Although social networking saw a significant gain in popularity among educators in various settings (Irons, 2008; Paradise, 2008; Salaway, 2008; Weekes, 2008; Wexler et al., 2008; Young, 2007), the K-12 sector has not embraced social networking sites with the same zeal as the corporate and higher education sectors have. K-12 administrators and educators remain concerned and cautious about allowing access to and use of these tools in schools because of the potential (real and perceived) dangerous associated with using them. As student use of social networking sites continues to increase, we predict that K-12 schools will continue to wrestle with the idea of allowing social networking sites to be used in the classroom for educational purposes.

Conclusion

In higher education and K-12 settings, we predict all spending will remain lower or at the same level until the health of the economy improves considerably. Traditionally, it takes 18–24 months for state budgets to recover after an economic downturn. Thus, it can be expected that state budgets will not start to recover until well into 2011 (Griffith, 2008). Although corporations reported increases in average direct learning expenditures, the current economy may cause changes in this trend, affecting spending adversely in the private sector as well. Business and corporate instructional technology specialists will be affected by these spending patterns, of course, but the relatively low cost and high yield of e-learning strategies may cause networked computer-based teaching and learning to continue to receive significant institutional support.

While corporate and higher education settings develop an increasing enthusiasm for the use of social networks for instructional purposes, K-12 settings find them a cause for concern. No matter what the setting, social networks are increasing in popularity. This is seen as an opportunity among communities that are composed entirely of adults and as a potential danger among communities that contain children and teenagers (the concern is that young people may not have the social skills necessary to use networking software safely). We can safely predict that computer-based social networking will continue to be a topic of high interest in all instructional settings though it may be more rapidly adopted for instructional use among educators who work with adults.

Online learning continues to grow. It is possible that online learning may actually thrive during an economic downturn since it provides a means of instructional delivery that does not generally require travel. In business settings, online learning provides a means of teaching large numbers of people the processes, procedures, and practices essential to their work. In higher education online learning offers opportunities for those looking to increase their professional skills and/or change careers. Although K-12 settings make the least use of online learning, there has been a significant rise in its use this past year.

Everyone seems to be taking advantage of the capabilities offered by Web 2.0 tools to make more and better use of multimedia and interaction in Web-based communication. Audio and video tools continue to become easier to use, and technologies that facilitate direct, real-time communication and easy-to-use asynchronous communication tools have become commonplace.

Overall, we foresee lean times ahead for just about everyone, but we also see tremendous opportunities for instructional technology specialists in corporate, higher education, and K-12 settings.

References

Allen, I. A., & Seaman, J. (2007). Online nation: Five years of growth in online learning. Needham, MA: Sloan Consortium.

Allen, I. A., & Seaman, J. (2008). *Staying the course: Online education in the United States.* Needham, MA: Sloan Consortium.

Bausell, C. V. (2008). Tracking U.S. trends. *Education Week, 27*(30), 39–42.

Bichelmeyer, B., & Molenda, M. (2006). Issues and trends in instructional technology: Gradual growth atop tectonic shifts. In M. Orey, V. J. McClendon, & R. Branch (Eds.), *Educational media and technology yearbook* (Vol. 31). Westport, CT: Greenwood Publishing Group Libraries Unlimited.

Brown, A., & Green, T. D. (2008). Issues and trends in instructional technology: Making the most of mobility and ubiquity. In M. Orey, V. J. McClendon, & R. Branch (Eds.), *Educational media and technology yearbook* (Vol. 33). Westport, CT: Greenwood Publishing Group Libraries Unlimited.

Brown, A., & Green, T. (2009). Issues and trends in instructional technology: Web 2.0, second life, and STEM share the spotlight. In M. Orey, V. J. McClendon, & R. Branch (Eds.), *Educational media and technology yearbook* (Vol. 34). New York: Springer Publishing.

Cavanagh, S. (2008). States heeding calls to strengthen STEM. *Education Week, 27*(30), 10–16.

Davis, M. R. (2009a). Breaking away from tradition: E-learning opens new doors to raise achievement. *Technology Counts 2009, 28*(26), 8–9.

Davis, M. R. (2009b). Dollars & sense: Ed-tech leaders employ creative tactics to cut IT costs and save programs. *Education Week,* Retrieved on April 27, 2009 from http://www.edweek.org/dd/articles/2008/10/20/02dollars.h02.html.

Dyril, O. E. (2008). *District buying power 2007.* Retrieved on April 29, 2009 from http://www.districtadministration.com/viewarticle.aspx?articleid=1263&p=2#0

eSchool News. (2006). 1-to-1 computing on the rise in schools. Retrieved April 29, 2009 from http://www.eschoolnews.com/news/showstory.cfm?ArticleID=6278

Greaves, T., & Hayes, J. (2009). *America's digital schools 2008 report.* Retrieved on April from http://www.ads2008.org/ads/index.php

Griffith, M. (2008). Education policy fellowship program leadership forum. Retrieved on April 29, 2009 from http://www.ecs.org/clearinghouse/79/57/7957.pdf

Hawkins, B. L., & Rudy, J. A. (2008). *EDUCAUSE core data service fiscal year 2007 summary report.* Washington, DC: EDUCAUSE.

Hightower, A. M. (2009). Tracking U.S. trends: States earn B average for policies supporting educational technology use. *Technology Counts, 28*(26), 30–33.

Irons, L. (2008). E-learning 2.0 and employee access to social network sites. Skilful Minds. Retrieved February 28, 2009 from http://skilfulminds.com/2008/09/26/e-learning-20-and-access-to-social-network-sites/

Klein, A. (2009). Effect of stimulus on NCLB renewal mulled. *Education Week, 28*(24), 19, 24.

National Center for Education Statistics (NCES) (2005). The condition of education 2005. NCES 2005-094. Washington, DC: U.S. Department of Education.

Online PD: The teachers talk back, *T.H.E. Journal*, Retrieved on April 27, 2009 from http://www.thejournal.com/articles/24246

Paradise, A. (2008). *State of the industry report: ASTD's annual review of trends in workplace learning and performance*. Alexandria, VA: American Society for Training & Development.

Piccianno, A. G., & Seaman, J. (2009). K-12 online learning: A 2008 follow-up survey of U.S. school district administrators. *The Sloan Consortium*. Retrieved on April 29, 2009 from http://www.sloanconsortium.org/publications/survey/pdf/k-12_online_learning_2008.pdf

Project Tomorrow (2009a). Learning in the 21st century: 2009 trends. Retrieved from http://www.tomorrow.org/speakup/learning21Report_2009_Update.html.

Project Tomorrow. (2009b). *Speak up 2008*. Retrieved on April 29, 2009 from http://www.tomorrow.org/SpeakUp/

Rideout, V., Roberts, D. F., & Foehr, U. G. (2005). Generation m: Media in the lives of 8–18 year olds. Retrieved on April 29, 2009 from http://www.kff.org/entmedia/entmedia030905pkg.cfm

Salaway, G. (2008). *The ECAR study of undergraduate students and information technology* (Vol. 8). Boulder, CO: EDUCAUSE.

Samuels, C. A. (2009). As stimulus taps turns on, districts can't escape cuts. *Education Week, 28*(28), 1, 14.

Sawchuk, S. (2009). Teacher training goes in virtual directions. *Technology Counts 2009, 28*(26), 22–24.

Technology Counts. (2008). STEM: The push to improve science, technology, engineering, and mathematics. *Education Week, 27*(30), 8.

Weekes, S. (2008). E-learning on the social. *Training and Coaching Today, Nov/Dec 2008*. 15.

Wexler, S., Hart, J., Karrer, T., Martin, M., Oehlert, M., Parker, S., et al. (2008). *E-learning 2.0: Learning in a Web 2.0 world*. Santa Rosa, CA: E-Learning Guild.

Young, O. G. (2007). *Global enterprise Web 2.0 market forecast: 2007 to 2013*. Cambridge, MA: Forrester Research, Inc.

Rapid Prototyping for Designing and Delivering Technology-Based Lessons

Tshepo Batane

Abstract This chapter reports on a project that was carried out to assist instructors who were new to the use of technology to design and deliver technology-based lessons using the Rapid Prototyping Instructional Design Model as a guide. The results of the project reported an increase in the instructors' confidence in using technology as they continued with the project. Soliciting feedback on the lessons encouraged students to participate more in their learning. The feedback was also used to inform the designs of the subsequent lessons.

Keywords Technology-based lessons · Rapid Prototyping Model · Feedback · Students' engagement · Instructors' confidence

Introduction

The use of Rapid Prototyping Model in designing and delivering technology-based lessons can be helpful in assisting instructors to effectively integrate technology in teaching and engage students more in the learning process. There has been rapid development in the kinds of technologies that could be used to facilitate learning; however, effective integration of these tools in the curriculum still remains a challenge (Keengwe, 2007). Studies report that there is a remarkable presence of computer technology in many institutions of higher learning; however, there is a big gap between this availability and effective integration into teaching and learning (Cuban, 2001; Green, 2001). Most instructors are still not fully utilizing these resources for the benefit of their students. This chapter argues that the Rapid Prototyping Instructional Design Model can assist to bridge this gap. This model operates with a pragmatic design principle that requires short-term planning at each stage of the course development process (Tripp & Bichelmeyer, 1990), thus allowing

T. Batane (✉)
University of Botswana
e-mail: batane@mopipi.ub.bw

M. Orey et al. (eds.), *Educational Media and Technology Yearbook*,
Educational Media and Technology Yearbook 35,
DOI 10.1007/978-1-4419-1516-0_4, © Springer Science+Business Media, LLC 2010

the instructor an opportunity to learn from the previous lessons and use that information to prepare for the subsequent ones. The purpose of this chapter is to present how Rapid Prototyping Instructional Design Model was utilized to assist university instructors who were novice technology users to incorporate technology into their teaching. The chapter also demonstrates involvement of students in learning. Several educators (Means, 1994; Brooks & Brooks, 1999; Solmon & Wiederhorn, 2000) have repeatedly stated the fact that students learn best if they are engaged in their learning. One of the compelling reasons why technology has found a clear place in the learning process is its ability to provide opportunities for students to be actively involved in their learning (Smith, 1997). In this chapter, engagement of students in learning refers not only to the various class activities assigned by instructors, but also to the involvement of students in their learning through participation in the course development process.

Rapid Prototyping Model

The Rapid Prototyping Instructional Design Model is a course development process whereby the designer does not develop the entire curricula at a go, but makes preparations and commitment only for a particular lesson at a time. This model involves designing lessons for instruction in a nonlinear approach that requires continuous evaluation and using the feedback to inform the design of the next lessons. As this cycle continues, it refines the products until a desirable outcome is produced (Culatta, 2009). The image of a spiral is often used to best represent the cyclical nature of this design. Tripp and Bichelmeyer (1990) say that a very desirable element of this model is that it allows for feedback from the users at each stage of the prototype design, which is very valuable in instruction because it assists in shaping up the intended outcome. They continue to argue that Rapid Prototyping is a very good model to use especially for computer-based instruction. Wilson and Heckman (1992) used the Rapid Prototyping Model to develop a Multimedia Weather Forecasting Course using SuperCard. They created a prototype for the course and repeatedly tested it on the users for a period of 4 months. After the prototype was refined, it was then used as a template for the final course. Tripp and Bichelmeyer describe the Rapid Prototyping Design Model as a four-level process, the stages of which are presented in Fig. 1.

Wilson, Jonassen, and Cole (1993) provide several ways through which the Rapid Prototyping Model can benefit the learning process, among these include:

- Testing out the effectiveness and appeal of a particular instructional strategy.
- Developing a model case or practice exercise that can serve as a template.
- Getting user feedback and reactions to two competing approaches.

They continue to say that the model can also be used to help achieve a number of things such as increasing instructors' confidence in using technology, getting

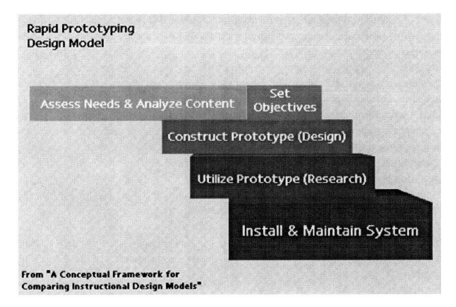

Fig. 1 Rapid prototyping design model

students involved more in learning, and providing a chance to solve problems immediately, instead of waiting until the end of semester.

Theoretical Framework

The theoretical framework that guided this study was Reigeluth's Elaboration Theory, which postulates that learning should be organized in increasing order of complexity with the simplest version of the task presented first (Reigeluth, 1992). According to Kearsley (1994), the main principle of this theory is creating a meaningful context into which subsequent developing ideas are built. This theory was selected because it was realized that even though lecturers were experts in their respective disciplines, when it came to the use of technology, they were novices and not comfortable with the tools they had to infuse in their teaching. Research proves that most instructors are very intimidated and overwhelmed with all the technological elements they have to infuse in their teaching (Webster, 2004). Reigeluth's Elaboration Theory calls for a simple step-by-step design that would assist in building their skills and confidence in using technology, and the Rapid Prototyping Model lent itself perfectly to this process.

Background of the Project

This project was borne out of the ongoing efforts to try to encourage instructors to make technology part of their teaching and learning. In the university where this project was implemented, a study was conducted in the previous year to assess the level of technology use among instructors. The study revealed that even though many staff members had been through a number of technology training workshops including Blackboard, which is the learning management system used by the university, very few people were actually putting this into use with their students. Lack of confidence was cited as the main reason why many people were not using technology with their students. As an effort to address this problem, the Rapid Prototyping Model was chosen to experiment with, to find out if it will yield any positive results in promoting the use of technology among instructors. The appeal of the model lay in its approach of starting small when building up a system and continually refining it until a desired outcome is produced. It was believed this approach would be very helpful in building people's confidence.

Two instructors were selected to participate in experimenting with the Rapid Prototyping Model. Both were new to the use of technology in learning; prior to the project, they had taught their courses entirely in a traditional manner. Students did fairly well in the classes, but the instructors felt that the lessons could benefit from the use of technology and make the courses even more interesting by presenting the course material through various technology tools. Each of the instructors selected one class to use for the project. Students chosen were at second- and third-year level. The project ran for one semester.

Aims of the Project

The main aims of this project were to

- Build up instructors' confidence in using technology for teaching and learning.
- Increase students' participation in learning.
- Develop model lessons that could be used as adaptable templates for any technology-based lesson.

The project was executed following the stages of the Rapid Prototyping Model as presented by Tripp and Bichelmeyer (1990).

Needs Analysis

In the first step, the participants with the help of the instructional designer performed an analysis of their courses to determine how technology could be infused in the various lessons. This use of technology was multipurpose; first, it was meant to assist in enhancing students' learning. Second, it was intended to help achieve certain outcomes as guided by the key areas of competence identified by the university. The institution has outlined graduate attributes deemed as essential skills that young people should posses as they finish school. Among these attributes are information and communication technology knowledge and skills; self-directed, lifelong learning skills; critical and creative thinking skills; problem-solving skills; and communication skills. Technology has been identified to play a crucial role in helping to attain these skills. Therefore, the infusion of technology in learning has become more of a requirement in the university curricula. The analysis of the course assisted in identifying when to use technology in the courses. The instructors then identified the kinds of technology that would be used. Being novice users, they first chose the simplest technologies possible to help build their confidence. For example, for the first lesson, basic PowerPoint was used to deliver the lesson. The technology competency level of students of the chosen classes was also assessed, and it was discovered that most students were computer savvy and their comfort level with technology was higher than that of their instructors.

Constructing a Prototype

The first lessons to be taught with technology were then designed. The objectives of the lessons were outlined and a clear articulation of how technology would be used to achieve these. All the key features of the lessons such as students' participation were considered, like creating a prototype. Wilson et al. (1993) say a prototype is an early phase of a system that has the same key feature components of the "real" thing.

A semi-structured evaluation form for students was developed. This form was meant for the students to provide feedback on how the lessons went, what they liked, and what they did not like. Students were also required to provide their own recommendations on how the lesson could be improved. The instructors were also required to provide their own evaluation of the lesson.

Utilizing the Prototype

The instructors then went on to execute the lesson with the students. This was the most important aspect of the project as the prototype was being tested out to find out what worked and what did not and most importantly whether the intended objectives were met. At the end of the lesson, students were requested to fill out the evaluation form and provide feedback on the lessons, including the use of the technology. The instructors also did their own evaluation of the lesson. Students were asked to provide recommendations on what other tools did they think would be useful to incorporate in their learning. Technical support was constantly provided for these instructors so that they did not get frustrated in their efforts to use technology with students.

Installing the Final System

The feedback, from the instructors and from the students, was then compiled and used to inform the design of the next lessons. The same procedure was carried out for the subsequent lessons until the instructors were able to produce lessons that they felt were very effective. Students were also given opportunities to lead the classes especially when using tools that the instructors were not very familiar with.

Results

When students were first asked to evaluate the lessons, they reported that it felt very awkward because they were used to evaluating only the entire course at the end of the semester, not an individual lesson. However, students did give their opinions on the lesson. For example, in one class, after the first lesson, most students reported that even though the instructor was using PowerPoint to teach, they did not find the lesson interesting because all they had to do was watch the instructor move from one slide to the other. One student stated, "the only thing different in this lesson was that things were projected on the screen, otherwise the teacher was reading to us what was in the screen." The students then provided recommendations on how they thought the lesson could be improved and what they want to see happening. They also provided recommendations on what alternative tools could be used to teach a similar lesson, and most of them indicated that they were willing to take lead if the instructor was not familiar with the suggested tools.

The instructors made sure that they took the students' suggestions into consideration and incorporated them into the subsequent lessons. For example, feedback from students that stated that the first PowerPoint lesson was boring challenged the instructors to go and find out ways to make their PowerPoint presentations more interesting. They went on to add more features such as animations, audio, pictures, and many other elements that would capture students' interest. This had a positive impact on the lessons; students became more and more active in the lessons as they felt they had ownership of the material and a say on what is being taught. As one student stated,

> When we were first asked to provided our thoughts and recommendations on the lesson, I did not take this very seriously because we are often asked to do evaluations of courses and frankly we do not think these people take our opinions into consideration at all. But in this case, I learned from my colleagues that indeed the instructor read what is said and incorporates it, so I started participating and offering my own suggestions which were considered. This made me happy and made me fully participate in class.

Students also felt encouraged to provide more and more feedback on the lessons.

The instructors also provided a critical evaluation of their lessons to inform the next lessons. Immediately at the end of the lesson they would write down their opinions of how the lesson went, what worked well, and what they needed to improve on. The instructors reported an increase in confidence with technology as they continued with the project. As the instructors gained confidence with the technology they were using, more advanced ones were added such as the use of online discussion forums, animations, and simulations. More innovative ways of using technology were developed. They said taking time to thoroughly plan how they would use the technology was very useful. This assisted the instructors to build lessons that were more effective. After several lessons, the instructors were able to use technology to create lessons that among other things were more student centered. Each execution of the lesson with the students provided a learning experience for the instructors.

The instructors also reported that reading the students' feedback on the lesson and their suggestions on what should be done felt very odd, as one instructor wrote, "the idea of students telling me what to do in the course is just like a student teaching me how to teach them and that feels awkward." Another instructor stated, "I felt this process makes one very vulnerable to students attack and if not handled properly it can backfire and result in students disrespecting you or losing confidence in you, that is why it was important that I clearly state why we were doing that."

Generally, instructors reported an improvement in students' academic achievement compared to previous semesters. In addition to increased class participation, students also showed improvement in graded assessments. However, an in-depth study needs to be conducted to solely attribute this to the project.

Limitations with the Project

The greatest challenge to this project was time; as the semester progressed and more material needed to be covered, there was not much time left for the evaluations and incorporation of the suggestions in the lesson. This led to the instructor drifting back to more traditional teaching methods (lecturing) to cover the required material. However, since this was the first experiment with the model, the next assignment was to look into the entire curriculum to see what adjustments could be made to allow room for innovative teaching strategies such as this project.

Discussion

The results of this study showed instructors starting small in using technology in order to build their confidence and ensure that they get to use it effectively. According to Culatta (2009), Rapid Prototyping allows the designer to start with a low fidelity medium (such as paper and pen) and move to increasingly higher fidelity prototypes as time goes on. So, as per the design of this model, the instructors started off at a small scale, building a prototype. This prototype served as a basis for discussion with its use measured against the intended outcomes. The prototype was evaluated, interrogated, and tested out to identify and solve immediate problems. Wilson et al. (1993) say that it is important early on to design a small-scale prototype that would be used to test out certain key features of the design, and according to them, the most important aspect of the Rapid Prototyping process is the execution of the designed unit with the potential learners. It was reported that at the beginning very basic and minimal technology was used to make sure that the instructors do not get overwhelmed and scared. They carefully used this technology and evaluated it to find out if indeed it was helpful in achieving the intended objectives and was used in the right context. According to Reigeluth's Elaboration Theory, when developing an idea, it is important to set up a context where subsequent ideas and skills will be growing from. When it comes to the use of technology in learning, context is of great importance. Different kinds of technologies have their place and time in learning, and it is crucial for instructors to understand those contexts so that technology can be maximized to deliver high-quality lessons. From their review of studies on the effects of technology on learning, Cradler, Freeman, Cradler, and McNabb (2002) report that the context in which technology is used is very important.

In this study, it was reported that students were more competent with technology than their instructors. This is not a surprising finding as it is the case in many other places of learning. Children today are mostly born into the technology, and it automatically becomes part of their growing up. Most teachers find themselves in a position where their pupils know more than they do when it comes to technology. This was well stated by John Couch, vice president of Apple Computer, when he said, "We are all digital immigrants" trying to teach the "digital natives" (Hunnicutt, 2003, 21). However, this does not necessarily discredit the teachers; they need to appreciate this fact and use it for the good of the learning experience. Instructors in this study realized that students were a great resource in the teaching and they utilized that resource through asking students to lead the class whenever instructors were using tools that they were not very familiar with. Research suggests that when students are given an opportunity to lead or teach the class, great amount of learning takes place (Law, 2008; Plimmer & Amor, 2006; Depaz & Moni, 2008).

Instructors in this study reported an increase in confidence as they continued with the project. Teacher confidence has been identified as one of the key ways to the effective and frequent use of technology. Teachers need to trust their ability to select, operate, and apply the available technology appropriately, and starting small will play a great role in achieving this. This notion is well supported by Reigeluth's Elaboration Theory, which advances the view that learning should be organized in increasing order of complexity with the simplest version of the task presented first. This idea worked very well with the instructors in this project because as they mastered how to infuse basic technology concepts in their teaching, they became confident to engage more complex ones.

The importance of technical support when dealing with technology can never be overstated; therefore, providing that support to the instructors played a great role in ensuring that instructors did not get too frustrated while working with technology, which could lead them to giving up especially at the infant stages when the project was very fragile.

Feedback from the students was reported to have played a crucial role in this project. First, this resulted in improved students' participation in class as they felt more ownership of the material being taught. Engagement of students in the learning process has been identified as one of the most influential factors in academic achievement. In their 1986 study on teachers' behavior and students' achievement,

Brophy and Good (1986) report that over all their findings, the amount of time students spent in academic tasks greatly influenced their academic achievement. They write, "academic engagement is a prominent element of the Quality Teaching model." The use of technology in learning has been credited with providing more opportunities for students to be engaged in the lessons both physically and mentally (Solomon and Weiderhorn, 2000). Our students today are wired differently; they require different techniques to get them involved. In this project, student involvement was taken to another level by making students part of the decision-making process of the lessons. Killen (2007) says that for students to stay interested in the lesson, they must be actively involved, and this can be done through using their ideas as an important part of the lesson. This has been proven to increase students' engagement in the learning process (Emmer, Evertson, Sanford, Clements, & Worsham, 1984). Killen goes on to say that learners are encouraged when their ideas are valued. Killen says, "it is important for me to know how my students feel about my teaching, I tell them feedback will be used to make it easier for them to understand future lessons."

Traditionally, we are not used to students having a say on what they are taught and how it should be taught. But it is clear that this mind-set should change. It is important for educators to know what students think and want, discuss the goals of the lesson with them, and let them have an input. Killen (2007) says "if the students do not know what they are supposed to be learning, or why it is important, or they see goals as unattainable or unimportant, you cannot expect them to be enthusiastic and engaged" (p. 111). Theorist Jerome Seymour Bruner advises us to "respect the ways children think and teaching to those ways" (Carrol & Wilson, 1993, p. 325). The process of soliciting ideas from students can give teachers an insight into the attitudes, understanding, and misconceptions that they bring to learning, and this information is vital in assisting them.

Instructors in this study reported that reading students' responses and suggestions on what needed to be done at times made them uneasy as it was against the norm. This shows that even though the instructors were trying to break away from traditional methods of learning that are teacher centered to more liberal teaching strategies that place the learner at the center of the learning process, they still needed to work hard to totally let students into the whole learning phenomenon including the design and execution of the courses. Traditional methods of teaching not only place the teacher at the center of the learning process during class, but also do not provide any room for students to have an input on the subject matter. The Rapid Prototyping Model allows for this input the feedback that students provide as they evaluate the lessons is very essential in shaping up the lessons. This provides a comprehensive evaluation of the lesson from different perspectives.

Although the major focus of this project was to improve the instructors' use of technology and also increase students' participation in learning, the overall impact that the project had on students' academic achievement was of interest. This study reported a general improvement in students' performance. This is in line with Killen who believes that engaging students through having them perform activities to construct their knowledge and encourage them to make choices in their learning is very important. Killen says when students are engaged in their learning, academic achievement increases. Wyne and Stuck (1982) state that engaging students also impacts other things such as self-esteem and positive attitudes toward school; therefore, success encourages further engagement in learning. However, it must also be noted that although the instructors witnessed a general improvement in students' performance, they could not confidently attribute this solely to the project because there may be other reasons why students performed better; for example, the assessments used were different from the ones used in the previous semesters. As Bailey (2004) states, it is not easy to identify what causes improvement in students' achievement since there are many factors at play and not much research has been conducted to establish this. However, whatever the reasons, the instructors were happy with the performance of their students at the end of the project.

Conclusion

In this study, the use of the Rapid Prototyping Instructional Design Model was effective in assisting novice technology users to incorporate technology in their teaching and learning. Soliciting students' ideas had a positive impact on engaging them more in learning and refining the lessons. However, the limitations of this project indicated that further adjustments need to be done to the curriculum itself to allow room for more innovative course delivery techniques such as in this project.

References

Bailey, J. (2004). Making the case: Research efforts on educational technology. *T.H.E. Journal*, *31*(10), 36–44.

Brooks, J., & Brooks, M. G. (1999). *In search of understanding: The case for constructivist classrooms*. Alexandria, VA: Association for Supervision and Curriculum Development.

Brophy, J., & Good, T. L. (1986). Teacher behavior and student achievement. In M. C. Wittrock (Ed.), *Handbook of research on teaching* (3rd ed., pp. 328–375). New York: Macmillan.

Carrol, J. A., & Wilson, E. E. (1993). *Jerome Seymour Bruner: Acts of teaching*. Eaglewood, CO: Teacher Ideas Press.

Cradler, J., Freeman, M., Cradler, R. & McNabb, M. (2002). Research implications for preparing teachers to use technology. *Learning & Leading with Technology*, *30*(1), 50–55.

Cuban, L. (2001). *Oversold and underused: Computers in the classroom*. Cambridge, MA: Harvard University Press.

Culatta, R. (2009). *Instructional Design; Rapid prototyping*. Retrieved March 10, 2007, from http://www.instructionaldesign.org/models/rapid_prototyping.html

Depaz, I., & Moni, R. W. (2008). Using peer teaching to support co-operative learning in undergraduate pharmacology. *Bioscience Education Journal*, 11, retrieved January 17, 2009, from http://www.bioscience.heacademy.ac.uk/journal/vol11/beej-11-8.pdf

Emmer, E., Evertson, C., Sanford, I., Clements, B. & Worsham, M. (1984). *Classroom management for secondary teachers*. Englewood Cliffs, NJ: Prentice-Hall.

Green, K. C. (2001). *The 2001 National Survey of Information Technology in US Higher Education: The campus computing project*. Retrieved October 11, 2008, from http://www.campuscomputing.net/summaries/2001/

Hunnicutt, L. (2003). Digital as a second language. *TechEdge, 23*(2), 20–21, 34–35.

Kearsley, G., (1994). *Theory into practice: Theory.* Retrieved January 16, 2008, from http://www.gwu.edu/~tip/reigelut.html

Keengwe, J. (2007). Faculty integration of technology into instruction and students' perceptions of computer technology to improve student learning. *Journal of Information Technology Education,* 6, 169–180. Retrieved October 12, 2008 from http://jite.org/documents/Vol6/JITEv6p169–180Keengwe218.pdf

Killen, R. (2007). *Effective teaching strategies; Lessons from research and practice.* Australia: Thomson Social Science Press.

Law, R. M. (2008)-07–19 Use and usefulness of peer-to-peer teaching and self-directed learning in a natural health products course. *Paper presented at the annual meeting of the American Association of Colleges of Pharmacy. Retrieved February 12, from* http://www.allacademic.com/meta/p270337_index.html

Means, B. (1994). Introduction: Using technology to advance educational goals. In B. Means (Ed.), *Technology and education reform: The reality behind the promise* (pp. 1–21). San Francisco, CA: Jossey-Bass.

Plimmer, B., & Amor, R. (2006). *Peer teaching extends HCI learning.* New York: ACM.

Reigeluth, C. (1992). Elaborating the elaboration theory. *Educational Technology Research and Development,*, *40*(3), 80–86.

Smith, K. (1997). Preparing faculty for instructional technology. *CAUSE/EFFECT, 20*(3), 36–44.

Solmon, L. C., & Wiederhorn, J. A. (2000). *Progress of technology in the schools.* 1999 report on 27 states. Milken Family Foundation. Retrieved March 23, 2008, from http://www.mff.org/pubs/progress_27states.pdf

Tripp, S. D., & Bichelmeyer, B. (1990). Rapid prototyping: An alternative instructional design strategy. *Educational Technology, Research and Development, 38*(1), 31–44.

Webster, P. W. (2004). A roadmap for change. *From Now On,* 13(6).

Wilson, B., & Heckman, B. (1992). *Cognitive apprenticeships in weather forecasting.* Paper presented at the meeting of the Association for Educational Communications and Technology, Washington, D.C.

Wilson, B. G., Jonassen, D. H. & Cole, P. (1993). Cognitive approaches to instructional design. In G. M. Piskurich (Ed.), *The ASTD handbook of instructional technology* (pp. 21.1–21.22). New York: McGraw-Hill.

Wyne, M., & Stuck, G. (1982). Time and learning: Implications for the classroom teacher. *Elementary School Journal, 83*(1), 67–75.

Theory-Based Evaluation of Instruction: Implications for Improving Student Learning Achievement in Postsecondary Education

Theodore Frick, Rajat Chadha, Carol Watson, and Ying Wang

Abstract While student global ratings of college courses historically predict learning achievement, the majority of recent U.S. college graduates lack proficiency in desired skills. Teaching and Learning Quality (TALQ), a new course evaluation instrument, was developed from extant instructional theory that promotes student learning. A survey of 193 students in 111 different courses at multiple institutions was conducted using TALQ. Results indicated strong associations among student ratings of First Principles of Instruction, academic learning time, perceptions of learning gains, satisfaction with courses, perceived mastery of course objectives, and their overall evaluation of courses and instructors. Instructors can implement the theoretically derived First Principles of Instruction by challenging students with real-world problems or tasks, activating student learning, demonstrating what is to be learned, providing feedback on student learning attempts, and encouraging student integration of learning into their personal lives.

T. Frick (✉)
Department of Instructional Systems Technology, School of Education, Indiana University, Bloomington, IN, USA
e-mail: frick@indiana.edu

R. Chadha (✉)
Department of Instructional Systems Technology, School of Education, Indiana University, Bloomington, IN, USA
e-mail: rajatchadha@gmail.com

C. Watson (✉)
Eppley Institute for Parks and Public Lands, Indiana University, Bloomington, IN, USA
e-mail: watsonc@indiana.edu

Y. Wang (✉)
Department of Education, Northwestern College, St. Paul, MN, USA
e-mail: ywang@nwc.edu

M. Orey et al. (eds.), *Educational Media and Technology Yearbook,*
Educational Media and Technology Yearbook 35,
DOI 10.1007/978-1-4419-1516-0_5, © Springer Science+Business Media, LLC 2010

Keywords Teaching and learning quality · Higher education · Student
learning · Course evaluation · First Principles of Instruction · Academic learning
time

Problem

This study began because the first author served on a university committee that
was expected to choose a few outstanding college instructors as recipients of significant monetary awards. The top candidates recommended by their departments
had provided the committee with customary forms of evidence that have been used
for evaluation of teaching for promotion and tenure. This experience nonetheless
raised the question: What empirical evidence is there that course evaluation data are
associated with student learning achievement?

Thus, we began to review research on student course evaluation in higher education. A review by Cohen (1981) stood out as the most highly cited in the *Web
of Knowledge* by scholarly research studies subsequently published on this issue.
Cohen's study

> ... used meta-analytic methodology to synthesize research on the relationship between stu-
> dent ratings of instruction and student achievement. The data for the meta-analysis came
> from 41 independent validity studies reporting on 68 separate multisection courses relating
> student ratings to student achievement. The average correlation between an overall instruc-
> tor rating and student achievement was 0.43; the average overall course rating and student
> achievement was 0.47.... . The results of the meta-analysis provide strong support for the
> validity of student ratings as measures of teaching effectiveness. (p. 281)

According to Cohen (1981), a typical example of an overall instructor rating item
was "The instructor is an excellent teacher." A typical overall course rating item
was "This is an excellent course." Cohen also found that ratings of instructor *skill*
correlated on average 0.50 with student achievement (e.g., "The instructor has good
command of the subject matter," "The instructor gives clear explanations"). The
other factor that showed a high average correlation (0.47) was course *structure* (e.g.,
"The instructor has everything going according to course schedule," "The instructor
uses class time well").

Studies similar to Cohen's meta-analysis have since been conducted, and those
that are methodologically sound have yielded relatively consistent findings (Abrami,
d'Apollonia, & Cohen, 1990; Abrami, 2001; Feldman, 1989; Kulik, 2001; Marsh,
1984). Further studies have also demonstrated positive relationships between independently observed classroom behaviors and student ratings of instructors and
courses (cf. Koon & Murray, 1995; Renaud & Murray, 2004). When these studies
are taken as a whole, reported correlations are moderate and positive, typically in
the 0.30–0.50 range. At first glance, there appears to be little doubt that at least
global student ratings of instructors and courses predict student achievement in
higher education.

However, such ratings are at best moderately or weakly correlated with student learning achievement – explaining a relatively small proportion of variance

in student learning achievement (Emery, Kramer, & Tian, 2003). In a more recent example, Arthur, Tubré, Paul, and Edens (2003) conducted a pre-/post-study of student learning gains in an introductory psychology course. They found a *weak* relationship between student evaluations of teaching effectiveness and measures of student learning gains. They also reported a *moderate* relationship between student grades and learning achievement.

Another potentially confounding factor is that students may respond to course evaluations in ways that do not reflect course or instructor quality. For example, Clayson, Frost, and Sheffet (2006) empirically tested the "reciprocity effect" between student grades and their ratings of instructors and classes. They found that when grades were lowered within a class, the ratings decreased, and when grades were raised, ratings increased. Clayson et al. (2006) offered the hypothesis that "...students reward instructors who give them good grades and punish instructors who give them poor grades, irrespective of any instructor or preexisting student characteristic" (p. 52).

Recent Reports on College Student Achievement – or Lack Thereof

Perhaps the issue of course evaluation should be further examined in light of what appears to be unsatisfactory levels of student achievement in postsecondary education. Two recent reports were studied in more detail. In the first report, Baer, Cook, and Baldi (2006) assessed literacy skills of 1,827 students who were nearing completion of their degrees at 80 randomly selected 2- and 4-year public universities and colleges. They used the same standardized assessment instrument as that in the National Assessment of Adult Literacy. The literacy assessments were supervised by a test administrator on each campus.

The Baer et al. (2006) report provides some sobering findings. They reported percentages of students from 2-year versus 4-year institutions, respectively, 23 and 38% of whom were *proficient* in prose literacy, 23 and 40% in document literacy, and 18 and 34% in quantitative literacy. This means that more than 75% of students at 2-year institutions performed *lower than proficiency level*, and more than 50% at 4-year institutions likewise scored lower. For example, these students could *not* "perform complex literacy tasks, such as comparing credit card offers with different interest rates or summarizing the arguments of newspaper editorials" (American Institutes for Research, 2006, n.p.). Even worse,

> ...approximately 30 percent of students in 2-year institutions and nearly 20 percent of students in 4-year institutions have only Basic quantitative literacy. Basic skills are those necessary to compare ticket prices or calculate the cost of a sandwich and a salad from a menu. (American Institutes for Research, 2006, n.p.)

In the second report, a comprehensive review of the literature by Kuh, Kinzie, Buckley, Bridges, and Hayek (2006) indicated a number of factors that influence student success in postsecondary education. One of their major findings was: "[a]mong the institutional conditions linked to persistence are supportive peers, faculty and staff members who set high expectations for student performance, and academic programs and experiences that actively engage students and foster academic and social integration" (p. 4). Based on these and other findings, Kuh et al., (2006) made several recommendations. One important recommendation was to "... *focus assessment and accountability efforts on what matters to student success*" (p. 4, italics added).

Research Questions

Results from these recent studies provide impetus for reexamining the kinds of items used on typical course evaluations in higher education. This led us to ask the primary research questions addressed in this report: Can we develop reliable scales for course evaluation that measure factors that are supported by instructional theory? Do these scales identify how instruction might be improved in ways that are more likely to be associated with improved student learning and overall course quality?

If we *can* develop better scales for use in course evaluation, then this would address, in part, the important recommendation made by Kuh et al. (2006) that universities and colleges should focus their assessment efforts on factors that influence student success. Course evaluations could be one of those assessments.

First Principles of Instruction. After an extensive review of the literature on theories and models of instruction, Merrill (2002) synthesized factors that promote student learning achievement. He identified what he called "First Principles" of Instruction. He claimed that to the extent these principles are present during instruction, learning is promoted. These First Principles include (1) *authentic problems or tasks* (students engage in a series of increasingly complex real-world problems or authentic whole tasks); (2) *activation* (students engage in activities that help them link past learning or experience with what is to be newly learned); (3) *demonstration* (students are exposed to differentiated examples of what they are expected to learn or do); (4) *application* (students solve problems or perform whole tasks themselves with scaffolding and feedback from instructors or peers); and (5) *integration* (students engage in activities that encourage them to incorporate what they have learned into their own personal lives). Instructors can do something about First Principles of Instruction in their courses. If instructors use more of the First Principles in their teaching, instructional theory predicts that students should learn more. First Principles of Instruction are not specific to a particular subject matter content, according to Merrill, and thus have a wide range of applicability.

Academic learning time. In examining the research literature, one factor has consistently shown a strong relation to student achievement at all levels: academic learning time (ALT). ALT refers to the frequency and amount of time that students spend *successfully engaged in learning tasks* that are similar to skills and knowledge they will be later tested on (Berliner, 1991; Brown & Saks, 1986; Fisher et al., 1978; Kuh et al., 2006; Squires, Huitt, & Segars, 1983). Yet the kinds of items in the Cohen (1981) meta-analysis largely focused on the instructor or course, not on *student* ALT. Student ALT is not something an instructor has direct control over, since it is the students who must put in the effort to succeed on tasks and activities in the course. However, if instruction is more effective, then one indicator of this effectiveness would be higher levels of ALT. Thus, a high rating of ALT by the students of their own performance would be an indicator of a successful course. Since ALT is predictive of student learning achievement, increased use of First Principles of Instruction would be expected to result in increased student ALT.

Levels of evaluation of training. Finally, we considered levels of evaluation of training effectiveness that have been used for more than five decades in nonformal educational settings such as business and industry (Kirkpatrick, 1994). The four levels of evaluation are (1) learner *satisfaction* with the training, often referred to as a "smiles test" or reaction; (2) *learning achievement*; (3) *transfer* of learning to the learner's job or workplace[1]; and (4) *impact* on the overall organization to which the learner belongs.

Level 1 is what many people believe that traditional course evaluations often measure, i.e., student satisfaction with a course and instructor. If a course and instructor is good, from the perspective of a student, then he or she would be expected to be more satisfied as a result.

With respect to Level 2, student learning achievement, we wondered if we could get students to rate their own learning progress. That is, compared with what they knew or could do before they took the course, how much did they perceive that they had learned? While there are issues of validity of self-reports, Cohen (1981) and Kulik (2001) indicated that many studies have found positive correlations of such self-reports with objective assessments in college such as common exams in multi-section courses. Learning progress would be a desirable outcome of a course, just as student ALT and satisfaction. Learning progress is nonetheless not a measure of actual student learning achievement, but only a perception by students about how much they have learned.

One might expect course grades to indicate student learning achievement in a more objective manner. However, with apparent grade inflation these days, course grades are probably not a good indicator of student learning achievement. Nonetheless, we wondered how students perceived their mastery of course objectives. It would be possible for students to report that they had learned a great deal in a course, but nonetheless they had not mastered the course objectives. Indeed, how to measure Kirkpatrick's Level 2 is somewhat elusive, particularly if instructor grades of student performance are not valid indicators of student learning achievement. Independent measures of student skills and knowledge are needed. Attempts to measure college student prose literacy, document literacy, and quantitative literacy, such as the study by Baer et al. (2006), would be an example of an independent measure of student achievement in college. However, we do not have standardized assessments of student learning at the university level in general in the United States, although some professions have their own tests as part of licensing or certification, such as for medical practitioners, optometrists, and lawyers.

---

[1]It should be also noted that Kirkpatrick's Level 3 is highly similar to Merrill's Principle 5 (integration). We did not attempt to measure Level 4 in this study.

Method

A survey instrument was constructed that contained items intended to measure scales for student ratings of self-reported ALT, satisfaction with the course, learning progress, authentic problems, activation, demonstration, application, and integration. In addition, several items were included from the university's standard course evaluation item pool from the Bureau for Evaluative Studies and Testing (BEST). These BEST items included *global* ones similar to those reported in Cohen (1981), which indicated overall ratings of the course and instructor. We also included on the survey several demographic questions, the grade that they received or expected to receive in the course, and their rating of their mastery of course objectives.

See Table 2 for the nine a priori item sets. Each set contained five items intended to measure the respective construct (scale). For this study, five items per scale were used with the anticipation that reliability analysis would permit scale reduction without compromising internal consistency reliability.

A paper version of the instrument was then reviewed by several faculty instructors, and wording of items considered to be confusing or ambiguous was modified. The instrument, now referred to as the *Teaching and Learning Quality Scales* (*TALQ Scales*), was then converted to a Web survey, which can be viewed online at http://www.indiana.edu/~edsurvey/evaluate/.

No explicit reference was made to Merrill's First Principles of Instruction or Kirkpatrick's levels of evaluation in the survey or study information sheet. Student ratings were not shared with their instructors and hence could not affect their grade in the course.

Volunteers were sought for participation in the study through e-mail requests to faculty distribution lists and student organizations at several postsecondary institutions. Respondents who had nearly or recently completed a course completed the survey. There were 193 valid cases remaining after elimination of those containing no data or that were test cases to ensure that data collection was working as intended via the Web survey.

Results

Since participation in the survey was voluntary, we also collected demographic data in the survey in order to facilitate interpretation of results and to document the representativeness of the obtained sample of 193 cases.

Nature of Courses and Respondents

Course topics. Data indicated that respondents evaluated a wide range of courses with relatively few respondents from any given course. We conducted a content analysis of qualitative responses to the survey question about the course title or content. A total of 111 different subject areas were mentioned by 174 respondents (19 respondents did not answer this question).

While courses in business (34), medicine (23), education (18), English (18), and computers and technology (12) were mentioned more frequently than others, a very wide range of subject matter was represented in the courses taken by respondents. Thus, there were 111 courses that appeared to have unique subject matter or titles, and the remaining 63 had similar course titles as mentioned by at least one other respondent (though seldom with the same instructor).

Course instructors. In addition, content analysis of courses rated by students indicated that they were, by and large, taught by different instructors. While several instructor names with the same or approximate spellings were listed more than once by different respondents, the very large majority of respondents appeared to have different instructors. This is consistent with the wide range of course topics, as indicated above.

Gender of student respondents. In Table 1, it can be seen that 132 females and 55 males responded to the survey (6 did not report gender). While it may appear that a disproportionate number of females responded, for the scales investigated in this

Table 1 Respondent and course demographics ($N = 193$)

Question		Frequency	Percentage
Gender	Female	132	70.6
	Male	55	29.4
	Missing	6	3.1
Class rating: I would rate this class as:	Great	107	56.0
	Average	71	37.2
	Awful	13	6.8
	Missing	2	1.0
Expected grade: In this course, I expect to receive	A	116	64.1
(or did receive) a grade of:	B	52	28.7
	C	11	6.1
	D	2	1.1
	Missing	12	6.2
Achievement: With respect to achievement of	Master	44	22.9
objectives of this course, I consider myself a:	Partial master	117	60.9
	Nonmaster	31	16.1
	Missing	1	0.5
Class standing: I am a:	Freshman	32	17.4
	Sophomore	25	13.6
	Junior	38	20.7
	Senior	30	16.3
	Graduate	59	32.1
	Missing/other	9	4.7
Course setting: I took this course:	Face-to-face	116	60.4
	Blended	12	6.3
	Online	64	33.3
	Missing	1	0.5

study, there were *no* significant relationships between gender and other variables or scales, as discussed below.

Class standing of respondents. In Table 1, it can be seen that approximately one-third of respondents were graduate students and the remaining two-thirds were undergraduates, with the latter being distributed about equally among freshmen to seniors (14–21% in each group).

Course settings. About 60% of courses evaluated were face-to-face, and about one-third were online or distance courses.

Course grades. Table 1 also displays responses of students with respect to their course grade. Almost 93% reported that they received or expected to receive an A or a B.

Mastery of course objectives by students. Since grades were not anticipated by this research team to be very discriminating among respondents, they were also asked, "With respect to achievement of objectives of this course, I consider myself a ____." Choices were master, partial master, and nonmaster. Table 1 indicates that about 23% reported themselves to be masters. The large majority considered themselves to be partial masters of course objectives, while 16% identified themselves as nonmasters.

Relationships Among Variables

In this study, we choose our a priori Type I error rate as $\alpha = 0.0005$ for determining statistical significance. Our sample size was fairly large ($n = 193$ cases), and we sought to minimize the probability of concluding statistical significance as an artifact of numerous comparisons. We conducted a total of 58 statistical tests. The overall Type I error rate for this study was $1 - (1 - 0.0005)^{58} = 0.0286$ (cf. Kirk, 1995, p. 120).

Gender. Gender (1 = male, 0 = female) was not significantly related ($p > 0.0005$) to overall course rating,[2] expected or received grade,[3] mastery level,[4] or class standing.[5] One of the chi squares approached significance ($\chi^2 = 5.22$, df $= 2$, $p = 0.052$, $n = 189$) between gender and mastery level. Slightly more males considered themselves to be masters than expected, and slightly fewer females considered themselves as masters than expected if there were no relationship.

One-way ANOVAs were run between gender and each of the remaining scales and variables discussed below. None of the *F*s was statistically significant.

Student mastery level. Spearman's ρ indicated a significant association between class rating and mastery of course objectives ($\rho = 0.306$, $p < 0.0005$, $n = 191$).

---

[2] 2 = great, 1 = average, 0 = awful
[3] 4 = A, 3 = B, 2 = C, 1 = D, 0 = F
[4] 2 = master, 1 = partial master, 0 = nonmaster,
[5] 5 = graduate, 4 = senior, 3 = junior, 2 = sophomore, 1 = freshman

Students who considered themselves masters of course objectives were more likely to rate the course as "great." There was also a significant correlation between student reports of mastery level and course grades ($\rho = 0.397$, $p < 0.0005$, $n = 181$).

Grades. Students' expected or received course grades were weakly associated with their ranks of overall course quality ($\rho = 0.241$, $p = 0.001$, $n = 180$). Grades and class standing were also weakly related ($\rho = 0.230$, $p = 0.002$, $n = 174$). Graduate students and upperclassmen reported somewhat higher grades than freshmen and sophomores.

Scale Reliabilities

Scale items and reliabilities are listed in Table 2. To determine the reliability of each scale, all five items in each scale were initially used to compute internal consistency with Cronbach's α coefficient. Items that were negatively worded (–) had their Likert scores reversed. Items were removed until no further item could be removed without decreasing the α coefficient. It should be noted that factor analysis was not considered appropriate at this point, since these scales were formed a priori.

Our goal was to form a single scale score for each reliable scale before further analysis of relationships among variables measured in the study. It can be seen in Tables 2 and 3 that internal consistency of each scale was generally quite high, ranging from 0.81 to 0.97.

Combined First Principles scale (Merrill 1–5). To determine the reliability of the combined scale, we first formed a scale score for each First Principle by computing a mean rating score for each case. Then we entered the five First Principles scale

Table 2 Nine TALQ Scales

Item no.	Scale name, Cronbach alpha, and items stems for each scale[6]
1.	*Academic Learning Time Scale ($\alpha = 0.81$)*
1-	I did not do very well on most of the tasks in this course, according to my instructor's judgment of the quality of my work
12	I frequently did very good work on projects, assignments, problems and/or learning activities for this course
14	I spent a lot of time doing tasks, projects and/or assignments, and my instructor judged my work as high quality
24	I put a great deal of effort and time into this course, and it has paid off – I believe that I have done very well overall
29-	I did a minimum amount of work and made little effort in this course

---

[6] Item numbers followed by a minus are negatively worded, and scales were reversed for reliability analyses.

Table 2 (continued)

Item no.	Scale name, Cronbach alpha, and items stems for each scale
2.	*Learning Progress Scale (α = 0.95)*
4	Compared to what I knew before I took this course, I learned a lot
10	I learned a lot in this course
22	Looking back to when this course began, I have made a big improvement in my skills and knowledge in this subject
27-	I learned very little in this course
32-	I did not learn much as a result of taking this course
3.	*Global rating items selected from the standard university form (α = 0.97)*
8	Overall, I would rate the quality of this course as outstanding
16	Overall, I would rate this instructor as outstanding
38	Overall, I would recommend this instructor to others
4.	*Authentic Problems/Tasks Scale (α = 0.87)*
3	I performed a series of increasingly complex authentic tasks in this course
19	My instructor directly compared problems or tasks that we did, so that I could see how they were similar or different
25	I solved authentic problems or completed authentic tasks in this course
31	In this course I solved a variety of authentic problems that were organized from simple to complex
33	Assignments, tasks, or problems I did in this course are clearly relevant to my professional goals or field of work
5.	*Activation Scale (α = 0.90)*
9	I engaged in experiences that subsequently helped me learn ideas or skills that were new and unfamiliar to me
21	In this course I was able to recall, describe or apply my past experience so that I could connect it to what I was expected to learn
30	My instructor provided a learning structure that helped me to mentally organize new knowledge and skills
39	In this course I was able to connect my past experience to new ideas and skills I was learning
41-	In this course I was not able to draw upon my past experience nor relate it to new things I was learning
6.	*Demonstration Scale (α = 0.89)*
5	My instructor demonstrated skills I was expected to learn in this course
17	My instructor gave examples and counter-examples of concepts that I was expected to learn
35-	My instructor did not demonstrate skills I was expected to learn
43	My instructor provided alternative ways of understanding the same ideas or skills
7.	*Application Scale (α = 0.82)*
7	My instructor detected and corrected errors I was making when solving problems, doing learning tasks or completing assignments

Table 2 (continued)

Item no.	Scale name, Cronbach alpha, and items stems for each scale
36	I had opportunities to practice or try out what I learned in this course
42	My course instructor gave me personal feedback or appropriate coaching on what I was trying to learn
8.	*Integration Scale ($\alpha = 0.87$)*
11	I had opportunities in this course to explore how I could personally use what I have learned
28	I see how I can apply what I learned in this course to real life situations
34	I was able to publicly demonstrate to others what I learned in this course
37	In this course I was able to reflect on, discuss with others, and defend what I learned
44-	I do not expect to apply what I learned in this course to my chosen profession or field of work
9.	*Learner Satisfaction Scale ($\alpha = 0.94$)*
2	I am very satisfied with how my instructor taught this class
6-	I am dissatisfied with this course
20-	This course was a waste of time and money
45	I am very satisfied with this course

Table 3 Combined First Principles Scale ($\alpha = 0.94$)

Principle
Authentic Problems/Tasks: students engage in real-world problems and tasks or activities
Activation: student prior learning or experience is connected to what is to be newly learned
Demonstration: students are exposed to examples of what they are expected to learn or do
Application: students try out what they have learned with instructor coaching or feedback
Integration: students incorporate what they have learned into their own personal lives

scores into the reliability analysis, treating each principle score as an item score itself. The resulting Cronbach's α coefficient was 0.94.

Formation of remaining scale scores. Scores were created for remaining scales such that each scale score represented a mean Likert score for each case.

Correlational Analyses

We next investigated the relationships among the scales themselves. Spearman's ρ was used as a measure of association, since these scales are ordinal. The reader should note that we considered a correlation to be significant when $p < 0.0005$, based on Type I error rate for this study, which in effect means that a finding was considered statistically significant when $p < 0.0286$.

First Principles of Instruction considered individually. It can be seen in Table 4 that First Principles are highly correlated with each other, with all correlations

Table 4 Spearman's ρ correlations for First Principles of Instruction scales

		Authentic problems	Activation	Demon-stration	Application	Integration
Authentic	P	1.000				
Problems Scale	N	192				
Activation	ρ	0.790[a]	1.000			
Scale	N	192	193			
Demonstration	ρ	0.803[a]	0.792[a]	1.000		
Scale	N	189	190	190		
Application	ρ	0.724[a]	0.763[a]	0.794[a]	1.000	
Scale	N	186	186	184	186	
Integration	ρ	0.819[a]	0.818[a]	0.770[a]	0.722[a]	1.000
Scale	N	192	193	190	186	193

[a] Correlation is significant ($p < 0.0005$, 2-tailed).

significant at $p < 0.0005$, with ρ ranging from 0.722 to 0.819. This should not be surprising, since the internal consistency α is 0.94. Therefore, the five First Principles were combined into a single scale score, as described above for subsequent analyses.

Relationships among scales. The results in Table 5 are very strong as a group. Except for student mastery, the Spearman correlations ranged from 0.46 to 0.89, with most in the range 0.60–0.80. Students who agreed that they frequently engaged successfully in problems and doing learning tasks in a course (reported ALT) also were more likely to report that they mastered course objectives. Furthermore, they

Table 5 Spearman's ρ correlations among TALQ Scales

		Combined First Principles	ALT	Learning progress	Satis-faction	Global rating (BEST)	Class rating	Mastery
Combined	ρ	1.000						
First Principles	N	193						
ALT	ρ	0.670[a]	1.000					
	N	192	192					
Learning	ρ	0.833[a]	0.747[a]	1.000				
Progress	N	193	192	193				
Satisfaction	ρ	0.850[a]	0.683[a]	0.856[a]	1.000			
	N	192	191	192	192			
Global Rating	ρ	0.890[a]	0.605[a]	0.811[a]	0.903[a]	1.000		
(BEST)	N	193	192	193	192	193		
Class Rating	ρ	0.694[a]	0.464[a]	0.649[a]	0.753[a]	0.773[a]	1.000	
	N	191	190	191	190	191	191	
Mastery of	ρ	0.344[a]	0.359[a]	0.334[a]	0.317[a]	0.341[a]	0.306[a]	1.000
Objectives	N	192	191	192	191	192	191	192

[a] Correlation is significant ($p < 0.0005$, 2-tailed).

agreed that this was an excellent course and instructor, and they were very satisfied with it.

There were strong relationships between ALT and First Principles of Instruction. Students who agreed that First Principles were used in the course also agreed that they were frequently engaged successfully in solving problems and doing learning tasks. These relationships will be clarified in the pattern analysis results described below (analysis of patterns in time [APT]).

Pattern Analysis (APT)

While there were numerous highly significant bivariate relationships that explained typically between 40% and 80% of the variance in ranks, specific patterns that show temporal relations among three or more variables are not shown in Tables 4 and 5. For example, what is the likelihood that *if* students agreed that ALT occurred during the course, *and if* they also agreed that First Principles occurred during the course, *then* what is the likelihood that they agreed that they learned a lot in the course?

Analysis of patterns in time (APT) is one way of approaching data analysis that is an alternative to the linear models approach (e.g., regression analysis, path analysis, and ANOVA; see Frick, 1983, 1990; Frick, An, & Koh, 2006):

> This [APT] is a paradigm shift in thinking for quantitative methodologists steeped in the linear models tradition and the measurement theory it depends on (cf. Kuhn, 1962). The fundamental difference is that *the linear models approach relates independent measures through a mathematical function and treats deviation as error variance. On the other hand, APT measures a relation directly by counting occurrences of when a temporal pattern is true or false in observational data.* Linear models relate the measures; APT measures the relation. (Frick et al., 2006, p. 2)

In the present study, we wanted to know that if students reported that ALT and First Principles occurred, then what is the likelihood that students also reported that they learned a lot, mastered course objectives, or were satisfied with their instruction?

We were able to do APT with our data set as follows: New dichotomous variables from existing scale scores were created for each of the cases.[7] A scale was recoded as "Yes" if the scale score for that case was greater than or equal to 3.5, and "No" if less than 3.5. For example, if the ALT agreement code is "Yes," it means that the student "agreed" or "strongly agreed" that ALT occurred for him or her in that course (frequent, successful engagement in problems, tasks, or assignments); and if the code is "No," then the student did *not* "agree" or "strongly agree" that ALT occurred for him or her.

---

[7] Variables can be characterized by more than two categories, but for this study and the sample size and the numbers of combinations, a simple dichotomy appeared to be best – especially since ratings were negatively skewed.

Table 6 APT Frequencies for the pattern: If *ALT* and *First Principles,* then *learning progress?*

	ALT agreement			
	No		Yes	
	Combined First Principles Agreement		Combined First Principles Agreement	
	No	Yes	No	Yes
	Learning progress agreement	Learning progress agreement	Learning progress agreement	Learning progress agreement
	Count	Count	Count	Count
No	26	8	10	6
Yes	9	8	12	113

If *ALT* and *First Principles,* then *Learned a Lot.* In Table 6 results are presented for the APT query. If student agreement with ALT is Yes, and if student agreement with First Principles is Yes, then student agreement with Learned a Lot is Yes? Normally in APT one would have a number of observations *within* a case for a temporal pattern, so that a probability can be calculated for each case and the probabilities averaged across cases. For example, in the Frick (1990) study, probabilities of temporal patterns on each case were determined from about 500 time samples. In the present study, we have only one observation per classification (variable) for each case.

There were a total of 119 occurrences of the antecedent condition (if student agreement with ALT is Yes, *and* if student agreement with First Principles is Yes). Given that the antecedent was true, the consequent (student agreement with Learned a Lot is Yes) was true in 113 out of those 119 cases, which yields an APT conditional probability estimate of 113/119 or 0.95 for this pattern.

Next we investigated the pattern: If student agreement with ALT is No, and if student agreement with First Principles is No, then student agreement with Learned a Lot is Yes? It can be seen that the antecedent occurred a total of 35 times, and the consequent occurred in 9 out of those 35 cases, for a conditional probability estimate of 9/35 = 0.26. Thus, about 1 out of 4 students agreed that they learned a lot in the course when they did not agree that ALT and First Principles occurred.

This can be further interpreted: When both ALT and First Principles occurred, students were nearly four times as likely (0.95/0.26 = 3.7) to agree that they learned a lot in the course, compared to when ALT and First Principles are reported to not occur.

If *ALT* and *First Principles,* then *Learner Satisfaction.* In Table 7, results for the APT query are presented: If student agreement with ALT is Yes, and if student agreement with First Principles is Yes, then student agreement with Learner Satisfaction is Yes? The consequent was true in 113 out of 118 cases when the

Table 7 APT Frequencies for the pattern: If *ALT* and *First Principles*, then *learner satisfaction?*

	ALT agreement			
	No		Yes	
	Combined First Principles agreement		Combined First Principles agreement	
	No	Yes	No	Yes
	Satisfaction agreement	Satisfaction agreement	Satisfaction agreement	Satisfaction agreement
	Count	Count	Count	Count
No	25	6	11	5
Yes	10	10	11	113

antecedent was true for a probability estimate of 0.96. On the other hand, when ALT was No and First Principles was No, then Learner Satisfaction occurred in 10 out of 35 cases, or a probability estimate of 0.29. The estimated odds of Learner Satisfaction when both ALT and First Principles are present compared to when both are not are about 3.3–1 (0.96/0.29).

If *ALT* and *First Principles*, then *Outstanding Instructor/Course*. In Table 8, results for the APT query are presented: If student agreement with ALT is Yes, and if student agreement with First Principles is Yes, then student agreement with Outstanding Instructor/Course is Yes? The probability of this pattern is 114/119 = 0.96. If both antecedent conditions are false, the probability is 4/35 = 0.11. The odds are about 8.7–1 that an instructor/course is viewed as outstanding by students

Table 8 APT Frequencies for the pattern: If *ALT* and *First Principles*, then outstanding instructor/course (global rating)?

	ALT agreement			
	No		Yes	
	Combined First Principles agreement		Combined First Principles agreement	
	No	Yes	No	Yes
	Global rating agreement	Global rating agreement	Global rating agreement	Global rating agreement
	Count	Count	Count	Count
No	31	4	15	5
Yes	4	12	7	114

Table 9 APT Frequencies for the pattern: If *ALT* and *First Principles*, then *mastery of course objectives?*

	ALT agreement			
	No		Yes	
	Combined First Principles agreement		Combined First Principles agreement	
	No	Yes	No	Yes
	Mastery level	Mastery level	Mastery level	Mastery level
	Count	Count	Count	Count
Nonmastery	14	3	3	11
Partial mastery	19	9	15	73
Mastery	2	4	4	34

when ALT and First Principles are both present versus both absent, according to student ratings.

If *ALT* and *First Principles*, then *Mastery*. In Table 9 results for the APT query are presented: If student agreement with ALT is Yes, and if student agreement with First Principles is Yes, then student agreement with Mastery is Yes? Here the pattern is less predictable, since it was true for 34 out of 118 students for a probability of 0.29 (roughly 1 out of 3 students). On the other hand, only 2 out of 35 students agreed that they had mastered course objectives (probability = 2/25 = 0.06) when they did not agree that First Principles and ALT occurred. Thus, students were five times more likely to agree that they mastered course objectives when they agreed versus did not agree that both ALT and First Principles occurred when they took the course.

Discussion

Implications from APT findings. The APT findings are consistent with earlier correlational results. APT allows temporal combinations or patterns of more than two variables at a time. In APT, relationships are not assumed to be linear nor modeled by a mathematical function – e.g., as in regression analysis. APT probability estimates are relatively easy to comprehend and can have practical implications. The reader is cautioned that a temporal association does not imply causation (cf. Frick, 1990).

Mastery of learning objectives. As noted earlier, less than 1 out of 4 students considered themselves masters of course objectives, even though 93% received As and Bs for their course grades. This could be interpreted in a number of ways, but what is noteworthy is the large discrepancy between grades received and student perceptions of their mastery. While student grades and perceptions of mastery are significantly correlated ($\rho = 0.397$), a grade of A or B appears not to be a good indicator of mastery of course objectives. A cross-tabulation of grades by mastery level indicated that 39 out of 182 students (21.4%) considered themselves to be masters and who received grade A. Approximately 42% of all students received an A, who perceived themselves to be partial masters (37%) or nonmasters (5%) of course objectives.

Implications from First Principles of Instruction. We did not tell students that we were measuring First Principles. We constructed rating scale items that were consistent with each of the five First Principles; then we scrambled the order and mixed them with items measuring other scales on the survey. Data from our study indicate that these rating scales are highly reliable.

While further research is needed with respect to the validity of the scales, those scales that rate use of First Principles of Instruction reveal things that course instructors can do something about. For example, if scores on the authentic problems/task scale are low, instructors could consider revising their course so that students are expected to perform authentic problems or tasks as part of their learning. If scores on the integration scale are low, then new activities can be included in a course to encourage students to incorporate what they have learned in their real lives. In other words, such changes would make course objectives more relevant from a student's perspective. If learning activities are viewed as being more relevant, then students would be expected to be more motivated and to spend more time engaged in activities than before. More successful engagement should lead to greater achievement, according to past studies of ALT (e.g., see Kuh et al., 2006). It is very clear from results in this study that students who agree that First Principles were used in their courses are also likely to agree that such courses and instructors were outstanding ($\rho = 0.89$).

The reader should note that numerous studies in the past have shown significant positive correlations between global course ratings and objective measures of student achievement such as course exams in multiple sections (Cohen, 1981; Kulik, 2001). Thus, it is likely that use of First Principles of Instruction is correlated with student learning achievement, but that was not measured in this study. It is important to note, however, in a separate study of undergraduate students in 12 courses at one university (Frick, Chadha, Watson, & Zlatkovska, 2009), the TALQ Scales were compared with independent assessments by classroom instructors of each student's mastery of course objectives. In that study, the TALQ was completed by most students in each of those 12 courses (total $n = 464$), and similar patterns of results were found. For example, students who agreed that their instructors used First Principles of Instruction were nearly three times more likely to agree that they experienced frequent success on course tasks (ALT). Furthermore, if students agreed that *both* First Principles *and* ALT occurred, they were over five times more likely to be rated by their course instructors as high masters of course objectives. When students neither agreed that First Principles occurred nor did they agree that they experienced ALT, they were about 26 times more likely to be rated as low masters of course objectives, compared with agreement that both First Principles and ALT did occur.

The relationship in the Frick et al. (2009) study indicated that First Principles of Instruction are indirectly related to mastery of course objectives. The Spearman correlation between First Principles and mastery was about 0.12, and although statistically significant, it is relatively low. The correlation between First Principles and ALT was much higher ($\rho = 0.58$), and the correlation between ALT and student mastery as determined by their course instructors was 0.36 and highly significant. Thus, it appears that when students agree that their instructors use First Principles of Instruction, it is associated with a greater likelihood of agreeing that they experienced ALT; and in turn, if they agreed they experienced ALT, then they were much more likely to be rated by their instructors as high masters of course objectives, and much less likely to be rated as low masters.

From a theoretical perspective, these patterns make sense. The items on the TALQ Scales used in the present study and also in the Frick et al. (2009) study were derived largely from a synthesis of instructional *theory* on which First Principles of Instruction are based. That theory predicts that when these principles are present, learning is promoted (Merrill, 2002; Merrill, Barclay, & van Schaak, 2008).

The further value of these theoretical principles is that they can be incorporated into a wide range of teaching methods and subject matter. These principles do not prescribe how to teach, nor what to teach. Incorporating First Principles of Instruction into one's teaching may, however, require college instructors to think differently about their subject matter than they are accustomed. Thirty percent of the respondents in this study did *not* agree that First Principles occurred in courses they evaluated, and that was similarly the case in the Frick et al. (2009) study where in 4 of the 12 courses (about 33%), students largely disagreed that First Principles of Instruction occurred. Instead of instruction organized around topics, it may need to be organized on the basis of a sequence of simple-to-complex, whole, real-world tasks or problems (cf. Merrill, 2007). While this can be challenging in redesigning a course, the clear benefit is that such problems or tasks are perceived as more meaningful and relevant by students. When respondents in this study agreed that First Principles occurred (70% of the sample), 9 out of 10 also agreed that they were satisfied with the course, learned a lot, and it was an outstanding instructor/course (see Tables 6, 7, and 8).

Conclusion

We surveyed 193 undergraduate and graduate students from at least 111 different courses at several higher education institutions using a new instrument designed to measure TALQ. Reliabilities ranged from 0.81 to 0.97 for the nine TALQ Scales. Spearman correlations among scales were highly significant, mostly in the 0.60s–0.80s.

Results from APT indicated that students in this study were three to four times more likely to agree that they learned a lot and were satisfied with courses when they also agreed that First Principles of Instruction were used *and* they were frequently engaged successfully (ALT). Students in this study were five times more likely to agree that they believed they had mastered course objectives when they also agreed that both First Principles and ALT occurred, compared with their absence. Finally, students were almost nine times as likely to rate the course and instructor as outstanding when they also agreed that both First Principles and ALT occurred versus did not occur.

Similar patterns were observed in the Frick et al. (2009) study, and, while fewer classes were observed, most students in each class completed the TALQ instrument. Not only did students self-report their mastery of course objectives, but their instructors independently rated their mastery based on performance in class and on exams, assignments, papers, projects, and other deliverables. Students in that study were about five times more likely to be rated by their instructors as high masters of course objectives, when those students independently reported that they agreed that their instructors incorporated First Principles of Instruction in the course and also agreed that they experienced ALT.

In summary, we believe that the TALQ Scales have considerable promise for use in evaluation of teaching in higher education. These scales are reliable, and scores on these scales are associated with higher student achievement as rated by their instructors. Finally, if instructors receive low evaluations of their teaching on the TALQ Scales on First Principles, these would be areas in which instructors could improve their courses. Such instructors could attempt to build their courses around a series of increasingly complex, authentic tasks (Principle 1); they could make greater efforts to activate student learning (Principle 2); they could model or demonstrate correct task performance more often (Principle 3); they could provide students with more opportunities to try out what they have learned and provide feedback (Principle 4); and they could provide students with more opportunities to integrate what they have learned into their own personal lives (Principle 5). If instructors do increase their use of First Principles, we would expect student ratings on the TALQ Scales to increase, and this in turn should increase the likelihood that more students will master course objectives. Future research studies are needed to empirically determine if this predicted pattern occurs.

References

Abrami, P. (2001). Improving judgments about teaching effectiveness using teacher rating forms. *New Directions for Institutional Research, 109*, 59–87.

Abrami, P., d'Apollonia, S. & Cohen, P. (1990). Validity of student ratings of instruction: what we know and what we do not. *Journal of Educational Psychology, 82*(2), 219–231.

American Institutes for Research (2006, January 19). New study of the literacy of college students finds some are graduating with only basic skills. Retrieved January 20, 2007: http://www.air.org/news/documents/Release200601pew.htm.

Arthur, J., Tubré, T., Paul, D. & Edens, P. (2003). Teaching effectiveness: The relationship between reaction and learning evaluation criteria. *Educational Psychology, 23*(3), 275–285.

Baer, J., Cook, A. & Baldi, S. (2006, January). The literacy of America's college students. American Institutes for Research. Retrieved January 20, 2007: http://www.air.org/news/documents/The%20Literacy%20of%20Americas%20College%20Students_final%20report.pdf.

Berliner, D. (1991). What's all the fuss about instructional time?. In M. Ben-Peretz & R. Bromme (Eds.), *The nature of time in schools: Theoretical concepts, practitioner perceptions*. New York: Teachers College Press.

Brown, B., & Saks, D. (1986). Measuring the effects of instructional time on student learning: Evidence from the Beginning Teacher Evaluation Study. *American Journal of Education, 94*(4), 480–500.

Clayson, D., Frost, T. & Sheffet, M. (2006). Grades and the student evaluation of instruction: A test of the reciprocity effect. *Academy of Management Learning and Education, 5*(1), 52–65.

Cohen, P. (1981). Student ratings of instruction and student achievement. A meta-analysis of multisection validity studies. *Review of Educational Research, 51*(3), 281–309.

Emery, C., Kramer, T. & Tian, R. (2003). Return to academic standards: A critique of student evaluations of teaching effectiveness. *Quality Assurance in Education, 11*(1), 37–46.

Feldman, K. (1989). The association between student ratings of specific instructional dimensions and student achievement: Refining and extending the synthesis of data from multisection validity studies. *Research in Higher Education, 30*, 583–645.

Fisher, C., Filby, N., Marliave, R., Cohen, L., Dishaw, M., Moore, J., et al. (1978). *Teaching behaviors: Academic learning time and student achievement: Final report of Phase III-B, Beginning Teacher Evaluation Study*. San Francisco: Far West Laboratory for Educational Research and Development.

Frick, T. (1983). Non-metric temporal path analysis: An alternative to the linear models approach for verification of stochastic educational relations. Bloomington, IN. Retrieved, March 4, 2007: http://www.indiana.edu/~tedfrick/ntpa/.

Frick, T. (1990). Analysis of patterns in time (APT): A method of recording and quantifying temporal relations in education. *American Educational Research Journal, 27*(1), 180–204.

Frick, T., An, J. & Koh, J. (2006). Patterns in Education: Linking Theory to Practice. In M. Simonson (Ed.), Proceedings of the Association for Educational Communication and Technology, Dallas, TX. Retrieved March 4, 2007: http://education.indiana.edu/~frick/aect2006/patterns.pdf.

Frick, T., Chadha, R., Watson, C. & Zlatkovska, E. (2009, under review). Improving course evaluations to improve instruction and complex learning in higher education. Submitted to *Educational Technology Research & Development*.

Kirk, R. (1995). Experimental design: Procedures for the behavioral sciences (3rd ed.). Pacific Grove, CA: Brooks/Cole.

Kirkpatrick, D. (1994). *Evaluating training programs: The four levels*. San Francisco, CA: Berrett-Koehler.

Koon, J., & Murray, H. (1995). Using multiple outcomes to validate student ratings of overall teacher effectiveness. *The Journal of Higher Education, 66*(1), 61–81.

Kuh, G., Kinzie, J., Buckley, J., Bridges, B., & Hayek, J. (2006, July). What matters to student success: A review of the literature (Executive summary). Commissioned report for the National Symposium on Postsecondary Student Success. Retrieved January 20, 2007: http://nces.ed.gov/npec/pdf/Kuh_Team_ExecSumm.pdf

Kulik, J. (2001). Student ratings: Validity, utility and controversy. *New Directions for Institutional Research, 109*, 9–25.

Marsh, H. (1984). Students' evaluations of university teaching: Dimensionality, reliability, validity, potential biases, and utility. *Journal of Educational Psychology, 76*(5), 707–754.

Merrill, M. D. (2002). First Principles of Instruction. *Education Technology Research and Development, 50*(3), 43–59.

Merrill, M. D. (2007). A task-centered instructional strategy. *Journal of Research on Technology in Education, 40*(<iss>1</iss>), 33–50.

Merrill, M. D., Barclay, M. & van Schaak, A. (2008). Prescriptive principles for instructional design. In J. M. Spector, M. D. Merrill, J. van Merriënboer & M. F. Driscoll (Eds.), *Handbook of research on educational communications and technology* (3rd ed., pp. 173–184). New York: Lawrence Erlbaum Associates.

Renaud, R., & Murray, H. (2004). Factorial validity of student ratings of instruction. *Research in Higher Education, 46*(8), 929–953.

Squires, D., Huitt, W. & Segars, J. (1983). *Effective schools and classrooms: A research-based perspective*. Alexandria, VA: Association for Supervision and Curriculum Development.

Developing Technology Fluency in Community Practice: Exploration of the "Paintbrush" Metaphor

Sarah Hug and Susan Jurow

Abstract In this qualitative study of a girls only technology program, the authors argue that an emphasis of self-expression through the use of technology limited middle school girls' developing technological fluency. The authors show how the metaphor of "technology as a paintbrush" was evident in (1) the organization of the physical environment of the program, (2) its curriculum, and (3) the interactions between the facilitators and the girls during the program. The authors conclude that educators need to analyze critically how the "technology as a paintbrush" metaphor is enacted in the context of facilitating girls' identity development as technologists.

Keywords Gender issues · Middle school · Technology

In the middle school technology course offered at the Girls Only Technology Program, Chelsea cannot be bothered to wait for the rest of the class to catch up. They are making individual name tents, folded pieces of paper that display students' names. They are making name tents so that their new teacher will get to know her students, and so the students can practice working with Microsoft Publisher software. Ms. Parsons, the technology instructor, says, "If it doesn't reflect your personality, then you need to do something about it." Chelsea arranges letters and symbols in a variety of ways, ~"chels"~, ~CH3L$~, and then back to a simple ~·chelsea·~, using the symbols available on Publisher. She helps her friend "$t3phani3" find symbols to reconstruct her name. As she works, she flips between two open screens, one showing the simple ~·chelsea·~ on a plain pink background and the other developing into a wild scene with flaming cars and trucks downloaded from the web, with ~CH3L$~ standing for a shortened version of her name.

S. Hug (✉)
ATLAS Institute, Assessment and Research Center, University of Colorado at Boulder, Boulder, CO, USA
e-mail: hug@colorado.edu

A.S. Jurow (✉)
School of Education, University of Colorado at Boulder, Boulder, CO, USA
e-mail: susan.jurow@colorado.edu

M. Orey et al. (eds.), *Educational Media and Technology Yearbook*,
Educational Media and Technology Yearbook 35,
DOI 10.1007/978-1-4419-1516-0_6, © Springer Science+Business Media, LLC 2010

Ms. Parsons walks by when Chelsea works with the simple ∼·chelsea·∼ design and tells her that she needs to *express* herself on the page. Eventually, Chelsea decides to use the symbol-laden ∼CH3L$∼, complete with flames and images of cars for one side of her name tent. On its back she keeps the simple, lowercase ∼·chelsea·∼ printed on a demure pink background.

In making her name tent, Chelsea tried on different identities using the computer—toying with the feminine, demure Chelsea and exploring the possibility of a more brash, car and truck-loving Chelsea. At the Girls Only Technology Program (hereafter Girls Only Program), housed at a Computer Clubhouse in a suburb of a large western city, girls are encouraged to explore who they are and who they want to be through art and technology. The logic behind Ms. Parson's teaching is aligned with research on youth development. According to Ginwright (2002), providing youth an outlet for expressing their identities is vital to their development, as adolescents' primary goals are to define themselves. Thus, through participation in the activities sponsored by the Girls Only Program, Chelsea and the girls who attend the program could be expected to learn technological skills and see themselves as computer users who are flexible designers of technology products, such as video. In addition, the products or artifacts they create could be expected to express the girls' interests or personalities. In this chapter, we explore the ways the program framed the girls' use of technology and examine what sorts of technologically fluent identities might be favored or encouraged in the Girls Only Program.

The purpose of this study was to describe how girls developed (or did not develop) *technological fluency* through their participation in the Girls Only Program at the Computer Clubhouse. Technological fluency is defined as the flexible use of multiple technologies for a variety of purposes (Council, 1999). Specifically, we asked: How did the organization of the Girls Only Program's curriculum and social interactions facilitate (or constrain) the girls in developing technical skills as well as the conceptual knowledge and intellectual capabilities needed to use technology in a fluid and competent manner?

Context: The Girls Only Technology Program at the Computer Clubhouse

In this study, we examined the activities that took place during an 8-week Girls Only Program that took place at the Silver Stream Computer Clubhouse in the Western United States. Computer Clubhouses provide underserved youth with free after-school opportunities to explore their own ideas through technology. The 106 Computer Clubhouses around the world follow the philosophy of the flagship clubhouse, which began in 1993 at the Massachusetts Institute of Technology:

1. The Clubhouse focuses on *constructionist* activities, which are activities that encourage young people to work as designers, inventors, and creators (Papert, 1980).

2. The Clubhouse encourages youth to work on projects related to their own interests.
3. The Clubhouse aims to create a sense of community, where young people work together with one another with support and inspiration from adult mentors.
4. The Clubhouse is dedicated to offering resources and opportunities to those who would not otherwise have access to them (www.computerclubhouse.org).

Resnick (2006), one of the creators of the Computer Clubhouse, captured a key principle of the Clubhouses with the phrase the "computer as a paintbrush" to describe how youth at the multiple sites around the globe could use the computer to create, design, and express themselves. The Computer Clubhouses make technology available to youth in underserved and under-resourced communities, decreasing the digital divide and providing a safe place for youth exploration of talents and interests. In addition, Computer Clubhouse facilitators serve as mentors to young people and provide student-directed support for using technology. Resnick's "computer as a paintbrush" metaphor is particularly useful in after-school environments, where motivation to learn is self-directed with no concrete consequences for nonparticipation. A participant cannot fail an after-school program such as the Girls Only Program, and can leave whenever she chooses. Participation is meant to be learner centered, and the clubhouse technology must foster self-direction and respect student interests, else the Computer Clubhouse would be a lonely place.

The Girls Only Program was a special program designed to increase female participation at the Silver Stream Computer Clubhouse during the summer months (when participation of young women often declined). Female participants were recruited from the group of middle school students who frequented the Computer Clubhouse after school or as part of their art course. In contrast to the less structured time for individual pursuits during regular Computer Clubhouse hours, the Girls Only Program was project-based. The girls were to create a series of video projects that followed the digital storytelling model (Lambert, 2005). The foundations of self-expression, individual choice, and downplaying technical savvy or skill in an effort to broaden youth participation that are emphasized in the Computer Clubhouse philosophy were similar to those that underlie the practice of digital storytelling. These similar perspectives contributed to the dominant view of "technology as a paintbrush" (an expansion of the "computer as a paintbrush" metaphor to include both hardware, software, and technological peripherals) at the Girls Only Program, which, we argue, rendered the technology secondary to the development process, and thus constrained the focus of technology to that of self-expression and the conveyance of ideas.

Conceptual Framework

We take a situated view of learning to understand how girls develop technologically fluent identities through their participation in the Girls Only Program. This perspective assumes that individuals develop skills, knowledge, and ways of speaking and acting through gradual participation in a community of practice—in this case, an emerging community of digital storytelling (Lave & Wenger, 1991; Rogoff, 1993).

From a situated perspective, learning involves more than an accumulation of facts, a checklist of skills mastered, or a score on a test. Learning also means becoming a certain kind of person. Learning occurs in a community of practitioners, in which participants learn skills and come to take on particular kinds of dispositions through gradually increasing and changing their forms of participation in the activities of the community.

A community of practice is a group of individuals engaged in a social practice with specific goals, in which members engage in the community at different kinds of participation (Wenger, 1998). Members initially learn about the community and how to engage effectively in practices through legitimate and peripheral participation in community activities. In his discussion of the process of moving from the periphery to the more central practices of a community, Wenger (1998) emphasizes that members of a community inevitably take different trajectories or pathways into and out of the community, with the most committed members becoming "fuller participants" within the community. Decisions regarding what trajectories to take into a community are not solely decided by individuals. Importantly, the community offers different trajectories to its individual members by the organization and transparency of its practices.

Communities provide a variety of conceptual and material resources to help individuals craft identities that help them become more central members of the community. Nasir (2004) suggests that the *ideational artifacts* of a community, which include the meanings of its symbols, central concepts, and foundational assumptions, are important to study to learn how individuals create identities in relation to a community. Ideational artifacts are concepts that shape the activities available in a specific context and constrain the interaction that can occur within that context (Nasir, 2004). They are concepts that individuals orient toward to influence activity in a community. The concepts themselves constrain what might occur. For example, in high school, choir and home economics courses are routinely offered at the same time as computer science courses. The assumption enacted in this policy is that individuals would be interested in either home economics and choir (predominantly girls) or computer science (predominantly boys). The ideational artifact suggests girls and boys have stereotypical, gendered academic interests. The perception that these groups of students divided along gender lines are mutually exclusive constrains students' behaviors, as the schedule assures choir members and home economics students may *not* participate in computer science.

Studying ideational artifacts in a particular context allows one to describe themes that emerge in a developing community of practice. Ideational artifacts can be thought of as nouns and verbs, just as *shape* and *mold* refer to the act of repositioning as well as the physical form of the newly constituted thing (Pea, 1985). In other words, ideational artifacts are shaped by the context and shape the context in which they are observed.

Ideational artifacts are reified in a community's artifacts. For example, the idea technology as paintbrush was seen in the Girls Only Program participants' self-maps (charts girls made to describe their possible futures), self-collages (descriptive, artistic clusters of words and images that represented the girls' interests), story-boards (paper and pencil depictions of their developing videos), scripts (written text that became the voiceover audio to the videos they created), and digital sto-ries (video projects the girls developed). Materiality of the ideational artifact, or ways the ideas were made tangible, made the conceptual ideas public (Holland & Cole, 1995) within the Girls Only Program community.

Literature Review

This study builds on the work of social scientists, learning theorists, educational policy makers, and engineers who study adolescents' and adults' development of technological skill, ability, and interest. In this section, we describe the dimen-sions of technological fluency used in this chapter, highlight work on technological identity development, and examine the gender gap regarding technology expertise.

Researchers at the MIT Media Laboratory and their partners at UCLA have stud-ied the development of technological fluency in a variety of ways, from paper and pencil assessments to case studies and formal interviews. Through performance assessments of students' programming and program debugging skills, researchers have found that students who had the opportunity to design and create with tech-nology scored higher on the performance assessments than those who learned a programming language through direct instruction (Harel & Papert, 1990).

Ching, Kafai, and Marshall (2000) looked at how students in a middle school technology project course developed technological fluency as they completed their long-term project. When they compared student participation roles that students were offered and that students took on, they found no gender differences between the types of technological design work in which girls and boys engaged. Both girls and boys participated in planning, programming, graphic work, and research when they were engaged in a structured collaborative activity.

Through case studies of student experimentation and play, (Resnick, Kafai, & Maeda, 2003) described the way a girl at the Intel Computer Clubhouse developed the intellectual capabilities of a technology designer as she tested mini-hypotheses with different ramp configurations in her efforts to build a marble machine. Current research from the MIT and LA-based sites is focused on online communities pro-gramming in school-based and after-school settings and the contribution of youth to the creative society (Kafai, Y.B., Fields, D.A., Cook, M., 2007; Resnick, 2007).

Turkle (1984) discussed adolescents and computing in her groundbreaking book *The Second Self: Computing and the Human Spirit*. In the early 1980s, Turkle observed children and adolescents using Papert's Logo computer program-ming software (Turkle, 1984). In her study of computer programmers, she saw examples of students assimilating computing into their personal identities, using computers to express themselves, and experimenting with who they may become through computing.

Similarly, Gee explored video gaming communities and the ways in which individuals developed technologically adept identities, including ways of thinking and acting in accordance with affinity groups (e.g., first-person shooter gamers and virtual reality gamers). Like those studying technological fluency, Gee found that gamers took on or appropriated the core values and ways of behaving in virtual worlds as they became engaged in the community of gaming practice.

Women are grossly underrepresented in the computer science field. In 2007, women comprised only 11% of all computer science majors, a proportion much reduced from its peak at 34% in the mid-1980s (www.ncwit.org). The American Association of University Women conducted a large-scale study of middle school girls' impressions of technology use (AAUW, 2000). Girls who participated in the AAUW Tech Savvy focus groups primarily described the computer as a tool to get things done. The girls expressed interest in computing as a means to an end. Participants said that girls "do not talk about computer stuff like boys do" (p. 10), but still enjoy using computers for different things, particularly communicating with one another and using the computer as an artistic medium. They compare their "computer as tool" use to their male peers, who view the computer as a toy with inherent value. The girls downplay the intellectual value in finding out how the computer works, the "hows" of technology.

Margolis and Fisher (2002) investigated how male and female computer science majors experienced the computing field at a prestigious institution. After interviewing dozens of Carnegie Mellon University computer science majors, the authors surmised the men were more likely to fit the science "boy wonder" stereotype—that of a scientist or technologist who exhibits intense interest in science or technology at an early age, experiments and tinkers with objects, and shows little interest in any other subject or activity. Girls were more likely to report a variety of interests and had less experience with programming and other technological pursuits. Margolis and Fisher stress that they did find some men who fit into the female technologist mold, as well as some women who resembled the boy wonder, but girls tended to enjoy technology as one of many interests, while boys tended to "dream in code" (p. 32).

These and related studies of young women engaged in technology shaped the study conducted at the Girls Only Program, as well as the planning of the program itself. The use of the computer as a tool to get things done was apparent in the local community and is described in more detail throughout the chapter. Like Turkle's, our study analyzed ways in which girls might assimilate computing into their personal identities, with a focus on how the learning environment was designed to encourage particular identities. Our work also builds on Gee's notion of learning as an appropriation of community values and ways of behaving regarding technology, and extends this by applying the ideational artifact concept to illustrate how these values and ways of behaving are encouraged in community practice and organization. Our work builds on these efforts, with a focus on adolescent and facilitator interactions and technological artifacts as data of interest. Rather than focusing exclusively on the girls' activity within the program context, this study illuminates how the context (in this case, the physical environment, curriculum, and interactions with other girls and with program facilitators) may shape the girls' development of technological fluency.

Methods

This work is exploratory in nature, and so the case study approach was chosen to analyze how the organization of the Girls Only Program's curriculum and social interactions facilitated (or constrained) the girls in developing technological fluency. Stake (1995) described case study selections as an effort to take full advantage of what researchers can discover from programs or people engaged in innovative, engaging activities.

Setting

The Girls Only Program was housed at the Silver Stream Computer Clubhouse in a suburb outside a mid-sized city in the western United States. The Girls Only Program was a special, 8-week program from March 2006 to May 2006 designed by Silver Stream facilitators to increase the number and proportion of females who attend the Silver Stream Clubhouse on a regular basis, to create a sense of community for the girls who attend Silver Stream, and to increase girls' technology knowledge and skill in digital video development. The program was free to all girls who wanted to attend during the 3-h Monday evening meetings.

The program aimed to reach girls separate from the boys for three reasons: to mitigate the adolescent posturing and flirting that often took place when the boys and girls were together in the clubhouse, to develop a community of young women who might encourage one another in their technology endeavors, and to increase the participation of females throughout the summer months, when the Silver Stream Computer Clubhouse participation of girls, already lower than that of boys, was lowest.

As part of a larger analysis of students becoming technologically fluent in an after-school setting (see Hug, 2007 for more information about this study), Hug chose this program to investigate young girls' development of technologically fluent identities. An analysis of 27 similar technology programs in the region revealed that the Girls Only Program offered a unique emphasis on technological exploration, choice, and creativity that could provide important insights into the ways *communities* of technology users develop ways of using technology.

The Girls Only Program was a good setting for studying technologically fluent identity development because it provided girls with a rich source of technological resources they could use as they chose to develop individually relevant projects at their own pace. The continuity of the Silver Stream Computer Clubhouse (founded in 2001) allowed girls to envision how they might continue their participation beyond the short time frame of the program into summer months and beyond. The established, theory-driven approach to facilitating and mentoring youth in Computer Clubhouse sites across the globe also made the program an ideal site for research; in contrast to burgeoning after-school programs that struggle for facilities, software, hardware, funding, staff, and participants, the Girls Only Program was well-positioned to succeed.

Participants

The Girls. All of the eight middle school girls who participated in the Girls Only Program took part in this study. The girls ranged in age from 11 to 14. Three of the girls were identified as Caucasian/white, four were of Hispanic and Native American heritage, and one was African American. All spoke fluent English, though two spoke some Spanish at home. The girls were invited by Ms. Parsons to take part in the Girls Only Program because they showed great interest in digital projects. One girl was a new member of the Silver Stream Computer Clubhouse and was recruited by her best friend to attend the program. The oldest girl had been a member of the Computer Clubhouse for 3 years, though on average girls had been attending for 6 months.

The Facilitators. There were four facilitators of the Girls Only Program. Ms. Parsons, assistant director of Silver Stream Computer Clubhouse, planned the program, acquired the software, and was the primary leader of Girls Only Program events. She also taught the middle school art and technology course, with a background in web design. The foundation enrichment director, a former middle school teacher, helped plan and lead Girls Only Program events. The remaining two facilitators were female volunteers at Silver Stream Computer Clubhouse with backgrounds in nonprofit community work and journalism, the latter recruited by the former to assist with the developing digital video.

Researcher Role

The first author's role in this research was that of a participant observer. Spradley (1980) described a participant observer as entering a site with two distinct intentions—to take part in the activities of the community she is studying and to examine the people and actions of the group. The first author joined the girls for the progress meetings and dinner portions of the meetings, engaged the girls in conversations about the project during work time, provided suggestions and feedback to the girls in the group, and assisted Ms. Parsons in planning and facilitating training aspects of the program.

Data Sources

To understand how the program promoted technological fluency development, we relied on the analysis of three main data sources: fieldnotes, video of program activities, and artifacts created by the girls as part of their digital video project.

Fieldnotes: During each Girls Only Program meeting, the first author took extensive notes regarding program activities, the interactions among facilitators and girls, and the first author's observation of girls' technology activity. Following each meeting the notes were expanded and revised when compared with video of program activities.

Video: Video cameras captured the activities of the community, including group meetings (in which all participants plan the days' events), video editing (done primarily by one or two girls at a time), and storyboard development (performed as a large group). Two cameras were running during the program at most times, one focused on the girls editing video when applicable. The author controlled the other camera as needed, moving among video editors at their workstations. The author left the tape running after the official end of activities to capture conversations girls had in down time.

Artifacts: The girls' video artifacts (including written documentation of the video planned as well as video and image files) collected weekly provided information regarding the way the girls were reifying, or making meaning of, the concept "Influences." We find this data is important as it allowed us to: (a) find out what technology the girls chose to use in their video; (b) understand the process of moving from storyboard to script to video, including the amount of time and effort expended at each stage; and (c) get a sense of the amount of change in the stories girls communicated via technology.

Approach to Data Analysis

To understand the Girls Only Program as a community of practice, content logs of each video were created, and episodes related to the ways in which facilitators and girls described and enacted the Girls Only Program activities, the purposes of girls' technology use as described by program participants, and the processes involved in developing the video product. These data provided information regarding participants' practice in the community, their appropriation of technological skills and capabilities, and the dialogue regarding girls in technology that evolved as the girls were working together to create the video. Field notes taken during the facilitators' planning meetings were also compared to the video documentation of what took place during the program, to look for inconsistencies and patterns of behavior, as well as for evidence of program flexibility in serving participants.

In order to understand patterns regarding the steps girls took in creating their digital projects, copies of the girls' developing video artifacts, journals, storyboards, and project notebooks were made so that the progression of their video could be analyzed. These records of practice were analyzed to study the process of reification, or the process of "making into a thing" (Wenger, 1998, p. 56). By analyzing these videos, it was possible to study how the girls framed the issue of "Influences" in their lives and made meaning through their developing video (Wenger, 1998, p. 57).

As we developed coding protocols, we expanded upon the set of generalizations or patterns that were documented in the data (Miles & Huberman, 1994). We collected a body of evidence to support the generalizations made in the case and examined the data given the predicted pattern of events. We built a generalization body of evidence with domain analysis and vignette analysis. Specifically, as the pattern of the theme "technology is used to express ideas" was discerned from coded lines in the transcript of the Girls Only Program, specific interactions that highlight this concept were extracted and analyzed as vignettes, presented in the following sections.

The Limits of the "Technology as Paintbrush" Metaphor in the Girls Only Program

In this section, we show how the view of "technology as paintbrush" was conveyed through the organization of the physical environment of the program, its curriculum, and the interactions between the facilitators and the girls during the program. Building on this, we argue that the ideational artifact of "technology as paintbrush" constrained how the participants in the Girls Only Program engaged with technology. Specifically, we found that the girls were encouraged to use technology as a tool for self-expression, to communicate personal stories about their lives. This focus could deter girls from viewing themselves as technologically fluent individuals who "look under the hood" and consider the power and capability of the tools they manipulated.

Messages About How to Use Technology: The Physical Environment

Physical spaces provide information about what sorts of activity occurs in them—the setup of the room, the tools available within, and the arrangement of the furniture all suggest what pursuits are encouraged. Spaces also indicate what sorts of people belong in them. The artifacts displayed highlight what activity is important and valued.

The physical environment reinforced the idea that the Girls Only Program was a place where individuals expressed themselves through artful technology use.[1] The

---

[1] The Girls Only Program took place in the physical setting of the Silver Stream Computer Clubhouse, decorated and maintained by Silver Stream Computer Clubhouse after-school facilitators and staff.

Silver Stream Computer Clubhouse is a room divided into two portions by a removable curtain. On one side, long tables provided room for the girls to hone their craft with "antique" art supplies, such as paints, clay, pencils, crayons, and markers. This portion of the room housed the art classes during the middle school day program and was open during clubhouse hours in the afternoons, when students chose their projects and had free time to experiment with all of the materials.

The other side of the room held the participant computers and large meeting table. The proximity of the art room enhanced the idea that computers are an extended, technologically advanced form of the paintbrush. Portions of the large space contained artistic resources and computer graphic resources on large bookcases, magazine racks, and cabinets. The resources were for a variety of audiences, from students new to computing and to art to the advanced professional (Fig. 1).

Fig. 1 The physical organization of the Girls Only Program room conveyed the program's emphasis on self-expression and creativity through the display of digital images, paintings, and drawings created by Silver Stream Computer Clubhouse members

The large space was decorated with approximately 50–60 works created by youth who spent time at the Computer Clubhouse, during open clubhouse hours, special programs, and school. Artifacts of both technological and art room practice were interspersed throughout both portions of the space—with pencil drawings hanging beside Photoshop creations. Most of the works had references to the creator in either visual or text form. For example, Adobe Photoshop creations included distortions of participants' faces, and there were collages developed digitally that prominently featured members' names (Fig. 2).

Fig. 2 This digital project, created by "Benny," was displayed on the wall at the Computer Clubhouse. It was chosen for the Intel Computer Clubhouse calendar and was distributed to Computer Clubhouses on six continents

Messages About How to Use Technology from the Curriculum

The curriculum that Ms. Parsons designed for the Girls Only Program conveyed messages regarding the valued uses of technology. Program decisions were explicitly designed to promote self-reflection and creative expression, to adhere to the tenets of the Computer Clubhouse philosophy. Ms. Parsons chose to use digital storytelling as a model for the collaborative films girls created. Digital storytelling is an interdisciplinary practice, making use of technological tools to diversify and leverage the powers of art, photography, and writing to create versatile multimedia projects that can easily be shared with family, friends, and strangers. In collaborative workshops, participants view digital stories created by others and critique these stories. They write scripts and develop storyboards that depict narration and image on paper as a way of planning the digital story. Participants receive hands-on instruction on the software tools they use to create their digital stories. As they work, participants critique one another's digital-stories-in-progress, and at the end of the workshop, participants present their stories to the group. Facilitators decided this model was in line with Silver Stream Computer Clubhouse goals and chose the model as a way to engage participants in digital video development.

The following artifacts were generated in the Girls Only Program:

- Self-collages, in which participants charted their interests, people who are important to them, their talents, and words they chose to describe themselves.
- Self-maps, where girls predicted possible future selves or the sorts of people they imagined themselves to become, including career aspirations as well as personality traits they admired.
- Video storyboards, drawings and text that describe each scene of the girls developing digital stories.
- Scripts, where girls type out all of the words they will record in their video projects.

The curriculum of the Girls Only Program further reinforced the notion of "technology as a paintbrush". Girls were given many opportunities to impart creative ideas on paper and on screen, particularly in the first weeks of the program. Facilitators devoted the first half of the program to the development of messages and themes that girls wanted to convey to their audience. During this time, girls independently used hardware and software to enhance their self-collages, using Adobe Photoshop. Program activities focused on dialogue, argumentation, and decision making in the video creation process. Girls were physically removed from the computer for most of the time, so they could talk to one another and to the facilitators around the center table.

Instructor-led activities at the Girls Only Program focused on defining oneself. Possible self-maps, self-map collages, scripts, and storyboards all called for girls to convey their thoughts and beliefs with words and images, with little technology use, though girls were asked to decide what technology would be in place (for example, where they would add photos, audio, video, and title art). The adult-led planning process was not unlike planning to write an essay or designing a poster. The technology was not an integral part of the process, merely the channel or means by which the ideas and stories would ultimately be communicated. The tools themselves were in fact invisible and unutilized until the final steps of artifact preparation.

Girls completed a survey the first day of the Girls Only Program. Facilitators modified the traditional Computer Clubhouse new member survey to address girls' motivations for enrolling in the Girls Only Program. A quarter of the items (5 of the 20 items) focused on the idea that technology is used for self-expression. Some examples of these items along with survey results can be found in Appendix.

The facilitators at the Girls Only Program framed the activities of the program to be ones in which girls would use computers as a tool for creative communication. In particular, the focus of the program was framed as one in which girls would express themselves and create video. The first adult-directed activity that supported the girls' use of "technology as a paintbrush" occurred on the first day of the program. Girls created their self-collages using paper and markers, describing themselves through pictures and text. The next step in this project was to enhance their creations through technology. Ms. Parsons scanned their hand-drawn self-maps into the computer, and girls opened their projects in Adobe Photoshop. Girls used the software to add color to their projects, insert photos of family and friends, and include additional content to their self-collages. The girls used the "technology as a paintbrush" to decorate their projects, using the Photoshop features to add color and detail to their hand-drawn works (as opposed to creating them initially using the computing technologies).

Messages About How to Use Technology from Social Interaction

We contend the ways in which local communities talk about the practice they engage in frames the ways the activities are perceived by community members. In this case, the digital stories developed by participants in the Girls Only Program were described as artifacts that express information about the creators. While technology was essential to video development, the talk surrounding the creation of video centered around self-expression.

Throughout the Girls Only Program, the project the girls created were considered opportunities for girls to communicate digitally. The instructors intended for girls to use this video project as an opportunity to express themselves, just as they might in a painting class.

In the second week of the Girls Only Program, Ms. Parsons began a discussion with the girls about the audience they could imagine for their developing video. Jessica said she would want her auntie to see her digital story, because she was someone Jessica admired. Ms. Parsons conveyed that this self-expression on Jessica's part could serve the audience in two ways, by providing a compelling story digitally and also by serving as a model for self-expression via video production. The excerpt illustrates how facilitators framed the Girls Only Program as a program devoted to self-expression through technology.

1. Ms. Parsons: Yeah, think about your auntie or other people coming and they say "hmm she's being real thoughtful she's expressing who she is. Boy I want to do, or what's important to me, or who do I want to be?"

In this conversation, Ms. Parsons expressed the value of storytelling, encouraging girls to use "technology as a paintbrush", to use hardware and software to convey information about themselves, so that they might in Turkle's words, "see themselves in the machine." Five of the girls seemed to accept this charge, by choosing to create digital stories directly tied to their own experiences, explaining what or who was important to them (friends, family), and recounting events in their lives. They chose to express personal stories with technology. The focus of the project was on the story, message, or idea conveyed, and not on the means by which the girls conveyed them.

The next week, as Ms. Parsons was describing the digital storytelling goals for the girls in the program, she emphasized the importance of expressing who you are through video. As she addressed the table full of aspiring digital storytellers, she reasoned that video was a powerful tool for communication, one they could leverage to express who they really were. This is important because it suggested a minimization of tool use for the sake of developing technological skill or expertise. In other words, the skills girls were developing using technology were made less vital to the technological creative process than the messages they conveyed.

2. Ms. Parsons: Video is such a powerful tool for communication this is your chance. It's good to keep your audience in mind but touch your soul. You know, "This is who I am."

This quote suggests that video is a particularly powerful tool, perhaps the best tool for communication and self-expression. None of the girls stopped their digital storytelling at the script phase, for example, claiming that they told their story effectively. Technology was an important and necessary aspect of each finished product, but implicitly so. Story and narrative, the message itself, were the most important, and the tools used and skill developed in telling the story were less important.

Technology as Paintbrush: Its Impact on Technological Identities

Throughout the first half of the program, girls used technology outside of program activities to express who they were, to tell stories, and to communicate with family and friends. They used computers during their free time to listen to music, to create music, to draw, and to add to their MySpace pages. They chatted about pixels ("Here, I'll make you look pretty. I have a 200 pixel camera"), their new cameras and video cameras ("I use mine to video me and my friends," "Mine has great features, but a small screen"), and their activities at the Computer Clubhouse with video ("I shot video for the last Open Mic night"). Yet when we discussed their strengths, aspirations, and what was important to them, none of the girls mentioned technology.

When they filled out self-maps (to describe their intentions after high school) and their pre- and post-self-collages (to describe what is important to them), none of them wrote the Computer Clubhouse or cameras on their pages. One girl added computers to her post-self-collage. Even as they digitally manipulated their projects, adding color, color transitions, text, and photos to their self-collages easily with Adobe Photoshop, they did not mention the effects as functions of the software program but as artistic choices and ways to represent themselves fully and represent what was important to them. *The tools were ubiquitous throughout the room, and yet the girls did not see them, talk about them, or seem to value them.*

The girls did not aspire to become technology gurus, but lawyers, veterinarians, singers, actors, chefs, and writers. They all have acquired many marketable technology skills at the Girls Only Program, yet they did not see them as leading to careers in technology. Digital storytellers must communicate ideas digitally, employing advanced technological skill to plan out their stories on storyboards, script out narratives, collect video and audio tape, clip and cut and import video, overlay audio onto video, add titles, create transitions in video, render DVDs, and burn the finished pieces on DVDs. In other words, using a digital storytelling project can be used to teach youth about technology. The emphasis in the Girls Only Program, however, remained a focus on the *story,* on the ways technology could be used to best communicate the ideas girls wanted to convey and not on the tools they used to do so. The problem with this is that it perpetuates the stereotypes regarding girls and underrepresented groups in regard to technology, that only white men (and boys) exercise the power of developing and exploring how technology works. These stereotypes indicate that women and underrepresented minorities are technology users, but not technology creators. By framing the Girls Only Program as a place where girls can use technology as a tool for self-expression, as a way of getting things done and nothing more, the program constrains opportunities for girls to explore how the technology works.

It seems that the fleshy underbelly of the technology as paintbrush ideational artifact is that technology becomes an invisible tool. While byproducts of the activity were technological skill development and an emergence of technological intellectual capabilities, participants and instructors did not explicitly identify these among the most beneficial aspects of the program. Girls used the technical tools, developing technological skills and intellectual capabilities as they completed videos. Girls were becoming digital storytellers, a role elevated in the local community of the Girls Only Program above a more technical role, like video editor or software expert. Put bluntly, when the purpose of the Girls Only Program was framed as learning to express oneself, the purpose was *not* to learn how to use Adobe Premiere software, *not* to become film-editing experts, and *not* to learn a little bit about the technical aspects of film production.

What Happens When We Lower the Floor?

At a Computer Clubhouse instructor workshop, Resnick talked about *lowering the floor* and *raising the ceiling* as a way of getting more individuals interested in self-expression through technology (Resnick, 2003). The goals of the Computer Clubhouse are to interest members in creating with technology by downplaying the skills and technological savvy necessary to achieve their goals and focusing on the products they are creating. Instructors ask, "Want to make a web page?" not "Want to learn html?" The goals of the program are explicitly focused on the product and not on the process involved in its creation, initially to lower barriers youth might perceive as excluding them from technology expertise. Thus, the tools and the skills involved in creating the product become invisible or merely obstacles to get around.

Lowering the floor as evidenced at the Girls Only Program appeared to allow for girls who might not typically be expected to engage with technology to do so. By deemphasizing the technical skill necessary to maximize technological capabilities, complex technology became more accessible to more youth at the Computer Clubhouse. The minimization of the tools in favor of the youth-driven project allowed self-expression to drive activity, but deemphasized the inherent power of the tools or the complexity of the skills youth learned to create their projects.

The girls mirrored the invisible use of technology in their practice within the community of digital storytellers. As Amber, Margo, Jessica, and Monique completed a storyboard, the discussion turned to how to bring in the images the way they wanted them to appear in their digital stories. "We'll figure that out later," Amber replied, and the girls went back to planning their video without a discussion of digital tool capability. Monique described herself as "all finished" with her digital story. All she had to do, she said, was put it together in that "thingy," indicating the video editing station. In her mind, the hard work was complete, though she had not yet used the technological tools necessary to create the digital story.

This approach allows more individuals to participate with digital technology, but does not highlight learning the software, understanding the hardware, or identifying with the "technologist" aspects of digital technology. Through their participation in the Girls Only Program, girls were offered artistic, digital storytelling identities tied to technology, and this deemphasized technological identities they may have otherwise adopted.

The Girls Only Program provided an opportunity for girls to express themselves through developing and producing a video about the influences of friends and family. Girls gradually participated more fully in the developing community of digital storytelling practice, using "technology as a paintbrush" to tell personal stories about their lives. All of the girls completed video projects at the Girls Only Program. In order to produce their videos, each girl or group of girls used technology fluently. That is, within the community of practitioners, and with various amounts of assistance from peers, instructors, and mentors, girls shot video, imported video, took digital pictures, imported images, negotiated new software, created titles and transitions, overlaid sound on video, cut video, and rendered and burned DVDs. Girls performed all of these technological skills in the service of self-chosen, self-directed digital story production.

Instructors and mentors positioned girls as technologically fluent young people, individuals taking part in a developing community of digital storytelling practice. This practice of telling a story digitally had social, emotional, and cognitive benefits (Bers & Cassell, 1998) in that girls identified and communicated the people, events, and values that influenced their lives in intelligent ways via technical tools. Further, the project allowed girls, like Jessica in her digital story project about peer pressure, to try on technological identities through their active participation in film making.

We do not intend to minimize tool use in this analysis of the Girls Only Program, only to describe how the program framed technology use as a means to an end, tools that were secondary to users' video development. In a broader analysis of the data from this study, Hug (2007) showed how the girls in the Girls Only Program became adept at using scripts, storyboards, and video editing software. The technological tools were vital to the girls' production of video, and each girl chose to use technology to express her personal (or not-so-personal) story. However, the *inherent power of the tools* was downplayed at the Girls Only Program in favor of the notion that the program was about imparting ideas and stories, which were the focus of practice in this community, particularly the development of digital stories.

One purpose of the Girls Only Program was to encourage girls to see themselves as creators of technology, capable young people who might one day become computer scientists. What girls learned was how to design *with* technology at the program. This is an excellent way to introduce girls to technology, to break barriers for young women in the field. However, it is not enough to persuade creative uses of technology without also highlighting what is "under the hood." A necessary next step requires enabling girls to design *technology*, much like a computer scientist or an engineer would. Designing the tools, technological devices, software, and hardware should be the end goal for programs hoping to diversify the technology workforce, as these problem-solving positions are the technology professionals with the status and abilities (CCAWMSET, 2000; Cohoon, 2002) to expand the use and development of technology for a diverse public.

The ideational artifact of technology as paintbrush enacted in the Girls Only Program imparted a set of values regarding technology, restricted girls' engagement with technology, and often led to the *invisibility* of technology use. The community values expressed implicitly and explicitly limited the types of technological identities taken up by community participants. The offered or sanctioned identity of a technical artist, one whose medium was electronic but whose intentions were to communicate, was the most prevalent. The notion of technology as paintbrush did make activity possible by providing a palatable way for girls to use technology—to tell personal stories through technological media. The community, however, framed the ways the participants engaged with the tools available and the ways they identified as technology *users and designers*. Girls persisted in the Girls Only Program, becoming digital storytellers and filmmakers, which necessitated technological skill but did not emphasize its development.

Girls became more expert users of technology at the Girls Only Program. They used the technological tools to develop personally relevant videos, while focusing on the product and not the process of this technology use. The invisibility of their tool use and the downplay of technological tool capabilities at the Girls Only Program meant girls did not have the equally important opportunity of discussing the technical aspects of the tools, the elements of technology design that made their experiences possible.

In order to address gender equity in technology, girls need to be encouraged not only to use technology fluently but also to develop new technologies, like computer scientists and engineers do. The design of software and hardware is the aspect of technology in which gender discrepancies are most apparent. Not surprisingly, technological design work is the technological field with the most prestige and highest pay and has the most direct impact on the technologies available in a society. In order to ensure that technology is made to better the lives of all, the technology itself should be designed by a diverse pool of technologists.

Participants in the Girls Only Program developed technological expertise in using a variety of technological tools, thinking flexibly with technology, and designing with technological tools. The focus of their work was on the product, though, and not on the technological tools they used. These girls are poised to become the next designers of computer technology. They have confidence in their abilities, see technological experience as vital to technological expertise, view themselves as technologically capable youth, and are self-reflective and creative. A next step for these girls would be participation in a community of practice that frames technological design (in the form of programming, for example) as a relevant enterprise for youth, that highlights tool capability as well as tool use as a mode of expression, and that offers girls trajectories into the next level of technological participation—technology design and development.

Appendix: Survey Items Related to the Technology as Paintbrush Ideational Artifact

The numbers after the items correspond to the number of girls who checked the box, indicating they agreed with the item.

1. I want to learn how to use a computer to express my creativity. (6 agree, 1 disagree)
2. I know how to use the computer to express my creativity. (6 agree, 1 disagree)
3. I use computers to

   _express my creativity (7)
   _get work done (7)
   _communicate with friends and family (7)
   _stay informed of local and world news (2)
   _stay informed of popular culture, music, and trends (5)

   10. Why did you decide to join the girls technology program? (please check all that apply)

   _to meet new people (7)
   _to get a chance to express myself (6)
   _to spend time with friends (7)
   _to try something new (7)
   _to have fun (7)
   _I really liked the last Girls Only Program (4)
   _to do something after school (5)
   _to learn about art and graphics (5)
   _to eat a nice meal with friends (3)
   _to learn more about computers (5)
   _to learn how to create a video (2)
   _I don't know (1)
   _you mean, there aren't any boys coming? (2)

References

Bers, M. U., & Cassell, J. (1998). Interactive storytelling systems for children: Using technology to explore language and identity. *Journal of Interactive Learning Research, 9*(2), 183–215.

CCAWMSET (2000). Executive summary from Land of Plenty. Report of the Congressional Commission on the Advancement of Women and Minorities in Science, Engineering and Technology Development. Washington, DC.

Ching, C. C., Kafai, Y. B. & Marshall, S. (2000). Spaces for change: Gender and technology access in collaborative software design projects. *Journal for Science Education and Technology, 9*(1), 45–56.

Cohoon. (2002). Recruiting and Retaining Women in Undergraduate Computing Majors. *SIGSCE Special Issue on Women and Computers, June.* Congressional Commission on the Advancement of Women and Minorities in Science, Engineering and Technology Development. (2000). Land of Plenty Diversity as America's Competitive Edge in Science, Engineering, and Technology. Washington, DC.

Council, N. R. (1999). *Being fluent with information technology.* Washington, DC: National Research Council: National Academies Press.

Ginwright, S. (2002). From Assets to Agents: Social Justice, Organizing and Youth Development. New Directions in Youth Development (Ginwright and James) *New Directions in Youth Development, 96* (Winter).

Harel, I., & Papert, S. (1990). Software design as a learning environment. *Interactive learning environments, 1*(1), 1–32.

Holland, D., & Cole, M. (1995). Between discourse and schema: Reformulating a cultural-historical approach to culture and mind. *Anthropology and Education Quarterly, 26*(4), 475–489. Vygotsky's Cultural-Historical Theory of Human Development: An International Perspective (Dec., 1995).

Hug, S. (2007). Developing technological fluency in a community of digital storytelling practice: Girls becoming tech-savvy. Ph.D. dissertation, University of Colorado at Boulder, United States – Colorado. Retrieved June 9, 2009, from Dissertations & Theses @ University of Colorado System database. (Publication No. AAT 3256474).

Kafai, Y.B., Fields, D.A. & Cook, M. (2007). Your second selves: avatar designs and identity play in a teen virtual world. In proceedings of Digital Games Research Association.

Lambert, J. (2005). *Digital storytelling: Capturing lives, creating community.* Berkeley: Digital Diner Press.

Lave, J., & Wenger, E. (1991). *Situated learning: Legitimate peripheral participation.* New York: Cambridge University Press.

Margolis, J., & Fisher, A. (2002). *Unlocking the clubhouse: Women in computing.* Cambridge, MA: MIT Press.

Miles, M. B., & Huberman, A. M. (1994). *Qualitative data analysis* (2nd ed.). Thousand Oaks, CA: Sage.

Nasir. (2004). Halal-ing the child: Reframing identities of opposition in an urban Muslim school. *Harvard Educational Review, 74*(2), 153–174.

Papert, S. (1980). Mindstorms: Children, computers, and powerful ideas. NY, NY: Basic.

Pea, R. D. (1985). Beyond amplification: Using computers to reorganize human mental functioning. *Educational Psychologist, 20*, 167–182.

Resnick, M. (2006). Computer as paintbrush: Technology, play, and the creative society. In D. Singer, R. Golikoff, & K. Hirsh-Pasek (Eds.), *Play = Learning: How play motivates and enhances children's cognitive and social-emotional growth.* Oxford: Oxford University Press.

Resnick, M. (2007). Sowing the seeds for a more creative society. *Learning and leading with technology, 35*(4), pp. 18–22.

Resnick, M., Kafai, J. & Maeda, J. (2003). *A networked, media-rich programming environment to enhance technological fluency at after-school centers in economically-disadvantaged communities.* Boston, MA: MIT Media Laboratory.

Rogoff, B. (1993). Children's guided participation and participatory appropriation in sociocultural activity. In R. Wozniak and K. Fischer (Eds.), *Development in Context: Acting and Thinking in Specific Environments* (pp. 121-153). Hillsdale, NJ: Lawrence Erlbaum Assoc..

Spradley, J. P. (1980). Participant observation. Orlando, FL: Harcourt Brace Jovanovich College Publishers.

Stake, R. (1995). *The art of case study research*. Thousand Oaks, CA: Sage Publications.

Turkle, S. (1984). *The second self: Computers and the human spirit*. New York: Simon and Schuster.

Wenger, E. (1998). *Communities of practice: Learning. Meaning and identity*. New York: Cambridge University Press.

Women, A. A. o. U. (2000). *Tech savvy report: Educating girls in the new computer age*. Washington, DC: American Association of University: Women Educational Foundation.

The Instructional and Learning Technologies Department (ILT) in the College of Education, Sultan Qaboos University

Ali S. Al Musawi

Abstract The Instructional and Learning Technologies (ILT) Department in the College of Education, Sultan Qaboos University (SQU), was established in 2005. Its mission is to achieve excellence in its provision of teaching, research and social services in the field of ILT. It offers a BA in ILT to meet the potential needs for information technology (IT) teachers and learning resources centres (LRC) specialists at both Omani basic education and general education levels. In this chapter, I will present main departmental, programme and prospective issues.

Keywords Oman · Instructional technology dept · BA studies

The Department

In light of the global and continuous developments in information technology, and in response to the current and potential needs of the Omani Ministry of Education for specialists in the fields of information technology, and learning resources, the College of Education at SQU proposed a new department for ILT to offer degree programmes at both undergraduate and graduate levels.

Four cohorts, with about 30 students in each, are currently enrolled in the B.Ed. programme. This year shall witness the graduation of the first batch of 11 ILT students. These graduates should be qualified teachers and specialists in operating and managing educational technologies besides producing instructional multimedia and developing human resources in both public and private sectors (Sadik, 2009, 2).

A.S. Al Musawi (✉)
Instructional Learning Technologies Department, College of Education, Sultan Qaboos University, Al Khodh, Oman
e-mail: asmusawi@squ.edu.om

M. Orey et al. (eds.), *Educational Media and Technology Yearbook*,
Educational Media and Technology Yearbook 35,
DOI 10.1007/978-1-4419-1516-0_7, © Springer Science+Business Media, LLC 2010

Vision and Objectives

The ILT Department attempts, with a futuristic perspective, to intensify its efforts in introducing a wide range of courses and programmes, in addition to the initial BA and professional diploma programmes. These courses include undergraduate, postgraduate and diploma levels, aiming at achieving the international standards in terms of quality assurance and excellence on both national and regional arenas. Specifically, the ILT Department intends to (1) contribute with other departments in the College of Education to preparing and qualifying pre-service IT teachers and specialists in LRCs; (2) provide required and elective courses to students in other areas of specializations in the College of Education; (3) develop the students' research abilities in their respective areas of specialization; (4) conduct research related to optimal efficiency and effectiveness of ILT; (5) provide a variety of community services by offering workshops, training programmes, seminars and symposia to the local communities and the society at large; (6) help in obtaining learning resources and various teaching devices in the college; and (7) cooperate with the Centre for Education Technology (CET) at SQU in conducting faculty development programmes at the university level (Instructional and Learning Technologies Department, 2005, 4 and 60).

Organization

The department board is the highest authority in the department. The board usually holds monthly meetings and makes all the decisions related to the planning and implementation of the ILT programmes. The department board appoints all needed committees at the beginning of each academic year, with the exception of some ad hoc committees that are usually appointed by the head of department, who is responsible for monitoring and implementing all action plans and decisions made by the board. In addition, the head of department performs all normal administrative duties including performance appraisal and incentives for both academic and technical and administrative staff according to the regulations, and by-laws set by the university and the College of Education (Eltahir, Asan, & Sadik, 2007, 15).

Resources

Human Resources

Faculty in the department are internationally qualified and experienced, the large majority of whom hold PhD degrees with specialization in one of the subject areas of the programme and teaching experience in many parts of the world. Omani faculty have international graduate qualifications from the USA, the UK and Australia. A student from this year's graduates will be selected for further study. She/he should spend 1–2 years serving as a 'demonstrator' in the department carrying out non-formal teaching assignments.

HRD: The university encourages continuing development of teaching methods, particularly in the use of ICT, with training schemes for new and existing staff, as well as opportunities to apply for annual grants for the development of innovative teaching projects. Contractually, staff members presenting research papers are entitled to funding support for one to two conferences annually. Most of the academic staff members usually use their summer and between-semester breaks for research. The Center for Human Resources and Staff Development at SQU offers training for new and existing faculty in different academic and technical fields. CET offers regular courses for staff seeking the advanced use of educational technology including WebCT and Moodle. Guest speakers are often invited for such training programmes.

Facilities and Technical Resources

Classrooms and Laboratories: The ILT Department has its own facilities for multimedia production for teaching and learning. In addition to its own multimedia labs, the ILT Department uses the university common teaching classrooms and lecture theatres. These are large rooms equipped with student furniture, whiteboards, TVs and video facilities, data shows and overhead projectors. These facilities are used for teaching ILT courses as well as other service courses offered by the department. In addition, due to the large number of students enrolled in the service courses, the department also uses other available facilities in the university. Programme students also have access to most computers in the university, including common and library labs. These labs have at least one printer, but due to heavy use they are frequently out of service. Commercial stationary and photocopying services are available at various locations on campus. A 24-h fast Internet service is available in all labs with online access to email, library and portal services. One departmental lab is being added for online teaching and computer classes. More labs and facilities are expected in the department as a plan was approved to allocate an extension building to the college.

Computers and Internet Resources: All departmental staff members have access to personal laptops, and an annual budget allows for reasonably frequent updating of these. They have online access to the library from their own offices and labs. Online access to student registration and other academic information is available for them via SQU portal. They also have online access to other services in the university such as booking lecture rooms and checking their employment information, such as leaves and salaries. The department has networked printers and one photocopy machine, with an additional four large photocopiers in the college administration (Eltahir et al., 2007, 78).

Library and Teaching Resources: The current SQU library is part of the newly built cultural centre comprising six floors with a large modern setting. It provides inter-loan facility and electronic access to an increasing number of journals in related subject areas, as well as the main databases. The college has its own library too. The department encourages the use of multiple sources and provides additional textbooks and materials in the college library for the use of the students and faculty. The department purchases reference books from book fairs and adds them to the collection of the college library.

Financial Resources

The university has a central budget system from which it allocates specific annual budget for each college depending on its current programmes and strategic development plans. The College of Education has no specific allocated budget for each department. However, the ILT Department, as well as other departments in college, submit their annual needs for instructional supplies, learning resources and capital equipment for computer labs within the budget of the college. The ILT Department also generates some funds from the research projects conducted by its faculty members to purchase needed equipment and production facilities. In addition, the academic staff members get some financial support from a central budget allocated for conferences (Eltahir et al., 2007, 19).

Teaching Activities

In addition to its initial BA programme in ILT, the department offers a number of required and elective courses for the different undergraduate and graduate programmes in the College of Education. The number of students enrolling in other college programmes is steadily increasing and has in turn raised the student–faculty ratio specifically for these service courses. Table 1 summarizes some of the ILT service courses.

Table 1 ILT service courses

Course title	Programme
Introduction to educational technology	B.Ed.
Educational and information technology	B.Ed. administration
Computer applications in school administration	B.Ed. administration
Educational technology	Diploma in Ed. supervision
Instructional, info. and comm. technologies	MA in education
Using computer in instruction	MA in educational psychology
Study skills	University elective

Research Activities

Faculty members at ILT conduct various types of individual, team and collaborative studies at university, national and international levels. Their research interests include, but are not limited to, the following fields: (a) use of educational technologies in teaching and learning, (b) applications of e-learning and web-based education, (c) use of LRCs in both higher and public education institutions, (d) exploration of ways of facing technological illiteracy and digital divide and (e) impact of emerging technologies in restructuring educational systems. In addition, they jointly supervise many postgraduate students in the areas of curriculum and instruction, psychology, and educational foundation and administration. Faculty members at ILT publish many scientific studies in peer-reviewed educational journals. Table 2 shows examples of these publications.

Table 2 Examples of some published research

Research title	Bibliographic details
Internet services by Sultan Qaboos University faculty members	Abdul Rahim, A. & Al Musawi, A.; International Journal of Instructional Media, USA, 2003, 30 (2), 163–176
Analyzing theoretical approaches and their implications to the development of distance learning courses research project at Sultan Qaboos University	Al Kindi, M., Al Musawi, A, Osman, M., and Al Naamany, A.; Malaysian Journal of Distance Learning, Malaysia, 2006, 8(1), 15–29
Teachers' attitudes towards personal use and school use of computers: new evidence from a developing nation	Sadik, A.; Evaluation Review, USA, 2006, 30(1), 86–113
Faculty perceptions of the professional development workshops conducted at Sultan Qaboos University	Al Musawi, A.; Journal of University Teaching and Learning Practice, 2008, Australia, 5(2), 92–104

Community Service

Faculty members at the ILT Department contribute to the Omani educational development process through: (1) holding workshops in the fields of instructional web, computer and multimedia design for basic and public education schools; (2) providing consultancies to public and private sectors and regional institutions in the fields of educational technologies research, development and evaluation and (3) presenting lectures and seminars in various areas of specializations for general education schools and higher education institutions.

The Programme

The BA programme in ILT began in September 2005 and is provided by the College of Education with the help of the Department of Library and Information Sciences at College of Arts and Social Sciences, and the Language Center.

Programme Objectives

In accordance with the broader university and the college aims, the programme seeks to equip students with the knowledge and skills to enable them to function successfully as teachers of IT and Learning Resources Specialists both in the classroom and in their wider professional life and to participate in helping improve the national economy, protect traditional Omani values, and interact in an increasingly globalized world. To this end the programme has been designed to (Eltahir et al., 2007, 33):

- Achieve university objectives in preparing qualified Omani teacher to prepare students professionally with sound knowledge and understanding of the principles and forces that shape education, the nature and management of classroom learning and of the curriculum.
- Develop competent practitioners with a sound grasp of pedagogy, who can contribute effectively to the Omani education system.
- Provide a basis for teaching educational and information technology.
- Stimulate and sustain the academic development of students, by providing courses that offer a broad exposure to the range and richness of IT/LRCs.
- Provide depth and breadth in studies by offering a core path that requires students to progress to increasingly demanding courses, as well as choices in a raft of elective courses.
- Provide students with a range of opportunities to develop and demonstrate independent and creative academic achievement.
- Develop a range of subject-specific and transferable skills, including high-order conceptual, literacy and communication skills of value in teaching and other graduate employment.
- Prepare specialists in field of the LRCs.
- Contribute to human resource development in the area of training in-service teachers who teach IT and supervise LRCs as well as to HRD in both government and private sectors.

Programme Data

Table 3 explains the programme data in terms of its title, number of students, and graduates.

Table 3 Programme data

Item	Data
Programme title	BA in ILT
Total number of students currently enrolled in the programme (2008–2009)	126
Number of new admitted in academic year (2008–2009)	23
Graduates (2008–2009)	11

Student Admissions

To get admission to the programme, students have to fulfil certain requirements. These requirements include:

a.Obtaining high percentage in the General Secondary School Certificate Exam (GSSCE).

b.Obtaining high percentage in maths and physics: for 2005/2006 intake, the required percentage in both subjects at GSSCE was (80%).

c.Passing the interview at the College of Education: the criteria of the interview include student's personality, his/her communication skills, general knowledge and subject knowledge.

Both the college and admissions deanship determine the criteria for accepting students to the programme. However, these criteria can be revised and modified by the college in consultation with the department. The programme is highly competitive and is one of the most popular programmes in the college. Most of the students enrolled selected this programme as their first option when they applied to the college. However, the programme capacity is decided on mainly by the college. Usually there is room for those students who will be transferred to the programme afterwards. In general, if the capacity of the programme for 2005/2006, for example, is 40 students, the department will accept 30 students and leave 10 seats for transferred students.

Programme Structure

Students enrolled in this programme must complete 130 credit hours distributed as shown in Table 4:

Table 4 Programme structure

Component	Credit hours
University requirements	18
College requirements	40
Department requirements	72: 54 (all major students)
	18 (IT teacher/LRCs specialist majors)

Provision

The programme offers a broad range of courses aimed at developing and enriching students' knowledge and personal competency in both education and instructional and learning technologies and providing a sound theoretical basis for IT teaching in Oman and for further study. The education component provides three courses in the area of educational foundation and administration; four courses in the area of educational psychology, counselling and research; one course in educational technology;

and three courses in the area of curriculum and teaching methods. In addition, 9 credit hours are given to teaching practice. University core and elective courses add 18 credit hours to the above education courses. These core credits include courses in Arabic language, Oman and the Islamic Civilization, Omani Society and Introduction to Personal Computers. Language Center also provides two 'English for Technology' credit courses as preparation for the programme in ILT.

Courses

Fig. 1 shows the course tree of the programme.

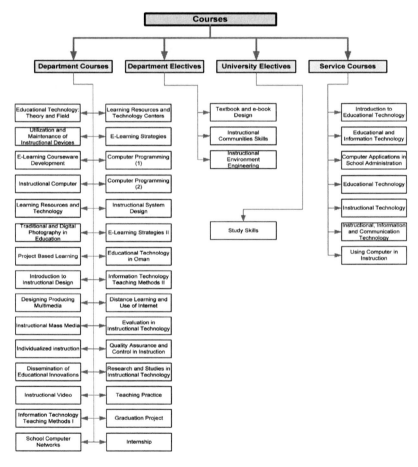

Fig. 1 ILT BA courses tree (*Source:* Sadik, 2009. ILT Annual Report, COE, SQU)

Curriculum

The curriculum aims to provide a suitable balance of education and IT courses. The educational component is designed to prepare qualified and competent individuals to work effectively in education. The IT curriculum is designed to provide a strong foundation for the development of superior technological competence in designing, developing, implementing and evaluating educational, information and communication technologies, and specialist subject knowledge, as well as opportunities to further develop particular interests and strengths in LRCs administration, training planning or needs assessment or advanced IT studies. The curriculum is designed to enable students to gradually progress to the status of professional IT teachers and LRCs specialists with specific emphasis on English language. In the ILT Department, advanced skills are developed by assigning students to both curricular and extracurricular readings and writings. Students also write papers and essays for supervised compulsory graduation project that encourages and supports independent learning and research abilities. The final year is more oriented to teaching, with higher level courses related to IT learning and teaching. Practical skills are given strong attention throughout the programme. For example, students are required to do field work in the schools' LRCs and internship in HRD as a way of improving their IT proficiency, leadership and communication skills and stimulating reflection about learning and teaching through observing teachers at work. In addition, school-based teaching practice for 3 days a week is offered in Semester 8. Opportunities for the development of cognitive skills, such as critical thinking, problem solving, inference, decision-making and other transferable skills, are provided for throughout the programme curriculum, with most courses teaching a range of subject-specific skills, including data collection, analysis, critical reading and other such skills. These facilitate progression to further study and employment as teachers. The programme courses are reviewed and revised periodically in a semi-annual quality assurance departmental seminar.

Language of Teaching

All BA courses are taught in English. The preparatory language programme in the Language Center addresses all language skills. Students are not allowed to take any course from their BA degree plan before passing level 6 in the English exam that is administered by the Language Center. These students must sit for English exam to determine their level in this language. According to their results, they are divided into levels 2–6, and those students who are below level 6 must study intensive English. Students who get level 6 should sit for the challenge test, and those who pass it can start registering in the programme courses, but those who fail must repeat or study level 6 again.

Intended Learning Outcomes

These outcomes are clearly expressed and communicated to the students and staff in the course syllabi, department handbooks, websites and in-house textbooks. Individual course outlines contain the specific aims and learning outcomes, the class meeting times and locations, the instructor's contact details and office hours as well as key course content and assessment methods. Student evaluation indicates the outcomes of the courses taught so far have been met in the teaching/learning process. The departmental intended learning outcomes are comprehensive enough to cover all the knowledge, skills, attitudes and role commitments expected of a teacher of IT and LRCs specialist in the Omani context, in accordance with the general objectives of the university and the college and as required by the Ministry of Education. The learning outcomes are periodically reviewed and developed as a result of changing expectations and policies at university, national or international level. The ILT Department attempted to make its courses (and their learning outcomes) as reflective as possible of the overall goals and expectations of the programme through liaison between the different providers of the programme and needs analyses at various times. It is anticipated that these courses support student progression to further study/employment through acquisition of educational, information and communication skills, professional and subject knowledge, and critical thinking skills. However, the course-level learning outcomes in parts of the programme reflect a balance between knowledge, understanding and technological skills.

Learning Issues

Learning Resources

The university has a policy of providing free textbooks for the students, who return them at the end of the semester. Most textbooks are of good quality and recent in the field. Textbooks are reviewed regularly; course instructors recommend the textbooks for their courses, and these are approved by a departmental committee. Most texts are compatible with course learning objectives and students reading ability. Most courses use additional sources of materials to supplement textbooks, such as printed or electronic handouts. Other courses use printed or electronic materials in place of textbooks. Students are required in some courses to research relevant supplementary materials.

Processes

All the programme courses have 4 contact hours per week, and full-time instructors are currently required to teach three to four sections with 80–120 students for a total of 9–14 contact hours. The number of students enrolled in the ILT Programme is expected to remain constant. A variety of teaching methods are used throughout the programme to achieve the intended learning outcomes. The smaller class sizes

(20–30) enjoyed by the ILT Department permits interactive seminar/workshop-style teaching, with some forms of group or pair work commonly used, and this allows a high level of interaction and close monitoring of students' development.

ICT is commonly used in the teaching/learning process. Many courses use computer labs for practical instruction or Internet/electronic database access or training work. Online instruction and/or discussion through WebCT or Moodle is also used in some courses to supplement class teaching. Student participation and independent learning are strongly encouraged through student presentations, self-learning, group work and research-based project work. In addition, around 5–10% of the final grade in a number of courses is allocated for student participation. Other opportunities for increased student participation and independent learning come through student groups and societies supported by the college, the department and the students affairs, such as the student-run ILT Society. Students enrolled in the programme have indicated that they highly value the contribution of these varied methods to their learning. Students have generous access to staff outside scheduled teaching hours. However, mandatory 4 office hours are set for all teaching staff.

Independent Learning

A major focus of the programme is to expand the students' otherwise limited world knowledge while developing their independent reading and critical thinking skills, creating a culture that reinforces independent learning and raises student awareness of its value. Most courses provide opportunities for autonomous learning through assignments, mini-projects and presentations. For instance, the compulsory course, 'Research and Studies in Instructional Technology', requires and supports an independently researched literature and field study.

Student Workloads

The normal student load is 15–18 credit hours and no more than 12 credit hours for students under probation. Significant numbers of students commute daily, limiting time for self-study and independent reading. Some students elect to take summer courses to spread their load, but this option is not open to all.

Student Progression

In general, ILT students are highly intelligent, well-motivated young people. However, students with insufficient background and competence in science and computing can encounter serious problems in their programme. Progression is governed by university regulations that stipulate course prerequisites and a satisfactory minimum GPA. Students failing to meet this standard are placed on probation. The university maintains a rigorous monitoring system for students at all levels through the advisory system. Advisors keep records of appropriate personal details of students, courses taken and grades awarded. These records are also available to advisor online. In addition, instructors' records of attendance and course work are kept and submitted at the end of each semester to the departmental authorities. Student email addresses are available to alert students to any progress or attendance concerns that arise at an early stage. The university requires staff to formally warn students who have missed 10% of classes. Students who fail to attend the required minimum of classes (20%) are barred from the course.

Assessment

A variety of assessment methods are used throughout the programme. Assessment takes the form of unseen examinations (in most courses at all levels of the programme), end-of-module tests, assessed research projects and classroom presentations. Students are required to produce a variety of class work for their courses, including essays, responsive journals, reports, graphical representations, presentations, group assignments, e-portfolios and quizzes, for which they receive quantitative and qualitative feedback. The department believes the variety of assessment methods used throughout the programme provides a balanced view of student learning and competence and ensures fairness and reliability in the assessment. Student evaluations indicate these assessment methods help them clarify their strengths and weakness. Teaching practice assessment is based on an observation sheet which contains certain criteria checked by a faculty supervisor from the college, the host principal and a cooperative teacher from the school where the student-teacher practices teaching. Assessment methods have been matched to course learning objectives, and they reflect the general objectives of the programme and individual courses. Lower and higher level questions are used in midterm and final exams. Most of these questions focus on measuring the knowledge and understanding and subject-specific skills. Other general and transferable skills are measured in other forms of assessment (research papers, student presentation, student participation, modelling, role playing, etc.). Students are provided with feedback about their performance and are able to discuss their evaluation with faculty in all assignments and tests throughout the programme, except the final examinations, where the results are announced while the students are on leave. The ILT Department uses the marking criteria and assessment scale published by the university. Where faculty employ additional criteria, these are communicated to the students via student handbooks and course syllabi. In some parts of the programme, instructors have enjoyed considerable flexibility with regard to assessment and examination of individual courses. In some multi-section courses, instructors have tailored course content and assessment to meet student needs and their own teaching strengths; these variations have sometimes made coordination and standardization of assessment more difficult in the college compulsory course, but the specification of course-level learning outcomes should improve consistency in these areas. To ensure that the assessment process is rigorous, objective and fair, it is usually done through the variety of methods, consultations and discussion at various levels. Final grades are reviewed by colleagues and submitted to the head of department for scrutiny, and then to the college board for discussion and approval. Students have the right to appeal if they feel that they have been assessed unfairly.

In such cases, a departmental committee investigates the complaint and reviews the students' assignments and exams. The university is concerned with the issue of plagiarism in work submitted for continuous assessment, since the problem is exacerbated by the spread of electronic communication. Students are reminded frequently that plagiarism is unacceptable; course outlines, handbooks and the Web specify the official policy; and essays showing substantial evidence of plagiarism can be failed or returned for resubmission.

Quality and Enhancement

Student Feedback

Courses and lecturers are subject to formal student evaluation each semester. The profiles published by the university following each evaluation exercise show that the programme faculty and courses are highly rated by the students. At the end of Spring 2009 semester, student evaluation was conducted and published online through SQU portal. Aside from the student evaluations conducted each semester by the university administration, periodic course reviews are being considered for future quality enhancement of ILT learning opportunities.

Programme Reviews

The university as a whole has gone through different internal and external review processes. The most recent external review process was conducted by the UNDP in 2005 in which the College of Education was among the reviewed colleges in the Middle East. In addition to the University's quality assurance mechanisms, ILT Department has an Internal Review Committee to monitor course offerings and assessment, and the college is undertaking a national programme for accreditation this year. At the end of each academic year, the department publishes an annual report presenting its achievements, weaknesses and future plans. The programme itself has been reviewed internally since its inception and received a formal external review by Professor Michael Hannafin[1] late 2007.

Challenges and Suggested Improvements

The above review reports show that the department and the programme have received good support from the university administration, which have a significant impact in their establishment and evolution. The reviewers mention that faculty

---

[1] Professor Michael J. Hannafin, Georgia Research Alliance Eminent Scholar in Technology-Enhanced Learning; and Director, Learning and Performance Support Laboratory.

members have been selected of the best calibre in the area of specialization, and despite the fact that the department has achieved part of its objectives, it should take some important decisions to continue its development (Hannafin, 2008; ILTD Seminar, 2009).

First, the teaching load of faculty members in the light of service courses should be reconsidered. Class sizes are expected to be further increased to 45 students in these courses. Staff teaching hours are on average relatively high compared with institutions elsewhere, with an expectation of ongoing research. Institutions that require publication for tenure and promotion should lower teaching loads, especially for junior faculty members. Assignments and student feedback have had to be reduced in some courses, and hours for student consultations restricted.

Second, the department needs to review the number and quality of specialization courses, and the balance between theoretical and applied aspects of these courses should be realized. The specialization courses have to link students to the profession through the training at schools at an early stage of their programme. Their quality needs to be ensured by following quality standards required to achieve the targeted academic accreditation by following the guidelines set by the accreditation institutions and determining the type of standards required.

Third, there is an awareness that students need to be trained to become independent learners and to use strategies to enable them to become effective learners outside the wall of the classroom. The majority of ILT students are products of schools where more traditional teaching methods are used, and many expect more structured teaching with emphasis on memorization. Significant numbers of students enter the programme lacking background and motivation for independent learning and remain narrowly preoccupied with grades. These reports note that, in general, students do not read widely and most see the Internet as a first and last resort. Many students have relatively limited prior reading experience and find assigned reading materials culturally and linguistically difficult. Moreover, the relatively high contact hours are further disincentives to reading in English. The general language weakness amongst the majority of students limits the amount of reading that can be assigned and to some extent the depth of classroom instruction. In addition, the lack of coordination between different course lecturers may cause students to have heavier workloads at some times in their semester. Moreover, the absence of common assessments in multi-section courses or any cross-sectional moderation, as in double-marking of examinations, may, sometimes, cause discrepancies in such cases. The reports also show that high number of compulsory courses required in the education strand of the programme may suggest some lack of flexibility and failure to provide sufficient optional courses for students to widen their knowledge and skills.

Fourth, the students had joined the department because they think that ILT specialization is of technological not educational nature; some of them are still more interested in technology. In addition, the university regulations currently allow students with 3.3 GPA to apply for transfer to the ILT major. The consequent unpredictable roll increases create major administrative problems, specifically when transferred students are academically weak. This problem is causing serious concern and needs to be addressed urgently.

Fifth, there is a need to relate the programme to the national trends in the areas of technology and manpower development to prepare teachers and the economic viability of this preparation in light of the Ministry of Education trends. The reports suggest the development of a comprehensive plan to link the department performance and its decisions in the area of teacher preparation with the rest of the programmes at the university and national levels by studying the pros and cons of future new programmes so as to help achieve goals of the university. There is a need to consider how to respond to the future needs of students through the analysis of information and documents and to develop contingency plans to respond to the continuing requirements of the programme, considering the provision of technology and the cost of updates and budgets needed. This should facilitate to meet the needs for specialized laboratories and software because of the special nature of the specialization and solve problems of buildings and offices available to the department and faculty members, especially with the increase in number. In addition, the department needs to ensure appropriate skills and competencies of faculty members, prepare new students in both theory and concept of their specialization and position them in real school situation, and determine the focus of the curriculum, its sequence and overlap. Due regard should be taken of both academic content and relevance to departmental aims and learning outcomes.

Proposals for improvements in the department and programme are drawn up as a result of these reviews. The followings summarize some suggestions for improvement (ILTD Seminar, 2009).

1. Revision of the ILT strategic plan.
2. Review of the new plan for BA programme in light of the observations of these reports. A revised major/minor BA programme to be designed and submitted to a succession of committees within the college, and then formally to the college board and the SQU Academic Council for approval.
3. An increase in the human and technical resources is being sought.
4. More technical staff is employed, and Omanis are sent abroad on scholarships.
5. Some of these challenges will be to some extent off-set by the relatively ILT courses' small class sizes which permit more interaction and individualizing of instruction.
6. Strategies for overcoming the problems of recycled textbooks include: the uploading of scanned materials to the department server, the use of online material through WebCT and the in-house publication of course manuals containing purpose-written or photocopied material.
7. A balance between teaching materials and the expectations of the students in terms of the willingness and competence is targeted.
8. New students should sit for an IT placement test upon admission.
9. The development of practical components in 'educational innovations' course to improve students' abilities of leadership.

10. More focus is given to the students' vocational placement.
11. Development of an effective plan for built-in evaluation process.
12. Compare the institutional trends towards education technology and its inter/national requirements when suggesting new programmes.
13. Measure the readiness of programme graduates to work in various work sites and thus determine the suitability of the depth and breadth of the programme.

References

Eltahir, M., Asan, A. and Sadik, A. (2007, January). ILT Department Self Study, College of Education Documents, Sultan Qaboos University.

Hannafin, M. (2008). "ILT Department External Reviewer Report", College of Education Documents, Sultan Qaboos University.

Instructional and Learning Technologies Department. (2005). "Departmental Guide", College of Education Documents, Sultan Qaboos University.

Instructional and Learning Technologies Department Seminar. (2009). "Departmental Evaluation and Implications", College of Education Documents, Sultan Qaboos University.

Sadik, A. (2009). ILT Annual Report, College of Education Documents, Sultan Qaboos University.

Learning with Technology: Learner Voice and Agency

Seng-Chee Tan, Beaumie Kim, and Jennifer Yeo

Abstract This chapter discusses one of the research perspectives of the Learning Sciences and Technologies academic group in the National Institute of Education (Singapore). Premised on social constructivists' view of learning, we explore design for learner agency and voice by adopting design experiment approach to study knowledge building and distributing the power of design decisions to the learners. We illustrate our efforts with vignettes of two of our research studies: one that demonstrates the importance of students' agency in knowledge construction and another that incorporates the diverse voices of stakeholders, including students, in developing a game for learning Earth system science.

Keywords Agency · Learner voice · Knowledge construction

Introduction

The field of instructional design and technology (IDT) is facing challenges posed by several forces – advent of knowledge-based economy, rapid development in technologies, and growing interest in the competing field of learning sciences. We are living in the Knowledge Age, a time when knowledge is regarded as the key asset for socioeconomic development of a country. The economic well-being of a

S.-C. Tan (✉)
Learning Sciences and Technologies, National Institute of Education, Nanyang Technological University, Nanyang Walk, Singapore
e-mail: sengchee.tan@nie.edu.sg

B. Kim (✉)
Learning Sciences and Technologies, National Institute of Education, Nanyang Technological University, Nanyang Walk, Singapore
e-mail: beaumie.kim@nie.edu.sg

J. Yeo (✉)
Natural Science and Science Education, National Institute of Education, Nanyang Technological University, Nanyang Walk, Singapore
e-mail: jennifer.yeo@nie.edu.sg

M. Orey et al. (eds.), *Educational Media and Technology Yearbook,*
Educational Media and Technology Yearbook 35,
DOI 10.1007/978-1-4419-1516-0_8, © Springer Science+Business Media, LLC 2010

country is now dependent on workers who possess in-depth understanding of a field of knowledge, who can search for relevant information, interpret, and critically analyze information and design innovative applications. In short, new economies need *knowledge workers* more than productive factory workers. The traditional mindset of IDT that focuses on training workers for efficiency and productivity has to be transformed to approaches that develop knowledge-building capacity among the workers.

Technologically, we are living in the Digital Age, where digital technologies have stealthily seeped into every aspect of our lives, making their ubiquitous presence in many objects surrounding us. We have witnessed how Internet has significantly multiplied the speed at which information can be communicated and, most critically, affords a platform where collective intelligence and of the worldwide community can be leveraged for rapid development of new ideas. Building on the Internet, we are now experiencing another wave of technological revolution, the Web 2.0 technologies, which challenge the reader–author relationship and spawn the development of new literacies. These networking technologies and user-generated contents are also hugely influencing the game industry, where online games and user-created virtual worlds are at its center. The use of technologies to *teach* has to be changed to the use of technologies to *learn* or *create with*.

Concomitantly, learning sciences as a field of study is gaining momentum. It brings together a synergy of expertise in cognitive science, educational psychology, computer science, and even instructional design to focus more on basic theory and research on learning. Learning sciences, as a field of study, aims to study the cognitive and social processes for learning and uses our understanding on learning to design more effective learning environments and to develop prototypes and tools for learning. Thus, rather than designing instructions, the focus is on researching and refining theories and practices of learning.

In the context of these changes, the Instructional Sciences academic group in the National Institute of Education, Singapore, has repositioned itself and was renamed to Learning Sciences and Technologies academic group (http://eduweb.nie.edu.sg/LST/home/default.asp). In this transition stage, we take an inclusive view that embraces pluralism in ideology and theoretical base. For instance, we offer Master of Arts in Instructional Design and Technology, as well as Master of Education (Learning Sciences and Technologies); our researchers conduct studies in the areas of new literacies, mathematics and problem solving, and knowledge building (http://www.lsl.nie.edu.sg/). Given the longer history of instructional science, we assume that the readers are familiar with research and practices in this discipline. In this chapter, we discuss the learning sciences perspective among our local research community, in particular one that focuses on empowering learners by giving them voice and agency for learning and design.

Learning with Technology

We believe in learning and creating with technology, as opposed to teaching with or through technology. The differences have been clearly explained by proponents of using technologies as cognitive tools (Jonassen & Reeves, 1996) and Mindtools (Jonassen, 2006). In essence, rather than using computers to replace tutors in giving instructions, computers are used as "intellectual partners to enable and facilitate critical thinking and higher order learning" (Jonassen & Reeves, 1996, p. 694). Unlike computer-based tutorial programs or intelligent tutoring system, the information or content knowledge are not hard-coded in the program and presented to the learners. The computers facilitate meaning making and knowledge constructions by and among the learners. For example, an asynchronous online discussion forum allows a group of learners to discuss an issue or debate about a topic; an online role-playing game requires players to dynamically form groups in order to play a role (e.g., making sure team members are in good health) and acquire skills that help them progress in the game. With proper scaffolding, the learners can be engaged in higher-order thinking processes: make meaning about what they have read, put forth their ideas, discuss their positions, apply what they have learnt to solve a problem, and many other cognitive processes.

Development in Technologies

The idea of using technologies as Mindtools revolutionizes learning using existing technologies. Many software used as Mindtools are initially developed as productivity tools that facilitate our works, for example, word processors. Thus, Mindtools is a learning technology that helps educators to look at existing computer programs (e.g., word-processing software and spreadsheet) from a different perspective. For educational applications, terms like "open tools" (Lim, 2009) are used to describe these tools. They are *open* because unlike tutorial programs, their epistemic values lie in the scaffolds/constraints they provide for/impose on learners to engage in critical thinking, rather than hard-coded content knowledge to be communicated to the learners.

In recent years, a new wave of technology development, collectively known as social software, has created new opportunities on the ways learning can be supported. Social software includes a wide range of social tools like discussion boards, messaging, web blogs (e.g., www.blogger.com), social book-marking tools (e.g., www. blinklist.com), wikis (e.g., en.wikipedia.org), and others. These tools capitalize on the collective intelligences and dynamics of a wide community connected through the Internet, beyond the physical boundaries. Initially, they are used for social purposes, for example, sharing of music, pictures, and opinions. It has become increasingly apparent that these technologies begin to challenge the traditional notion of literacies and literacy practices, giving rise to *new literacies*. Beyond reading and writing, new literacies include "socially recognized ways of generating, communicating and negotiating meaningful content through the medium of encoded texts within contexts of participating in Discourse" (Lankshear & Knobel, 2006, p. 64). Thus, participating in online forums or multi-user games, publishing personal blogs, and writing in wikis can be examples of new literacies. It requires the technical skills to participate in these activities, as well as a change in mindset

(Lankshear & Knobel, 2006, 2007), especially in the participants' agency. The participants have greater control in participating (e.g., as a participant in an online forum or game rather than a reader of a website), but at the same time, need to have awareness of the social codes and norms to participate in these activities.

An important development in social software is multi-user immersive virtual environments. These environments use rich 3D graphics to create a virtual space where participants can interact with each other, usually through informal communication styles, and experience a sense of being in a virtual world, in the company of other people (Bartle, 2004). According to Gee (2003), participating in video games is also a form of new literacy where the learners "situate meaning in a multimodal space through embodied experiences to solve problems and reflect on the intricacies of the design of imagined worlds and the design of both real and imagined social relationships in the modern world" (p. 48).

Social Constructivist View of Learning

Underpinning learning with technology is the ontological and epistemological view of social constructivism, one that treats reality as constructed by individual's mind rather than the mind as a reflection of the objective reality, and learning involves active and agentive participation among learners who engage in collaborative knowing through social interactions. The constructivist views of learning, though a relatively recent development in the field of IDT, have received growing interest among many researchers and catalyzed the convergence between the discipline of learning sciences and instructional design. They partly explain the coexistence of "traditional" IDT and learning sciences programs in many universities (e.g., Indiana University, Pennsylvania State University, and Nanyang Technological University).

Building on constructivist views of learning, Lipponen, Hakkarainen, and Paavola (2004) further differentiated between the participatory approach and the knowledge creation approach of learning. The participatory approach of learning is epitomized in learning through apprenticeship in a community of practice. For example, in medical field, a novice pre-registration doctor is enculturated into the practice of medicine by first participating from the periphery as an intern, shadowing licensed medical doctors to learn the culture and practices of being a doctor. It takes many years for a foundation house officer to become a registrar and eventually a consultant, through formal examinations and years of embodied experience. Thus, learning is premised on situation cognition and the notion of identity creation, often in the context of a real-life community. However, this approach of learning seems to focus more on preserving the cultural capital of a community rather than being innovative. To address this concern, the knowledge creation approach advocates collaborative knowledge building, with the constant goal of improving cultural artifacts and collective knowledge. This approach of learning is exemplified in a scientist community where scientists constantly discuss and explore new ideas and build on existing body of knowledge to create new theories.

Extending this to K-12 setting, Scardamalia and Bereiter (2006) proposed the knowledge-building pedagogy. Knowledge building aims to develop students' disposition and skills in knowledge work in a learning community that consists of a cohesive group of learners with a culture and practice of collaboration and collective advancement of understanding (Bielaczyc & Collins, 1999). One of the central principles of knowledge building is collective idea improvement, which happens when individuals put forth their ideas in a public space (e.g., an online forum) to be discussed and critiqued with the goal of improving these ideas. The students need to be engaged in knowledge-building talk, a discourse that focuses on epistemic reflection on assumptions, evidence, and premises that support the ideas. Knowledge building sounds like a daunting task for the K-12 students, but it is important to note that we are not demanding the students to report new discoveries or propose new theories like scientists do, neither are we engaging the students in nonproductive discussion that seems to "reinvent the wheels." The goal is not only to put students in the trajectory of development of knowledge works but develop their dispositions, attitudes, and skills in knowledge building.

Learner Voice and Agency

Several conditions need to be present for knowledge building to happen, among them, students need to possess the epistemic agency for knowledge building. The word *agency* connotes motivation and ownership. That means the students see it as their responsibility to discuss and improve their ideas or to come up with solutions to a problem. There is an element of self-directed learning – students initiate personally challenging inquiry and develop personal knowledge and skills to pursue the challenges (Gibbons, 2002). In addition, the students must possess the *epistemic* capacity to engage in knowledge building; in other words, the cognitive abilities to think and talk about knowledge work like asking relevant questions, communicating and putting forth personal ideas, seeking relevant answers, and critically discussing ideas related to the object of inquiry. In short, a student with epistemic agency takes on the responsibility to engage in inquiry works, looks for information, makes meaning of the information, and uses appropriate criteria to assess the validity of an idea to the inquiry. Lest we are misunderstood for interpreting knowledge building as a personal pursuit of knowing, it is important to emphasize that knowledge building occurs in a learning community, where there is a reciprocal relationship between self-directed learning and collaborative learning: students assume both personal and collective cognitive responsibility to advance both personal and collective understanding of a topic.

Similarly, many learners are accustomed to speak through the voice of authority (i.e., textbooks and teachers) rather than through their personal beliefs and ideas in our school context. Bakhtin (1981) terms such discourses as *authoritative discourse* and *internally persuasive discourse*. As designers and researchers, we also often see learners as having empty vessels to be filled in with a flux of knowledge. However, learners' daily literacy practices outside of classrooms could influence their beliefs and ideas about the world. In the classroom context, both students and teachers assume that the authoritative voices from the textbook and traditional ways of interacting in the classrooms (i.e., quietly engaged in reading and listening) are what good students should foreground. In designing learning technologies, we should engage learner voices about what personal beliefs and ideas they have about the world, what excites them, and what kind of experience they have outside of classroom.

The notion of students' agency and voice possess great challenges to the instructional designers. What then are the roles of the instructors? Many ID models that build on the foundation of ADDIE approach (analysis, design, develop, implement, evaluate) will break down because they are premised on the assumption that a body of knowledge can be analyzed into parts (whole to parts) and presented to the learners sequentially so that the learners can construct the knowledge (parts to whole). There are, however, very few instructional design models that advise on constructivist learning, one of which is Jonassen's (1999) model that focuses on designing constructivist learning environments rather than prescribing instructions. In a constructivist learning environment, we present the learners with authentic problems and support the learners with related cases, information resources, and collaboration tools. The instructor supports the learners by modelling, coaching, and scaffolding. Researchers in learning sciences, on the other hand, suggest conducting design experiments that emphasize reciprocal relationship between theory-based design and analysis of practice in the learning environment. For example, a researcher works with a teacher to design a learning environment based on existing theories of learning; the analysis of the implementation of this learning environment provides empirical evidence of the process and outcomes of learning, which inform the next cycle of intervention. Through iterative research cycles, we refine both the theoretical models of learning premised on empirical evidence and the actual educational practices.

Another emerging development is the breaking of artificial barrier between experts and learners in learning designs. Designers have started to involve learners in the design process in order to reflect their voices in the design in various ways, namely, user-centered design, participatory design, and informant design approaches (Facer & Williamson, 2004). User-centered design views learners as testers for designs to assess whether their needs are met (Norman & Draper, 1986), whereas participatory design considers them as partners throughout the design process by assigning them more responsible roles (Druin, 1999). Informant design, on the other hand, combined these two approaches to involve informants (e.g., learners and teachers) in various roles in different stages. For example, learners may be asked to observe and evaluate existing designs and prototypes, and then become testers when the technology is ready (Scaife, Rogers, Aldrich, & Davies, 1997). The most challenging work for the researchers in this approach is to make sure that we hear "learner" voices without imposing our own views.

In the next section, we provide two short descriptions of our research effort: one is part of a design research that demonstrates the importance of students' agency in knowledge construction; another incorporates the diverse voices of stakeholders, including students, in developing a game for learning Earth system science.

Vignette 1: Students' Agency for Knowledge Creation

One design research undertaken by a team of learning scientists from Learning Sciences Lab in National Institute of Education was the design of pedagogical supports for enabling inquiry learning through a learning community approach. This is a collaborative project conducted with a group of science teachers from a local high school to refine a Problem-based Learning (PBL) model, they had developed to foster deep science learning. The PBL model, known as THINK cycle is a five-stage collaborative learning process whereby students, presented with a (T)rigger problem, will (H)arness information by identifying and exploring learning issues, followed by carrying out tests to (I)nvestigate their hypothesis, and concluding the learning activity by presenting what they (K)now through a group report or presentation. In this learning environment, the teacher acts as a metacognitive coach.

One of the challenges in conducting a constructivist learning environment is supporting students' agency. For effective learning in a constructivist learning environment such as PBL, students need to work collaboratively with one another by keeping themselves up to date with the group's goals, knowledge, action, and status; engaging in sharing, questioning, negotiation, explanation, and reflection of ideas; and producing both cognitive and physical artifacts as evidence of their collaborative efforts (Dillenbourg, 1999). This is a challenge for both teachers and students in managing time, space, and cognitive processes. One of the ways this project supports collaborative learning is through a computer-supported collaborative learning (CSCL) system, Knowledge Constructor, which is an online discussion tool that represents discussion threads in a graphical form. A screenshot of Knowledge Constructor environment of one of the forum discussions is shown in Fig. 1.

Knowledge Constructor provides an easily accessible common space for registered students to share and negotiate ideas. The database of ideas and interaction on the asynchronous system provides a permanent record of individual and group deliberation over the problem, thus allowing ideas to be read and built on anywhere and anytime. The graphical representation of student's ideas, with links showing how each idea is built upon, displays the interconnectedness of multiple viewpoints. Exposing individual responses to ideas allows them to be scrutinized by others and helps to trigger cognitive activity around the ideas. However, technology alone may not be sufficient to support students' agency, as will be demonstrated by case example 1 below. Instead cognitive scaffolds, as will be illustrated in case example 2, are equally crucial to support students' agency.

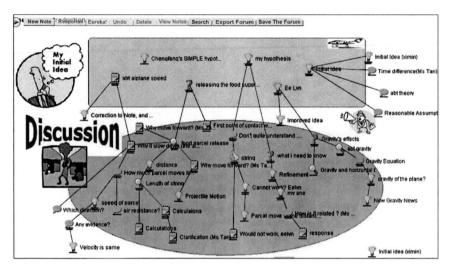

Fig. 1 Screenshot of knowledge constructor environment

Case Example 1

Case example 1 illustrates a group of five 14-year-old students solving a physics problem based on the topic of two-dimension kinematics. They were tasked to find out the length of a string needed to drop a parcel onto a pre-designated area from a remote-controlled car running on tracks placed above a table. In line with the PBL approach, students were to identify and explore learning issues and propose solutions to solve the problem with the newly constructed knowledge. However, we observed little motivation from the students to discuss learning issues identified. For example, learning issues raised by individual students such as "does gravity affect velocity of the package as it falls to the ground" were dismissed by other group members to be irrelevant without any convincing justification. Similar questions that sought to understand the effect of "flying forward of the parcel (being) a factor in the experiment" and the effect of "velocity of the dropping parcel (on) the displacement of where the parcel would hit" merely drew cursory responses (e.g., "yes") from other group members. As a result of an absence of exploration and critical discussion of the learning issues raised, there were many missed opportunities to advance the group's understanding of two-dimension kinematics. Having to propose a solution to the given problem, two of the students sought the help of their older sibling or school seniors to provide scientifically consistent answers. However, they were unable to explain their solutions when questioned. Another proposed solution was obtained through trial-and-error. When asked about their apparent lack of agency in searching for information, constructing new understandings, and solving the problem, one student said that she often did not know what to search for since she had little idea what topic was relevant to the problem context. Thus it was difficult to participate meaningfully in the online discussion with the little knowledge they had. In other words, while technological supports such as CSCL system may be necessary for ideas to be recorded, displayed, and built upon, technology alone may not be a sufficient condition for knowledge creation. Without appropriate cognitive structures to signpost the content area relevant to the problem, it may be difficult for students to be engaged in any meaningful talk.

Case Example 2

To address the design gaps described in case example 1, two key interventions were introduced to the next design cycle to assist students in identifying and exploring relevant learning issues. First, the problem task provided clear indication of the topic area associated to the problem. This was meant to direct students' attention to the relevant topic so that meaningful and relevant ideas might be shared and discussed among the students. Second, a knowledge-building process was implemented before the problem solving. The knowledge-building process, which engaged students in building shared knowledge among the group members, was meant to encourage students to construct their understanding of the problem context before applying the knowledge to solve the problem. The result of these interventions was an improved demonstration of students' agency.

Case example 2 shows a group of five high school students trying to find out the causes of a roller coaster accident. They were instructed by their teacher (1) to derive a mathematical expression to explain how the roller coaster ride worked by considering energy changes as the roller coaster cart moved down a slope and (2) to test their hypothesis for the reason why the roller coaster cart overshot its usual stopping distance. By directing students' attention to the "energy changes" in the roller coaster ride, students were able to identify and explore learning issues relevant to the problem right from the start of the THINK cycle. A question raised by one of the students about the effect of friction on the roller coaster cart drew many built-on notes from her team members, who enthusiastically posted information that they found on the Internet. They posted information about the effect of friction on energy changes, the work–energy theorem, and interpretation of the relationship among the different forms of energy associated with a roller coaster ride in a coherent manner. While some of these threads might seem shallow in cognitive processes since most information was taken directly off the Internet, there were other threads that demonstrated a high degree of critical thinking. The excerpt in Table 1, which shows students evaluating a piece of information taken from the Internet, is one example.

In note 21, student M questioned whether it was possible to "eliminate other factors like air resistance, friction" as shared by student J in note 17. This led student J to evaluate the two effects of the two forces on the roller coaster (i.e., "friction would affect the roller coaster more than the air resistance" in note 30), justifying that "the roller coaster has more contact with the track than the air" in note 37. Although this interpretation might seem somewhat inconsistent with the scientific view, this thread of discussion nonetheless showed students' engagement, critically

Table 1 Excerpt of students discussing information obtained from the Internet

Note	Author	Date/time	Content
17	J	2006-07-26 10:11:51	Once a roller coaster has reached its initial summit and begins its descent, the forces acting upon it are gravity, normal force and dissipative forces such as air resistance. ... air resistance is able to do work upon cars, draining a small amount of energy from the total mechanical energy which the cars possess ... Since the effect is small, it is often neglected. By neglecting the influence of air resistance, it can be said that the total mechanical energy of the train of cars is conserved during the ride. ... Energy is neither gained nor lost, ... http://www.glenbrook.k12.il.us/gbssci/phys/mmedia/energy/ce.html
21	M	2006-07-26 10:18:45	Iff u eliminate other factors like air resistance, friction etc, the roller coaster will never stopp in the first place since energy is neither gain nor lost if, u concentrate on factors like mass, speed the result wil be completly different from the one which includes air resistance and friction
30	J	2006-07-26 10:30:13	Friction would affect the roller coaster more than the air resistance and cannot be negligent. friction would cause energy to be converted to heat energy and thus lesser energy would be available for kinetic energy, and distanced object moves is reduced
34	Ms Cho	2006-07-26 10:35:57	Why do you say that the effect of air resistance is less than friction?
37	J	2006-07-26 10:39:15	The air resistance is smaller than friction because the roller coaster has more contact with the track than the air. furthermore, there is gravity acting on the train, pulling it to the track which makes friction greater as gravity has to be overcome to create horizontal motion

discussing the ideas related to the problem context. This was an improvement from the shallow responses to learning issues raised in case example 1. The result of this sharing of information and critical discussion of ideas was a mathematical expression that describes how the roller coaster cart worked. However, due to an error in assumption made about the effect of friction on the roller coaster ride, the students found that the empirical evidence they obtained from the model setup of the roller coaster was not consistent with their derived expression. This led student D to question, "what have we neglected in e process of driving e final equation?" Her question triggered another round of inquiry into the construction of the mathematical expression – a demonstration of students' agency as they questioned the assumption made about the problem context, reexamined their interpretation of the work–energy theorem, refined the mathematical expression, and tested their refined expression against empirical evidences, all done without much prompting from the teacher. Eventually, they found that they had to take into account air resistance in this problem context as they wrote in their report that "Without adding in air resistance into external forces, the stopping distance is the same, so air resistance does affect the stopping distance, ..." The result of this design cycle was a significant advancement of the group's understanding of the work–energy theorem as the students had delved more deeply into the meaning of the theorem through repeated cycles of knowledge building and problem solving. One key attribute to the advancement of the group's knowledge was the motivation and ownership the students had in self-directing their learning process. High level of cognitive processes was also involved as students compared and evaluated different ideas they encountered about the problem context and eventually applied the ideas they had constructed to the problem.

In a nutshell, the two case examples show the importance of students' agency in knowledge creation. Technology alone is not sufficient for supporting students' agency. Equally important are the cognitive and content scaffolds that provide students with a common direction in their learning process.

Vignette 2: Design of Technologies and Learner Voice

The main thread cuts across the various projects in Learning Sciences and Technologies academic group, and Learning Sciences Lab is to work in partnership with the teachers and through observing how learners work with technologies for development and local adaptations. One such design approach is to incorporate the diverse voices of stakeholders in developing a game for learning Earth system science, named Voyage to the Age of Dinosaurs (VAD) (Kim, Miao, Chavez, & Shen, 2007). This game intends to provide an immersive experience by recreating and replaying portions of Earth's history using intelligent agent technology and a 3D multi-user game environment. The design process is largely dedicated to understanding and designing with learner voices by foregrounding learners' interests, opinions, and ideas about dinosaurs, earth dynamics, and games. This project attempts to address design problems of many artifacts and rules in educational games not fostering learning and many designers only talking to the users through the final product (Norman, 2004). The second author of the chapter is the principal investigator of this project, and we will briefly describe the past and future design workshops and how they are contributing to the design.

The research team is in the second year of collaboration with two secondary schools for the informant design process (e.g., Druin, 2002; Scaife et al., 1997). Oneof the key intentions of the informant design workshops was to create opportunities in which learners' role would shift from passive recipients of knowledge in the classroom to providers of ideas as the empowered and acknowledged experts in their own rights (Kim et al., 2009). The research team first met with the teachers regularly without their students to review the design workshop results and prototype development progress, after which the teachers came back to the design workshop with their students (approximately 10 students from each school). We started the first workshop when the students were at the beginning of their Secondary 1 school year (Grade 7).

Workshop I: Learner Conceptions

An after-school workshop was conducted in each school. Small groups of three to four students worked with a research team facilitator in order to elicit students' understandings of the targeted Earth systems science concepts and phenomena (Geography in Singapore; e.g., earth morphology, plate tectonics, volcanoes, earthquakes, and rock formation) and to understand students' processes of reasoning and explanations. The team developed a set of open-ended questions and asked them to explain individually using diagrams and writing. Gobert and Clement(1999) found that diagramming helped students' understanding of both the spatial/static and causal/dynamic aspects of Earth's processes and, therefore, better represents their understanding.

Regardless of their exposure to formal lesson on these topics, students' depth of understanding and explanations were mostly shallow with few exceptions, and the level of vocabulary and scientific terms used varied quite a bit. The students wrote their responses individually or as a group (with text and diagrams) and discussed their ideas (see Table 2). In Table 2, drawing and a quote from one of the workshop I participants exemplifies how he was dependent on an authoritative voice (his mother) to describe his ideas of earthquake, but at the same time, he, presumably, interpreted it in his own ways by using "plates" instead of "blades." The research team found that participants during the first workshop were generally more passive, looking for "credible" sources of information (i.e., recalling some facts or images and fitting their explanations to what they remembered from lessons, textbooks, television programs, popular books, magazines, etc.), and trying to find out whether or not their answers are acceptable to the facilitator.

Workshop II: Stories of Earth and Dinosaurs

The second workshop was held over 2 days during school holidays in order to give students an opportunity to work together in groups of four (a mix of students from two schools), outside of school in a different environment, and to brainstorm and develop ideas about dinosaurs, fossils, and the prehistoric environment by beginning to draft stories about dinosaurs based on their interests and ideas. The same group of students from the first workshop was engaged in various activities: on the first day at the Singapore Science Centre they visited the Dinosaur Alive! Exhibit and watched an IMAX movie about dinosaur excavation; on the second day at the Singapore Botanic Garden and NIE's MxL Lab they visited the evolution garden, generated and presented their stories and scripts, created short movies from their scripts, and so forth.

Table 2. Design workshops and example artifacts

Workshop	What it looked like	Artifact	Discourse
Workshop I: Learner conceptions			"My mother said that the blades move, then it shakes the ground which will start to crack."
Workshop II: Stories of earth and dinosaurs			"Later I cry then you start... Ok ready. Then you say 'eh, I found something leh.' Don't say you found a bone. Then you cry with me like that."
Workshop III: Dinosaur game Play and ideas			"They (dinosaurs) invent a, the time traveling machine from the past, go to the future."

The common characteristic of their movies across different groups was "role-playing". They liked to play the role of paleontologists who find fossils of dinosaurs. One of the groups described, "Back in the laboratory situated in the city of Beijing. We, the group of paleontologists, took out the fossils we found for research." The climax of their stories tended to include dinosaurs fighting before their resulting death and burial. Dinosaurs' actions in these scenes usually reflect how they were depicted as fossils in previous scenes about fossil findings. Below is one example of such scenes:

> The Meilong gave a loud screech that frightened its prey so badly that it appears to have its leg rooted into the ground. As it ate its prey in satisfaction, a Dilong Paradoxus jumped in to snatch the Meilong's delicious lunch. Seeing its own food being snatched away, the Meilong decided to attack the Dilong Paradoxus.

Table 2 shows how students were making movies together with the props and backdrops provided by the research team. Students chose what dinosaurs they would like to feature in their movie (from early Cretaceous, China Liaoning province), wrote their scripts of present and past (paleontologist finding fossils as well as how the dinosaurs found in the fossils were interacting with each other in the past), and filmed their movies by acting out various emotions, Earth processes, and actions of dinosaurs and paleontologists. The figure inside of the example artifact is the screen capture of the movie made by one of the groups, called T-Rex. In that particular scene, two students were acting as paleontologists who finally found some fossils after a long search. The excerpt beside it is from the conversation during their filming, in which the group was detailing the interactions: they were crying while going back to their car without any finding, but stumbling onto something that turned out to be a fossil. This particular group started their script writing by imitating the movie and a short script example written in the script-writing template. However, they started to speak through what Bahktin (1981) called "internally persuasive discourse" as they tried to represent volcanic eruptions, paleontologists' excavations, and fossilization of the dinosaurs they featured. By observing how they were making meanings about actions, emotions, and cognitions of the whole movie script, the research team was able to capture ideas about how to distribute such emotions and cognitions within the 3D game environment.

Workshop III: Dinosaur Game Play and Ideas

The third design workshop was held at one of the schools to elicit students' ideas on game design. The research team brought laptop computers with the prototype version 1 installed, video cameras, and blank flip charts for them to draw and write their ideas. The students initially played the prototype and discussed with their group members as to what were the things they would like to see in the next prototype. They basically wanted more complexity, challenge, and advanced weapons in the game that were more comparable to the commercial games. They were given opportunities to evaluate two existing commercial games featuring dinosaurs as characters and come up with their own "hottest" game in town. In Table 2, Workshop III, the group was discussing and putting the information on the project website and also writing their ideas on the sheet (on the table in the picture) to share with others. During the sharing session, students as well as researchers walked through each group's station to hear their ideas and provide feedback. Out of classroom context and content, students were voicing out their ideas without being concerned too much about what adults (i.e., teachers and researchers who were present in the workshop) thought about their ideas and were not looking for confirmations from them. They were more critical to each other: one student was giving feedback to the sharing group by saying, "hey, the game is supposed to be educational. You have too much killing going on!"

Overall, first-person shooter genre, multi-missions/quests, and various skills for characters were reflected in their "hottest" games. For example, in Table 2, quote for Workshop III, one of the teams personified the dinosaur characters, which were intelligent enough to develop a time machine and attack people in the future. They also discussed level system, punishment and reward system (e.g., money and experience points as reward), and various weapons (e.g., FireGun, IceGun, WindGun, FreezeGun, Rocket Launcher, Bombs, Big Nets, etc.).

Workshop IV and Beyond: Experiencing the Story and the Concept of the Game

The research team is currently developing the next prototype and planning for the next design workshops. As the team is shaping up the game, the previous workshops on learners' conceptions, story ideas, and game ideas are constantly revisited. The subsequent design workshops will be focused on experiencing the story and the concepts in the game in the physical setting as well as in the game itself, so that learners, teachers, and members of the research team can think more deeply about what kind of interactions could enhance their game experience and learning within 3D virtual world. Figure 2 shows the tentative map for the trail within NIE where

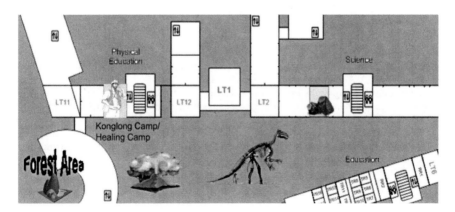

Fig. 2 Trail map for workshop IV

learners will have a simulated experience similar to the current game prototype. One of the trail stop is again for them to play the prototyped game and provide their ideas and feedback. The following design workshop (workshop V) is being planned to make a conceptually richer experience as to visiting actual place where learners can touch, see, and imagine the Earth processes, such as fossil site, rocky hills, dormant volcanic mountain, or hot springs.

Conclusion

The above vignettes of our research effort feature one of the key characteristics of the nature of Learning Sciences research projects: working in partnership with students and teachers and through design experiments to observe how learners work with technologies for development and local adaptations.

In the past, misunderstanding about constructivist learning has led to futile effort by instructor designers, learners, and instructors. For example, in some classrooms, we saw students bustling with activities, but when we analyzed the talks, there was not much meaning making and knowledge construction. We now take a holistic, multi-faceted approach that recognizes instructor's effort in designing and structuring the learning environments and also takes into consideration learners' agency and voice. The first vignette shows that even if a teacher were to relinquish power to the students, students may not readily take up ownership of their learning. Learner agency needs to be supported with technology and other resources for knowledge construction to occur. The second vignette shows our approach in involving students in learning design, thus creating conditions to encourage the students to shift from passive recipients of knowledge in the classroom to providers of ideas; in a way we are empowering them and signifying their contributions as partners of the design process. There is evidence to show that such effort would lead to meaningful learning with technology, rather than an approach that is exclusively done by instructional designers and subject matter experts.

References

Bakhtin, M. (1981). Discourse in the novel. In M. Bakhtin (Ed.), *The dialogic imagination* (pp. 287–422). Austin: University of Texas Press.

Bartle, R. (2004). *Designing virtual worlds*. Indianapolis: New Riders Publishing.

Bielaczyc, K., & Collins, A. (1999). Learning communities in classrooms: A reconceptualization of educational practice. In C. M. Reigeluth (Ed.), *Instructional design theories and models* (Vol. II). Mahwah NJ: Lawrence Erlbaum Associates.

Dillenbourg, P. (1999). What do you mean by collaborative learning?. In P. Dillenbourg (Ed.), *Collaborative-learning: Cognitive and computational approaches* (pp. 1–19). Oxford: Elsevier.

Druin, A. (1999). *Cooperative inquiry: Developing new technologies for children with children*. Paper presented at the CHI'99, New York.

Druin, A. (2002). The role of children in the design of new technology. *Behaviour and Information Technology, 21*(1), 1–25.

Facer, K., & Williamson, B. (2004). *Designing educational technologies with users. Retrieved March 20, 2009, from* http://www.futurelab.org.uk/resources/publications-reports-articles/handbooks/Handbook196.

Gee, J. P. (2003). *What videogames have to teach us about learning and literacy.* New York: Palgrave Macmillan.

Gibbons, M. (2002). *The self-directed learning handbook: Challenging adolescent students to excel.* San Francisco: Jossey-Bass.

Gobert, J. D., & Clement, J. J. (1999). Effects of student-generated diagrams versus student-generated summaries on conceptual understanding of causal and dynamic knowledge in plate tectonics. *Journal of Research in Science Teaching, 36*(1), 39–53.

Jonassen, D. H., & Reeves, T. C. (1996). Learning with technology: Using computers as cognitive tools. In D. H. Jonassen (Ed.), *Handbook of research for educational communications and technology* (1st ed., pp. 693–719). New York: Macmillan.

Jonassen, D. H. (1999). Designing constructivist learning environments. In C. M. Reigeluth (Ed.), *Instructional design theories and models: A new paradigm of instructional theory* (pp. 217–239). Mahwah, NJ: Lawrence Erlbaum Associates, Inc.

Jonassen, D. H. (2006). *Modeling with technology: Mindtools for conceptual change.* Columbus, OH: Merill/Prentice Hall.

Kim, B., Miao, C. Y., Chavez, M., & Shen, Z. (2007). Serious Immersion and Embodied Learning: Traces of Dinosaurs in Earth System Science *(Grant # NRF2007-IDM003-MOE-002)* National Institute of Education, Singapore: National Research Foundation, Ministry of Education.

Kim, B., Wang, X., Tan, L., Kim, M., Lee, J., & Pang, A. (2009). *Designing with Stakeholders for Learning Innovations: Voyage to the Age of Dinosaurs.* Paper presented at the Annual Meeting of American Educational Research Association, San Diego, CA.

Lankshear, C., & Knobel, M. (2006). *New literacies: Everyday practices and classroom learning* (2nd ed.). New York: Open University Press.

Lankshear, C., & Knobel, M. (2007). Sampling "the New" in new literacies. In M. Knobel, & C. Lankshear (Eds.), *A new literacies sampler* (pp. 1–25). New York: Pter Lang Publishing Inc.

Lim, C. P. (2009). Formulating guidelines for instructional planning in technology enhanced learning environments. *Journal of Interactive Learning Research, 20*(1), 55–74.

Lipponen, L., Hakkarainen, K., & Paavola, S. (2004). Practices and orientations of CSCL. In J. W. Strijbos, P. A. Kirschner, & R. L. Martens (Eds.), *What we know about CSCL and Implementing it in Higher Education* (pp. 34–50). Dordrecht, Netherlands: Kluwer Academic Publishers.

Norman, D. A. (2004). *Emotional design: Why we love (or hate) everyday things.* New York: Basic Books.

Norman, D. A., & Draper, S. W. (Eds.). (1986). *User centered system design: New perspectives on human-computer interaction.* Hillsdale, NJ: Lawrence Erlbaum Associates.

Scaife, M., Rogers, Y., Aldrich, F., & Davies, M. (1997). Designing for or designing with? Informant design for interactive learning environments. In S. Pemberton (Ed.), *Proceedings of CHI 97 conference on human factors in computing systems: Looking to the future* (pp. 343–350). New York, NY: ACM Press.

Scardamalia, M., & Bereiter, C. (2006). Knowledge building: Theory, pedagogy, and technology. In Sawyer, R. K. (Eds.), *The Cambridge handbook of the learning sciences* (pp. 97–118). New York: Cambridge University Press.

Trends in Performance Improvement: Expanding the Reach of Instructional Design and Technology

James D. Klein

Abstract This chapter describes the development and implementation of a graduate-level course on human performance technology (HPT) at Arizona State University – Tempe. It includes a list of HPT competencies that graduates of instructional design and technology (IDT) programs should attain and a description of a performance improvement project designed to help them acquire those skills. The chapter concludes by providing some "lessons learned" aimed at faculty who are thinking about implementing a course on HPT and students who are considering enrolling in one.

Keywords Human performance technology · Instructional design · Trends

What Is Human Performance Technology?

Human performance technology (HPT) expands the scope of instructional design and technology (IDT) by employing the systems approach to address a problem or realize an opportunity. HPT is the systematic combination of several processes – performance analysis, cause analysis, intervention selection and design, intervention implementation, and evaluation (International Society for Performance Improvement, 2009; Van Tiem, Moseley, & Dessinger, 2000). It is concerned with measurable performance and how to structure elements within a results-oriented system (Stolovitch & Keeps, 1999). HPT can be applied to individuals, small groups, and large organizations (International Society for Performance Improvement, 2009).

J.D. Klein (✉)
Educational Technology, Mary Lou Fulton Graduate School of Education, Arizona State University, Tempe, AZ, USA
e-mail: james.klein@asu.edu

M. Orey et al. (eds.), *Educational Media and Technology Yearbook*,
Educational Media and Technology Yearbook 35,
DOI 10.1007/978-1-4419-1516-0_9, © Springer Science+Business Media, LLC 2010

The HPT approach includes the design and implementation of a variety of instructional and noninstructional interventions (Hutchison & Stein, 1998; Van Tiem et al., 2000). Instructional technology is only one of many interventions that can be used to improve performance. While a number of systems have been proposed to classify interventions, a logical way to categorize them is based on the causes of performance problems (Gilbert, 1996; Sanders & Thiagarajan, 2001).

HPT and IDT

Graduates of academic IDT programs who can apply HPT models, principles, and concepts are becoming increasingly valuable in today's workplace. To address this demand, programs offer courses, concentrations, and certificates focused on HPT. For example, results of a survey administered to faculty members in a variety of academic disciplines such as instructional design, adult learning, business, communications, human resource development, and management revealed that many programs address HPT in their curriculum (Medsker, Hunter, Stepich, Rowland, & Basnet, 1995). Furthermore, a review of degree requirements at 11 well-established IDT programs indicated that all of them offer at least one elective course on HPT; three of the programs offer more than one HPT course (Klein & Fox, 2004).

According to Dick and Wager (1998), IDT programs struggle with the extent to which they should include HPT in their curriculum because of the IDT field's traditional focus on instruction and training solutions. The purpose of this chapter is to describe the development and implementation of a course on HPT offered by the Educational Technology graduate program at Arizona State University – Tempe. The chapter provides some "lessons learned" to assist IDT faculty who may be thinking about teaching a course on HPT and to provide guidance to students who are considering enrolling in such a course.

What Should IDT Students Learn About HPT?

To identify the skills and knowledge that IDT students should acquire in a course on HPT, a web-based survey was administered to a sample of 45 practitioners and 24 faculty members throughout the United States.[1] The survey included 44 Likert-type items, each containing a separate HPT competency statement. Respondents rated the importance of each competency using a four-point scale from very important to not important.

Twelve items on the survey related to the phases of the HPT model. The bulleted list below shows the items rated as very important or important by respondents, listed in order of importance:

---

[1] Readers who want detailed information about the competency study described in this section of the chapter should read Klein and Fox (2004).

- Distinguish between performance problems requiring instructional and noninstructional solutions.
- Conduct a performance analysis for a specific situation to identify how and where performance should change.
- Evaluate a performance improvement intervention to determine whether or not it solved the performance problem.
- Conduct a cause analysis for a specific situation to identify factors that contribute to the performance gap.
- Select a range of possible performance interventions that would best meet needs revealed by the performance and cause analyses.
- Assess the value of a performance improvement solution.
- Define and describe HPT.
- Identify and implement systems to support and maintain performance improvement interventions.
- Describe the general model of HPT.

The survey also included 16 categories of performance interventions suggested by Hutchison and Stein (1998). The list below shows the top 10 intervention categories (listed in order) that were rated as very important or important by respondents.

- Measurement and Evaluation
- Instructional Technology
- Feedback
- Organizational Development
- Job and Workflow
- Communication
- Quality Improvement
- Information
- Rewards and Recognition
- Documentation and Standards

Six other intervention categories were rated as somewhat important:

- Human Development
- Management Science
- Selection
- Resource Systems
- Career Development
- Ergonomics

Trends in Performance Improvement

Advocates of HPT suggest that those interested in improving human performance must learn how to analyze performance problems and their underlying causes and should acquaint themselves with a variety of instructional and noninstructional interventions. Accordingly, the overall goal of the course – *Trends in Performance Improvement* – is for students to apply skills and acquire knowledge in the field of HPT. The course was developed using typical instructional design processes (see Fig. 1). Course topics and objectives were identified using results from the HPT competency study by Klein and Fox (2004) described above. This led to the design and implementation of six units of instruction.

> *Unit 1: Introduction to Performance Improvement*: This unit provides an overview to the course. Students complete the survey developed by Klein and Fox (2004) to identify their own competencies, skills, and interests in HPT. They are also introduced to performance interventions and create a list of those they want to learn about during the semester.

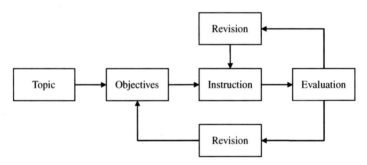

Fig. 1 Typical ID processes

> *Unit 2: What Is Human Performance Technology?* Unit 2 introduces students to the HPT field. They are expected to define HPT in their own words, describe the critical attributes of performance improvement, and explain how fields such as instructional systems design, learning psychology, human resource development, information technology, psychometrics, and human factors have influenced HPT (Rosenberg, Coscarelli, & Hutchison, 1999; Stolovitch & Keeps, 1999).
>
> *Unit 3: HPT Processes and Models*: This unit focuses on models of HPT promoted by the International Society for Performance Improvement (Van Tiem et al., 2000) and the American Society for Training and Development (Rothwell, 1996). Students apply components of these models throughout the course.
>
> *Unit 4: Performance Analysis*: The first phase in the performance improvement process – performance analysis – is central to this unit. Students identify opportunities and initiators for a performance analysis (Rossett, 1999). They

also conduct a performance analysis to (a) analyze a performance problem or opportunity, (b) analyze the organization and environment where a performance problem or opportunity exists, and (c) identify gaps between optimal and actual performance (Mager & Pipe, 1997; Van Tiem et al., 2000).

Unit 5: Cause Analysis: This unit focuses on cause analysis, the critical link between identified performance gaps and their appropriate interventions. Students conduct a cause analysis to determine the root causes of a performance problem and why it exists (Gilbert, 1996).

Unit 6: Selecting Performance Interventions: The strategies and tactics used to improve human performance is the crux of this unit. Students identify criteria and practical guidelines for designing successful performance interventions, classify interventions according to the type of root cause that they are trying to address, and recommend appropriate interventions to solve an identified performance problem and its related causes (Hutchison & Stein, 1998; Sanders & Thiagarajan, 2001; Spitzer, 1999).

Performance Improvement Project

During the course, student teams work for a client to apply performance improvement processes to an actual problem or opportunity. The project begins after students acquire foundational knowledge about HPT (Units 1, 2, and 3). It is accomplished in the phases described below.

Phase 1: Problem Identification and Project Plan

During this phase of the project, the team meets with their client to identify:

- The client's initial performance opportunity or problem and why she/he perceives it as such;
- The client's anticipated goal for the project; and
- The key players in the client's organization including the individuals and groups to consult about the problem or opportunity. This includes the client, their employees by job roles, and other possible stakeholders.

In addition, the team develops a project plan during Phase 1 that outlines:

- Data and information to collect;
- A proposed schedule of activities to accomplish; and
- The roles and responsibilities of each team member.

Phase 2: Performance and Cause Analyses

During this phase of the project, the team collects data and information from key players to analyze the organization and environment where the performance problem or opportunity exists. An organizational analysis is conducted to identify the mission, vision, and goals of the client's organization (department, unit, or work group). An environmental analysis is conducted to uncover factors related to the performance problem or opportunity. These factors may include:

- The workforce – their knowledge, skills, motivation, expectations, capacity, and ability;
- The workplace – the resources, tools, information, and feedback provided by the organization as well as the consequences, rewards, and incentives of performance or nonperformance; and
- The work – the job tasks, processes, policies, procedures, and employee responsibilities related to the opportunity or problem.

The performance issue is then outlined in terms of actual and optimal performance. The team conducts a gap analysis to identify:

- The desired performance the organization would like to realize;
- The current performance happening within the organization; and
- The gap(s) between optimal and actual performance.

A range of possible causes of the problem are also identified during Phase 2 of the project. The team is required to

- Address all possible causes related to the environment and individual performers;
- Identify potential barriers to achieving positive results; and
- Explain how data obtained during performance analysis was used to identify and support each of the identified causes.

Phase 3: Report to Client

During the final phase of the project, the team communicates with their client about findings related to the performance opportunity or problem. The outcome of Phase 3 is a concise, written report that includes the following:

- An executive summary to provide succinct information about the project to the client;

- An explanation of why the team carried out the project including background information about the organization, a description of the performance problem or opportunity, and a statement of purpose;
- A description of data sources, the key questions asked, and the tools and techniques used to collect information;
- A presentation of the results of data collection efforts. Findings are related to purposes and key questions. Tables and charts are used to represent data; and
- A discussion of the implications of findings as well as recommended solutions and performance interventions. Suggested solutions and interventions are based on identified causes of the performance problem or barriers to the performance opportunity.

Implications for Teaching and Learning HPT

Trends in Performance Improvement has been offered as an elective course to graduate students in the Educational Technology Program at Arizona State University – Tempe, since the 2002 fall semester. The remaining part of this chapter discusses some "lessons learned" while implementing the course over the last 8 years. These lessons are meant to assist faculty who are thinking about implementing such a course and students who are considering whether or not to enroll in one.

1. *Finding real-world projects is labor intensive.* According to Klein, Spector, Grabowski, and de la Teja (2004), "effective instructors provide opportunities for learners to transfer new skills and knowledge to a job setting or to their lives. Strategies for promoting transfer range from using realistic cases and problems to selecting examples and activities from the setting where the new skills will be applied" (p. 47).

    It is not easy to find clients who will give permission to investigate an actual performance problem in a real organization. Faculty must solicit projects in advance and rely on alumni, current students, colleagues, and local professional organizations for help. They must also word their requests so clients clearly know what is expected of them prior to committing to a project. Below is an excerpt from the invitation used to solicit clients for Trends in Performance Improvement.[2]

    > The Educational Technology program at Arizona State University – Tempe (ASU) is currently accepting requests from organizations interested in having a human performance technology (HPT) analysis conducted on a current performance issue.
    >
    > What your organization will provide – Organizations chosen for this HPT analysis will identify the performance issue they would like to address, the desired state, and provide data to be used in the analysis. Data may include but is not limited to interviews with employees, focus groups, surveys, and analysis of existing business processes and systems.

---

[2]The author acknowledges Frank Nguyen, who developed the initial draft of this invitation.

What ASU will provide – ASU graduate students will conduct the data collection and analysis work at no direct cost. At the conclusion of the analysis, the HPT team will provide a formal report that includes current and desired state, gap analysis, cause analysis, and solution recommendations. Your organization is free to adopt or reject any of the recommendations as you see fit.

2. *Clients must buy into what will happen during the life of the project.* Successful HPT projects require a sponsor who will champion it to others in the organization (Spitzer, 1999). The type of project described above requires time and effort on the part of clients and their employees. Student teams should have access to the key players in the organization. Information and data must be provided in a timely manner. In addition, findings may point to other problems within the organization and with individuals and groups in it. It is important that the client understands that these issues may arise.

3. *There are pros and cons to conducting the project in a student's work setting.* Students enrolled in graduate IDT programs often work in education or training organizations. This means that they have opportunities to find clients who may allow an investigation of a performance problem in their organization. Having an "inside person" can help when participants are nonresponsive or when information is slow to arrive. However, the insider must be aware of their own biases. Furthermore, sharing performance issues with coworkers and managers can lead to awkward moments for students who work for the organization where the HPT project is implemented.

4. *HPT projects should be conducted in an ethical manner.* Researchers collecting data on design and development questions are obligated to follow ethical practices (Richey & Klein, 2007). Approval to conduct organizational and environmental analyses should be given by someone in the organization who has the authority to grant it. In some cases, a signed nondisclosure agreement is required.

   HPT analyses require that information be collected from human participants. Approval should be given by the participants who will share information with team members. Teams are asked to consider confidentiality, anonymity, and related issues when determining what information should and should not be reported to the client.

5. *Project teams should be prepared for conflicts to arise.* The following is part of an email message sent from a member of an HPT project team to others on the team:

   When I left the meeting last night, I thought it was the best thing to do considering the circumstances. I was done being a contributor to the discussion because I don't think it's a good idea to open my mouth when I'm tired, emotional, and angry. I had to decide whether to sit there and risk tears, or leave. After I decided to step away from the situation, I lashed out and said I wanted to drop the class. I never planned to do that.

   Obviously I don't hold back on making my arguments, but I don't have a problem going along with decisions I disagree with, nor do I take it personal if everyone does not agree with me.

   The communication system the group has decided on and the way you want to deal with meeting minutes is very confusing to me and seems inefficient. I had already decided, though, because the plan is "majority rules" I have to do my best to work within your system. You are not likely to get me to agree it is a good and professional system, but I want to move on with the project, regardless.

I am not expecting replies to this message. I'd rather just move on with the project. Please let me know what I can do this week to work on the project and if you planned any additional meetings.

Experiences such as this one has led to discussions of Tuckman's Model of Group Development (cited in Chapman, 2005) and implementation of a collaborative team-processing activity. This activity is used to improve team processes by having each member list things that work well, things that could improve, and things the individual could do differently to improve the team experience. The activity is conducted at the end of each phase of the project.

The example above shows the amount of investment students make in Trends in Performance Improvement. Many students report that the course is among the most time consuming, difficult, and satisfying in their program of study.

6. *HPT projects can be used to confirm established practices and advance the field.* IDT is an empirical field. As such, graduate programs should prepare students to apply research skills in multiple professional settings including business, industry, military, and schools. However, a recent study by Klein, Martin, Tutty, and Su (2005) suggests that this may not always be the case.

In Design and Development Research: Methods, Strategies and Issues, Richey and Klein (2007) state

> The workplace is a primary source of research problems. An astute researcher can identify many problems and questions by observing how design and development is done in a particular setting, by discussing ID practices with designers, or by reflecting on his or her own practice. Not only are the experiences and concerns of those in various workplace settings important stimuli to this type of research, but actual projects themselves can also serve as the focus of design and development research (p. 17).

The course described in this chapter has led to student research presentations at professional conferences including a survey study of HPT competencies (Fox & Klein, 2002), a cross-cultural analysis of trends in performance improvement (Vadivelu & Klein, 2006), and case studies of the application of HPT in a hospital, a high school district, and a manufacturing setting (Hancock-Niemic, Llama, Mansfield, Martin, & Klein, 2004; Klein, Nquyen, Bevill, Winter, Reisslein, & Fox 2003).

Presenting research findings is often considered to be the responsibility of academics rather than practitioners. The field of HPT will advance as more work is documented to provide empirical support for our practice.

Acknowledgments I want to express my heartfelt thanks to the students and clients of *Trends in Performance Improvement*. I especially appreciate the assistance of Eric Fox, Jayne Klein, and Frank Nguyen, who have contributed instructional activities used in the course.

References

Chapman, A. (2005). *Bruce Tuckman's 1965 Forming, Storming, Norming, Performing team development model*. http://www.businessballs.com/ tuckmanformingstormingnormingperforming.htm. Retrieved September 21, 2005.

Dick, W., & Wager, W. (1998) Preparing performance technologists: The role of a university. In P. J. Dean & D. E. Ripley (Eds.), *Performance improvement interventions: Performance technologies in the workplace* (pp. 239–251). Washington, DC: International Society for Performance Improvement.

Fox, E. J., & Klein, J. D. (2002). What should instructional technologists know about human performance technology? *The 25th Annual Proceedings of Selected Research and Development Papers Presented at the National Convention of the Association for Educational Communications and Technology*. Dallas, TX, 233–240.

Gilbert, T. (1996). *Human competence: Engineering worthy performance*. Washington, DC: International Society for Performance Improvement.

Hancock-Niemic, M., Llama, G., Mansfield, J., Martin, F., & Klein, J. (2004). Using human performance technology to identify potential barriers to online high school course development. *The 27th Annual Proceedings of Selected Research and Development Papers*, pp. 328–333. Association for Educational Communications and Technology.

Hutchison, C. S., & Stein, F. (1998). A whole new world of interventions: The performance technologist as integrating generalist. *Performance Improvement, 37*(5), 18–25.

International Society for Performance Improvement (2009). *What is human performance technology?* Retrieved June 2, 2009 from www.ispi.org.

Klein, J. D., & Fox, E. J. (2004). Performance improvement competencies for instructional technologist. *TechTrends, 48*(2), 22–25.

Klein, J. D., Martin, F., Tutty, J., & Su, Y. (2005). Teaching research to instructional design & technology students. *Educational Technology Magazine, 45*(4), 29–33.

Klein, J. D., Nguyen, F., Bevill, L., Winter, C., Reisslein, J., & Fox, E. (2003, October). *Teaching performance improvement: Can we help clients identify and solve their problems?* Paper presented at the annual meeting of the Association for Educational Communications and Technology, Anaheim, CA.

Klein, J. D., Spector, J. M., Grabowski, B., & de la Teja, I. (2004). *Instructor competencies: Standards for face-to-face, online, and blended settings*. Greenwich, CT: Information Age Publishing.

Mager, R., & Pipe, P. (1997). *Analyzing performance problems or you really oughta wanna* (3rd ed.). Atlanta, GA: Center for Effective Performance.

Medsker, K., Hunter, P., Stepich, D., Rowland, G., & Basnet, K. (1995). HPT in academic curricula: Survey results. *Performance Improvement Quarterly, 8*(4), 6–21.

Richey, R. C., & Klein, J. D. (2007). *Design and development research: Methods, strategies and issues*. Mahwah, NJ: Lawrence Erlbaum.

Rosenberg, M. J., Coscarelli, W. C., & Hutchison, C. S. (1999). The origins and evolution of the field. In H. Stolovitch & E. Keeps (Eds.), *Handbook of human performance technology* (2nd ed.). San Francisco: Jossey-Bass.

Rossett, A. (1999). Analysis for human performance technology. In H. Stolovitch & E. Keeps (Eds.), *Handbook of Human Performance Technology* (2nd ed., p. 139–162). San Francisco: Jossey-Bass.

Rothwell, W. J. (1996). *ASTD models for human performance improvement*. Alexandria, VA: American Society for Training and Development.

Sanders, E. S., & Thiagarajan, S. (2001). *Performance intervention maps*. Alexandria, VA: American Society for Training & Development.

Spitzer, D. R. (1999). The design & development of high-impact interventions. In H. Stolovitch & E. Keeps (Eds.), *Handbook of Human Performance Technology* (2nd ed., pp. 136–154). San Francisco: Jossey-Bass.

Stolovitch, H. D., & Keeps, E. J. (1999). What is human performance technology?. In H.Stolovitch & E.Keeps (Eds.), *Handbook of Human Performance Technology* (2nd ed., pp. 3–23). San Francisco: Jossey-Bass.

Vadivelu, R., & Klein, J. D. (2006, October). *An international cross cultural analysis of trends in corporate training and performance improvement*. Paper presented at the annual meeting of the Association for Educational Communications and Technology, Dallas, TX.

Van Tiem, D. M., Moseley, J. L., & Dessinger, J. C. (2000). *Fundamentals of performance technology: A guide to improving people, process, and performance*. Washington, DC: International Society for Performance Improvement.

Part II
Trends and Issues in Library and Information Science

Introduction

Stephanie A. Jones

The inauguration of Barack Obama, the first African-American president of the United States, and the continued financial crisis across the nation were two major events of the year 2009. Although the long-term affect of Obama's presidency will not be known for years to come, the school library community has hopes that his stimulus plan will improve the status of the nation's public school libraries (Farmer & Shontz, 2009; Whelan, 2009). The current economic difficulties have resulted in layoffs of teachers and school library media specialists across the country, as well as decreased funding to school library media centers (Farmer & Shontz, 2009). These budgetary cutbacks are creating the need for school library media specialists to reach beyond the school walls in order to facilitate access to alternative resources that are more economical. The chapters in this part address a variety of issues pertaining to expanding information access: the promotion of ethical behavior online, the enhancement of curricular offerings via distance learning, and the facilitation of e-government resources.

The chapter by Dotson and Dotson-Blake highlights the often overlooked collaboration between school library media specialists and school counselors. Although school librarians are encouraged to work with the entire school community in order to promote student learning, the majority of their collaborative relationships tend to be with classroom teachers (Montiel-Overall, 2008). However, Dotson and Dotson-Blake's chapter demonstrates the benefits that can result when the media specialist ventures into areas beyond the familiar. In this instance the catalyst was the need to expand the scope of course offerings in high schools that lacked special interest and advanced placement courses due to a lack of funding or personnel. Utilizing a North Carolina public school model, the authors demonstrate that by combining the skills and expertise of these two professionals additional course offerings via online distance education can be made available to students in order to supplement those currently taught through traditional means.

S.A. Jones (✉)
Leadership, Technology, and Human Development Department, Georgia Southern University, Statesboro, GA, USA
e-mail: sjones@georgiasouthern.edu

M. Orey et al. (eds.), *Educational Media and Technology Yearbook*,
Educational Media and Technology Yearbook 35,
DOI 10.1007/978-1-4419-1516-0_10, © Springer Science+Business Media, LLC 2010

Shanahan and Farmer's timely chapter concerns the role of the school library media program on the issue of cyberbullying, which is the "use of technology to intimidate and harass others" (Bissonette, 2009, p. 4). Shanahan and Farmer posit that teacher librarians are uniquely positioned to provide leadership and information to limit this behavior. They recommend that teacher librarians work with counselors and the rest of the school community to teach and promote digital citizenship. The authors describe some of the whys and hows of cyberbullying, as well as recommending a variety of websites and strategies to identify and teach students, staff, and community members about its existence, consequences, and prevention.

In the chapter on e-government documents, Velasquez's contention, based on the ideal that an informed public is the basis of a participatory democracy, is that schools have the responsibility to educate students in the use of government documents. She notes that being able to access and use government information online is an essential skill students will need when they are adults. Although she accedes that some of the government websites are difficult to use, their benefits far outweigh the disadvantages. There are government websites relevant to virtually any curriculum area for all grade levels, and they can be used with confidence because they are authoritative, current, and free of copyright restrictions. Velasquez challenges school library media specialists to make e-government documents accessible and relevant to students so they will be prepared to participate responsibly as twenty-first century citizens.

The authors of these three chapters show that school library media specialists will continue to seek creative ways to meet the information needs of teachers and students, despite the current economic difficulties presented by the depressed economy. To paraphrase President Obama, if we, as librarians, are walking down the right path and are willing to keep walking, eventually we will make progress.

References

Bissonette, A. M. (2009). *Cyber law: Maximizing safety and minimizing risk in classroom.* Thousand Oaks, CA: Corwin.

Farmer, L., & Shontz, M. (2009). Spending survey. *School Library Journal, 55*(4), 38–44.

Montiel-Overall, P. (2008). Teacher and librarian collaboration: A qualitative study. *Library & Information Science Research, 30*(2), 145–155.

Whelan, D. L. (2009, May 12). President Obama freezes school library funding in 2010. *School Library Journal.* Retrieved July 12, 2009, from http://www.schoollibraryjournal.com/article/CA6657608.html?industryid=47064

School Library Media Specialists and School Counselors: Collaborative Partners to Expand Distance Education Opportunities for High School Students

Kaye B. Dotson and Kylie P. Dotson-Blake

Abstract Budgetary concerns compel school administrators to decrease staff, resulting in fewer course offerings and causing small, disadvantaged schools to struggle to provide courses. Alternative educational modalities in the distance learning and online arena offer solutions. School media specialists and school counselors can lead in redesigning access to and delivery of education through a creative online approach. This chapter will present practical perspectives for school counselors and school media specialists for collaborative development and delivery of online courses in high school settings. Perspectives and suggestions linked to the critical process of developing twenty-first-century learners, based on documented research, are presented.

Keywords Collaboration · School media specialist · School counselor · Online course · Course delivery · Access · Distance learning

Introduction

Progressive nations have long understood and appreciated the value of education. Consequently, large expenditures of funds have been designated in the United States (USA) over the course of many years to the cause of education. All children in the United States are promised an education; unfortunately the quality of the education children receive varies widely. One factor closely related to this variance is funding, meaning that children who are fortunate to live in affluent suburbs and neighborhoods have access to more "highly funded" and consequently "higher

K.B. Dotson (✉)
Department of Library Science, East Carolina University, Greenville, NC, USA
e-mail: dotsonl@ecu.edu

K.P. Dotson-Blake (✉)
Department of Counselor and Adult Education, East Carolina University, Greenville, NC, USA
e-mail: blakek@ecu.edu

M. Orey et al. (eds.), *Educational Media and Technology Yearbook*,
Educational Media and Technology Yearbook 35,
DOI 10.1007/978-1-4419-1516-0_11, © Springer Science+Business Media, LLC 2010

quality" education than do children in socioeconomically disadvantaged inner city and rural communities (Ingersoll & Perda, 2006). This is the unfortunate truth. Children are often simply not afforded the same quality of education due to the tax-base funding their school and local education agency (LEA) receive (Payne & Biddle, 1999). In the face of increasing economic turmoil, LEAs hardest hit by the downturn have seen dramatic cuts in teaching personnel (Toppo & Gillum, 2009). Fewer teachers may mean more limited course offerings, particularly in special interest areas and advanced courses. Small, rural schools with limited tax revenues particularly struggle to maintain teachers and provide necessary course offerings.

Fortunately, alternative delivery modalities, including distance education, offer powerful tools for overcoming barriers to provide expanded, comprehensive education opportunities for U.S. students. For the purpose of this chapter, distance education will be of primary focus when discussing alternative education formats. Distance education opens the doors to expanded electives, advanced placement (AP), college preparatory, and dual enrollment courses to high school students who otherwise may have faced more limited opportunities. Additionally, other personal interest courses that can enrich student's education but were previously unavailable to students may be offered as well.

Positioned to Address the Concern

School library media specialists are leaders in facilitating access to resources, and school counselors are on the frontlines of student course of study planning. The unique vantage points of these professionals as both leaders of their own programs and collaborative contributors to multiple school programs afford them the opportunity to witness firsthand the broad impact of dwindling resources. These professionals are also aware of possibilities offered by distance education. School counselors have the professional preparation to identify appropriate distance education courses to fit into students' courses of study, and school library media specialists have the professional preparation necessary to facilitate access to these distance education resources. As such, these two professionals hold the keys to open the doors of global education to students through online coursework options. There is evidence that a coalition of the school counselor and the school library media specialist can improve the educational environment and outcomes for students (White & Wilson, 1997). More specifically, we suggest that collaboration between these professionals can also facilitate the provision of comprehensive education experiences through high-quality online courses (Dotson & Dotson-Blake, 2009).

The pivotal roles, played by school counselors and librarians, are like that of no other educator in the school. The intersecting individual and collaborative responsibilities of counselors and librarians affords these professionals a broader school-wide vision than the classroom teacher. To better meet the needs of their stakeholders, counselors and librarians must utilize their unique school-wide perspective to implement alternative means of instruction. As helping professionals, school counselors care about students and work to help students access resources necessary for personal and academic growth. Professionally, school counselors prepared to provide comprehensive programs and collaborate with other professionals to meet the needs of students (American School Counselor Association, 2005). School media specialists are likewise mandated to open the doors of the library to partner with teachers and other education professionals to provide necessary services to students (American Association of School Librarians & Association for Educational Communications and Technology, 1998). These mandates serve as a foundation from which to begin to build collaborative relationships for practice.

School library media specialists are in the unique position to see students actively engaging in use of technology through social networking, blogs, wikis, and other innovative uses of current technology. The next logical step for school library media specialists is to help students use this technology for educational purposes in addition to entertainment. Students' skills in the use of technology improve through familiarity and use.

Offering online courses in the high school setting helps prepares students to be good stewards of online information and effective twenty-first-century learners. School library media specialists are able to facilitate the development of partnerships to provide course credits through distance learning and to help students engage as online information consumers in an ethical, safe manner. School library media specialists are professionally prepared to help students refine searching skills and become aware of copyright laws and ethical use of information. Through participation in online courses, students' navigation of the web sharpens, word processing improves, and mastery of web-based learning tools solidifies, all of which serve to better prepare students for twenty-first-century higher education. It is time to integrate the technology students use daily for entertainment into the high school curriculum to increase the personal responsibility and academic progress of students.

This shift in thinking is shared by school counselors who also see the merit of facilitating the growth of students in an environment that can be monitored and that allows for a degree of protection for the student. The school counselor is professionally prepared to assess students to determine which students are developmentally ready for the independence and self-regulation necessary for successful participation in distance education. Identifying students with a high likelihood of success is of particular importance for schools offering courses through distance education. Additionally, counselors prepared to facilitate distance education offerings recognize that distance education may help alleviate scheduling problems and will serve to provide increased course access to homebound students.

Additionally, online education poses a few significant concerns, with which school counselors are professionally prepared to assist. There are concerns regarding issues of safety in the online arena. Drawing from their professional training, school counselors can develop safety workshops to prepare students for distance education engagement. Sexual predators, bullies, abuses of ownership, and other issues could all possibly arise during course engagement in the online arena and can be addressed in a highly structured high school setting, better preparing the student for post-high school freedom and independence in their use of Internet. This is especially significant because these issues may not be addressed in large part beyond the high school level.

Working collaboratively, school library media specialists and school counselors can comprehensively address the developmental, practical, and ethical and safety concerns associated with online engagement. An effective collaborative approach might entail the library media specialist closely monitoring issues of copyright and providing professional Internet navigation and technological assistance, with the school counselor assessing students to determine developmental readiness, providing course of study planning, and enlightening students to safe use of online tools and resources. This collaboration allows schools to provide distance education opportunities with integrity and intentionality to prepare students for contemporary global engagement as ethical, safe cyber-citizens.

Consequently, counselors and librarians must work, both together and with classroom teachers, to locate, facilitate, and deliver a variety of course offerings online and through early college initiatives. Doing so broadens the horizons of rural students and students in public high schools that lack sufficient funding or staff to offer a wide variety of courses and advanced placement course options. The move to broaden the high school curriculum through alternative routes to learning is changing the face of education and is designed to level the playing field, increasing opportunities to students nationwide, and school library media specialists and school counselors are professionals at the heart of this work.

Case Example

Consider for a moment the case of one rural high school in eastern North Carolina. With less than 300 students and a socioeconomically disadvantaged tax base, the school struggles to offer core courses and electives are severely limited. The school library media specialist, after attending a conference presentation on dual enrollment and distance education at the high school level, approached the school counselor about possibilities for their students. The school counselor enthusiastically agreed that distance education held great potential for students. Collaboratively, the two professionals identified necessary resources and developed a plan for identifying and offering distance education courses to students. After working with the administration to secure necessary resources, including space, time for planning, and access to existing technology resources within the school, the school library media specialist and school counselor began informing students of distance education offerings.

Jermaine, a high school junior, planning for a career in pharmacy, wanted to take Latin. Initially, this appeared a most unlikely possibility, as Latin was a course never before offered in his small, rural high school. However, his school library media specialist working with the school counselor located an available online Latin course for him. Jermaine became a member of a pilot group beginning the online program in his rural county. He completed his course with a final grade "A," and followed enthusiastically with Latin II. Not only did Jermaine get a foundational course that would serve to his advantage later in his specialized academic studies, but he also became a vocal advocate for online opportunities.

Another success story from this case involved a concerned parent who was thrilled to find that her son could take a psychology course online through the local community college. Her son could earn college credit while still attending high school through an established dual enrollment program. In North Carolina, high school students may participate in community college courses through "dual" or "concurrent" enrollment. Dual enrollment provides a vehicle for advanced high school students to take college-level courses while still in high school. In the state of North Carolina, these college courses are tuition free if official written permission is obtained from the high school principal and chief administrative school officer (superintendent).

The school counselor and school administration had previously established the collaborative relationship with the community college, and funding was provided at the state level for dual enrollment programs. The school library media specialist secured textbooks and facilitated access to technology available at the school site. Technology was a significant issue, as this student did not have access to high-speed Internet in his home but could easily take advantage of it in his school setting. The librarian further supported this student's efforts by making the library computers available to him after school hours. This flexibility was approved by the administration. The student did not have to leave the school facility to earn college credit, no small matter as this would result in considerable savings for the parent in the future. Not surprisingly, this parent worked closely with the school counselor to ensure that any available online dual enrollment course that fit into her child's course of study was included. The end result was that this student left high school with 12 h in college credit and with a 4.0 grade point average in those courses. The parent of this student said her son's enthusiasm for school improved even more when he realized that he was getting ahead in college before he even finished high school!

The use of multiple distance learning opportunities helped this impoverished rural school meet the needs of different students. These instances could not have happened without the willingness of faculty to take advantage of available resources. In this case example, the school library media specialist assumed the role of facilitator to make sure the resources became available to students. The school library media specialist served as the primary link between the district, the school, and the online provider, as well as being the primary program contact for online students and their parents. Students were closely monitored by the school library media specialist to assure that they were on the right track and were following proper information use guidelines. The school counselor also held a number of short information sessions with students to alert them to the possible missteps individuals can take in the online world. She also made students aware of possible courses, which would better prepare them for the fields identified as their future professional interests. Finally, she worked closely with students and parents/guardians to ensure that students chose courses that complemented their program of study and 4-year plan.

Fortunately, the school administration saw the advantages in expanding educational formats and allocated funding to support this innovative trend through staff support. Flexibility in terms of hours and scheduling was supported by the administration. Both librarian and counselor served as strong advocates for distance education offerings, advising students and encouraging them to consider alternative formats for coursework.

Key Elements to Implement Collaborative Distance Education Offerings

To facilitate the offering of distance education courses to high school students, initially a school faculty must understand and appreciate the significance of this emerging trend. Building on this appreciation, key elements must be included in the structure of alternative education modalities within the high school settings. These key elements include collaboration, course/instructional design, and planning to overcome potential challenges.

Collaboration

The total faculty, not just the librarian and counselor, must work together and share responsibilities for the end results (Anderson-Butcher & Ashton, 2004; Gardner, 1999; Lawson & Barkdull, 2000). As the saying goes, "it takes a village to raise a child," so also it takes a faculty to prepare a student. The need for support and collaboration is essential to foster investment by all school personnel in the success of new distance education offerings. The foundation of collaboration is developing a clear understanding of how children, their families, and the professionals who work with them are interdependent (Anderson-Butcher & Ashton, 2004). Collaboration between teachers, counselors, and librarians produces a higher degree of meaning, significance, and authenticity for assignments (Gross & Kientz, 1999). When beginning alternative formats for education, particularly in the online arena, it is extremely important that students and teachers understand the terrain and the complexities and possible dangers inherent therein. Professionals and students must share a collective knowledge of resources and how to access and utilize resources for the success of collaboration and the safety of all stakeholders (Mostert, 1996).

Course/Instructional Design

Though each state will approach the provision of distance education and dual enrollment programs to high school students in widely varying formats, there is much to be learned from analysis of one state's approach. By exploring the process North Carolina used to develop the infrastructure and expectations for distance learning at the high school level, professionals can grasp the necessity of intentionality in protocol establishment and development of course/instructional design. Protocol and course/instructional design are critical foundational elements of distance education.

North Carolina embraced the concept of distance learning as early as September 2002. The Business Education Technology Alliance (BETA) was created by the North Carolina General Assembly for the purpose of preparing globally competitive workers and citizens for the twenty-first century. The BETA Commission led to the development of North Carolina's Virtual Public School (NCVPS, 2009). The authorizing legislation for NCVPS states: "NCVPS shall be available at no cost to all students in North Carolina who are enrolled in North Carolina's public schools, Department of Defense schools, and schools operated by the Bureau of Indian Affair" (NCVPS, 2009). North Carolina supports distance learning in a variety of formats. These include

- NC Virtual Public School
- Learn and Earn (Community Colleges)
- Learn and Earn (UNCG iSchool)
- NC School of Science and Math (IVC-NCIH)

North Carolina Virtual Public Schools is an innovative effort to expand education opportunities for high school students. Schools that are unable to offer courses due to funding or staffing deficiencies are able to provide full access to a wide range of high school courses made available through NCVPS at no cost to students. The courses are developed and taught by certified teachers.

North Carolina's Community College's Learn and Earn Online allows high school students to take college-level courses online or face-to-face and earn both high school and college credits. Again, there is no cost to the student, which makes this extremely attractive to the parent struggling to make ends meet.

Distance education offered, in the format of UNCG iSchool, provides a dual enrollment program whereby students may earn college credit while in high school (five quality points honors credit HS and three credit hours college) (UNCG iSchool, 2009). These courses are completely online and support the objectives of school counselors in that they are structured in developmentally appropriate ways for high school students. To provide the structure and support developmentally necessary for high school students, online courses should be offered in a specific course period allowing the librarians to serve as facilitators to monitor the course and assist the students. The University of North Carolina at Greensboro has intentionally approached the instructional design of courses developing high-tech and innovative courses that are engaging and highly interactive and, again, present no costs to students.

The North Carolina School of Science and Mathematics pioneered distance learning using video and audio through the North Carolina Information Highway (NCIH). The initiative made courses accessible to rural and remote areas. For example, schools such as those on isolated Ocracoke Island on North Carolina's Outer Banks have been able to access a range of courses not available on-site.

Any of these formats opens doors to high school students in North Carolina in a way not possible in years past. Students may become empowered and in control of their own learning. Other states quite possibly have approached design of online learning in the high school differently; however, exploring North Carolina's process clearly illuminates the need for collaboration and planning across multiple levels of government and education. Additionally, school counselors and school library media specialists must thoroughly research any potential distance education offering to make sure it is developmentally appropriate, financially affordable, and congruent with graduation requirements for students prior to including it in any student's course of study.

Planning to Overcome Potential Challenges

As in any new program, with initial implementation of distance education in high schools there are challenges. Schools must initiate the partnership and provide a facilitator. School systems may need to provide additional or specialized training for facilitators, counselors, and school library media specialists to partner with some institutions providing distance education services. School systems must also provide adequate technology and ensure that their site has defined strategies to sustain the technological capacity to support distance coursework.

Despite the increasing integration of such high-tech interactive media as electronic whiteboards, chat rooms, and audio and video streaming, technology requirements for districts and schools are actually fairly simple: Students need a computer with high-speed, broadband Internet access and properly adjusted settings for the firewall, which is designed to control access (e.g., to certain Web sites). Most schools provide computer access through computer labs, which are open to students throughout the day and, in some cases, after regular school hours or on weekends. Because online courses are designed to operate with one or more, but usually not all, Web browsers (i.e., the software that allows a computer to read and interact with Web text, images, and tools), districts or schools also must ensure that their computers are outfitted with a browser (e.g., Explorer, Safari, Firefox) compatible with the online courses it plans to offer (U.S. DOE, 2007).

Finally, time for collaborative planning for school library media specialists and school counselors is critical for the success of these programs. These professionals must collaboratively assess needs of students and available resources and develop plans to communicate with teachers, students, and parents/family members to share information about the newly available opportunities. All of these steps take time and collaborative planning. Administration must be onboard, and faculty investment is key to identifying and overcoming challenges within the school.

Additionally, students may face their own personal challenges to participation in distance education courses. Lack of high speed Internet access in students' homes may present a problem. Fortunately, this challenge can be overcome by providing adequate technology within the school and opportunities to access resources outside of school hours for homework and special projects. Students must also be self-motivated and understand that they bear a substantial responsibility for their own education. School systems are not obligated to provide facilitator for all partnerships with institutions offering distance education courses; thus, responsibilities for adult moderation and facilitation of learning experiences may fall to the counselor and librarian.

Conclusion: Revisiting Roles with Plans for Success

Partnerships between the school counselor, school library media specialist, and classroom teachers are important for identifying potential students who might benefit from alternative routes to learning. The counselor is prepared to evaluate student records, ability, and achievement, but the classroom teacher may bring a more personalized understanding of student strengths, weaknesses, interests, and attitudes. Classroom teachers may have a strong sense of these aspects as a result of classroom interaction with students. This information is important for making decisions determining which students are suitable potential candidates for participation in distance learning.

School counselors assist students in making decisions regarding course options for course-of-study plans. They may bring understanding and awareness of academic requirements, future options, and needed engagement. They offer information concerning the psychosocial and developmental needs of students. Additionally they provide a professional focus on collaboration and teaming (American School Counselor Association, 2005). In most schools, counselors are the key professionals for future career and educational planning for students. Counselors can link career counseling needs to possible online course opportunities through their knowledge of students' needs and interests. They are able to investigate online providers to find out what advanced courses are available and the quality of each provider's course design and review and evaluation process (U.S.DOE, 2007). To be sure to meet as many needs as possible, it is important that counselors take advantage of multiple course providers.

School library media specialists have technology skills, access to resources, and the opportunity to open doors, inviting and welcoming students to full access to resources for unlimited study (Medley, 2002). School library media specialists also bring understanding of information skills (information literacy) and tools to integrate skills, action, and learning (Doiron & Davies, 1998), thereby making education more accessible and effective for all. The library becomes an extension of the classroom and is a center of learning. The integration of materials and technologies supported by the facilitation and instruction of a school library media specialist results in a rich, inclusive, and educational culture for students.

Administrators must support the process and provide strong leadership and understanding of this emerging trend in education. They set the tone for the partnership, and their support can both strengthen and extend collaborative partnerships between school library media specialists and school counselors around distance education initiatives. Ultimately, administrators are responsible for the expenditure of funds, and by supporting and strategically planning for the inclusion of distance education opportunities, administrators are able to provide a broad range of course offerings even in the face of limited budgets.

Students are vital partners in the process. Naturally they hold valuable information concerning their needs and abilities. It is imperative that they and their parents should be included in all collaborative efforts as they can both share a wealth of important information. As helping professionals, school counselors are professionally prepared to work closely with stakeholders (American School Counselor Association, 2005). As such, school counselors can involve parents and students to solicit feedback to improve collaborative efforts. Working as contributing, important members of the team will empower students to engage responsibly in their personal academic and career planning and will increase all stakeholders' investment in the process. Working together ultimately leads to student success.

Counselors and librarians have an opportunity today to serve in the role of transformational leaders, promoting teaching and learning through alternative formats. It is only by using innovative measures that we can expect expanded, different results for contemporary students (Davidson, Schofield, & Stocks, 2001). The time for a difference is now, as we take advantage of continuously emerging educational trends, in our quest to prepare students to achieve in the twenty-first century.

References

American Association of School Librarians & Association for Education Communications and Technology. (1998). *Information power: Building partnerships for learning.* Chicago: American Library Association.

American School Counselor Association. (2005). *The ASCA national model: A framework for school counseling programs, Second Edition.* Alexandria, VA: Author.

Anderson-Butcher, D., & Ashton, D. (2004). Innovative models of collaboration to serve children, youths, families, and communities. *Children & Schools, 26*(1), 39–53.

Davidson, A. L., Schofield, J., & Stocks, J. (2001). Professional cultures and collaborative efforts: A case study of technologists and educators working for change. *The Information Society, 17*(1), 21–32.

Doiron, R., & Davies, J. (1998). *Partners in learning: Students, teachers and the school library.* Englewood, CO: Teacher Ideas Press.

Dotson, K. B., & Dotson-Blake, K. P. (2009). Providing core courses online in the small rural school: Collaborative roles and responsibilities. Presented at the *10th Annual Teaching and Learning with Technology Conference.*

Gardner, H. (1999). *Intelligence reframed: Multiple intelligences for the 21st century.* New York, NY: Basic Books.

Gross, J., & Kientz, S. (1999). Collaborating for authentic learning. *Teacher Librarian, 27*(1), 21–25.

Ingersoll, R. A., & Perda, D. (2006). *What the data tell us about shortages of mathematics and science teachers.* Paper presented at the NCTAF Symposium on the Scope and Consequences of K12 Science and Mathematics Teacher Turnover, October, 2006

Lawson, H., & Barkdull, C. (2000). Gaining the collaborative advantage and promoting systems and cross-systems change. In A. Sallee, K. Briar-Lawson, & H. Lawson (Eds.), *New century practice with child welfare families* (pp.245–270). Las Cruces, NM: Eddie Bowers.

Medley, K. P. (2002). Would you like to collaborate?. *Library Talk*, *15*(1), 16–18.

Mostert, M. (1996). Interprofessional collaboration in schools: Benefits and barriers in practice. *Preventing School Failure*, *40*(3), 135–138.

North Carolina Virtual Public Schools. (2009). Retrieved March 25, 2009 from http://www.ncvps.org/about/.

Payne, K. J., & Biddle, B. J. (1999). Poor school funding, child poverty, and mathematics achievement. *Educational Researcher*, *28*(4), 4–13.

Toppo, G., & Gillum, J. (2009). Tide turns against schools as foreclosures rise. *USA Today*, March 16, 2009.

UNCG iSchool. (2009). Retrieved March 25, 2009 from http://web.uncg.edu/dcl/web/ischool/index.php.

U.S. Department of Education, Office of Innovation and Improvement. 2007. *Connecting students to advanced courses online: Innovations in education*, Washington, D.C.

White, M., & Wilson, P. (1997). School counselors and teacher-librarians: A necessary partnership for effective schools. *Emergency Librarian*, *25*(1), 8–13.

The Role of the School Library Media Center Program in the Education and Prevention of Cyberbullying

Seanean Shanahan and Lesley S.J. Farmer

Abstract It is the school library's responsibility to provide the tools necessary for students to utilize online resources effectively and efficiently. This education should also account for the increasing need for instruction regarding cyber ethics, particularly with the rise of cyberbullying. The teacher librarian is in the unique position to organize programs throughout the curriculum that will address the needs of the students and staff, state standards, and the American Library Association's recommendations.

Keywords Bullying · Cyberbullying · Teacher librarian · Cyber ethics

As technology advances, so do the techniques for harassing and bullying. While traditional bullies still range on the playground, cyberbullies are becoming increasingly common. One of the duties of the teacher librarian (TL) is to educate students and faculty about information literacy, which includes the responsibilities of cyber citizenship and ethical behavior. The entire school community needs to understand, address, and prevent cyberbullying. This chapter defines cyberbullying, discusses its ramifications on individuals and the school community at large, and recommends strategies for cyberbullying education and prevention.

The Context of Cyberbullying

In essence, a cyberbully (aka cyber harasser, cyber attacker, electronic bully, etc.) is any person who bullies or harasses someone using some form of technology. Extending the definition of physical bullying can be misleading because of the

S. Shanahan (✉)
Instructional Media Services for the Los Angeles Unified School District, Los Angeles, CA, USA
e-mail: sshanaha@lausd.net

L.S.J. Farmer (✉)
Librarianship Program, California State University, Long Beach, CA, USA
e-mail: lfarmer@csulb.edu

M. Orey et al. (eds.), *Educational Media and Technology Yearbook*, 163
Educational Media and Technology Yearbook 35,
DOI 10.1007/978-1-4419-1516-0_12, © Springer Science+Business Media, LLC 2010

Internet's properties. Those who physically bully or harass usually do so repeatedly over time, yet a person who commits an act that may be viewed as cyberbullying may do it just one time. Because of the way the Internet works, one message or picture posted about an individual one time online can be transmitted by others and can "attack" the victim repeatedly through multiple viewings and/or multiple transmissions (Kowalski, r., Limber, S. & Agatston, p. 2008).

Cyberbullying, or cyber harassment, is a relatively new reality in the school system. Many educators are unaware of its existence, and those who are aware often misunderstand the dangers involved. Unlike physical bullying, which is often done on campus and can be handled by staff members, cyberbullying can be perpetrated almost anywhere through cellular phones, the Internet, social networking sites, chat rooms, instant messages, and other emerging technologies. Because most cyberbullying occurs off-campus, the school community mistakenly believes that little can be done to prevent such harassment (Shariff, 2008).

Furthermore, unlike today's students who have been raised on this equipment, many educators lack understanding of technology itself and its ramifications. Just as people used to pass notes in class that were often thrown away and forgotten, now students send text messages that get forwarded repeatedly and can come back to harass the victim time and again, making those notes much more harmful than a piece of paper in the trash could ever be. Educators themselves are often photographed or audiotaped, and those images are then uploaded to various online sites or transmitted from phone to phone, making educators victims even as they are supposed to be the protectors. This new form of proactive aggression against both students and teachers has caught educators off-guard, and they are often unprepared to deal with the situations themselves, let alone know how to prevent them.

Teacher librarians need to be particularly mindful because the library media center (LMC) is often the point of access to the Internet for many students. It is frequently the one place that students can go during their free time to work on assignments or go online. Students who use the LMC's computers often do so for recreation, including gaming, web surfing, and emailing, although some libraries limit computer use to research for school assignments. In any case, because of the lack of education about technology and the Internet, much of what is done online is done without knowledge about netiquette and online ethics, also known as cyber ethics. Therefore, the library staff needs current knowledge of cyber ethics and cyberbullies in order to act proactively.

Growing Numbers: Technology and Cyberbullying

Computers and technology have existed for a relatively small span of time in the history of the world; however, their impact has become greater than any could have foreseen. Where earlier generations were just beginning to see computers become more than room-sized leviathans, the current generation has access to palm-sized technology run by microchips and tiny processors. Twenty years ago, classroom computers were just starting to be installed with monochrome screens and a few basic programs. The Internet hadn't yet begun to appear in public school settings. However, times have changed. As of 2003, the U. S. Census reported that almost all schools had Internet connectivity, with just a few rural or very poor schools lacking such connections

As technology improves, so does access to technology. Even students in the poorest neighborhoods now have access to some form of technology either at school, at the public library, through friends, or with pay-per-use technology like cell phones. "Nearly two-thirds of U.S. kids ages 3–17 live in a home that has a personal computer . . ." (Sparling, 2004, p. 19). "It is estimated that 91% of kids 12–15 years old and almost all teens (99%) ages 16 to 18 use the Internet" (Keith & Martin, 2005, p. 224). "More than four in five adolescents currently own at least one type of electronic device, such as a cell phone, BlackBerry, personal data assistant, or computer . . . 55% of Americans ages 12–17 were using online social networking sites such as Facebook or MySpace . . ." (*Harvard Mental Health Letter,* 2008, p. 4).

With the advent of new technology has also come ways to abuse that technology. As cell phones and other portable devices become smaller, the number of ways to conceal the devices has grown. When educators think of students abusing technology, they often worry about students cheating on exams or sending text messages during class. What they often don't consider is the personal toll that new technology is taking on the students themselves. It used to be the schoolyard bully who students feared the most; now it is the cyberbully who is beginning to grow in power. While most of the attacks are fairly minor, ". . . six percent of the young people surveyed experienced harassing incidents, including threats, rumors, or other offensive behavior, and two percent reported episodes of distressing harassment that they described as making them feel very or extremely upset or afraid" (Keith & Martin, 2005, p. 225).

Most studies agree that cyberbullying is becoming an increasing problem in schools, even between friends. Students often become accidental cyberbullies just by hitting the reply button because what they type doesn't always get interpreted the way it was intended. Without body language and vocal tones, things that are funny in person often are not when read as text. Noted school counselor Julia Chibarro (2007) reported that cyberbullying has become one of the most prevailing ways that middle schoolers harass others. She states:

> Eleven percent of the students (13 percent of the girls and 8.6 percent of the boys) reported cyberbullying someone else at least once in the previous two months. Of those students who reported cyberbullying others, 41.3 percent reported bullying another student at school, 32.7 percent reported bullying a friend, and 12.6 percent reported bullying a sibling" (Chibbarro, 2007, p. 65).

Why Do Youth Cyberbully?

There are a number of reasons why cyberbullies attack others. Many do it because they think that it is socially acceptable to do so. They are given positive encouragement by friends especially when their attacks are public or shared with others; in chat rooms, a cyberbully gets reinforcement from other chatters who are watching the attacks take place. "Proactive aggression is used consistently as a tool for personal gain (status, control, self-confirmation, gratification, etc.)" (McAdams & Spencer, 2007, p. 121). This kind of "social status" cyberbullying often fades away as children mature and have more empathy for their victims.

The apparent anonymity of the Internet loosens up some youth to express themselves without restraint (Adams, Angeles 2008; Beale, Hall 2007). Cyberspace makes youth feel invisible – and sometimes invincible. Youth become less concerned about how they present themselves, and the lack of immediate face-to-face feedback leads to lack of "norming" so that perpetrators continue their negative behavior, sometimes to the point that they dissociate their real identity from their virtual reality (Mason, 2008).

More likely, a cyberbully is a person who is trying to improve his/her own rank in school or is trying to bring another person down in rank; as a group, they may be described as social climber bullies: children who are seeking to raise themselves from a middle rank to a higher one in the school social class structure (Chibbaro, 2007). "Wannabes" and others attack the "losers" to strengthen their own reputation and try to get the attention of the "popular" crowd. Alternatively, cyberbullies try to dethrone the popular kids in an attempt to supplant them or at least move up in rank.

As with any other bullies, cyberbullying is often done to compensate for a lack of control in other areas of bullies' lives. If they can't control one set of circumstances, maybe they can control another. "Aggression for proactive aggressors has, over an extended time become an internalized means of achieving personal security, competence, and control in their lives" (McAdams & Spencer, 2007, p. 121). This lack of control can be in their home lives, social status at school, environment surrounding school/home, or a combination of these.

Cyberbullies apparently need to control others; so many children will resort to cyberbullying because they don't have to be physically dominant to commit the acts. "Those lacking physical superiority (i.e., the majority) will turn to deception, coercion, and manipulation to gain the control they need for a positive self-image" (McAdams & Spencer, 2007, p. 122). They can also do it with some anonymity, so they can avoid physical confrontation later. "Because face-to-face contact with the victim is unnecessary, cyberbullies may hide in anonymity, making the identification of these bullies more difficult" (Chibbaro, 2007, p. 66). However, there are many instances in which the cyberbully begins attacks online, but then continues to attack at school with more aggression. Often, victims of cyberbullies are also victims of physical bullies.

Gender also figures into the cyberbullying equation. As in the physical world, "Male bullies tend to engage in direct bullying whereas female bullies tend to engage in indirect bullying" (Chibarro, p. 65). Where males tend to focus on threats and descriptions of physical violence, females often focus more on psychological abuse (Cullerton-Sen, Crick, 2005). Girls will often use indirect methods to lure a victim to complacency and then attack, while boys usually just flame or threaten violence. "Boys are more likely to make online threats and build websites targeting others. . . In general, girls inflict virtual abuse more than boys though instant messaging, online conversations, and e-mails" (Keith & Martin, 2005, p. 225). Direct threats to others, even online, can be taken to authorities and steps can be taken to deal with the physical dangers. However, the psychological attacks of girls are much more difficult for authorities to punish, so female cyberbullies are often much more powerful.

Nor are attacks limited to peers; an increasing number of adults, especially school employees, are becoming victims of cyberbullies. When students become angry or feel as if they are a victim of a school employee, they may seek revenge by recording and posting damaging talk or images. Cyberbullies also create social networking sites using an alias of a teacher or an administrator and make false statements about those individuals; the victims or their coworkers may be totally unaware of those fraudulent pages.

What Techniques Do Cyberbullies Use?

Electronic bullying, like traditional bullying, can be done individually or in groups. Some bullies work individually with focused attacks on one or more people. Cyberbully groups might have a specific purpose or target in mind, or they might just randomly attack others. Groups often use chat rooms and online "burn" books (similar to slam books in that they write salacious comments) to gang up on victims. Cyberbully groups also can be made up of complete strangers who follow one bully who leads attacks.

One of the most prolific forms of cyberbullying is verbal: name-calling, teasing, or threatening. Cyberbullies attack others online directly or spread harmful messages in chats, instant messages, and text messages. They may even go so far as to virtually stalk their victims. "Relational bullying is a form of social isolation that includes behaviors such as gossiping, intentionally leaving students out of activities, spreading rumors, and other measures that seek to change peer groups" (Jacobsen & Bauman, 2007, p. 1). A popular technique, especially among female cyberbullies, is exclusion. Because social acceptance is so important to children's self-esteem, excluding one child from group activities is particularly harmful. Cyberbullies often ignore others online during chats, refusing to respond to texts/Ims/emails.

Another cyberbullying technique focuses on posting and disseminating images online or to cell phones. Many youth naively post image of themselves on a social networking site such as MySpace or Facebook. Cyberbullies download these images, manipulate them using programs such as Photoshop or Paint, and then re-post them or distribute them to others. Images might be edited simply by adding messages or arrows, or they might be manipulated almost beyond recognition. Cyberbullies have also been known to take pictures of their victims surreptitiously in restrooms or dressing rooms, and then disseminate them online (Kelsey, 2007). Similarly, cyberbullies might film fights (even setting them up) and then post them on YouTube or other videocasting sites. A new trend of "sexting" is more open, but just as damaging; a child will either take an inappropriate picture of himself or herself or let someone else take that kind of picture, and then it gets forwarded to others. Sometimes the initial photo is knowingly taken, and other times it is done surreptitiously, but the unforeseen consequences done can be irreparable in either case. Moreover, students in possession of these images, whether they wanted them or not, can be prosecuted for possessing child pornography. Many students leave with good social standing on a Friday, only to return Monday to find themselves outcasts who are avoided by even their friends because of these undermining cyber attacks.

Some cyberbullies are very calculating, using deceit to gain the victim's confidence. "Proactive aggressors can be expected to manipulate others' emotions in their drive for personal gain" (McAdams & Spencer, 2007, p. 122). Later, the bully will skillfully manipulate their victims by sending harmful messages when the victim is the most vulnerable. McAdams and Spencer elucidate,

> ... the timing of proactive aggression has often been preplanned to produce maximum gain and minimal consequence for the aggressor... Disingenuously saying exactly what others want to hear, they open the door for undeterred aggression by first winning the trust of those who would be most likely to suspect and intervene (p. 122).

Cyberbullies might also impersonate their victims to bad effect. Sometimes they forward a victim's own email or text messages, hack an account to changes information on sites, or send messages from the victim's account, making it appear that the victim sent it (Stomfay-Stitz, Wheeler, 2007).

How Are Victims Affected?

Cyberbullies find that it is safer to attack online because many people do not understand how the Internet works. Parents are often unaware that the child is being attacked, and the child is unaware of how the technology works, so he doesn't know that it can be reported, traced, and stopped (at least temporarily for each aggressor). With so many different cyberbullying techniques used, the victim may not be able to avoid or counteract all forms of attacks.

Much like victims of physical bullies, cyberbully victims respond in many ways, from suicide and social isolation to rage and truancy. Responses include, but are not limited to, ignoring the messages, responding to the attacks with messages of their own, keeping the attacks a secret, re-reading/viewing the messages (thereby attacking themselves in a very real sense), avoiding school and situations that put them in contact with the bullies, becoming depressed and suicidal, becoming angry and violent, and attacking others as they have been attacked (Jacobsen & Bauman, 2007).

Part of the problem stems from the very nature of the attacks themselves. Cyberbullying can seem invisible; bruises are usually internal rather than external as seen in physical bullying. Nevertheless, "harmful messages intended to undermine the reputation of a victim can be far more damaging than face-to-face altercations. Instead of remaining a private matter or event known by only a small group, text or photographs can be communicated to a large audience in a short time" (Strom & Strom, 2005, 36). Even if social stigma does not actually occur, victims may feel that their reputations have been damaged. "Victims of cyberbullies are often fearful of telling adults because they fear the bullying will become more harmful and intense" (Chibbaro, 2007, p. 66). Even after the attack is over and forgotten by most, the victim may continue to receive the occasional forwarded message about the attack or believe that people are still thinking about the incident.

Often, cyberbullies may be the best-behaved students on campus. In her 2007 article, Chibarro says, ". . . these types of bullies are often overlooked because they are leaders in the school and looked upon with favor by administrators, teachers, and counselors" (p. 66). They are intelligent and know how to manipulate others. When possible, they often try to get on the good sides of administrators and teachers so they have even more control; their victims may be reluctant to report the bullying incident, thinking that their word will not be taken as seriously as the popular student's. Even if the victim is initially believed, the cyberbully will often talk around the actions to excuse them, convincing the adults that it was not meant to be mean or cruel and that the victim is just reading or perceiving it incorrectly.

How Should Cyberbullying Be Addressed?

Part of the problem dealing with cyberbullies is that ". . . parents and educators have found themselves unprepared for the task of monitoring students' Internet use and misuse" (Chibbaro, 2007, p. 65). School officials and parents are often surprised by the many various ways that cyberbullies attack. "The solutions most often proposed are simplistic and result in minimal protection" (Strom & Strom, 2005, p. 39).

One of the first instinctive reactions of adults to cyberbullying is to take away the technology from the victim to prevent him/her from being attacked again. However, this is just the kind of reaction that needs to be avoided. When the victim is punished by having technology removed, it only encourages the cyberbully more and convinces the victim to not report any future abuse (Van Dusen, 2008).

If the victim knows the cyberbully, he or she might want to respond to the cyberbullying incident, but that reaction is usually ineffective. "[This] might seem to be a reasonable counter. Yet, student experience shows that this approach can motivate a bully to apply even more severe methods of intimidation" (Strom & Strom, 2005, p. 39). Parents should also avoid responding to cyberbullies.

Often, the general belief of victims, bullies, and adults is that this form of bullying is untraceable. However, this is actually far from true; every message has a trace code that can be used to follow the message back to the original computer or cell phone. Most cyberbullies are probably not savvy enough, nor do they believe it necessary, to re-route their attacks through programs that can erase their "fingerprints."

In any case, policies should be established to address the problems, both at school and off-campus. The 2007 U.S. Supreme Court ruling Frederick v. Morse expands the measures that schools can take relative to student action outside of school hours. The federal S 1492 Broadband Data Improvement Act (Public Law 110-385), also titled Protecting Children in the Twenty-first Century Act, mandates that all schools receiving e-rate discounts must teach students "about appropriate online behavior, including interacting with other individuals on social networking sites and in chat rooms and cyberbullying awareness and response." The federal act targets minors and emphasizes Web 2.0 activities such as social networking and cyberbullying. TLs are well positioned to instruct students about appropriate online activity.

California School Boards Association's (2007) policy brief suggests several factors to consider when developing policies to address cyberbullying: education and supervision of online behavior, Internet filtering, reporting mechanisms (including anonymous tips), assessment of potential threats, and response strategies. Willard and Steiner's 2007 book *Cyberbullying and Cyberthreats* contains several forms that can be used for policies and procedures, and in 2008 Virginia's Department of Education developed a model school policy on cyberbullying, which provides useful tools.

More profoundly, the issue of cyberbullying prevention must be addressed proactively (Cyberbullying, 2006). The overarching goal is effective and responsible personal and social engagement with digital resources. While some of the motive is protection and safety, which has resulted in required filtering software and acceptable use policies, a more positive spin is the need for students to learn coping skills and demonstrate that they can *contribute* meaningful knowledge to the digital society (Shariff, 2008).

One of the issues facing these students is that many do not yet have the experience or emotional maturity to empathize with their victims (Harris Interactive, 2007). They often do not realize that what they are saying is hurtful; many believe that they are just teasing and that the recipients of the attacks should just "relax" because "it didn't mean anything." In their research of cyberbullying among Nottingham (UK) students aged 11–16, Sharples, Grader, Harrison, and Logant (2009) found that almost three-quarters of the students regularly used social networking sites and that teachers wanted to use Web 2.0 technology but were afraid of possible risks to the children; a panel of experts determined that schools should provide Web 2.0 access along with education about responsible learning. Campuses need to instruct the school community in cyber ethics and emotional consequences.

Several websites offer tutorials or curriculum guidance about cyberbullying:

- http://www.cybersmartcurriculum.org/cyberbullying/
- http://www.media-awareness.ca/english/resources/educational/lessons/secondary/cyber_bullying/cyberbullying_civic.cfm
- http://teachingtoday.glencoe.com/tip/cyberbullying
- http://www.csriu.org
- http://mentalhealth.samhsa.gov/15plus/aboutbullying.asp
- http://digizen.org/cyberbullying/
- http://www.ctap4.org/cybersafety/
- http://www.onguardonline.gov/quiz/socialnetworking_quiz.html
- http://www.nsteens.org
- http://www.NetSmartz.org

- http://www.SafeInternetKids.com
- http://www.thatsnotcool.com
- http://www.mcgruffspo.com/cybersafetysat.html
- http://www.cybersafety.ca.gov/
- http://www.cyber-safety.com/
- http://www.wiredsafety.org/
- http://www.isafe.org
- http://www.ftc.gov/bcp/edu/pubs/consumer/tech/tec14.htm
- http://www.ala.org/ala/washoff/WOissues/techinttele/internetsafety/internetsafety.htm
- http://www.stopbullyingnow.hrsa.gov
- http://teachdigital.pbwiki.com/cyberbullying

Who is best positioned to teach *all* students about cyberbullying? Teacher librarians. They are truly resource persons, providing value-added physical and intellectual access to information and ideas. TLs have been the educational copyright and cyber conscience for years, *and* they have tried to address these issues positively by collaboratively developing learning activities that enable students to engage with others creatively to gather ideas and generate new knowledge rather than just copy old knowledge (American Association of school Librarians and Association for Educational Communications and Technology, 1998). Here are some ways that TLs can work with counselors and the rest of the school community to teach and promote digital citizenship relative to cyberbullying.

- Surveying students about their experiences and needs relative to cyberbullying
- Teaching students and teachers about cyberbullying and ways to respond to such bullies
- Supervising student social networking
- Mapping the curriculum to incorporate instruction and opportunities to demonstrate ethical online behavior
- Creating and disseminating webliographies about cyberbullying
- Conducting workshops on cyberbullying for peers and the school community
- Serving on educational committees to develop ways to address cyberbullying

Student Involvement in Addressing Cyberbullying

As noted above, solutions to cyberbullying are sometimes cloaked in adult protectivism. The related issue of inappropriate websites has led to mandated filtering software so that youth will not be exposed unnecessarily to such sites. However, such practices do not help youth develop critical evaluation skills to cope with profane Internet sites. Generally, TLs advocate a more proactive approach: teaching youth how to evaluate Internet information and deal with inappropriate telecommunications.

Likewise, youth perceptions and involvement can provide effective ways to address cyberbullying. As youth self-identify cyberbullying behaviors and impacts, they become more aware of the problem. When they are involved in developing ways to solve the problem, they gain more ownership and control, feeling empowered to cope themselves as well as to help their peers (Whittier, 2006).

Qualitative assessment can elicit interest and provide pre- and post-test data. By eliciting youth perceptions via surveys and focus groups, librarians can ascertain what needs exist for addressing cyberbully. Appendix 1 provides a field-tested survey based on Beran and Li's (2005) research, which can be administered online. Questions were developed in order to discover: (1) how technology might be being used on campus; (2) if students are committing acts of cyberbullying; (3) if students have recognized cyberbullying previously; and (4) if there is enough evidence to suggest a need to create a cyberbullying education program on campus. The survey's second section (Appendix 2) focuses on possible effects that cyberbullying might be having on students.

The National Crime Prevention Council asked Harris Interactive to conduct a nationwide representative survey about teens' perceptions about cyberbullying. Almost half of the 824 middle and high school respondents stated that they had experienced cyberbullying within the last year, and usually knew the bully. Girls were more likely to be bullied and to report such incidents. The respondents gave several coping techniques, the primary one being to block telecommunications access (e.g., keep social networking sites private and phone numbers unlisted), stop enabling others to cyberbully, and report incidents. They also said that adults (parents, schools, and mass media) should send clear messages about not cyberbullying (Moessner, 2007).

Middle school teacher Johanna Mustacchi developed a unit on social networking and cyberbullying for her classes; students researched cyberbullying issues and presented skits to their classmates and other school community members, including adults. Building on that success, Mustacchi developed a middle school Internet safety curriculum that involved students as peer teachers and counselors. As a result, students became more aware and savvy about cyberbullying, and Internet behavior improved (2009). Her article notes several teen-centric cybersafety websites:

- http://netsmartz.org/netteens.htm
- http://www.safeteens.com
- http://teenangels.org
- http://www.webwiekids.org

Girl Scouts of the USA have worked closely with girls and other stakeholders to address cyberbullying. Girl Scouts make great efforts to provide a safe learning environment for their members, including respectful behavior and Internet safety. Their research institute has examined girls' experiences and perceptions about Internet use (Roban, 2002; Schoenberg, Riggins, & Salmond, 2003). In 2007, in collaboration with the Vermont Commission on Women, Vermont Girl Scouts interviewed

200 girls in grades 6–12 about bullying, including cyberbullying: their experiences, their perceptions, and their ideas for addressing such behavior. Girls were concerned with the rise in cyberbullying, but felt as if it was a personal problem that they had to deal with on their own. School reporting procedures were usually in place, but girls did not always find these effective or safe. The study concluded that adults and youth need to work together on combating cyberbullying. In 2009 based on these studies, Girl Scouts joined with Microsoft to develop a girl-centric online informal educational program titled Let Me Know (LMK); girls serve as peer experts in order to advise other girls about these problems. The websites   http://lmk.girlscouts.org (for girls) and   http://letmeknow.girlscouts.org (for adults) offer useful facts and guidance.

Conclusions

Students have gained power with the advent of telecommunications, particularly with the use of social networking. However, with that power comes responsibility. Sometimes students do not know how much power they can wield, and others may realize their power but not fully appreciate the consequences. Rather than taking power away from students (which could be a difficult task to enforce), the school community needs to become aware of cyber abuse, and develop strategic plans to educate students about digital citizenship as well as teach coping techniques when cyberbullying does occur.

With their knowledge about technology and information processes, LTs can proactively collaborate with the school community to teach students how to use and create digital information appropriately. Thomas Jefferson asserted that an informed citizenry is needed for a sound democracy. Informed citizens can make better decisions and act on them. Extended to the cyber environment, digital citizenship necessitates participating responsibly and respectfully in cyberspace to act wisely for social and personal improvement.

Appendix 1

General Survey Questions – Yes /No Response

Do you own a cell phone?
If you own a cell phone, does it have a camera?
Have you heard of students using technology to harass/bully other students?
Would you like to learn more about Cyberbullying?
Do you think teachers and administrators should be trained to be able to recognize
  Cyberbullying and teach students how to avoid it?

(continued)

Survey Questions Regarding Personal Actions That Could Be Considered Cyberbullying – Ordinal Scale from 0 to 4

Have you ever taken someone's picture without his/her permission?
Have you ever audio- or videotaped someone without his/her permission?
Have you ever posted someone's picture online without his/her permission?
Have you ever edited or changed a digital picture of someone?
Have you ever sent an email or text to someone that could be viewed as "mean" or "rude"?

Survey Questions Regarding Receipt of Actions That Could Be Considered Cyberbullying – Ordinal Scale from 0 to 4

Has anyone ever taken your picture without your permission?
Has anyone ever audio- or videotaped you without your permission?
Has anyone ever posted a picture of you online without your permission
Has anyone ever edited or changed a picture of you?
Has anyone ever sent you an email or text that could be viewed as "mean" or "rude"?

Survey Questions Regarding the Impact of Cyberbullying – Yes/No Response

Are you willing to answer these questions?
Have these types of harassing behaviors involving technology been directed toward you?
If so, how have you been impacted?
I felt sad and hurt.
I felt angry.
I felt embarrassed.
I felt afraid.
I missed school because of it.
I had difficulty concentrating.
My grades have dropped because of it.
I blame myself.
Do the people who harassed you by using technology also harass you in other ways (not including technology)?
Do you use technology to harass others?

---

0 = Never; 1 = Once/Twice; 2 = A few times; 3 = Many times; 4 = Almost every day.

Appendix 2: Cyberbullying Focus Group – Final Exercise

Objectives

The purpose of this focus group is to study the possible need for a Cyberbullying education program that would be spearheaded by the teacher librarian.

Protocol questions

1. We've been doing some work on Cyberbullying over the last few weeks. What have you learned about it?
2. What do you think you still need to learn about it?

3. What do you think most students should be made aware of regarding Cyberbullying?
4. How much do you think teachers/administrators understand about Cyberbullying?
5. What more do you think they should learn?
6. How important do you think it is to create a Cyberbullying education program here? (scale 1–5; 1 being least, 5 being most important)
7. Who should be the focus of this program? (students, teachers/administrators, parents)
8. Do you have anything else you'd like to share about this topic?

Process

Students who have been studying Cyberbullying over the course of the semester were pulled out of their class in small groups (5–7) and were given 5–10 minutes to answer and discuss the questions. Students were assured that all answered would remain anonymous for this discussion. They were not audiotaped, but detailed notes were taken, leaving out any references to student identities.

References

Adams, D., & Angeles, R. (2008). Mobile devices at school: Possibilities, problems, and tough choices. *Educational Technology, 48*, 35–38.

American Association of School Librarians and Association for Educational Communications and Technology. (1998). *Information power: Building partnerships for learning.* Chicago: American Library Association.

Beale, A., & Hall, K. (2007). Cyberbullying: What school administrators (and parents) can do. *The Clearing House, 81*, 8–12.

Beran, T., & Li, Q. (2005). Cyber-harassment: A study of a new method for an old behavior. *Journal of Educational Computing Research, 32*(3), 265–277.

California School Boards Association. (2007). *Cyberbullying: Policy considerations for statements.* Sacramento: California School Boards Association.

Chibbaro, J. (2007). School counselors and the cyberbully: Interventions and implications. *Professional School Counseling, 11*, 65–68.

Cullerton-Sen, C., & Crick, N. (2005). Understanding the effects of physical and relational victimization: The utility of multiple perspectives in predicting social-emotional adjustment. *School Psychology Review, 34*, 147–160.

Cyberbullying: Understanding and Preventing Online Harassment and Bullying. (2006). *School Libraries in Canada.* Canadian Association for School Libraries. Retrieved October 10, 2008, from http://www.cla.ca/casl/slic/254cyberbullying.html

Girl Scouts of the USA and Vermont Commission on Women. (2007). *What teen girls say about . . . bullying and harassment.* New York: Girl Scouts of the USA.

Jacobsen, K., & Bauman, S. (2007). Bullying in schools: School counselors' responses to three types of bullying incidents. *Professional School Counseling, 11*, 1–9.

Keith, S., & Martin, M. (2005). Cyber-bullying: Creating a culture of respect in a cyber world. *Reclaiming Children and Youth: The Journal of Strength-based Interventions, 13*(4), 224–228.

Kelsey, C. (2007). *Generation Myspace: Helping your teen survive online adolescence*. New York: Marlowe & Company.

Kowalski, R., Limber, S. & Agatston, P. (2008). *Cyberbullying: Bullying in the digital age*. Malden, Eng.: Blackwell.

Mason, K. (2008). Cyberbullying: A preliminary assessment for school personnel. *Psychology in the Schools, 45*(4), 323–348.

McAdams, R., III, & Spencer, L. (2007). How to help a bully: Recommendations for counseling the proactive aggressor. *Professional School Counseling, 11*, 120–127.

Moessner, C. (2007). Cyberbullying. *Trends & Tudes, 6*(4), 1–4.

Mustacchi, J. (2009). R U safe? *Educational Leadership, 66*(6), 78–82.

Protecting children and teens from cyber-harm. (2008). *Harvard Mental Health Letter, 25*(1), 4–5.

Roban, W. (2002). *The Net effect: Girls and new media*. New York: Girl Scouts of the USA.

Schoenberg, J., Riggins, T., & Salmond, K. (2003). *Feeling safe: What girls say*. New York: Girl Scouts of the USA.

Shariff, S. (2008). *Cyber-bullying: Issues and solutions for the school, the classroom and the home*. New York: Routledge.

Sharples, M., Grader, R., Harrison, C., & Logant, K. (2009). E-safety and web 2.0 for children aged 11–16. *Journal of Computer Assisted Learning, 25*, 70–84.

Sparling, P. (2004). Mean machines. *Current Health 2, 31*(1), p11–p13.

Stomfay-Stitz, A., & Wheeler, E. (2007). Cyberbullying and our middle school girls. *Childhood Education, 83*, 308 J-K.

Strom, P., & Strom, R. (2005). When teens turn cyberbullies. *Education Digest, 71*(4), 35–41.

U. S. Census. (2003). *Computer and Internet use in the United States*. Washington, DC: U. S. Census.

Van Dusen, A. (2008, September 15). How to stop cyber-bullying. *Forbes.com*. Retrieved October 10, 2008, from: http://www.forbes.com/2008/09/15/bully-school-cyber-forbeslife-cx_avd_0915health.html

Virginia Department of Education. Division of Technology. (2008). *Acceptable use policies: A handbook*. Retrieved July 17, 2009, from Virginia Department of Education, Division of Technology web site: http://www.doe.virginia.gov/VDOE/Technology/AUP/home.shtml

Whittier, D. (2006). Cyberethics in the Googling age. *Journal of Education, 187*(2), 1–65.

Willard, N., & Steiner, K. (2007). *Cyberbullying and cyberthreats*. Champaign, IL: Research Press.

E-Government, Government Documents, and School Libraries

Diane L. Velasquez

Abstract This chapter discusses the use of electronic government sources and documents for school media specialists, teachers, and children in K-12 education. Ninety-seven percent of all government information is online, resulting in rich and free source of authoritative material that can enrich the electronic sources of the school media center (GPO, 2002). The ability to easily add sources for curriculum support as well as to expand general source material is something no library should overlook. Annotated e-government sources are included in this chapter along with lists of children's and teachers' government web sites.

Keywords E-government · Government documents · Government information · Government publications · Federal government

Introduction

This chapter focuses on electronic government (e-government) and government documents for teachers, school library media specialists, and children. E-government is defined as "technology, particularly the Internet, to enhance the access to and delivery of government information and services to citizens, business, government employees, and other agencies" (Hernon, Reylea, Dugan, & Cheverie, 2002, p. 388). Another way e-government is described is a communication between the government and its citizens via computers and a Web-enabled telecommunication Internet device (Evans & Yen, 2006; Jaeger, 2003; Roy, 2003).

The federal government of the United States is the largest publisher in the world (Hernon, Dugan, & Shuler, 2003; Morehead, 1999; Robinson, 1998). Additionally, the U.S. government has millions of web sites, making it the biggest producer of

D.L. Velasquez (✉)
Graduate School of Library and Information Science, Dominican University, River Forest, IL, USA
e-mail: dvelasquez@dom.edu

M. Orey et al. (eds.), *Educational Media and Technology Yearbook*,
Educational Media and Technology Yearbook 35,
DOI 10.1007/978-1-4419-1516-0_13, © Springer Science+Business Media, LLC 2010

Internet sites internationally (Hernon et al., 2003). Given that so much is available from the federal government, it makes sense for school library media specialists (SLMS) to be familiar with government documents useful to teachers and students in support of the school curriculum. Government information promotes U.S. history and civics curriculum by providing digital access to primary documents. Government documents can also support the entire curriculum when used as a research source for students, faculty, and school library media specialists. Government documents, federal as well as state, can provide access to information unavailable elsewhere. The advantage to using government information is that it is freely available; the only thing needed is a computer that has Internet access.

Literature Review

The literature supports the notion that government documents have been traditionally overlooked by K-12 educators and school library media specialists as a source of information. School library media specialists who do not use government documents to support curriculum or as reference sources in the school media center are missing a rich and free source of information.

Few articles over the past five years discuss government documents; however, in library literature there have been three articles written for librarians who work in school library media centers. An article by Butler concerned copyright issues when duplicating maps for math or geography classes (2004). In this article Butler discussed whether or not federal government maps are copyrighted. Maps created for the federal government are in the public domain if they were created as work for hire. According to Butler, "the definition of 'work for hire' means that the federal government hired an individual or group to create a map and that map is owned by the hiring organization" (p. 46). In the case of state or local documents, each entity can choose whether or not to place their works in the public domain. As an example, the State of Idaho has copyrighted their state statutes (Idaho Code § 9-350). If the federal map is in the public domain, it can be copied for classroom or library use (Butler, 2004).

Another article, "Government Documents Go to School" by Sandra Williams (2005), discussed an informal survey she did with students, teachers, and school library media specialists about using government documents in K-12 classrooms in central Minnesota communities and districts in the Minneapolis/St. Paul suburbs. In the article Williams did not articulate the grade levels the teachers were instructing. Williams found that the majority of those surveyed did not know how to use government documents nor wanted to learn. Government documents were perceived as difficult to use, a myth that has persisted over time. Williams stated that government documents had a

> mystery and a reputation for complexity that are perhaps well-deserved. Many government publications are filled with page after page of single-spaced text with rarely an illustration; some documents consist mostly of statistics; and a great number appear to be dry reports of congressional hearings or pedantic treatises giving results of government funded research.

Teacher-librarians have every right to ask how these publications might be made accessible and meaningful to their students (p. 8).

Once Williams (2005) demystified government documents for her patrons, they began using e-government resources in the classroom and school media center, adding to the curriculum in simple ways. One example included instructing teachers how to use the *Occupational Outlook Quarterly* as a career counseling resource. Williams concluded that once teachers and librarians learned more about e-government publications, they found opportunities to use them.

Another article written by Suzanne Sears (2006) entitled "Government Information for Parents and Teachers" was published in *DTTP: Documents to the People*. Sears discussed the mandate the Clinton (1997) administration communicated to the federal executive agencies in an April 18, 1997, memorandum to expand information to the Internet and make it accessible to children, teachers, and parents. The mandate President Clinton supported explains the many children's and teachers' sites on executive agencies and departments Internet sites that are currently available. During the G.W. Bush administration, the number of kid's sites was reduced, but there is still a significant presence of electronic sources available on the Internet.

Accessibility of Government Documents

Government documents are located in Federal Depository Libraries (FDLs) which are part of the Federal Depository Library Program (FDLP) and agree to allow members of the public into federal libraries to access the government information. There are 1277 member libraries in the United States. The majority (56.7%) of the libraries are academic, such as 4-year institutions, community colleges, or law libraries (GPO, 2009). The rest are either public libraries (22.2%) or special libraries (22.1%). The libraries can be located on the Web at the Government Printing Office (GPO) web site (www.gpoaccess.gov). There is at least one depository library in every state, as well as in American Samoa, Guam, Micronesia, Puerto Rico, and the American Virgin Islands (Government Printing Office [GPO], 2009a, b).

In today's world, U.S. federal government information is also available through the World Wide Web and the Internet. In 2002, the Government Printing Office (GPO) mandated that by 2005 over 95% of all government documents would be placed on the Internet. Today, more than 97% of government information is available on the Internet (GPO, 2007). This government information includes anything that was in print, microforms, CD, or DVD that has been converted to an electronic format. For example, many of the documents published by the National Park Service are now available in print and electronically.

Born digital is what a document is called if it is never put out in a print, CD, DVD, or microformat. Many of the agencies and departments never print a document on paper; information is put directly onto the Internet. There are pros and cons to a born digital document. One issue is how does someone know it is a "real" government document? GPO is dealing with the situation by putting watermarks that appear when a user requests the document from their web site. The other problem is archival. If the document is born digital, the assumption is that it will be saved somewhere in perpetuity. That is not always the case.

One of the barriers to government information is ease of access. Prior to 2002, finding government information was a journey through a myriad of print, microfiche, DVDs, CDs, and electronic documents with little organization. In Federal Depository Libraries (FDLs), the majority of government documents and information are cataloged using the Superintendant of Documents Classification System (SuDoc). The SuDoc system is based on provenance similar to archival processes. For example, a census document would first be filed under the classification of "C" to designate Commerce – which is the department the Census Bureau is under – followed by a complex numerical system. In other libraries, government documents are interfiled in either the Dewey Decimal Classification (DDC) system or the Library of Congress (LC) system, depending on which classification system the library prefers. Document records provided to the Online Computer Library Center (OCLC) by the GPO now include SuDoc, DDC, and LC cataloging information with the understanding that not all libraries use the same classification system. OCLC is a major source of cooperative cataloging for libraries of all types.

In the electronic environment, many of the libraries that catalog in SuDoc, DDC, or LC for government documents will include the link. The Government Printing Office (GPO), where possible, provides a persistent URL (PURL) which enables the user to be redirected automatically if the URL is ever changed. It is important for government document librarians and other users to let GPO know when a web page moves so appropriate changes can be made to the PURL.

Many times the web site design for the government agency or department makes it a difficult-to-find required information. Knowing where to look on each web site is the main factor, since none of the departments or agencies has the same look or feel to their web site. Each web site is different and everything is located in a different place. For example, on one web site the teacher's resources may be on the top of the page, on another it may be on the right side, and then on the third it may be on the bottom. There is little consistency in where information is placed. For example, the new Obama White House web site has a "White House 101" section for educational information entitled "Facts and Fun for All Ages" (White House, 2009). This new section is very different from the previous administration's child-centered site.

The majority of information available on federal government web sites is free of copyright restrictions, i.e., it is in the public domain, so that means information can be used over and over again without fear of copyright infringement. There is no need to get permissions from the copyright holder. Very few federal government documents or web sites are copyrighted. If a document is copyrighted, it will be noted on the site or document; at that point, permission would be needed if the work does not fall under the guidelines of Fair Use in the Copyright Act.

Creating an Informed Citizen

Part of educating children about government information is to teach them that they live in a representative democracy. Once they become an adult, it is hoped they will become involved in their community, county, state, and federal government. The ideal of an informed public is that as citizens we become knowledgeable about the political, social, and other important issues of the day.

The earliest mention of an informed public comes from Thomas Jefferson. Jefferson (1789) was quoted as saying: "Whenever the people are well-informed, they can be trusted with their own government." An informed public is considered to be a public good. The definition of a public good is based on the theory of political economics and is considered to be "a very special class of goods which cannot be withheld from all and for which the marginal cost of an additional person consuming them, once they have been produced, is zero" (Johnson, 2005).

Part of the job as a citizen is to be informed. The truest form of an informed public is that in order to vote we become astute about our representative democracy and what is happening with the candidates and the external environment around us. Our democracy is participatory in that once we are 18 or older, we participate by voting for and communicating with our elected and appointed representatives. Participatory democracy has roots to our colonial heritage (Shields, 2003, p. 522). Some examples of participatory democracy are town meetings and conversations across fences; bureaucracies are places where conversations occur continuously and where participatory democracy can be employed daily (Shields, p. 522). Shields' article discussed how John Dewey and Jane Addams viewed democracy; Dewey saw it as a way of life and Addams as a link to a larger moral common good (p. 524).

In the *Federalist Papers* (1787) the informed public is reiterated through many of the different pieces that were published. The ideal of an informed public is the basis on which Congress determined to publish and distribute copies of important documents to college and university libraries as well as historical associations in 1813. This was the beginning of the Government Printing Office as we know it today.

The ability to teach the children the basics of democracy can be tied into learning how to access information from our government. Educating children and teachers how to use government information helps build the tools to enable them to find the information they will need to cultivate the knowledge of their government as well as candidates running for office.

All citizens should be able to access e-government. K-12 education has a role in teaching our children the basics of democracy. The administrators, teachers, and school library media specialist have an opportunity to make a difference in the education of the children of the future by teaching them how to traverse the quirky ways our e-government system works. Children at ease with born digital instruction can easily learn e-government access points.

Teaching children in the K-12 environment to become familiar with government documents is necessary because as they become adults it will be expected that they can access government information online. Everything from simple tax forms to complicated FEMA forms are online. Very few government agencies accept paper forms when a citizen is applying for services. For example, when a college-age student is applying for federal aid for scholarships or loans, the Free Application for Federal Student Aid (FAFSA, www.fafsa.ed.gov) form is filled out online. All of these federal departments and agencies make the assumption that the average citizen has access to a computer and has a basic level of computer and literacy and familiarity with government information. For example, all of the tax forms are available on the IRS web site at www.irs.gov. At USA.gov, the web portal for the federal government, all the agencies and departments have links to their e-government sites by topic; this allows people to do basic tasks like file for federal student financial aid or replace vital records like a birth certificate through a state or county web site. In today's environment, public libraries have become the place where people can go to fill out these forms. Not everyone is able to fill out the forms with a level of competency, nor are all librarians trained in finding and filling out the forms in the online e-government environment.

E-Government and Public Libraries

According to the Pew Internet & American Life Project "Information Searches That Solve Problems" completed by the University of Illinois – Urbana-Champaign (UIUC), Princeton Survey Research Associates International (PSRAI), and Pew Internet & American Life Project (2007): "The vast majority of Americans want and expect information about government programs to be available on the internet" (p. iii). This finding supports the belief that people turn to the Internet when looking for information from the federal government (Estabrook, Witt, & Rainie, 2007, p. v). The report also supports the assumption that the place where most citizens go for public access computers and broadband capability is the public library (Estabrook et al.). Public access computing is one of the services public libraries provide, and government information is available through the Internet for those patrons who do not have access at home.

According to research done by Bertot, McClure, and Jaeger (2005), 99.6% of all public libraries have some access to the Internet. The type of the Internet access varies according to the availability of broadband, DSL, or dial-up connections. The Internet connectivity available (broadband, DSL, or dial up) determines the speed of the download for the e-government forms accessible from the web sites.

E-government and public libraries play a critical role in reducing the digital divide: (1) public libraries give public access to Internet-connected computers; (2) public librarians help the patrons with e-government information; and (3) during a natural disaster or emergency, the library may be the only place where there is public Internet access and computers (Bertot, Jaeger, Langa, & McClure, 2006). During the hurricane season of 2004–2005, libraries in the Gulf Coast area that were not destroyed were their community's main computer center for communication with the outside world (Bertot et al., 2006). Those who needed to file insurance claims and FEMA forms went to the public library (Bertot et al., 2006). As mentioned earlier, many federal and state government forms must be filled out electronically. As an example, FEMA allows only online filing of their forms, which necessitates a computer with an Internet connection.

K-12 Education, E-Government, and Government Documents

The number of government documents and web sites available on the Internet for K-12 educators and school library media specialists is astounding. The free nature and quality of the available documents is a unique source of information for teachers and school library media specialists.

School library media specialists should take advantage of free, e-government information because they are often working on a limited or shoestring budget in their school district. Government documents can be accessed via the Internet, pathfinders, and other finding aids that can be developed and created for the children to facilitate access to them. A prime example of this type of web portal is Kids.gov, which has information for children in grades K-8. The page is revised regularly and includes a date in the lower right corner for the last time it was updated.

Many government web sites have "kid's sites" as well as sites directed toward teachers and parents (see Appendices 1 and 2 for some examples). The sites that are directed toward teachers often have lesson plans and other documents that can supplement curriculum. The teacher sites also have information that is directed toward specific grades, age ranges, and topics. Some of the sites take into consideration the national education standards in the particular subject areas. A few sites, like that of the Smithsonian Institution at http://www.smithsonianeducation.org/educators/, contain links to educational resources aligned to state standards.

An example of using e-government in the classroom would be creating a unit on volcanoes. A search in the United States Geological Survey (U.S.G.S.) education site for grades 4–8 (http://education.usgs.gov/common/primary.htm#volcanoes) reveals a teacher packet with six lessons, a poster, and teachers' guide. Each lesson includes background information, two-timed activities, reproducible master sheets for making overheads or copies, and activity sheets. The teaching guide gives a breakdown of each lesson.

The Library of Congress American Memory collection has extensive historical artifacts from baseball cards to historical documents to sheet music. Many of the collections have been digitized. The American Memory collection is a great place to let a group of high school students loose with a project to write on something that piques their interest. Suppose a baseball fan would want to do a paper on the different types of collections the Library of Congress has on baseball. There are collections including baseball cards from cigarette packages and sheet music of the song *Take Me Out to the Ball Game.* There are a wide variety of photographs of different types of baseball teams from different time periods.

Careers are a popular research subject in school, and the *Occupational Outlook Handbook* (OOH) (http://www.bls.gov/oco/home.htm) is a source that can be used to find information about jobs. Basic information includes the education needed for each type of career, what the job prospects for the next 5–10 years would be, and what would be mean and median wages. The OOH is a good source for middle and high school students, and while the electronic version is accessible, a print copy in the school media center would not be without merit.

Web Sites for Librarians and Educators

The following government web sites are excellent places to start to search for information and educational materials for teachers and librarians to use. The sites have course planning materials that can be used within such sites as the Library of Congress, National Archives and Records Administration, Census Bureau, and the U.S. Courts.

FREE (www.free.ed.gov) is a collection of links to federally supported teaching and learning resources. The site is organized by topic area and each topic area is organized by subtopic. For example, Math contains such topics as algebra, data analysis, geometry, measurements, number, and operations. There is a wide variety of topics ranging from arts to world studies and everything in between.

Browse Topics (www.browsetopics.gov) is a joint project between the Government Printing Office (GPO) and Oklahoma State University (OSU), listing government sites by general topics. The topics are broader than the FREE sites and points to web sites created by the federal government. The sites may or may not be teacher or kid centric but general government document sites.

The Official Kids Portal for the U.S. Government (www.kids.gov) is designed primarily for kids and includes government as well as commercial web sites. It has tabs across the top for specific grade ranges (K-5 and 6–8) as well as one for educators. Many of the linked sites also provide lesson plans and classroom activities for teachers. Kids.gov includes state as well as federal sites.

USA.gov (http://www.usa.gov) is the U.S. government's portal to departmental and agency web sites. It has tabs for citizens, businesses and nonprofits, government employees, and visitors to the United States. Under the citizen's tab, there are places for kids, teens, parents, and other more specific audiences, as well as a place to search the government Web. The site is good for general searches, but also has the ability to do specialized searches.

The Teachers page from the Library of Congress (http://www.loc.gov/teachers) includes over 10 million primary source documents. The Teachers page links to a learning page that has lesson plans that connect to the Library of Congress's American Memory collection, which includes digital archives of documents, artwork, and all kinds of special collections. The material is primary source material that can be connected to through the Internet. This site gives the students and teachers the ability to work with primary source material they may not normally have access to in the classroom.

The National Archives and Research Administration's (NARA) Digital Classroom (http://www.archives.gov/education) has lesson plans connecting to the Our Documents collection (http://www.ourdocuments.gov). Our Documents collection is the 100 most important historical documents related to American history, such as the Declaration of Independence, Washington's Farewell Speech, Brown *v.* Board of Education Opinion, and others. NARA has split up the lesson plans into historical eras with specific plans that tie to the various documents. All of the lesson plans have been correlated with the National History Standards and the National Standards in Civics and Government.

Ben's Guide to U.S. Government for Kids (http://bensguide.gpo.gov/) is a web site that resides at GPO. It has kids' and parents' and teachers' links. The kids' sites are divided by grade level (K-2, 3–5, 6–8, and 9–12) and then subdivided by topic. The parents' and teachers' site is also divided by topic. Both the kids' and parents' and teachers' sites have additional agency links that are more extensive than most of the other sites previously mentioned.

U.S. Courts Educational Outreach (http://www.uscourts.gov/outreach/) features materials aimed at high school-level students. This site can be used in the classroom or if the class is scheduling a field trip to the local federal courthouse. The thrust of the outreach is to have young people understand basic court literacy issues like first and sixth amendment rights.

The U.S. Geological Service has an education site (http://education.usgs.gov/) that provides information for K-12 as well as higher education. The site includes information divided by primary (K-6) and upper (7–12) grades. The teacher site includes teacher packets that were originally available in print and are now downloadable. Some of them can still be ordered in print.

The U.S. Census Bureau has a program entitled Census in Schools (http://www.census.gov/dmd/www/schmat1.html) that is currently based on the 2000 Census. The material is sequenced for grades K-4, 5–8, and 9–12 and arranged in three strands: mapping literacy, community involvement, and managing data. Each grade level has different handouts and tasks for students. All lessons are downloadable.

Google (www.google.com) has a topic-specific search feature that allows a search of just government and military sites. It is called Google U.S. Government or Google Uncle Sam (http://www.google.com/unclesam). The advantage to using this advanced search is that it easily narrows the search to only government sites, eliminating the need for additional query filters.

Conclusion

E-government and school library media centers are a match that needs to be made. E-government sources are free and easy to find on the Internet. Within this article there are many sources noted that can be used to build a pathfinder or a web page of sources for teachers and children. In the past, e-government and government documents had the reputation of being difficult to use. However, librarians can make these resources more accessible to students and teachers through creating information portals and through instruction. There are millions of easily accessible web pages of government information waiting to be mined.

Appendix 1: Teachers' Government Web Sites

Agriculture in the Classroom: http://www.agclassroom.org/
The Antidrug: http://www.theantidrug.com/
Army Corps of Engineers, Water Safety: http://www.orn.usace.army.mil/pao/watersafety/teacher_resources.htm
Bureau of Printing and Engraving: http://www.moneyfactory.gov/newmoney/main.cfm/learning/download
Central Intelligence Agency Teacher's Site: https://www.cia.gov/kids-page/parents-teachers/index.html
Department of Education Teacher's Information: http://www.ed.gov/teachers/landing.jhtml?src=fp
Environmental Protection Agency, Teaching Site: http://www.epa.gov/teachers/
Food and Drug Administration, Teachers and Parents: http://www.fda.gov/ForConsumers/ByAudience/Educators/default.htm
Federal Highway Safety Administration, Education Site: http://www.fhwa.dot.gov/education/index.htm
Federal Reserve, Frequently Asked Questions: http://www.federalreserve.gov/generalinfo/faq/faqcur.htm
Fish and Wildlife Service: http://www.fws.gov/educators/educators.html
Food Safety: http://www.foodsafety.gov/~fsg/fsgkids.html
Health and Human Services: http://www.hhs.gov/kids/teachers.html
Department of Interior: http://www.doi.gov/teachers/
Department of Labor, Educators: http://www.dol.gov/dol/audience/aud-educators.htm
Los Alamos Lab, Teacher's Site: http://www.lanl.gov/education/teachers/
NASA, Ames Research Center: http://erc.arc.nasa.gov/
NASA, Glenn Research Center: http://www.nasa.gov/centers/glenn/education/
NASA, Goddard Space Flight Center: http://education.gsfc.nasa.gov/
NASA, Johnson Space Center: http://education.jsc.nasa.gov/
NASA, Langley Research Center: http://www.nasa.gov/centers/langley/education/index.html
NASA, Marshall Space Flight Center: http://education.nasa.gov/edoffices/centeroffices/marshall/home/index.html
NASA, Jet Propulsion Laboratory: http://www.jpl.nasa.gov/education/index.cfm
NASA, Space Kids: http://spacekids.hq.nasa.gov/osskids/education.htm
NASA, Stennis Space Center: http://wwwedu.ssc.nasa.gov/

NASA, Teacher's Guides: http://kids.earth.nasa.gov/guide/index.htm

National Endowment for the Humanities, Lesson Plans: http://edsitement. neh.gov/lesson_index.asp

National Institute on Drug Abuse for Teens: http://teens.drugabuse. gov/parents/index.php

National Institute on Drug Abuse Goes Back to School: http://backtoschool. drugabuse.gov/

National Institute of Environmental Health Sciences: http://www.niehs.nih.gov/ health/scied/teachers/index.cfm

National Oceanic and Atmospheric Administration: http://www.education. noaa.gov/teachers1.html

National Oceanic and Atmospheric Administration Teacher at Sea Program: http://teacheratsea.noaa.gov/

National Park Service (NPS): http://www.nps.gov/learn/

Non-renewal Energy Lab, Education Sites: http://www.nrel.gov/education/

Occupational Safety and Health Administration: http://www.osha.gov/ SLTC/teenworkers/educators.html

Peace Corps: http://www.peacecorps.gov/wws/

Science 4 Kids, Teachers Desk: http://www.ars.usda.gov/is/kids/teachers/ TeachDesk.htm

Smithsonian Institute, Anthropology: http://www.sil.si.edu/SILPublications/ Anthropology-K12/anth-k12.htm

Smithsonian Institute, Educators: http://smithsonianeducation.org/educators/ index.html

State Department: http://future.state.gov/educators/index.htm

Thomas – Legislative Resources for Teachers: http://www.thomas. gov/teachers/

U.S. Fire Administration: http://www.usfa.dhs.gov/kids/parents-teachers/

U.S. House of Representatives, Educational Resources: http://www.house. gov/house/Educate.shtml

U.S. Mint Teachers Site: http://www.usmint.gov/kids/teachers/

U.S. Patent & Trademark Office (USPTO): http://www.uspto.gov/web/ offices/ac/ahrpa/opa/kids/special/kidguide.htm

Veteran's Affairs: http://www.va.gov/kids/teachers/index.asp

Appendix 2: Kids' Sites

Army Corps of Engineers, Kid's Corner: http://education.usace.army. mil/index.cfm

Bureau of Alcohol, Tobacco and Firearms, Kid's Site: http://www.atf.gov/ kids/index.htm

CIA Kid's Page: https://www.cia.gov/kids-page/index.html

Census State Facts for Students: http://www.census.gov/schools/facts/

Center for Disease Control, Kid's Site: http://www.cdc.gov/ncbddd/kids/kitppage.htm

Science 4 Kids: http://www.ars.usda.gov/is/kids/

Department of Education, Kid's Zone: http://nces.ed.gov/nceskids/eyk/index.asp?flash=false

Department of Energy, The Energy Lab, High School Students: http://www.netl.doe.gov/education/students.html

Department of Interior: http://www.doi.gov/kids/index.html

Department of Labor Kids Sites Index: http://www.dol.gov/dol/audience/aud-kidsyouth.htm

EPA, Kid's Site: http://www.epa.gov/teachers/

Federal Reserve: http://www.federalreserve.gov/kids/

Federal Reserve, Spanish or Español: http://www.federalreserve.gov/kids/default_spanish.htm

FDA, Kid's Site: http://www.fda.gov/oc/opacom/kids/default.htm

U.S. Fire Administration: http://www.usfa.dhs.gov/kids/flash.shtm

Fish and Wildlife Service: http://www.fws.gov/educators/students.html

Food Safety: http://www.foodsafety.gov/~fsg/fsgkids.html

Forest Service: http://www.fs.fed.us/kids/

The Globe Program: http://www.globe.gov/fsl/html/templ.cgi?for_students&lang=en

Housing and Urban Development: http://www.hud.gov/kids/

Housing and Urban Development, Students: http://www.hud.gov/groups/students.cfm

Library of Congress Kid's Page: http://www.americaslibrary.gov/cgi-bin/page.cgi

Minerals Management Service: http://www.mms.gov/mmskids/

NASA, Star Child: http://starchild.gsfc.nasa.gov/docs/StarChild/StarChild.html

National Institute for Environmental Health Sciences, Kids Site: http://kids.niehs.nih.gov/

National Institute for Standards and Technology: http://www.nist.gov/public_affairs/kids/weblinks.htm

National Oceanic and Atmospheric Administration (NOAA): http://www.education.noaa.gov/students.html

NOAA, Playtime for Kids: http://www.weather.gov/om/reachout/kidspage.shtml

OSHA, Teenagers: http://www.osha.gov/SLTC/teenworkers/teenworkers.html

Peace Corps: http://www.peacecorps.gov/kids/

Smithsonian Institute: http://smithsonianeducation.org/students/index.html

State Department: http://future.state.gov/

U.S. Patent and Trademark Office (USPTO): http://www.uspto.gov/go/kids/

U.S. Treasury Sites for Kids: http://www.ustreas.gov/kids/

Veteran's Affairs (VA): http://www.va.gov/kids/

White House 101: http://www.whitehouse.gov/about/white_house_101/

Year of the Ocean, 1998, Kids Corner: http://www.yoto98.noaa.gov/kids.htm

References

Bertot, J. C., Jaeger, P. T., Langa, L. A., & McClure, C. R. (2006, September 4). Public access computing and Internet access in public libraries: The role of public libraries in e-government and emergency situations. *First Monday, 11*(9). Retrieved January 5, 2009, from http://firstmonday.org

Bertot, J. C., McClure, C. R., & Jaeger, P. T. (2005, May). Public libraries and the internet 2004: Survey results and findings. Tallahassee, FL: College of Information, Information Use Management & Policy Institute, Florida State University.

Butler, R. P. (2004, May/June). Copying government maps. *Knowledge Quest, 32*(5), 46–47.

Clinton, W. J. (1997, April 18). Memorandum on expanding access to Internet-based educational resources for children, teachers, and parents. *Public papers of the president – William J. Clinton – 1997, Vol. 1.* Washington, DC: Government Printing Office. Retrieved March 29, 2009, from the Government Printing Office http://frwebgate5.access.gpo.gov/cgi-bin/TEXTgate.cgi?WAISdocID=264278497609+0+1+0&WAISaction=retrieve

Estabrook, L., Witt, E., & Rainie, L. (2007). Information searches that solve problems: How people use the Internet, libraries, and government agencies when they need help. Pew Internet & American Life Project, Graduate School of Library and Information Science, University of Illinois at Urbana-Champaign, and Princeton Survey Research Associates International. Retrieved March 1, 2009, from http://www.pewinternet.org/~/media//Files/Reports/2007/Pew_UI_LibrariesReport.pdf.pdf

Evans, D., & Yen, D. C. (2006). E-Government: Evolving relationship of citizens, government, domestic, and international development. *Government Information Quarterly, 23*(2), 207–235.

FREE. (n.d.). Retrieved March 28, 2009, from www.free.ed.gov

Google U.S. Government. (2009). Retrieved April 27, 2009, from http://www.google.com/unclesam

Government Printing Office. (2002). Retrieved March 1, 2009, from www.gpoaccess.gov

Government Printing Office. (2007). Retrieved March 1, 2009, from www.gpoaccess.gov

Government Printing Office. (2009a). Ben's guide to U.S. government for kids. Retrieved March 28, 2009, from http://bensguide.gpo.gov/

Government Printing Office. (2009b). Federal depository directory. Retrieved March 29, 2009, from http://catalog.gpo.gov/fdlpdir/FDLPdir.jsp

Government Printing Office, & Oklahoma State University. (n.d.). Browse Topics. Retrieved March 28, 2009, from www.browsetopics.gov

Hernon, P., Dugan, R. E., & Shuler, J. A. (2003). *U.S. government on the web: Getting the information you need* (3rd ed.). Westport, CT: Libraries Unlimited.

Hernon, P., Reylea, H. C., Dugan, R. E., & Cheverie, J. F. (2002). *United States government information: Policies and sources.* Westport, CT: Libraries Unlimited.

Idaho Code. § 9-350. (2009). Retrieved April 27, 2009, from http://www.legislature.idaho.gov/idstat/Title9/T9CH3SECT9-350PrinterFriendly.htm

Jaeger, P. T. (2003). The endless wire: E-government as global phenomenon. *Government Information Quarterly, 20*(4), 323–331.

Jefferson, T. (1789). Favorite Jefferson quotes from the writings of Thomas Jefferson. Retrieved September 27, 2005, from http://etext.virginia.edu/jefferson/quotations/jeff5.htm

Johnson, P. M. (2005). A glossary of political economy terms. Retrieved September 27, 2005, from http://www.auburn.edu/~johnspm/gloss/public_goods

The Library of Congress. (2009). The teachers page. Retrieved March 28, 2009, from http://www.loc.gov/teachers

Madison, J., Hamilton, A., & Jay, J. (1787). *The federalist papers.* New York: The Modern Library.

Morehead, J. (1999). *Introduction to United States government information sources* (6th ed.). Englewood, CO: Libraries Unlimited.

National Archives & Records Administration. (2009a). Digital classroom. Retrieved March 28, 2009, from http://www.archives.gov/education

National Archives & Records Administration. (2009b). Our documents. Retrieved March 28, 2009, from http://www.ourdocuments.gov

The official kids portal for the U.S. government. (2007). Retrieved March 28, 2009, from http://www.kids.gov

Robinson, J. S. (1998). *Tapping the government grapevine* (3rd ed.). Phoenix, AZ: Oryx.

Roy, J. (2003, Spring). Introduction: E-government. *Social Science Computer Review, 21*(1), 3–5.

Sears, S. (2006, Summer). Government information for parents and teachers. *DTTP, 34*(2), 23–25.

Shields, P. M. (2003, November). The community of inquiry: Classical pragmatism and public administration. *Administration & Society, 35*(5), 510–538.

USA.gov. (2009). Retrieved April 27, 2009, from http://www.usa.gov

U.S. Census Bureau. (2008). Census in the schools. Retrieved March 28, 2009, from http://www.census.gov/dmd/www/teachers.html

U.S. Courts. (n.d.). Retrieved March 28, 2009, from http://www.uscourts.gov/outreach/index.html

U.S. Department of Labor Statistics. (2009). *Occupational outlook handbook*. Retrieved March 28, 2009, from http://www.bls.gov/oco/home.htm

U.S. Geological Service. (2009). Education. Retrieved March 28, 2009, from http://education.usgs.gov/

White House 101. (2009). White House. Retrieved March 29, 2009, from http://www.whitehouse.gov/about/white_house_101/

Williams, S. Q. (2005, June). Government documents go to school. *Teacher Librarian, 32*(5), 9–13.

Part III
Leadership Profiles

Introduction

Robert Maribe Branch

The purpose of this part is to profile individuals who have made significant contributions to the field of educational media and communication technology. Leaders profiled in the *Educational Media and Technology Yearbook* have typically held prominent offices, composed seminal works, and made significant contributions that have influenced the contemporary vision of the field. The people profiled in this part have often been directly responsible for mentoring individuals, who have themselves become recognized for their contributions in one way or another.

There are special reasons to feature people of national and international renown. This volume of the *Educational Media and Technology Yearbook* profiles individuals who continue to uphold the tradition of leadership in educational media and communication technology. The leaders profiled this year are Jerrold E. Kemp and W. Michael Reed.

The following people (alphabetically listed) were profiled in earlier volumes of the *Educational Media and Technology Yearbook*:

John C. Belland	Jean E. Lowrie
Robert K. Branson	Wesley Joseph McJulien
James W. Brown	M. David Merrill
Bob Casey	Michael Molenda
Betty Collis	David Michael Moore
Robert E. De Kieffer	Robert M. Morgan
Robert M. Diamond	Robert Morris
Walter Dick	James Okey
Frank Dwyer	Ronald Oliver
Donald P. Ely	Tjeerd Plomp
James D. Finn	Rita C. Richey
Robert Mills Gagné	Paul Saettler
Castelle (Cass) G. Gentry	Wilbur Schramm
Thomas F. Gilbert	Charles Francis Schuller

R.M. Branch (✉)
Learning, Design, and Technology Program, The University of Georgia, Athens, GA, USA
e-mail: rbranch@uga.edu

M. Orey et al. (eds.), *Educational Media and Technology Yearbook*,
Educational Media and Technology Yearbook 35,
DOI 10.1007/978-1-4419-1516-0_14, © Springer Science+Business Media, LLC 2010

(continued)

Kent Gustafson	Don Carl Smellie
John Hedberg	Howard Sullivan
Robert Heinich	William Travers
Stanley A. Huffman	Constance Dorothea Weinman
Harry Alleyn Johnson	Paul Welliver
Roger Kaufman	Paul Robert Wendt
Addie Kinsinger	David R. Krathwohl

There is no formal survey or popularity contest to determine the persons for whom the profiles are written. People profiled in this part are usually emeritus faculty who may or may not be active in the field. You are welcome to nominate individuals to be featured in this part. The editors of this yearbook will carefully consider your nomination. Please direct comments, questions, and suggestions about the selection process to the editorial office: Educational Media and Technology Yearbook, 604 Aderhold Hall, The University of Georgia, Athens, Georgia 30602, or mikeorey@uga.edu.

Jerrold Kemp: Designing Effective Instruction

Diane Igoche

Dr. Jerrold Kemp is one of the most accomplished scholars in instructional technology. His career spans over 30 years, and thus, his contribution to the field of instructional technology should be duly recognized. Dr. Kemp received his doctorate in instructional technology from Indiana University. He also worked as a high school science teacher and media coordinator in Miami, Florida. Dr. Kemp began his career in academia at the San Jose State University as a professor of education, where he also worked as the coordinator of media production and instructional development services. He taught at San Jose State University for 30 years of his academic career. His steady career at the university is one that should be envied.

Professional Activities and Service

Dr. Kemp is a former president of the Association of Educational and Communications Technology (AECT) and he also served as one of the early presidents of AECT's Division of Systemic Change. According to his friend and coauthor, Dr. Gary Morrison, "Dr. Kemp is a gentleman scholar, who is very generous with his time to students and showed dedication to the success of international students." He is also devoted to service to the community as a scholar and on a global scale; this is evident from his consultancies with international organizations and K-12 school districts.

Research

Dr. Kemp has authored many scholarly works and consulted on various educational projects in numerous educational institutions and agencies in the United States and abroad, including United Nations Educational, Scientific and Cultural Organization

D. Igoche (✉)
Learning, Design, and Technology Program, The University of Georgia, Athens, GA, USA
e-mail: dai011@uga.edu

M. Orey et al. (eds.), *Educational Media and Technology Yearbook*,
Educational Media and Technology Yearbook 35,
DOI 10.1007/978-1-4419-1516-0_15, © Springer Science+Business Media, LLC 2010

(UNESCO). His early research interests were in audiovisual instructional media. He published a renowned textbook in 1963 on audiovisual instruction: *Planning and Producing Audiovisual Materials.* This book came at a time when, as Kemp says, "it was important to address the changing nature of audiovisual materials to incorporate adequate instructional design and the best selection of media to serve instructional objectives." Dr. Kemp has since authored and coauthored five very important texts on instructional media, training, and instructional design. He has also written numerous articles on audiovisual and instructional development techniques for professional journals. One of the most notable works of his illustrious career is his contribution of one of the most utilized instructional design models: Kemp's model.

Kemp's Model

Dr. Jerrold Kemp developed Kemp's Instructional Design Model in 1985. The Kemp model is a holistic instructional design model that incorporates practically all factors in a learning environment and is very flexible because of its iterative nature. In 1994, Dr. Kemp, alongside Dr. Gary Morrison and Dr. Steven Ross, modified Kemp's model to include two additional components to the model, and then went on to publish *Designing Effective Instruction.* Morrison and Ross have continued to produce different editions of Kemp's model and are currently working on the sixth edition.

Dr. Kemp is undoubtedly a pioneer in the field of educational media and technology. Although he retired from the professoriate in 1994, he has continued to publish scholarly articles and books on instructional technology. He has also met success outside academia, where in 2003 he published a successful relationship guide with his wife Edith Ankersmit Kemp. Dr. Kemp's work has joined the rank of quality seminal works in instructional technology and will continue to remain relevant for a long time.

The author and the yearbook editors wish to express our gratitude to Dr. Gary Morrison, who provided information about the accomplishments of Dr. Jerrold Kemp.

W. Michael Reed: At the Beginnings Using Computers in Education for Higher-Order Learning

Min Liu and John Burton

Dr. William Michael "Mike" Reed was an accomplished, dedicated, and recognized educator in instructional technology. Strongly rooted in the classroom, Mike was driven in the early 1980s and 1990s to explore the uses of computers in education

M. Liu (✉)
Instructional Technology Program, Department of Curriculum and Instruction, University of Texas, Austin, TX, USA
e-mail: mliu@utexas.edu

J. Burton (✉)
Instructional Systems Development/Educational Psychology, Virginia Tech, Blacksburg, VA, USA
e-mail: jburton@vt.edu

M. Orey et al. (eds.), *Educational Media and Technology Yearbook,*   197
Educational Media and Technology Yearbook 35,
DOI 10.1007/978-1-4419-1516-0_16, © Springer Science+Business Media, LLC 2010

beyond computer literacy itself. His work evolved from the possible connections between computer literacy and problem solving (computer programming and use as a means to increase problem-solving ability), to the use of computers in the creative writing process (computers as a tool in a higher-order process), to hypermedia and multimedia, to structure to-be-learned material (computers as a design extension). In the process he was at the forefront of the movement from computing in education as a means unto itself to computing as a learner, and designer, tool.

After completing his Bachelors degree at Virginia Tech in English in 1972, Reed completed 3 years in the US Army before he returned to Virginia Tech to complete a Masters degree in English Education. He began his career as an educator in earnest as a high school English teacher in Front Royal, Virginia. During his 5 years at Front Royal Reed, he coached tennis, cross-country, track, and football. He also taught English at the local community college, and in 1981 he returned to Virginia Tech to pursue a doctorate in Community College Administration. He soon doubted whether he wanted to train as an administrator and whether he wanted to focus at the community college level. He transferred to Curriculum and Instruction, where, in 1984, he received his doctorate with specializations in Instructional Technology and English Education from Virginia Tech. Theoretically strong, his dissertation combined cognitive load theory with the emerging composition theories (Flower & Hays, 1981). He would never turn away from his grounding in, and respect for, the role of theory in research.

Reed went to West Virginia University in 1981 to establish and manage a computer laboratory in Technology Education. He quickly expanded the role of the lab to encompass all of education. Along the way he established WVU's first Instructional Technology graduate program. Dr. Reed was tenured within 4 years and attained the rank of professor of instructional technology in 1992. During his tenure at West Virginia University (1984–1998), Dr. Reed received the three highest professional awards at the university level: the Outstanding Teaching Award in 1990, the Benedum Distinguished Scholar Award in 1993, and the Heebink Distinguished Service Award in 1994. Receiving one of these awards is enviable. It is likely unheard of for one individual to receive all three of these prestigious awards in less than 15 years. Reed was also awarded two Fulbright Professorships: to Austria (1988) and Finland (1992). In 1998, he joined New York University faculty as Professor of Educational Communication and Technology and also served as its Program Chair from 1998 to 2004. Retired from NYU, in 2007, he went to Radford Virginia to be near his mother, sister, and niece. Later that year he became the Institutional Review Board Administrator at Radford University.

During his lifetime, W. Michael Reed published extensively in major IT journals. His works can be found in such journals as *Journal of Educational Computing Research*, *Computers in Human Behavior*, *Journal of Research on Computing in Education*, *Journal of Educational Multimedia and Hypermedia*, *Journal of Educational Psychology*, *Computers in the Schools*, and *Journal of Research and Teaching in Developmental Education*. His research topics covered computer use in writing, problem solving with computers, technology in teacher education, and hypermedia/multimedia learning and individual differences.

Apart from producing many research publications, he served as editor and co-editor of numerous books and special journal issues. These included: Reed and Burton, (1988),Reed and Bonk (1992), Reed, Burton, and Liu (1994), Reed, Ayersman, and Liu (1995), Reed (1996), and Hoffman, Reed, and Rosenbluth (1997). Reed also was the editor of *Journal of Computing in Childhood Education* from 1994 to 1996 and co-editor of *Journal of Research on Technology in Education* from 1999 to 2003.

Dr. Reed was active in professional organizations. He made over 60 presentations at state, regional, national, and international conferences. He often brought his students along and co-presented with them at conferences. His students' presence was noticeable at annual meetings such as Eastern Education Research Association. In addition, he was Director of Division 12 (Educational Technology), Eastern Education Research Association, 1999–2003.

In addition to his significant contributions in research, teaching, and professional services, Dr. Reed has taught and mentored many doctoral students and junior colleagues and prepared the next generation of accomplished educators. He was the chair of over 50 doctoral dissertation committees. His students are spread from West Virginia to Arkansas, Alaska to Texas, New York to Virginia, and Florida to South Carolina. He made a lasting influence on his students and colleagues and touched many people's lives. As Dr. John Burton, his advisor, stated, "Mike's legacy is not in his published work but in the scores of his students and colleagues." He will be forever remembered and missed.

Reflective Addendum: Mike's Life

Curtis Book

As is clear, Mike was a builder, a composer, and a designer. In a word, he was a doer. At its heart, Mike's life was one of composition. He composed it as he went along and lived as he wished from start to end. But each day and each product must be seen for the greater whole. This is a man who wrote as a journalist for the US Army in Germany. Countless newspaper articles and other documents were drafted, redrafted, approved, signed, and disseminated.

Knowing Mike, he was likely composing and recomposing them at each waking moment of day as well as in his sleep. After completing his army duties, he had the challenging task of teaching teenagers about the great works of Shakespeare and other compositions as a high school English teacher in Virginia. It is likely he touched many hearts and minds with his sage advice, keen insights, and timely and heavy feedback. Perhaps more enjoyably he coached these kids in many after-school sporting events.

When Mike left the world of an English teacher, he went on to write a massive composition called a dissertation as a graduate student at Virginia Tech. After successful defense, he crafted many other such types of documents when at WVU and

NYU. During his time in academia, Mike trained dozens of other graduate students to write coherent, interesting, and seminal compositions of their own. His life of composing did not end when the research was completed. Often these works would end up as published papers in conference proceedings.

If you knew Mike, you would not be surprised by the fact that upon return from such conferences, he was not done. He would quickly assemble the troops for a special journal issue of their compiled papers, yet another form of composition. Once submitted, he was still not done! These journal issues often were reprinted a year or two after release as edited books, typically with colleagues and former students as co-editors. All the while, Mike was subtly teaching each of his collaborators and students the composing process. He was the grand maestro!

All aspects of his life were composition. All products – from his programming in Basic as well as Logo in his early academic years to his more rich hypermedia and multimedia designs – could be viewed as compositions. These were his works of art. His contributions to world. Ditto all the frameworks, models, and learning guides he built as well as the myriad journals he reviewed for. Compositions – all of them.

What's more, much of this work was on the writing or composing process itself. Mike was, in fact, a writing researcher. And if writing is indeed thinking, Mike Reed was the consummate thinker. He not only was constantly writing or reading the writing of others, but was researching the entire shebang. In effect, he wanted everyone to know what good writing or composition was and was continually researching it, teaching it, and sharing it.

In addition to his life as an academic, Mike wanted to write the ultimate composition – the novel. And in 2001, he did just that! It was titled *Kelly Barracks*. That was his masterpiece. His sonata. His magnum opus. With that, his life had come full circle, from one who was trained in how to write a composition as well as teach others about the process to one who composes such wonderful displays of human intelligence for others to read, dissect, discuss, and reflect upon.

Without much doubt, there are some forms of composition within Mike's life that are not mentioned in these brief paragraphs. Each person who was touched by him likely has his or her own stories involving one or more products or compositions of Mike's life. These too should be added here for that is what a biography should be – a compilation of one's life. And Mike Reed definitely compiled! He left us much to personally read, assign to our students, expand upon, and simply enjoy.

References

Flower, L., & Hayes, J. R. (1981). *"A Cognitive Process Theory of Writing."* College Composition and Communication 32.4(December 1981): 365–387.

Hoffman, N. E., Reed, W. M., & Rosenbluth, G. S. (1997). *Stories of change: Lessons from experiences in school restructuring.* Albany, NY: SUNY

Reed, W. M. (1996). *Assessing the impact of computers on learning: 1987.* Eugene, OR: International Society for Technology in Education.

Reed, W. M., Ayersman, D. J., & Liu, M. (1995). *Hypermedia: Theory, research, and practice.* New York: Pergamon Press.

Reed, W. M., & Bonk, C. J. (1992). *Computer use in the improvement of writing.* New York: Pergamon Press.

Reed, W. M., & Burton, J. K. (1988). *Educational computing and problem solving.* New York: Haworth Press.

Reed, W. M., Burton, J. K., & Liu, M. (1994). *Multimedia and megachange: New directions for educational computing.* New York: Haworth Press.

Part IV
Organizations and Associations

Introduction

Michael Orey

Part 4 includes annotated entries for associations and organizations, most of which are headquartered in North America, whose interests are in some manner significant to the fields of learning, design and technology, or library and information science. For the most part, these organizations consist of professionals in the field or agencies that offer services to the educational media community. In an effort to list only active organizations, I deleted all organizations that had not updated their information since 2006. Readers are encouraged to contact the editors with names of unlisted media-related organizations for investigation and possible inclusion in the 2011 edition.

Information for this part was obtained through e-mail directing each organization to an individual web form through which the updated information could be submitted electronically into a database created by Michael Orey. Although the section editors made every effort to contact and follow up with organization representatives, responding to the annual request for an update was the responsibility of the organization representatives. The editing team would like to thank those respondents who helped assure the currency and accuracy of this part by responding to the request for an update. Figures quoted as dues refer to annual amounts, unless stated otherwise. Where dues, membership, and meeting information are not applicable, such information is omitted.

M. Orey (✉)
Learning, Design, and Technology Program, The University of Georgia, Athens, GA, USA
e-mail: mikeorey@uga.edu

M. Orey et al. (eds.), *Educational Media and Technology Yearbook,*   205
Educational Media and Technology Yearbook 35,
DOI 10.1007/978-1-4419-1516-0_17, © Springer Science+Business Media, LLC 2010

Worldwide List of Organizations in Learning, Design, Technology, Information, or Libraries

Name of Organization or Association – Adaptech Research Network

Acronym – None

Address:
Dawson College, 3040 Sherbrooke St. West
Montreal, QC
H3Z 1A4
Canada

Phone Number – 514-931-8731 #1546; **Fax Number** – 514-931-3567 Attn: Catherine Fichten

Email Contact – catherine.fichten@mcgill.ca; **URL** – http://www.adaptech.org

Leaders – Catherine Fichten, Ph.D., Co-director; Jennison V. Asuncion, M.A., Co-Director; Maria Barile, M.S.W., Co-director

Description – Based at Dawson College (Montreal), we are a Canada-wide, grant-funded team, conducting bilingual empirical research into the use of computer, learning, and adaptive technologies by postsecondary students with disabilities. One of our primary interests lies in issues around ensuring that newly emerging instructional technologies are accessible to learners with disabilities.

Membership – Our research team is composed of academics, practitioners, students, consumers, and others interested in the issues of access to technology by students with disabilities in higher education.

Dues – None

Meetings – None

Publications – Fossey, M.E., Asuncion, J.V., Fichten, C.S., Robillard, C., Barile, M., Amsel, R., Prezant, F., & Morabito, S. (2005). Development and validation of the Accessibility Of Campus Computing For Students With Disabilities Scale (ACCSDS). Journal of Postsecondary Education and Disability, 18(1), 23–33. Jorgensen, S., Fichten, C.S., Havel, A., Lamb, D., James, C., & Barile, M.

M. Orey et al. (eds.), *Educational Media and Technology Yearbook*,
Educational Media and Technology Yearbook 35,
DOI 10.1007/978-1-4419-1516-0_18, © Springer Science+Business Media, LLC 2010

(2005). Academic performance of college students with and without disabilities: An archival study. Canadian Journal of Counselling, 39(2), 101–117. Fichten, C.S., Asuncion, J.V., Barile, M., Fossey, M.E., Robillard, C., Judd, D., Wolforth, J., Senécal, J., Généreux, C., Guimont, J.P., Lamb, D., & Juhel, J-C. (2004). Access to information and instructional technologies in higher education I: Disability service providers' perspective. Journal of Postsecondary Education and Disability, 17(2), 114–133.

Name of Organization or Association – Agency for Instructional Technology

Acronym – AIT

Address:
Box A
Bloomington, IN
47402-0120
US

Phone Number – (812)339-2203; **Fax Number** – (812)333-4218

Email Contact – info@ait.net; **URL** – http://www.ait.net

Leaders – Charles E. Wilson, Executive Director

Description – The Agency for Instructional Technology has been a leader in educational technology since 1962. A nonprofit organization, AIT is one of the largest providers of instructional TV programs in North America. AIT is also a leading developer of other educational media, including online instruction, CDs, videodiscs, and instructional software. AIT learning resources are used on six continents and reach nearly 34 million students in North America each year. AIT products have received many national and international honors, including an Emmy and Peabody award. Since 1970, AIT has developed 39 major curriculum packages through the consortium process it pioneered. American state and Canadian provincial agencies have cooperatively funded and widely used these learning resources. Funding for other product development comes from state, provincial, and local departments of education; federal and private institutions; corporations and private sponsors; and AITs own resources.

Membership – None.

Dues – None.

Meetings – No regular public meetings.

Publications – None.

Name of Organization or Association – American Association of Colleges for Teacher Education

Acronym – AACTE
Address:
1307 New York Ave., N.W., Suite 300
Washington, DC
20005-4701
US

Phone Number – 202/293-2450; **Fax Number** – 202/457-8095

Email Contact – jmills@aacte.org; **URL** – http://www.aacte.org/

Leaders – Sharon P. Robinson, President and Chief Executive Officer

Description – The American Association of Colleges for Teacher Education is a national alliance of educator preparation programs dedicated to the highest quality professional development of teachers and school leaders in order to enhance PK-12 student learning. The 800 institutions holding AACTE membership represent public and private colleges and universities in every state, the District of Columbia, the Virgin Islands, Puerto Rico, and Guam. AACTE's reach and influence fuel its mission of serving learners by providing all school personnel with superior training and continuing education. AACTE employs three key strategies to achieve its goals: Advocacy: AACTE maintains a constant presence on Capitol Hill to expand its congressional network and provide members with up-to-the-minute analysis of education policy. Leadership: AACTE believes in consensus building through open and free-flowing dialogue on education matters, consistent support for diverse learners, and serving as a principal authority on issues pertaining to teacher quality. Service: AACTE provides members with vital communication regarding policy issues and events, publications targeting various areas of interest, and unique professional development opportunities.

Membership – Membership in AACTE is institutional with over 5,500 institutional representatives. There are two categories of membership: regular membership and affiliate membership. Regular membership is available to 4-year degree-granting colleges and universities with significant commitment to the preparation of education personnel and that meet all the criteria for regular membership. Affiliate membership is also available. For more information please contact the membership department at membership@aacte.org or 202/293-2450.

Dues – None

Meetings – Annual Members Meeting, New Leadership Academy. State Leaders Institute, and more

Publications -

Name of Organization or Association – American Association of Community Colleges

Acronym – AACC

Address:
One Dupont Circle, NW, Suite 410
Washington, DC
20036-1176
US

Phone Number – (202)728-0200; **Fax Number** – (202)833-9390

Email Contact – nkent@aacc.nche.edu; **URL** – http://www.aacc.nche.edu

Leaders – George R. Boggs, President and CEO

Description – AACC is a national organization representing the nations more than 1,195 community, junior, and technical colleges. Headquartered in Washington, DC, AACC serves as a national voice for the colleges and provides key services in the areas of advocacy, research, information, and leadership development. The nations community colleges serve more than 11 million students annually, almost half (46%) of all US undergraduates.

Membership – 1,195 institutions, 31 corporations, 15 international associates, 79 educational associates, 4 foundations.

Dues – vary by category

Meetings – Annual Convention, April of each year; 2009: April 4–7 Phoenix, AZ

Publications – Community College Journal (bi-mo.); Community College Times (bi-weekly newspaper); Community College Press (books, research and program briefs, and monographs).

Name of Organization or Association – American Association of School Librarians

Acronym – AASL

Address:
50 East Huron Street
Chicago, IL
60611-2795
US

Phone Number – (312) 280-4382 or (800) 545-2433, ext. 4382; **Fax Number** – (312) 280-5276

Email Contact – aasl@ala.org; **URL** – http://www.ala.org/aasl

Leaders – Julie A. Walker, Executive Director

Description – A division of the American Library Association, the mission of the American Association of School Librarians is to advocate excellence, facilitate change, and develop leaders in the school library media field

Membership – 9,500
Dues – Personal membership in ALA (beginning FY 2009, 1st year, $65; 2nd year, $98; 3rd and subsequent yrs., $130) plus $50 for personal membership in AASL. Student, retired, organizational, and corporate memberships are available.

Meetings – National conference every two years; next national conference to be held in 2009.

Publications – School Library Media Research (electronic research journal at http://www.ala.org/aasl/SLMR) Knowledge Quest (print journal and online companion at http://www.ala.org/aasl/kqweb) AASL Hotlinks (email newsletter) Non-serial publications (http://www.ala.org/ala/aasl/aaslpubsandjournals/aaslpublications.cfm)

Name of Organization or Association – American Educational Research Association

Acronym – AERA

Address:
1430 K Street, NW, Suite 1200
Washington, DC
20005
US

Phone Number – (202) 238-3200; **Fax Number** – (202) 238-3250

Email Contact – outreach@aera.net; **URL** – http://www.aera.net

Leaders – Lorraine M. McDonnell, President of the Council, 2008–2009

Description – The American Educational Research Association (AERA) is the national interdisciplinary research association for approximately 25,000 scholars who undertake research in education. Founded in 1916, AERA aims to advance knowledge about education, to encourage scholarly inquiry related to education, and to promote the use of research to improve education and serve the public good. AERA members include educators and administrators; directors of research, testing, or evaluation in federal, state, and local agencies; counselors; evaluators; graduate students; and behavioral scientists. The broad range of disciplines represented includes education, psychology, statistics, sociology, history, economics, philosophy, anthropology, and political science. AERA has more than 160 Special

Interest Groups, including Advanced Technologies for Learning, NAEP Studies, Classroom Assessment, and Fiscal Issues, Policy, and Education Finance.

Membership – 25,000 Regular Members: Eligibility requires satisfactory evidence of active interest in educational research as well as professional training to at least the masters degree level or equivalent. Graduate Student Members: Any graduate student may be granted graduate student member status with the endorsement of a voting member who is a faculty members at the students university. Graduate Students who are employed full-time are not eligible. Graduate Student membership is limited to 5 years.
Dues – vary by category, ranging from $35 for graduate students to $120 for voting members, for one year. See AERA website for complete details: www.aera.net

Meetings – 2009 Annual Meeting, April 13–17, San Diego, California

Publications – Educational Researcher; American Educational Research Journal; Journal of Educational and Behavioral Statistics; Educational Evaluation and Policy Analysis; Review of Research in Education; Review of Educational Research. Books: Handbook of Research on Teaching, 2001. (revised, 4th edition) Ethical Standards of AERA, Cases and Commentary, 2002 Black Education: A Transformative Research and Action Agenda for the New Century, 2005 Studying Teacher Education: The Report of the AERA Panel on Research and Teacher Education, 2006 Standards for Educational and Psychological Testing (revised and expanded, 1999). Co-published by AERA, American Psychological Association, and the National Council on Measurement in Education

Name of Organization or Association – American Foundation for the Blind

Acronym – AFB

Address:
11 Penn Plaza, Suite 300
New York, NY
10001
US

Phone Number – (212)502-7600, (800)AFB-LINE (232-5463);
Fax Number – (212)502-7777

Email Contact – afbinfo@afb.net; **URL** – http://www.afb.org

Leaders – Carl R. Augusto, President; Kelly Parisi, Vice President of Communications

Description – The American Foundation for the Blind (AFB) is a national non-profit that expands possibilities for people with vision loss. AFB's priorities include broadening access to technology; elevating the quality of information and tools for the professionals who serve people with vision loss; and promoting independent and healthy living for people with vision loss by providing them and their families with relevant and timely resources. In addition, AFB's web site serves as a gateway to a wealth of vision loss information and services. AFB is also proud to house the Helen Keller Archives and honor the over forty years that Helen Keller worked tirelessly with AFB. For more information visit us online at www.afb.org.

Membership – None

Dues – None

Meetings – None

Publications – AFB News (free); Journal of Visual Impairment & Blindness; AFB Press Catalog of Publications (free). AccessWorld™; Subscriptions Tel: (800) 232-3044 or (412) 741-1398

Name of Organization or Association – American Library Association

Acronym – ALA

Address:
50 E. Huron St.
Chicago, IL
60611
US

Phone Number – (800) 545-2433; **Fax Number** – (312) 440-9374

Email Contact – library@ala.org; **URL** – http://www.ala.org

Leaders – Keith Michael Fiels, Executive Director

Description – The ALA is the oldest and largest national library association. Its 65,000 members represent all types of libraries: state, public, school, and academic, as well as special libraries serving persons in government, commerce, the armed services, hospitals, prisons, and other institutions. The ALA is the chief advocate of achievement and maintenance of high-quality library information services through protection of the right to read, educating librarians, improving services, and making information widely accessible. See separate entries for the following affiliated and subordinate organizations: American Association of School Librarians, American Library Trustee Association, Association for Library Collections and Technical Services, Association for Library Service to Children, Association of College and Research Libraries, Association of Specialized and Cooperative Library Agencies, Library Administration and Management Association, Library and Information Technology Association, Public Library Association, Reference and User Services Association, Young Adult Library Services Association, and Continuing Library Education Network and Exchange Round Table.

Membership – 65,000 members at present; everyone who cares about libraries is allowed to join the American Library Association.

Dues – Professional rate: $55, first year; $83, second year; third year & renewing: $110 Library Support Staff: $39 Student members: $28 Retirees: $39 International librarians: $66 Trustees: $50 Associate members (those not in the library field): $50

Meetings – Annual Conference: July 10–15, 2009 – Chicago, IL; June 24–30, 2010 – Washington, D.C.; June 23–29, 2011-New Orleans, LA//Midwinter Meeting: January 23–28, 2009 – Denver, CO; January 15–20, 2010 – Boston, MA; January 21–26, 2011 – San Diego, CA

Publications – American Libraries; Booklist; Choice; Book Links.

Name of Organization or Association – Association for Childhood Education International

Acronym – ACEI

Address:
17904 Georgia Ave., Suite 215
Olney, MD
20832
US

Phone Number – (301)570-2111; **Fax Number** – (301)570-2212

Email Contact – headquarters@acei.org; **URL** – http://www.acei.org

Leaders – Diane P. Whitehead, Acting Executive Director

Description – ACEI publications reflect careful research, broad-based views, and consideration of a wide range of issues affecting children from infancy through early adolescence. Many are media-related in nature. The journal (Childhood Education) is essential for teachers, teachers-in-training, teacher educators, day care workers, administrators, and parents. Articles focus on child development and emphasize practical application. Regular departments include book reviews (child and adult); film reviews, pamphlets, software, research, and classroom idea-sparkers. Six issues are published yearly, including a theme issue devoted to critical concerns.

Membership – 10,000

Dues – $45, professional; $29, student; $23, retired; $85, institutional.

Meetings – 2009 Annual Conference, March 18–21, Chicago, IL USA

Publications – Childhood Education (official journal) with ACEI Exchange (insert newsletter); Journal of Research in Childhood Education; professional focus newsletters (Focus on Infants and Toddlers, Focus on Pre-K and K, Focus on Elementary, Focus on Middle School, Focus on Teacher Education, and Focus on Inclusive Education); various books.

Name of Organization or Association – Association for Computers and the Humanities

Acronym – ACH

Address:
[Address]
[City], ON
[Zip Code]
[Country]

Phone Number – [phone number]; **Fax Number** – [fax number]

Email Contact – kretzsh@uga.edu; **URL** – http://www.ach.org/

Leaders – Executive Secretary, ACH

Description – The Association for Computers and the Humanities is an international professional organization. Since its establishment, it has been the major professional society for people working in computer-aided research in literature and language studies, history, philosophy, and other humanities disciplines, and especially research involving the manipulation and analysis of textual materials. The ACH is devoted to disseminating information among its members about work in the field of humanities computing, as well as encouraging the development and dissemination of significant textual and linguistic resources and software for scholarly research.

Membership – 300

Dues – Individual regular member, US $65 Student or Emeritus Faculty member, US $55 Joint membership (for couples), Add US $7

Meetings – Annual meetings held with the Association for Literary and Linguistic Computing.

Publications – ACH Publications: – Literary & Linguistic Computing – Humanist

Name of Organization or Association – Association for Continuing Higher Education

Acronym – ACHE

Address:
OCCE Admin Bldg Rm 233, 1700 Asp Ave
Norman, OK
73072
US

Phone Number – 800-807-2243; **Fax Number** – 405-325-4888

Email Contact – admin@acheinc.org; **URL** – http://www.acheinc.org/

Leaders – James P. Pappas, Ph.D., Executive Vice President

Description – ACHE is an institution-based organization of colleges, universities, and individuals dedicated to the promotion of lifelong learning and excellence in continuing higher education. ACHE encourages professional networks, research, and exchange of information for its members and advocates continuing higher education as a means of enhancing and improving society.

Membership – Approximately 1,600 individuals in approximately 650 institutions

Dues – $80, professional; $495, institutional

Meetings – For a list of Annual and Regional Meetings, see http://www.acheinc.org/annual_conference.html

Publications – Journal of Continuing Higher Education (3/year); Five Minutes with ACHE (newsletter, 10/year); Proceedings (annual).

Name of Organization or Association – Association for Educational Communications and Technology

Acronym – AECT

Address:
1800 N Stonelake Dr., Suite 2
Bloomington, IN
47404
US

Phone Number – (812) 335-7675; **Fax Number** – (812) 335-7678

Email Contact – pharris@aect.org; **URL** – http://www.aect.org

Leaders – Phillip Harris, Executive Director; Ward Cates, Board President

Description – AECT is an international professional association concerned with the improvement of learning and instruction through media and technology. It serves as a central clearinghouse and communications center for its members, who include instructional technologists, library media specialists, religious educators, government media personnel, school administrators and specialists, and training media producers. AECT members also work in the armed forces, public libraries, museums, and other information agencies of many different kinds, including those related to the emerging fields of computer technology. Affiliated organizations include the International Visual Literacy Association (IVLA), Minorities in Media (MIM), New England Educational Media Association (NEEMA), SICET (the Society of International Chinese in Educational Technology), and KSET (the Korean Society for Educational Technology). The ECT Foundation is also related to AECT.

Each of these affiliated organizations has its own listing in the Yearbook. AECT Divisions include: Instructional Design & Development, Information & Technology Management, Training & Performance, Research & Theory, Systemic Change, Distance Learning, Media & Technology, Teacher Education, International, and Multimedia Productions.

Membership – 2,500 members in good standing from K-12, college and university and private sector/government training. Anyone interested can join. There are different memberships available for students, retirees, corporations and international parties. We also have a new option for electronic membership for international affiliates.

Dues – $99.00 standard membership discounts are available for students and retirees. Additional fees apply to corporate memberships or international memberships.

Meetings – Summer Leadership Institute held each July. In 2007 it will be in Chicago, IL. AECT holds an annual Conference each year in October. In 2007, it will be held in Anaheim, CA.

Publications – TechTrends (6/year, free with AECT membership; available by subscription through Springer at www.springeronline.com); Educational Technology Research and Development (6/year $46 members; available by subscription through Springer at www.springeronline.com); Quarterly Review of Distance Education (q., $55 to AECT members); many books; videotapes.

Name of Organization or Association – Association for Experiential Education

Acronym – AEE

Address:
3775 Iris Avenue, Ste 4
Boulder, CO
80301-2043
US

Phone Number – (303)440-8844; **Fax Number** – (303)440-9581

Email Contact – executive@aee.org; **URL** – http://www.aee.org

Leaders – Paul Limoges, Executive Director

Description – AEE is a nonprofit, international, professional organization committed to the development, practice, and evaluation of experiential education in all settings. AEE's vision is to be a leading international organization for the development and application of experiential education principles and methodologies with the intent to create a just and compassionate world by transforming education.

Membership – Nearly 1,500 members in over 30 countries including individuals and organizations with affiliations in education, recreation, outdoor adventure programming, mental health, youth service, physical education, management development training, corrections, programming for people with disabilities, and environmental education.

Dues – $55–$115, individual; $145, family; $275 – $500, organizational

Meetings – AEE Annual Conference in November. Regional Conferences in the Spring.

Publications – The Journal of Experiential Education (3/year); Experience and the Curriculum; Adventure Education; Adventure Therapy; Therapeutic Applications of Adventure Programming; Manual of Accreditation Standards for Adventure Programs; The Theory of Experiential Education, Third Edition; Experiential Learning in Schools and Higher Education; Ethical Issues in Experiential Education, Second Edition; The K.E.Y. (Keep Exploring Yourself) Group: An Experiential Personal Growth Group Manual; Book of Metaphors, Volume II; Women's Voices in Experiential Education; bibliographies, directories of programs, and membership directory. New publications since last year: Exploring the Boundaries of Adventure Therapy; A Guide to Women's Studies in the Outdoors; Administrative Practices of Accredited Adventure Programs; Fundamentals of Experience-Based Training; Wild Adventures: A Guidebook of Activities for Building Connections with Others and the Earth; Truth Zone: An Experimental Approach to Organizational Development; Exploring the Power of Solo, Silence, and Solitude.

Name of Organization or Association – Association for Library and Information Science Education

Acronym – ALISE

Address:
65 E. Wacker Place Suite 1900
Chicago, IL
60612
US

Phone Number – 312-795-0996; **Fax Number** – 312-419-8950

Email Contact – contact@alise.org; **URL** – http://www.alise.org

Leaders – Kathleen Combs, Executive Director

Description – Seeks to advance education for library and information science and produces annual Library and Information Science Education Statistical Report. Open to professional schools offering graduate programs in library and information science; personal memberships open to educators employed in such institutions; other memberships available to interested individuals.

Membership – 500 individuals, 69 institutions

Dues – institutional, sliding scale, $350–2,500; $150 international; personal, $125 full-time; $75 part-time, $40 student, $60 retired

Meetings – Tuesday, January 20, through Friday, January 23, 2009 – Denver, Colorado

Publications – Journal of Education for Library and Information Science; ALISE Directory; Library and Information Science Education Statistical Report.

Name of Organization or Association – Association for Library Collections & Technical Services

Acronym – ALCTS

Address:
50 E. Huron St.
Chicago, IL
60611
US
Phone Number – (312)280-5037; **Fax Number** – (312)280-5033

Email Contact – alcts@ala.org; **URL** – www.ala.org/alcts

Leaders – Charles Wilt, Executive Director

Description – A division of the American Library Association, ALCTS is dedicated to acquisition, identification, cataloging, classification, and preservation of library materials; the development and coordination of the country's library resources; and aspects of selection and evaluation involved in acquiring and developing library materials and resources. Sections include Acquisitions, Cataloging and Classification, Collection Management and Development, Preservation and Reformatting, and Serials.

Membership – 4,800 Membership is open to anyone who has an interest in areas covered by ALCTS.

Dues – $65 plus membership in ALA

Meetings – Annual Conference; Chicago, July 9–15, 2009, Washington, DC, June 24–30, 2010, New Orleans, June 23–29, 2011, Anaheim, June 21–27, 2012.

Publications – Library Resources & Technical Services (q.); ALCTS Newsletter Online (6/year)

Name of Organization or Association – Association for Library Service to Children

Acronym – ALSC

Address:
50 E. Huron St.
Chicago, IL
60611
US

Phone Number – (312)280-2163; **Fax Number** – (312)944-7671

Email Contact – alsc@ala.org; **URL** – http://www.ala.org/alsc

Leaders – Diane Foote

Description – Information about ALSC can be found at. Information on ALSCs various awards, including the nationally known Newbery Medal for authors and the Caldecott Medal for illustrators can be found at. The Association for Library Service to Children develops and supports the profession of children's librarianship by enabling and encouraging its practitioners to provide the best library service to our nations children. The Association for Library Service to Children is interested in the improvement and extension of library services to children in all types of libraries. It is responsible for the evaluation and selection of book and nonbook library materials and for the improvement of techniques of library service to children from pre-school through the eighth grade or junior high school age, when such materials and techniques are intended for use in more than one type of library. Committee membership is open to ALSC members. Full list of ALSC boards and committees can be found at.

Membership – Over 4,000 members

Dues – $45 plus membership in ALA; $18 plus membership in ALA for library school students; $25 plus membership in ALA for retirees

Meetings – National Institute, Fall.

Publications – Children and Libraries: The Journal of the Association for Library Service to Children (3x per year); ALSConnect (quarterly newsletter). ALSC Blog -.

Name of Organization or Association – Association of American Publishers

Acronym – AAP

Address:
50 F Street, NW, Suite 400
Washington, DC

20001
US

Phone Number – (202)347-3375; **Fax Number** – (202)347-3690

Email Contact – aoconnor@publishers.org; **URL** – http://www.publishers.org

Leaders – Tom Allen, President and CEO (DC); Judith Platt, Director of Communications/Public Affairs

Description – The Association of American Publishers is the national trade association of the US book publishing industry. AAP was created in 1970 through the merger of the American Book Publishers Council, a trade publishing group, and the American Textbook Publishers Institute, a group of educational publishers. AAPs more than 300 members include most of the major commercial book publishers in the United States, as well as smaller and nonprofit publishers, university presses, and scholarly societies. AAP members publish hardcover and paperback books in every field and a range of educational materials for the elementary, secondary, postsecondary, and professional markets. Members of the Association also produce computer software and electronic products and services, such as online databases and CD-ROMs. AAPs primary concerns are the protection of intellectual property rights in all media, the defense of free expression and freedom to publish at home and abroad, the management of new technologies, development of education markets and funding for instructional materials, and the development of national and global markets for its members products.

Membership – Regular Membership in the Association is open to all US companies actively engaged in the publication of books, journals, loose-leaf services, computer software, audiovisual materials, databases and other electronic products such as CD-ROM and CD-I, and similar products for educational, business and personal use. This includes producers, packagers, and co-publishers who coordinate or manage most of the publishing process involved in creating copyrightable educational materials for distribution by another organization. "Actively engaged" means that the candidate must give evidence of conducting an ongoing publishing business with a significant investment in the business. Each Regular Member firm has one vote, which is cast by an official representative or alternate designated by the member company. Associate Membership (non-voting) is available to US not-for-profit organizations that otherwise meet the qualifications for regular membership. A special category of associate membership is open to nonprofit university presses. Affiliate Membership is a non-voting membership open to paper manufacturers, suppliers, consultants, and other non-publishers directly involved in the industry.

Dues – Dues are assessed on the basis of annual sales revenue from the print and electronic products listed above (under Regular Membership), but not from services or equipment. To maintain confidentiality, data is reported to an independent agent.

Meetings – Annual Meeting (February), Small and Independent Publishers Meeting (February), School Division Annual Meeting (January), PSP Annual Meeting (February)

Publications – AAP Monthly Report

Name of Organization or Association – Association of College and Research Libraries

Acronym – ACRL

Address:
50 E. Huron St.
Chicago, IL
60611-2795
US

Phone Number – (312)280-2523; **Fax Number** – (312)280-2520

Email Contact – acrl@ala.org; **URL** – http://www.ala.org/acrl

Leaders – Mary Ellen Davis, Executive Director

Description – The Association of College and Research Libraries (ACRL), the largest division of the American Library Association, is a professional association of academic librarians and other interested individuals. It is dedicated to enhancing the ability of academic library and information professionals to serve the information needs of the higher education community and to improve learning, teaching, and research. ACRL is the only individual membership organization in North America that develops programs, products and services to meet the unique needs of academic and research librarians Information on ACRLs various committees, task forces, discussion groups, and sections can be found at. Information on ACRLs various awards can be found at.

Membership – With over 13,000 members, is a national organization of academic and research libraries and librarians working with all types of academic libraries – community and junior college, college, and university – as well as comprehensive and specialized research libraries and their professional staffs.

Dues – $55 plus membership in ALA; $35 plus membership in ALA for library school students and for retirees SECTIONS (two at no charge, additional sections $5 each): African American Studies Librarians (AFAS); Anthropology and Sociology Section (ANSS); Arts Section; Asian, African, and Middle Eastern Section (AAMES); College Libraries Section (CLS); Community and Junior College Libraries Section (CJCLS); Distance Learning Section (DLS); Education and Behavioral Sciences Section (EBSS); Instruction Section (IS); Law and Political Science Section (LPSS); Literatures in English (LES); Rare Books and Manuscripts Section (RBMS); Science and Technology Section (STS); Slavic and East European

Section (SEES); University Libraries Section (ULS); Western European Studies Section (WESS); Women's Studies Section (WSS)

Meetings – ACRL 14th National Conference – March 12–15, 2009, Seattle, WA, Theme: Pushing the Edge: Explore, Engage, Extend

Publications – List of all print and electronic publications at ACRLog: Blogging for and by academic and research librarians. ACRL Insider – The mission of the ACRL Insider Weblog is to keep the world current and informed on the activities, services, and programs of the Association of College & Research Libraries, including publications, events, conferences, and eLearning opportunities. ACRL Podcasts – Academic Library Trends & Statistics (annually). Statistics data for all academic libraries reporting throughout the US and Canada. Trends data examines a different subject each year. Available from ALA Order Fulfillment, P.O. Box 932501, Atlanta, GA 31193-2501 and from the ALA Online Store. Choice: Editor and Publisher, Irving E. Rockwood. ISSN 0009-4978. Published monthly. Only available by subscription: $315 per year for North America; $365 outside North America. CHOICE Reviews on Cards: $390 per year for North America – U.S., Canada, and Mexico; $440 outside North America. ChoiceReviews.online: See pricing for site licenses at. College & Research Libraries (6 bi-monthly journal issues). Sent to all ACRL members. Subscriptions, $70 – US. $75 – Canada and other PUAS countries. $80 – Other foreign countries. College & Research Libraries News (11 monthly issues, July–Aug. combined). Sent to all ACRL members. Subscriptions: $46 – US. $52 – Canada and other PUAS countries. $57 – Other foreign countries. RBM: A Journal of Rare Books, Manuscripts, and Cultural Heritage. (2 issues). Subscriptions, $42 – US. $47 Canada and other PUAS countries. $58 – Other foreign countries.

Name of Organization or Association – Association of Specialized and Cooperative Library Agencies

Acronym – ASCLA

Address:
50 E. Huron St.
Chicago, IL
60611
US

Phone Number – (800)545-2433, ext. 4398.; **Fax Number** – (312)944-8085

Email Contact – ascla@ala.org; **URL** – http://www.ala.org/ascla

Leaders – Executive Director

Description – A division of the American Library Association, ASCLA represents state library agencies, multitype library organizations, independent libraries and libraries serving special populations to promote the development of coordinated library services with equal access to information and material for all persons.

Membership – 917

Dues – You must be a member of ALA to join ASCLA. See www.ala. org/membership for most current ALA dues rates. ASCLA individual membership: $40; organization membership: $50; State Library Agency dues: $500.

Meetings – ASCLA meets in conjunction with the American Library Association.

Publications – Interface, quarterly online newsletter; see Web site http://www.ala.org/ascla for list of other publications.

Name of Organization or Association – Canadian Library Association/ Association canadienne des bibliothèques

Acronym – CLA/ACB

Address:
328 Frank Street
Ottawa, ON
K2P 0X8
Canada

Phone Number – (613)232-9625; **Fax Number** – (613)563-9895

Email Contact – info@cla.ca; **URL** – http://www.cla.ca

Leaders – Linda Sawden Harris, Manager of Financial Services; Judy Green, Manager, Marketing & Communications; Don Butcher, Executive Director

Description – Our Mission CLA/ACB is my advocate and public voice, educator and network. We build the Canadian library and information community and advance its information professionals. Our Values. We believe that libraries and the principles of intellectual freedom and free universal access to information are key components of an open and democratic society. Diversity is a major strength of our Association. An informed and knowledgeable membership is central in achieving library and information policy goals. Effective advocacy is based upon understanding the social, cultural, political and historical contexts in which libraries and information services function. Our Operating Principles. A large and active membership is crucial to our success Our Association will have a governance structure that is reviewed regularly and ensures that all sectors of the membership are represented. Our Association will be efficiently run, fiscally responsible and financially independent Technology will be used in efficient and effective ways to further our goals. Our Association places a high value on each of our members. Our Association will ensure that its staff are provided with tools and training necessary for them to excel at their jobs. Our Associations strategic plan will be continually reviewed and updated.

Membership – The Associations five constituent divisions are: Canadian Association for School Libraries (CASL), including the School Library Administrators (SLAS) section (approx. 200 members) Canadian Association of College and University Libraries (CACUL), including the Community and Technical College (CTCL) section (approx. 800 members) Canadian Association of Public Libraries (CAPL), including the Canadian Association of Children's Librarians (CACL) section (approx. 650 members) Canadian Association of Special Libraries and Information Services (CASLIS), with chapters in Calgary, Edmonton, Manitoba, Ottawa, Toronto and Atlantic Canada (approx. 590 members) Canadian Library Trustees Association (approx. 180 members)

Dues – $ 25–$ 1000

Meetings – 2009 CLA/ACB National Conference 7 Tradeshow, Montreal, May 29–June 1

Publications – Feliciter (membership & subscription magazine, 6/year).

Name of Organization or Association – Close Up Foundation

Acronym – CUF

Address:
44 Canal Center Plaza
Alexandria, VA
22314
US

Phone Number – (703)706-3300; **Fax Number** – (703)706-3329

Email Contact – cutv@closeup.org; **URL** – http://www.closeup.org

Leaders – Timothy S. Davis, President & CEO

Description – A nonprofit, non-partisan civic engagement organization dedicated to providing individuals of all backgrounds with the knowledge, skills, and confidence to actively participate in democracy. Each year, Close Up brings 15,000 secondary and middle school students and teachers to Washington, DC for week-long government studies programs. In addition, Close Up produces an array of multimedia civic education resources for use in classrooms and households nationwide, including Close Up at the Newseum, a weekly youth-focused current affairs program C-SPAN.

Membership – Any motivated middle or high school student who wants to learn about government and American history is eligible to come on our programs. No dues or membership fees.

Dues – Tuition is required to participate on Close Up educational travel programs. A limited amount of tuition assistance is available to qualified students through the Close Up Fellowship program. With a designated number of students, teachers receive a fellowship that covers the adult tuition and transportation price. Please contact 1-800-CLOSE UP for more information.

Meetings – Meetings take place during week-long educational programs in Washington, DC

Publications – Current Issues (new edition produced annually); The Bill of Rights: A Users Guide; Perspectives; International Relations; The American Economy; Face the Music: Copyright, Art & the Digital Age; documentaries on domestic and foreign policy issues.

Name of Organization or Association – Computer Assisted Language Instruction Consortium

Acronym – CALICO

Address:
214 Centennial Hall, Texas State University, 601 University Dr.
San Marcos, TX
78666
US

Phone Number – (512)245-1417; **Fax Number** – (512)245-9089

Email Contact – info@calico.org; **URL** – http://calico.org

Leaders – Robert Fischer, Executive Director

Description – CALICO is devoted to the dissemination of information on the application of technology to language teaching and language learning.

Membership – 1,000 members from United States and 20 foreign countries. Anyone interested in the development and use of technology in the teaching/learning of foreign languages are invited to join.

Dues – $65 annual/individual

Meetings – 2007, Texas State University, San Marcos; 2008, University of San Francisco

Publications – CALICO Journal (three times a year), CALICO Monograph Series (Monograph V, 2006; Monograph VI, 2007).

Name of Organization or Association – Consortium of College and University Media Centers

Acronym – CCUMC

Address:
1200 Communications Bldg., Iowa State University
Ames, IA
50011-3243
US

Phone Number – (515)294-1811; **Fax Number** – (515)294-8089

Email Contact – ccumc@ccumc.org; **URL** – www.ccumc.org

Leaders – Executive Director (currently vacant)

Description – CCUMC is a professional group of higher education media personnel whose purpose is to improve education and training through the effective use of educational media. Assists educational and training users in making films, video, and educational media more accessible. Fosters cooperative planning among university media centers. Gathers and disseminates information on improved procedures and new developments in instructional technology and media center management.

Membership – 750 individuals at 325 institutions/corporations: Institutional Memberships – Individuals within an institution of higher education who are associated with the support of instruction and presentation technologies in a media center and/or technology support service. Corporate Memberships – Individuals within a corporation, firm, foundation, or other commercial or philanthrophic whose business or activity is in support of the purposes and objectives of CCUMC. Associate Memberships – Individuals from a public library, religious, governmental, or other organizations not otherwise eligible for other categories of membership. Student Memberships – Any student in an institution of higher education who is not eligible for an institutional membership.

Dues – Institutional or Corporate Membership: $325 for 1–2 persons, $545 for 3–4 persons, $795 for 5–6 persons, $130 each additional person beyond six Student Membership: $55 per person Associate Membership: $325 per person

Meetings – 2007 Conference, Gainesville Florida, October 18–22, 2007

Publications – College & University Media Review (journal – semi-annual) Leader (newsletter – 3 issues annually in electronic format)

Name of Organization or Association – Council for Exceptional Children

Acronym – CEC

Address:
1110 N. Glebe Rd. #300
Arlington, VA
22201
US

Phone Number – (703)620-3660. TTY: (703)264-9446;
Fax Number – (703)264-9494

Email Contact – cec@cec.sped.org.; **URL** – http://www.cec.sped.org

Leaders – Bruce Ramirez, Executive Director

Description – CEC is the largest international organization dedicated to improving the educational success of students with disabilities and/or gifts and talents. CEC advocates for governmental policies supporting special education, sets professional standards, provides professional development, and helps professionals obtain conditions and resources necessary for high-quality educational services for their students.

Membership – Teachers, administrators, professors, related services providers (occupational therapists, school psychologists...), and parents. CEC has approximately 50,000 members

Dues – $111 a year

Meetings – Annual Convention & Expo attracting approximately 6,000 special educators

Publications – Journals, newsletters books, and videos with information on new research findings, classroom practices that work, and special education publications. (See also the ERIC Clearinghouse on Disabilities and Gifted Education.)

Name of Organization or Association – Delete

Acronym – NASTA

Address:
120 S. Federal Place, Room 206
Santa Fe, NM
87501
US

Phone Number – 505.827.1801; **Fax Number** – 505.827.1826

Email Contact – webmaster@nasta.org; **URL** – http://www.nasta.org

Leaders – David P. Martinez, President

Description – NASTAs purposes are to (1) foster a spirit of mutual helpfulness in adoption, purchase, and distribution of instructional materials; (2) arrange for study and review of textbook specifications; (3) authorize special surveys, tests, and studies; and (4) initiate action leading to better quality instructional materials. Services provided include a working knowledge of text construction, monitoring lowest prices, sharing adoption information, identifying trouble spots, and discussions in the industry. The members of NASTA meet to discuss the textbook adoption process and to improve the quality of the instructional materials used in the elementary, middle, and high schools. NASTA is not affiliated with any parent organization and has no permanent address.

Membership – Textbook administrators from each of the 21 states that adopt instructional material at the state level on an annual basis.

Dues – $25 annually per individual

Meetings – NASTA meets annually during the month of July

Publications – Manufacturing Standards and Specifications for Textbooks (MSST)

Name of Organization or Association – East–West Center

Acronym – none

Address:
1601 East-West Rd.
Honolulu, HI
96848-1601
US

Phone Number – (808)944-7111; **Fax Number** – (808)944-7376

Email Contact – ewcinfo@EastWestCenter.org;
URL – http://www.eastwestcenter.org/

Leaders – Dr. Charles E. Morrison, President

Description – The US Congress established the East-West Center in 1960 with a mandate to foster mutual understanding and cooperation among the governments and peoples of Asia, the Pacific, and the United States. Officially known as the Center for Cultural and Technical Interchange Between East and West, it is a public, nonprofit institution with an international board of governors. Funding for the center comes from the US government, with additional support provided by private agencies, individuals, and corporations, and several Asian and Pacific governments. The Center, through research, education, dialog, and outreach, provides a neutral meeting ground where people with a wide range of perspectives exchange views on topics of regional concern. Scholars, government and business leaders, educators, journalists, and other professionals from throughout the region annually work with

Center staff to address issues of contemporary significance in such areas as international economics and politics, the environment, population, energy, the media, and Pacific islands development.

Membership – The East–West Center is not a membership-based institution. However, our alumni organization, The East–West Center Association (EWCA), is an international network of professionals who have a past affiliation with the East–West Center. Regardless of length of stay or type of participation, all are automatically members (associates) of the EWCA. There are no membership fees or other requirements to participate in the EWCA.

Dues – None

Meetings – Events are listed on our Website, visit: eastwestcenter.org/events

Publications – East–West Center expertise and research findings are published by the East–West Center and by presses and collaborating organizations throughout the region and the world. Publications address a range of critical issues in the Asia Pacific region. The East–West Center sponsors or publishes several series, from short papers to books (see below). For more information about EWC publications, visit: http://www.eastwestcenter.org/publications/ The Asia Pacific Bulletin (APB), produced by the East–West Center in Washington, publishes summaries of Congressional Study Groups, conferences, seminars, and visitor roundtables, as well as short articles and opinion pieces. APB summaries are always two pages or less, designed for the busy professional or policymaker to capture the essence of dialogue and debate on issues of concern in US-Asia relations. East–West Dialogue, an online publication, is an interactive forum for discussion and debate of key issues in Asia-US economic relations. The East–West Dialogue seeks to develop and promote innovative policy, business, and civic initiatives to enhance this critical partnership. Contemporary Issues in Asia and the Pacific is a book series that focuses on issues of contemporary significance in the Asia Pacific region, most notably political, social, cultural, and economic change. The series seeks books that focus on topics of regional importance, on problems that cross disciplinary boundaries, and that have the capacity to reach academic and other interested audiences. The Contemporary Issues in Asia and the Pacific book series is published by Stanford University Press. The Studies in Asian Security book series, published by Stanford University Press and sponsored by the East–West Center, promotes analysis, understanding, and explanation of the dynamics of domestic, transnational, and international security challenges in Asia. The peer-reviewed publications in the Series analyze contemporary security issues and problems to clarify debates in the scholarly community, provide new insights and perspectives, and identify new research and policy directions. With a Series committee comprising individuals from diverse theoretical persuasions who have undertaken extensive work on Asian security, books in the Studies in Asian Security series are designed to encourage original and rigorous scholarship, and seek to engage scholars, educators, and practitioners. Policy Studies presents scholarly analysis of key contemporary domestic and international political, economic, and strategic issues affecting Asia in a policy relevant manner. Written for the policy community, academics, journalists, and the informed public, the peer-reviewed publications in this series provide new policy insights and perspectives based on extensive fieldwork and rigorous scholarship. Pacific Islands Policy examines critical issues, problems, and opportunities that are relevant to the Pacific Islands region. The series is intended to influence the policy process, affect how people understand a range of contemporary Pacific issues, and help fashion solutions. A central aim of the series is to encourage scholarly analysis of economic, political, social, and cultural issues in a manner that will advance common understanding of current challenges and policy responses. East–West Center Special Reports present in-depth analysis and exposition that offer insights to specialists yet are accessible to readers outside the author's discipline. These peer-reviewed publications address diverse topics relevant to current and emerging policy debates in the Asia Pacific region and the United States. Papers in the Asia Pacific Issues series address topics of broad interest and significant impact relevant to current and emerging policy debates. These eight-page, peer-reviewed papers are accessible to readers outside the author's discipline.

Name of Organization or Association – Education Development Center, Inc.

Acronym – EDC

Address:
55 Chapel St.
Newton, MA
02458-1060
US

Phone Number – (617)969-7100; **Fax Number** – (617)969-5979

Email Contact – emarshall@edc.org; **URL** – http://www.edc.org

Leaders – Dr. Luther S. Luedtke, President and CEO

Description – Education Development Center, Inc. (EDC) is an international, non-profit organization that conducts and applies research to advance learning and promote health. EDC currently manages 325 projects in 50 countries. Our award-winning programs and products, developed in collaboration with partners around the globe, address nearly every critical need in society, including early child development, K-12 education, health promotion, workforce preparation, community development, learning technologies, basic and adult education, institutional reform, medical ethics, and social justice.

Membership – Not applicable

Dues – Not applicable

Meetings – Not applicable

Publications – (1) Annual Report (2) Mosaic, an EDC Report Series (3) EDC Update, an EDC Newsletter (4) EDC Online Report (5) Detailed Web site with vast archive of publications, technical reports, and evaluation studies.

Name of Organization or Association – Educational Communications, Inc., Environmental and Media Projects of

Acronym – None
Address:
P.O. Box 351419
Los Angeles, CA
90035
US

Phone Number – (310)559-9160; **Fax Number** – (310)559-9160

Email Contact – ECNP@aol.com; **URL** – www.ecoprojects.org

Leaders – Nancy Pearlman, Executive Director and Producer

Description – Educational Communications is dedicated to enhancing the quality of life on this planet and provides radio and television programs about the environment. Serves as a clearinghouse on ecological issues. Programming is available on 100 stations in 25 states. These include: ECONEWS television series and ENVIRONMENTAL DIRECTIONS radio series. ECO-TRAVEL Television shows focus on ecotourism. Services provided include a speaker's bureau, award-winning public service announcements, radio and television documentaries, volunteer and intern opportunities, and input into the decision-making process. Its mission is to educate the public about both the problems and the solutions in the environment. Other projects include the Ecology Center of Southern California (a regional conservation group), Project Ecotourism, Humanity and the Planet, Earth Cultures (providing ethnic dance performances), and more

Membership – $20.00 for yearly subscription to the Compendium Newsletter

Dues – $20 for regular. All donations accepted

Meetings – as needed

Publications – Compendium Newsletter (bi-monthly newsletter) Environmental Directions radio audio cassettes, (1,550 produced to date) ECONEWS and ECO-TRAVEL television series (over 550 shows in the catalog available on 3/4″, VHS, and DVD)

Name of Organization or Association – Edvantia, Inc. (formerly AEL, Inc.)

Acronym – Edvantia

Address:
P.O. Box 1348
Charleston, WV
25325-1348
US

Phone Number – (304)347-0400, (800)624-9120; **Fax Number** – (304)347-0487

Email Contact – carla.mcclure@edvantia.org; **URL** – http://www.edvantia.org

Leaders – Dr. Doris L. Redfield, President and CEO
Description – Edvantia is a nonprofit education research and development corporation, founded in 1966, that partners with practitioners, education agencies, publishers, and service providers to improve learning and advance student success. Edvantia provides clients with a range of services, including research, evaluation, professional development, and consulting.

Membership – None

Dues – None

Meetings – None

Publications – The Edvantia Electronic Library contains links to free online tools and information created by staff on a wide array of education-related topics. Visitors to the Edvantia Web site can also access archived webcasts and webinars and sign up for a free monthly newsletter.

Name of Organization or Association – ENC Learning Inc.

Acronym – ENC

Address:
1275 Kinnear Rd
Columbus, OH
43212
US

Phone Number – 800-471-1045; **Fax Number** – 877-656-0315

Email Contact – info@goenc.com; **URL** – www.goenc.com

Leaders – Dr. Len Simutis, Director

Description – ENC provides K–12 teachers and other educators with a central source of information on mathematics and science curriculum materials, particularly those that support education reform. Among ENCs products and services is ENC Focus, a free online magazine on topics of interest to math and science educators. Users include K–12 teachers, other educators, policymakers, and parents.

Membership – ENC is a subscription-based online resource for K-12 educators. Subscriptions are available for schools, school districts, college and universities, and individuals. Information for subscribers is available at www.goenc.com/subscribe

Dues – None

Meetings – None

Publications – ENC Focus is available as an online publication in two formats: ENC Focus on K-12 Mathematics, and ENC Focus on K-12 Science. Each is accessible via www.goenc.com/focus

Name of Organization or Association – Film Arts Foundation

Acronym – Film Arts

Address:
145 9th St. #101
San Francisco, CA
94103
US

Phone Number – (415)552-8760; **Fax Number** – (415)552-0882

Email Contact – info@filmarts.org; **URL** – http://www.filmarts.org

Leaders – K.C. Price – Interim Executive Director

Description – Service organization that supports the success of independent film and video makers. Some services are for members only and some open to the public. These include low-cost classes in all aspects of filmmaking; affordable equipment rental (including digital video, 16 mm, Super-8, Final Cut Pro editing, ProTools mix room, optical printer, etc); Resource Library; free legal consultation; bi-monthly magazine Release Print; grants program; year-round events and exhibitions; non-profit sponsorship; regional and national advocacy on media issues, and significant discounts on film- and video-related products and services.

Membership – nearly 3,000

Dues – $45 for "Subscriber" level benefits including bi-monthly magazine, discounts, and access to libraries and online databases. $65 for full "Filmmaker" benefits including above plus: significant discounts on classes and equipment rentals, eligibility for nonprofit fiscal sponsorship, free legal consultation and filmmaking consultation.

Meetings – Annual membership meeting and regular networking events.

Publications – The award-winning bi-monthly magazine Release Print

Name of Organization or Association – Great Plains National ITV Library

Acronym – GPN

Address:
P.O. Box 80669
Lincoln, NE
68501-0669
US

Phone Number – (402)472-2007, (800)228-4630; **Fax Number** – (800)306-2330

Email Contact – npba@umd.edu; **URL** – http://shopgpn.com/

Leaders – Stephen C. Lenzen, Executive Director

Description – Produces and distributes educational media, video, CD-ROMs and DVDs, prints and Internet courses. Available for purchase for audiovisual or lease for broadcast use.

Membership – Membership not required.

Dues – There are no dues required.

Meetings – There are no meetings. We do attend subject specific conventions to promote our products.

Publications – GPN Educational Video Catalogs by curriculum areas; periodic brochures. Complete listing of GPN's product line is available via the Internet along with online purchasing. Free previews available.

Name of Organization or Association – Health Sciences Communications Association

Acronym – HeSCA

Address:
One Wedgewood Dr., Suite 27
Jewett City, CT
06351-2428
US

Phone Number – (203)376-5915; **Fax Number** – (203)376-6621

Email Contact – hesca@hesca.org; **URL** – http://www.hesca.org/

Leaders – Ronald Sokolowski, Executive Director

Description – An affiliate of AECT, HeSCA is a nonprofit organization dedicated to the sharing of ideas, skills, resources, and techniques to enhance communications and educational technology in the health sciences. It seeks to nurture the professional growth of its members; serve as a professional focal point for those engaged in health sciences communications; and convey the concerns, issues, and concepts of health sciences communications to other organizations that influence and are affected by the profession. International in scope and diverse in membership, HeSCA is supported by medical and veterinary schools, hospitals, medical associations, and businesses where media are used to create and disseminate health information.

Membership – 150.

Dues – $150, indiv.; $195, institutional ($150 additional institutional dues); $60, retiree; $75, student; $1,000, sustaining. All include subscriptions to the journal and newsletter.

Meetings – Annual meetings, May–June.

Publications – Journal of Biocommunications; Feedback (newsletter)

Name of Organization or Association – Institute for the Future

Acronym – IFTF

Address:
124 University Avenue, 2nd Floor
Palo Alto, CA
94301
US

Phone Number – (650)854-6322; **Fax Number** – (650)854-7850

Email Contact – info@iftf.org; **URL** – http://www.iftf.org

Leaders – Dale Eldredge, COO

Description – The Institute for the Future (IFTF) is an independent nonprofit research group. We work with organizations of all kinds to help them make better, more informed decisions about the future. We provide the foresight to create insights that lead to action. We bring a combination of tools, methodologies, and a deep understanding of emerging trends and discontinuities to our work with companies, foundations, and government agencies. We take an explicitly global approach to strategic planning, linking macro trends to local issues in such areas as: * Work and daily life * Technology and society * Health and health care * Global business trends * Changing consumer society The Institute is based in California's Silicon Valley, in a community at the crossroads of technological innovation, social experimentation, and global interchange. Founded in 1968 by a group of former RAND Corporation researchers with a grant from the Ford Foundation to take leading-edge research methodologies into the public and business sectors, the IFTF is committed to building the future by understanding it deeply.

Membership – Become a Member. To become a member of IFTF, companies and organizations can join one or more of our membership programs or contract with us for private work. Each membership program offers a distinct set of deliverables at different membership prices and enrollment terms. Please visit the individual program sites for more detailed information on a particular program. For more information on membership contact Sean Ness at sness@iftf.org or 650-854-6322. * Ten-Year Forecast Program * Technology Horizons Program * Health Horizons Program * Custom Private Work

Dues – Corporate-wide memberships are for one year periods: * Ten-Year Forecast – $15,000/year * Technology Horizons – $65,000/year * Health Horizons – $65,000/year At present, we do not have university, individual or small-company programs set up. For those companies that support our research programs, we will often conduct custom research.

Meetings – Several a year, for supporting members.

Publications – IFTF blogs * Future Now – http://future.iftf.org – emerging technologies and their social implications * Virtual China – http://www.virtual-china.org – an exploration of virtual experiences and environments in and about China * Future of Marketing – http://fom.iftf.org – emerging technology, global change, and the future of consumers and marketing * Ten-Year Forecast (members only) – http://blogger.iftf.org/tyf – a broad scan of the leading edge of change in business, government, and the global community * Technology Horizons (members only) – http://blogger.iftf.org/tech – emerging technologies and their implications for business, society and family life

Name of Organization or Association – Instructional Technology Council

Acronym – ITC

Address:
One Dupont Cir., NW, Suite 360
Washington, DC
20036-1143
US

Phone Number – (202)293-3110; **Fax Number** – (202)822-5014

Email Contact – cmullins@itcnetwork.org; **URL** – http://www.itcnetwork.org

Leaders – Christine Mullins, Executive Director

Description – An affiliated council of the American Association of Community Colleges established in 1977, the Instructional Technology Council (ITC) provides leadership, information and resources to expand access to, and enhance learning through, the effective use of technology. ITC represents higher education institutions in the United States and Canada that use distance learning technologies. ITC members receive a subscription to the ITC News and ITC listserv with information on what's happening in distance education, participation in ITCs professional development audioconference series, distance learning grants information, updates on distance learning legislation, discounts to attend the annual e-Learning Conference which features more than 80 workshops and seminars.

Membership – Members include single institutions and multi-campus districts; regional and statewide systems of community, technical and two-year colleges; for-profit organizations; four-year institutions; and, nonprofit organizations that are interested or involved in instructional telecommunications. Members use a vast array of ever-changing technologies for distance learning. They often combine different systems according to students needs. The technologies they use and methods of teaching include: audio and video conferences, cable television, compressed and full-motion video, computer networks, fiber optics, interactive videodisc, ITFS, microwave, multimedia, public television, satellites, teleclasses, and telecourses.

Dues – $450, Institutional; $750, Corporate

Meetings – Annual e-Learning Conference

Publications – Quality Enhancing Practices in Distance Education: Vol. 2 Student Services; Quality Enhancing Practices in Distance Education: Vol. 1 Teaching and Learning; New Connections: A Guide to Distance Education (2nd ed.); New Connections: A College President's Guide to Distance Education; Digital Video: A Handbook for Educators; Faculty Compensation and Support Issues in Distance Education; ITC News (monthly publication/newsletter); ITC Listserv.

Name of Organization or Association – International Association for Language Learning Technology

Acronym – IALLT

Address:
Instr. Media Svcs, Concordia Coll.
Moorhead, MN
56562
US

Phone Number – (218) 299-3464; **Fax Number** – (218) 299-3246

Email Contact – business@iallt.org; **URL** – http://iallt.org

Leaders – Mikle Ledgerwood, President; Ron Balko, Treasurer

Description – IALLT is a professional organization whose members provide leadership in the development, integration, evaluation and management of instructional technology for the teaching and learning of language, literature, and culture.

Membership – 400 members Membership/Subscription Categories * Educational Member: for people working in an academic setting such as a school, college or university. These members have voting rights. * Full-time Student Member: for full-time students interested in membership. Requires a signature of a voting member to verify student status. These members have voting rights. * Commercial Member: for those working for corporations interested in language learning and technology. This category includes for example language laboratory vendors, software and textbook companies. * Library Subscriber: receive our journals for placement in libraries.

Dues – 1 year: $50, voting member; $25, student; $60, library subscription; $200 commercial. 2 year: $90, voting member; $380 commercial.

Meetings – Biennial IALLT conferences treat the entire range of topics related to technology in language learning as well as management and planning. IALLT also sponsors sessions at conferences of organizations with related interests, including CALICO and ACTFL

Publications – IALLT Journal of Language Learning Technologies (2 times annually); materials for language lab management and design, language teaching and technology. Visit our website for details. http://iallt.org

Name of Organization or Association – International Association of School Librarianship

Acronym – IASL

Address:
PO Box 83
Zillmere, QLD
4034
Australia

Phone Number – 61 7 3216 5785; **Fax Number** – 61 7 3633 0570

Email Contact – iasl@kb.com.au; **URL** – www.iasl-slo.org/

Leaders – Peter Genco-President; Karen Bonanno-Executive Secretary

Description – Seeks to encourage development of school libraries and library programs throughout the world; promote professional preparation and continuing education of school librarians; achieve collaboration among school libraries of the world; foster relationships between school librarians and other professionals connected with children and youth and to coordinate activities, conferences, and other projects in the field of school librarianship.

Membership – 550 plus

Dues – $50 Zone A (e.g. United States, Canada, Western Europe, Japan) $35 Zone B (e.g. Eastern Europe, Latin America, Middle East) $20 Zone C (e.g. Angola, India, Bulgaria, China) Based on GNP
Meetings – Annual Conference, Lisbon, Portugal, July 2006

Publications – IASL Newsletter (3/year); School Libraries Worldwide (semi-annual); Conference Professionals and Research Papers (annual)

Name of Organization or Association – International Center of Photography

Acronym – ICP

Address:
1114 Avenue of the Americas at 43rd Street
New York, NY
10036
US

Phone Number – (212)857-0045; **Fax Number** – (212)857-0090

Email Contact – info@icp.org; **URL** – http://www.icp.org

Leaders – Willis Hartshorn, Director; Phyllis Levine, Director of Communications.

Description – Located on a dynamic two-part campus in midtown Manhattan, the International Center of Photography (ICP) stands amongst the nation's foremost museums dedicated to preserving the past and ensuring the future of the art of photography. One of the largest facilities of its kind, ICP presents changing exhibitions of the finest works of some of the most talented photographers in the world. With over 20 exhibitions each year, ICP presents an extensive array of historical and contemporary photographs, revealing the power and diversity of the medium from documentary photography to digital imaging. The School of the International Center of Photography fosters study of the history, techniques, aesthetics, and practices of photography in a wide range of programs: continuing education classes; two full-time certificate programs; a Master of Fine Arts program in collaboration with Bard College, Master of Arts and Master of Fine Arts degree programs in conjunction with NYU; Digital Media Program; lectures; and symposia.

Membership – 4,430

Dues – Current levels available on request.

Meetings – The ICP Infinity Awards (annual–2007 is the 23rd)

Publications – Martin Munkacsi; Ecotopia; Atta Kim: ON-AIR; Snap Judgments: New Positions in Contemporary African Photography; African American Vernacular Photography: Selections from the Daniel Cowin Collection; Modernist Photography: Selections from the Daniel Cowin Collection; Young America. The Daguerreotypes of Southworth and Hawes; and others!

Name of Organization or Association – International Council for Educational Media

Acronym – ICEM

Address:
Postfach 114
Vienna, None
A-1011
Austria

Phone Number – +43 660 5113241; **Fax Number** – None

Email Contact – lylt@a1.net; **URL** – www.icem-cime.org

Leaders – John Hedberg, President; Ray Laverty, Secretary General

Description – Welcome to ICEM Our purposes are: * To provide a channel for the international exchange and evaluation of information, experience and materials in the field of educational media as they apply to pre-school, primary and secondary education, to technical and vocational, industrial and commercial training, teacher training, continuing and distance education. * To foster international liaison among individuals and organizations with professional responsibility in the field of educational media. * To cooperate with other international organizations in the development and application of educational technology for practice, research, production, and distribution in this field.

Membership – What are the main advantages of ICEM membership? IICEM membership enables those professionally involved in the production, distribution and use of media in teaching and learning to establish a broad network of contacts with educators, researchers, managers, producers and distributors of educational media from around the world. It also provides opportunities to discuss topics of mutual concern in an atmosphere of friendship and trust, to plan and carry out co-productions, to compare and exchange ideas and experiences, to keep abreast of the latest developments, and to work together towards the improvement of education on an international level. Membership in ICEM includes a subscription to the ICEM quarterly journal, Educational Media International, an entry in the Who's who on the ICEM Webpage, registration at ICEM events and activities either free of charge or at reduced rates, eligibility to engage in working groups or become a member of the Executive Committee, participate at the General Assembly and numerous other advantages. Our purposes are: * To provide a channel for the international exchange and evaluation of information, experience and materials in the field of educational media as they apply to pre-school, primary and secondary education, to technical and vocational, industrial and commercial training, teacher training, continuing and distance education. * To foster international liaison among individuals and organizations with professional responsibility in the field of educational media. * To cooperate with other international organizations in the development and application of educational technology for practice, research, production, and distribution in this field. Who can be a member of ICEM? Members are organizations and individuals who are involved in educational technology in any one of a variety of ways. There are several different types and categories of ICEM members, Individual Members, National Representatives, Deputy Representatives and Coordinators. Individual Members may join ICEM by paying individual membership fees. National Representatives are appointed by their Ministry of Education. National Coordinators are elected by other ICEM members in their country. Regional Representatives and Coordinators represent a group of several countries. ICEM Secretariat, c/o Ray Laverty SG Pf 114 1011 WIEN AUSTRIA Email: lylt-at-a1.net

Dues – None

Meetings – Annual General Assembly in Autumn; Executive Committee meeting in Spring; Locations vary.

Publications – Educational Media International (quarterly journal) http://www.icem-cime.org/emi/issues.asp Aims & Scope Educational media has made a considerable impact on schools, colleges and providers of open and distance education. This journal provides an international forum for the exchange of information and views on new developments in educational and mass media. Contributions are drawn from academics and professionals whose ideas and experiences come from a number of countries and contexts. Abstracting & Indexing Educational Media International is covered by the British Education Index; Contents Pages in Education; Educational Research Abstracts online (ERA); Research into Higher Education Abstracts; ERIC; EBSCOhost; and Proquest Information and Learning.

Name of Organization or Association – International Recording Media Association

Acronym – IRMA

Address:
182 Nassau St., Suite 204
Princeton, NJ
08542-7005
US

Phone Number – (609)279-1700; **Fax Number** – (609)279-1999

Email Contact – info@recordingmedia.org;
URL – http://www.recordingmedia.org

Leaders – Charles Van Horn, President; Guy Finley, Associate Executive Director
Description – IRMA, the content delivery and storage association, is the worldwide forum on trends and innovation for the delivery and storage of entertainment and information. Founded in 1970, this global trade association encompasses organizations involved in every facet of content delivery. Beginning with the introduction of the audiocassette, through the home video revolution, and right up to today's digital delivery era, IRMA has always been the organization companies have turned to for news, networking, market research, information services, and leadership.

Membership – Over 400 corporations, IRMAs membership includes raw material providers, manufacturers, replicators, duplicators, packagers, copyright holders, logistics providers, and companies from many other related industries. Corporate membership includes benefits to all employees.

Dues – Corporate membership dues based on gross dollar volume in our industry.

Meetings – Annual Recording Media Forum (Palm Springs, CA); December Summit (New York, NY);

Publications – 9X annual Mediaware Magazine; Annual International Source Directory, Quarterly Market Intelligence

Name of Organization or Association – International Society for Performance Improvement

Acronym – ISPI

Address:
1400 Spring Street, Suite 260
Silver Spring, MD
20910
US

Phone Number – 301-587-8570; **Fax Number** – 301-587-8573

Email Contact – emember@ispi.org; **URL** – http://www.ispi.org

Leaders – Richard D. Battaglia, Executive Director

Description – The International Society for Performance Improvement (ISPI) is dedicated to improving individual, organizational, and societal performance. Founded in 1962, ISPI is the leading international association dedicated to improving productivity and performance in the workplace. ISPI represents more than 10,000 international and chapter members throughout the United States, Canada, and 40 other countries. ISPI's mission is to develop and recognize the proficiency of our members and advocate the use of Human Performance Technology. This systematic approach to improving productivity and competence uses a set of methods and procedures and a strategy for solving problems for realizing opportunities related to the performance of people. It is a systematic combination of performance analysis, cause analysis, intervention design and development, implementation, and evaluation that can be applied to individuals, small groups, and large organizations.

Membership – 10,000 Performance technologists, training directors, human resources managers, instructional technologists, human factors practitioners, and organizational consultants are members of ISPI. They work in a variety of settings including business, academia, government, health services, banking, and the armed forces.

Dues – Membership Categories Active Membership ($145 annually). This is an individual membership receiving full benefits and voting rights in the Society. Student Membership ($60 annually). This is a discounted individual full membership for full-time students. Proof of full-time enrollment must accompany the application. Retired Membership ($60 annually). This is a discounted individual full membership for individuals who are retired from full-time employment. Special Organizational Membership Categories These groups support the Society at the top level. Sustaining Membership ($950 annually). This is an organizational membership and includes five active memberships and several additional value-added services and discounts. Details available upon request. Patron Membership ($1,400 annually). This is an organizational membership and includes five active memberships and several additional value-added services and discounts. Details available upon request.

Meetings – Annual International Performance Improvement Conference, Fall Symposiums, Professional Series Workshops, Human Performance Technology Institutes

Publications – Performance Improvement Journal (10/year). The common theme is performance improvement practice or technique that is supported by research or germane theory. PerformanceXpress (12/year) Monthly newsletter published online. Performance Improvement Quarterly PIQ is a peer-reviewed journal created to stimulate professional discussion in the field and to advance the discipline of HPT through publishing scholarly works. ISPI Bookstore. The ISPI online bookstore is hosted in partnership with John Wiley & Sons.

Name of Organization or Association – International Visual Literacy Association

Acronym – IVLA

Address:
Dr. Constance Cassity, IVLA Treasurer, Northeastern State University, 3100 E. New Orleans St.
Broken Arrow, OK
74014
US

Phone Number – 918-449-6511; **Fax Number** – 918-449-6146

Email Contact – IVLA_Treasurer@netzero.com; **URL** – www.ivla.org

Leaders – IVLA Treasurer, Constance Cassity

Description – IVLA provides a multidisciplinary forum for the exploration, presentation, and discussion of all aspects of visual learning, thinking, communication, and expression. It also serves as a communication link bonding professionals from many disciplines who are creating and sustaining the study of the nature of visual experiences and literacy. It promotes and evaluates research, programs, and projects intended to increase effective use of visual communication in education, business, the arts, and commerce. IVLA was founded in 1968 to promote the concept of visual literacy and is an affiliate of AECT.

Membership – Membership of 500 people, mostly from academia and from many disciplines. We are an international organization and have conferences abroad once every third year. Anyone interested in any visual-verbal area should try our organization: architecture, engineering, dance, the arts, computers, video, design, graphics, photography, visual languages, mathematics, acoustics, physics, chemistry, optometry, sciences, literature, library, training, education, etc.

Dues – $60 regular; $30 student and retired; $60 outside United States; $500 lifetime membership

Meetings – Yearly conference usually October/November in selected locations.

Publications – The Journal of Visual Literacy (bi-annual – juried research papers) and Selected Readings from the Annual Conference.

Name of Organization or Association – Knowledge Alliance

Acronym – None
Address:
815 Connecticut Avenue, NW, Suite 220
Washington, DC
20006
US

Phone Number – 202-518-0847; **Fax Number** – None

Email Contact – waters@KnowledgeAll.net; **URL** – http://www.knowledgeall.net

Leaders – James W. Kohlmoos, President

Description – Knowledge Alliance (formerly known as NEKIA) was founded in 1997 as a nonprofit, non-partisan strategic alliance to address the increasingly urgent need to apply rigorous research to persistent educational challenges facing our country's schools. Composed of leading education organizations, Alliance members are involved in high-quality education research, development, dissemination, technical assistance and evaluation at the federal, regional, state, tribal, and local levels. The Alliance works closely with the US Congress, US Department of Education and other federal agencies in advocating knowledge-based policy for innovation and improvement in education. Our Mission Knowledge Alliances mission is to improve k-12 education by widely expanding the development and use of research-based knowledge in policy and practice. We believe that the effective use of research-based knowledge is essential to increasing student achievement and closing achievement gaps and should be a central organizing concept for the education reform efforts at all levels. We envision a new knowledge era in education policy and practice that focuses on the effective use of research-based knowledge to achieve successful and sustainable school improvement.

Membership – 28

Dues – Not available

Meetings – Board Meetings and Retreats; Invitational R&D Summit (2009); Hill Days; Communicators Institute

Publications – none

Name of Organization or Association – Learning Point Associates

Acronym – none

Address:
1120 E. Diehl Road Suite 200
Naperville, IL
60563-1486
US

Phone Number – (630)649-6500, (800)356-2735; **Fax Number** – (630)649-6700

Email Contact – info@learningpt.org; **URL** – www.learningpt.org
Leaders – Gina Burkhardt, Chief Executive Officer

Description – Learning Point Associates, with offices in Naperville, Illinois; Chicago; New York; and Washington, DC, is a nonprofit educational organization with more than 20 years of direct experience working with and for educators and policymakers to transform educational systems and student learning. The national and international reputation of Learning Point Associates is built on a solid foundation of conducting rigorous and relevant education research and evaluation; analyzing and synthesizing education policy trends and practices; designing and conducting client-centered evaluations; delivering high-quality professional services; and developing and delivering tools, services, and resources targeted at pressing education issues. Learning Point Associates manages a diversified portfolio of work ranging from direct consulting assignments to major federal contracts and grants, including REL Midwest, the National Comprehensive Center for Teacher Quality, Great Lakes East Comprehensive Assistance Center, Great Lakes West Comprehensive Assistance Center, The Center for Comprehensive School Reform and Improvement, and the NCLB Implementation Center.

Membership – Not applicable

Dues – None

Meetings – None

Publications – Visit the Publications section of our website.

Name of Organization or Association – Library Administration and Management Association

Acronym – LAMA

Address:
50 E. Huron St.
Chicago, IL
60611
US

Phone Number – (312)280-5032; **Fax Number** – (312)280-5033

Email Contact – lama@ala.org; **URL** – http://www.ala.org/lama

Leaders – Lorraine Olley, Executive Director; Catherine Murray-Rust, President

Description – MISSION: The Library Administration and Management Association encourages and nurtures current and future library leaders, and develops and promotes outstanding leadership and management practices. VISION: LAMA will be the foremost organization developing present and future leaders in library and information services. IMAGE: LAMA is a welcoming community where aspiring and experienced leaders from all types of libraries, as well as those who support libraries, come together to gain skills in a quest for excellence in library management, administration and leadership. Sections include: Buildings and Equipment Section (BES); Fundraising & Financial Development

Section (FRFDS); Library Organization & Management Section (LOMS); Human Resources Section (HRS); Public Relation and Marketing Section (PRMS); Systems & Services Section (SASS); and Measurement, Assessment and Evaluation Section (MAES).

Membership – 4,800

Dues – $50 regular(in addition to ALA membership); $65 organizations and corporations; $15, library school students

Meetings – ALA Annual Conference 2006, New Orleans, June 22–27; Midwinter Meeting 2007, San Diego, Jan 9–14

Publications – Library Administration & Management (q); LEADS from LAMA (electronic newsletter, irregular).

Name of Organization or Association – Library and Information Technology Association

Acronym – LITA

Address:
50 E. Huron St
Chicago, IL
60611
US

Phone Number – (312)280-4270, (800)545-2433, ext. 4270; **Fax Number** – (312)280-3257

Email Contact – lita@ala.org; **URL** – http://www.lita.org

Leaders – Mary C. Taylor, Executive Director, mtaylor@ala.org

Description – A division of the American Library Association, LITA is concerned with library automation; the information sciences; and the design, development, and implementation of automated systems in those fields, including systems development, electronic data processing, mechanized information retrieval, operations research, standards development, telecommunications, video communications, networks and collaborative efforts, management techniques, information technology, optical technology, artificial intelligence and expert systems, and other related aspects of audiovisual activities and hardware applications.

Membership – LITA members come from all types of libraries and institutions focusing on information technology in libraries. They include library decision-makers, practitioners, information professionals and vendors. Approximately 4,300 members.

Dues – $60 plus membership in ALA; $25 plus membership in ALA for library school students

Meetings – National Forum, fall.

Publications – LITA Blog. Information Technology and Libraries (ITAL): Contains the table of contents, abstracts and some full-text of ITAL, a refereed journal published quarterly by the Library and Information Technology Association. Technology Electronic Reviews (TER): TER is an irregular electronic serial publication that provides reviews and pointers to a variety of print and electronic resources about information technology. LITA Publications List: Check for information on LITA Guides and Monographs.

Name of Organization or Association – Lister Hill National Center for Biomedical Communications

Acronym – LHNCBC

Address:
National Library of Medicine, 8600 Rockville Pike
Bethesda, MD
20894
US

Phone Number – (301)496-4441; **Fax Number** – (301)402-0118

Email Contact – lhcques@lhc.nlm.nih.gov; **URL** – http://lhncbc.nlm.nih.gov/

Leaders – Clement J. McDonald, MD, Director, ClemMcDonald@mail.nih.gov

Description – The Lister Hill National Center for Biomedical Communications is a research and development division of the National Library of Medicine (NLM). The Center conducts and supports research and development in the dissemination of high-quality imagery, medical language processing, high-speed access to biomedical information, intelligent database systems development, multimedia visualization, knowledge management, data mining and machine-assisted indexing. The Lister Hill Center also conducts and supports research and development projects focusing on educational applications of state-of-the-art technologies including the use of microcomputer technology incorporating stereoscopic imagery and haptics, the Internet, and videoconferencing technologies for training health care professionals and disseminating consumer health information. The Centers Collaboratory for High Performance Computing and Communication serves as a focus for collaborative research and development in those areas, cooperating with faculties and staff of health sciences educational institutions. Health profession educators are assisted in the use and application of these technologies through periodic training, demonstrations and consultations. High Definition (HD) video is a technology area that has been explored and developed within the Center, and is now used as the

NLM standard for all motion imaging projects considered to be of archival value. Advanced three dimensional animation and photorealistic rendering techniques have also become required tools for use in visual projects within the Center.

Membership – None

Dues – None

Meetings – None

Publications – Fact sheet (and helpful links to other publications) at: http://www.nlm.nih.gov/pubs/factsheets/lister_hill.html

Name of Organization or Association – Media Communications Association – International

Acronym – MCA-I

Address:
PO Box 5135
Madison WI 53705-0135, WI
53705-0135
US

Phone Number – Use Contact Form; **Fax Number** – Please Ask

Email Contact – info@mca-i.org; **URL** – http://www.mca-i.org

Leaders – Lois Weiland, Executive Director

Description – Formerly the International Television Association. Founded in 1968, MCA-Is mission is to provide media communications professionals opportunities for networking, forums for education and resources for information. MCA-I also offers business services, such as low-cost insurance, buying programs, etc., to reduce operating costs. MCA-I also confers the highly acclaimed Media Festival awards (The Golden Reel is back!) on outstanding multimedia productions. Visit MCA-Is Web site for full details.

Membership – Over 3,000 individual and corporate members. Membership programs also are available to vendors for relationship and business development.

Dues – $160, individual.; $455, organizational; PLATINUM – $5,000; GOLD – $4,000; SILVER – $2,500; BRONZE – $1,200;

Meetings – Various Partnerships with Association Conferences

Publications – MCA-I eNews (Monthly), LeaderLinks (Monthly), CONNECT (Quarterly), Find a Pro Directory (online)

Name of Organization or Association – Medical Library Association

Acronym – MLA

Address:
65 E. Wacker Pl., Ste. 1900
Chicago, IL
60601-7246
US

Phone Number – (312)419-9094; **Fax Number** – (312)419-8950

Email Contact – info@mlahq.org; **URL** – http://www.mlanet.org

Leaders – Carla J. Funk, MLS, MBA, CAE, Executive Director

Description – MLA, a nonprofit, educational organization, comprises health sciences information professionals with more than 4,500 members worldwide. Through its programs and services, MLA provides lifelong educational opportunities, supports a knowledge base of health information research, and works with a global network of partners to promote the importance of quality information for improved health to the health care community and the public.

Membership – MLA, a nonprofit, educational organization, comprises health sciences information professionals with more than 4,500 members worldwide. Through its programs and services, MLA provides lifelong educational opportunities, supports a knowledge base of health information research, and works with a global network of partners to promote the importance of quality information for improved health to the health care community and the public. Membership categories: Regular Membership Institutional Membership International Membership Affiliate Membership Student Membership

Dues – $165, regular; $110, introductory; $255–600, institutional, based on total library expenditures, including salaries, but excluding grants and contracts; $110, international; $100, affiliate; $40, student

Meetings – National annual meeting held every May; most chapter meetings are held in the fall.

Publications – MLA News (newsletter, 10/year); Journal of the Medical Library Association (quarterly scholarly publication); MLA DocKit series, collections of representative, unedited library documents from a variety of institutions that illustrate the range of approaches to health sciences library management topics); MLA BibKits, selective, annotated bibliographies of discrete subject areas in the health sciences literature; standards; surveys; and copublished monographs.

Name of Organization or Association – Mid-continent Research for Education and Learning

Acronym – McREL
Address:
4601 DTC Blvd., Suite 500
Denver, CO
80237
US

Phone Number – (303)337-0990; **Fax Number** – (303)337-3005

Email Contact – info@mcrel.org; **URL** – http://www.mcrel.org

Leaders – J. Timothy Waters, Executive Director

Description – McREL is a private, nonprofit organization whose purpose is to improve education through applied research and development. McREL provides products and services, primarily for K-12 educators, to promote the best instructional practices in the classroom. McREL houses one of 10 regional educational laboratories funded by the US Department of Education, Institute for Educational Science. The regional laboratory helps educators and policymakers work toward excellence in education for all students. It also serves at the North Central Comprehensive Center, providing school improvement support to the states of Iowa, Minnesota, Nebraska, North Dakota, and South Dakota. McREL has particular expertise in standards-based education systems, leadership for school improvement, effective instructional practices, teacher quality, mathematics and science education improvement, early literacy development, and education outreach programs.

Membership – not a membership organization

Dues – no dues

Meetings – annual conference

Publications – Changing Schools (q. newsletter); Noteworthy (annual monograph on topics of current interest in education reform). Numerous technical reports and other publications. Check website for current listings.

Name of Organization or Association – Minorities in Media

Acronym – MIM

Address:
1800 N. Stonelake Dr. Suite 2
Bloomington, IN
47408
US

Phone Number – (703) 993-3669; **Fax Number** – (313)577-1693

Email Contact – dtolbert@nu.edu; **URL** – None

Leaders – Denise Tolbert, President

Description – MIM is a special interest group of AECT that responds to the challenge of preparing students of color for an ever-changing international marketplace and recognizes the unique educational needs of today's diverse learners. It promotes the effective use of educational communications and technology in the learning process. MIM seeks to facilitate changes in instructional design and development, traditional pedagogy, and instructional delivery systems by responding to and meeting the significant challenge of educating diverse individuals to take their place in an ever-changing international marketplace. MIM encourages all of AECT's body of members to creatively develop curricula, instructional treatments, instructional strategies, and instructional materials that promote an acceptance and appreciation of racial and cultural diversity. Doing so will make learning for all more effective, relevant, meaningful, motivating, and enjoyable. MIM actively supports the Wes McJulien Minority Scholarship, and selects the winner.

Membership – contact MIM president.

Dues – $20, student; $30, nonstudent

Meetings – None

Publications – Newsletter is forthcoming online. The MIM listserv is a membership benefit

Name of Organization or Association – National Aeronautics and Space Administration

Acronym – NASA

Address:
NASA Headquarters, 300 E Street SW
Washington, DC
20546
US

Phone Number – (202)358-0103; **Fax Number** – (202)358-3032

Email Contact – education@nasa.gov; **URL** – http://education.nasa.gov

Leaders – Angela Phillips Diaz, Assistant Administrator for Education

Description – From elementary through postgraduate school, NASAs educational programs are designed to inspire the next generation of explorers by capturing students interest in science, mathematics, and technology at an early age; to channel more students into science, engineering, and technology career paths; and to enhance the knowledge, skills, and experiences of teachers and university faculty. NASAs educational programs include NASA Spacelink (an electronic information system); videoconferences (60-min interactive staff development videoconferences to be delivered to schools via satellite); and NASA Television (informational and educational television programming). Additional information is available from the Office of Education at NASA Headquarters and counterpart offices at the nine NASA field centers. Further information may be obtained from the NASA Education Homepage and also accessible from the NASA Public Portal at See learning in a whole new light!

Membership – None

Dues – None

Meetings – None

Publications – Publications and Products can be searched and downloaded from the following URL – http://www.nasa.gov/audience/foreducators/5-8/learning/index.html

Name of Organization or Association – National Alliance for Media Arts and Culture

Acronym – NAMAC

Address:
145 Ninth Street, Suite 250
San Francisco, CA
94103
US

Phone Number – (415)431-1391; **Fax Number** – (415)431-1392

Email Contact – namac@namac.org; **URL** – http://www.namac.org

Leaders – Helen DeMichel, Co-Director

Description – NAMAC is a nonprofit organization dedicated to increasing public understanding of and support for the field of media arts in the United States. Members include media centers, cable access centers, universities, and media artists, as well as other individuals and organizations providing services for production, education, exhibition, distribution, and preservation of video, film, audio, and intermedia. NAMACs information services are available to the general public, arts and non-arts organizations, businesses, corporations, foundations, government agencies, schools, and universities.

Membership – 300 organizations, 75 individuals

Dues – $75–$450, institutional (depending on annual budget); $75, indiv.

Meetings – Biennial Conference

Publications – Media Arts Information Network; The National Media Education Directory, annual anthology of case-studies "A Closer Look," periodic White Paper reports, Digital Directions: Convergence Planning for the Media Arts

Name of Organization or Association – National Association for Visually Handicapped

Acronym – NAVH

Address:
22 West 21st St., 6th Floor
New York, NY
10010
US

Phone Number – (212) 889-3141; **Fax Number** – (212) 727-2931

Email Contact – navh@navh.org; **URL** – http://www.navh.org

Leaders – Dr. Lorraine H. Marchi, Founder/CEO; Cesar Gomez, Executive Director

Description – NAVH ensures that those with limited vision do not lead limited lives. We offer emotional support; training in the use of visual aids and special lighting; access to a wide variety of optical aids, electronic equipment and lighting; a large print, nationwide, free-by-mail loan library; large print educational materials; free quarterly newsletter; referrals to eye care specialists and local low vision resources; self-help groups for seniors and working adults; and educational outreach to the public and professionals.

Membership – It is not mandatory to became a member in order to receive our services. However, your membership helps others retain their independence by allowing NAVH to provide low vision services to those who cannot afford to make a donation. In addition, members receive discounts on visual aids, educational materials and our catalogs. Corporations and publishers may also join to help sponsor our services. Please contact us for more information.

Dues – Membership is $50 a year for individuals. Publishers and corporations interested in membership should contact NAVH.

Meetings – Seniors support group 2 times at month; Seminar on low vision for ophthalmology residents; yearly showcase of the latest in low vision technology, literature and services

Publications – Free quarterly newsletter distributed free throughout the English-speaking world; Visual Aids Catalog; Large Print Loan Library Catalog; informational pamphlets on vision, common eye diseases and living with limited vision; booklets for professionals who work with adults and children with limited vision

Name of Organization or Association – National Association of Media and Technology Centers

Acronym – NAMTC
Address:
NAMTC, 7105 First Ave. SW
Cedar Rapids, IA
52405
US

Phone Number – 319 654 0608; **Fax Number** – 319 654 0609

Email Contact – bettyge@mchsi.com; **URL** – www.namtc.org

Leaders – Betty Gorsegner Ehlinger, Executive Director

Description – NAMTC is committed to promoting leadership among its membership through networking, advocacy, and support activities that will enhance the equitable access to media, technology, and information services to educational communities. Membership is open to regional, K-12, and higher education media centers that serve K-12 students as well as commercial media and technology centers.

Membership – Institutional and corporate members numbering approximately 225.

Dues – $100 institutions; $300, corporations

Meetings – Regional meetings are held throughout the United States annually. A national Leadership Summit is held in the spring.

Publications – Membership newsletter is "ETIN," a quarterly publication.

Name of Organization or Association – National Commission on Libraries and Information Science

Acronym – NCLIS

Address:
1800 M Street, NW; Suite 350 North Tower
Washington, DC
20036-5841
US

Phone Number – (202)606-9200; **Fax Number** – (202)606-9203

Email Contact – info@nclis.gov.; **URL** – http://www.nclis.gov

Leaders – C. Beth Fitzsimmons, Chairman

Description – A permanent independent agency of the US government charged with advising the executive and legislative branches on national library and information policies and plans. The Commission reports directly to the president and Congress on the implementation of national policy; conducts studies, surveys, and analyses of the nations library and information needs; appraises the inadequacies of current resources and services; promotes research and development activities; conducts hearings and issues publications as appropriate; and develops overall plans for meeting national library and information needs and for the coordination of activities at the federal, state, and local levels. The Commission provides general policy advice to the Institute of Museum and Library Services (IMLS) director relating to library services included in the Library Services and Technology Act (LSTA).

Membership – 16 commissioners (14 appointed by the president and confirmed by the Senate, the Librarian of Congress, and the Director of the IMLS).

Dues – none

Meetings – Average 2–3 meetings a year

Publications – None

Name of Organization or Association – National Communication Association

Acronym – NCA

Address:
1765 N Street, NW
Washington, DC
22003
US

Phone Number – 202-464-4622; **Fax Number** – 202-464-4600

Email Contact – dwallick@natcom.org; **URL** – http://www.natcom.org

Leaders – Roger Smitter, Executive Director

Description – A voluntary society organized to promote study, criticism, research, teaching, and application of principles of communication, particularly of speech communication. Founded in 1914, NCA is a nonprofit organization of researchers, educators, students, and practitioners, whose academic interests span all forms of human communication. NCA is the oldest and largest national organization serving the academic discipline of Communication. Through its services, scholarly publications, resources, conferences and conventions, NCA works with its members to strengthen the profession and contribute to the greater good of the educational enterprise and society. Research and instruction in the discipline focus on the study of how messages in various media are produced, used, and interpreted within and across different contexts, channels, and cultures

Membership – 7,700

Dues – From $60 (Student) to $300 (Patron). Life membership also available.

Meetings – Four regional conferences (ECA, ESCA SSCA, WSCA) and 1 Annual National Conference.

Publications – Spectra Newsletter (mo.); Quarterly Journal of Speech; Communication Monographs; Communication Education; Critical Studies in Mass Communication; Journal of Applied Communication Research; Text and Performance Quarterly; Communication Teacher; Index to Journals in Communication Studies through 1995; National Communication Directory of NCA and the Regional Speech Communication Organizations (CSSA, ECA, SSCA, WSCA). For additional publications, request brochure.

Name of Organization or Association – National Council of Teachers of English: Commission on Media, Assembly on Media Arts

Acronym – NCTE

Address:
1111 W. Kenyon Rd.
Urbana, IL
61801-1096
US

Phone Number – (217)328-3870; **Fax Number** – (217)328-0977

Email Contact – public_info@ncte.org; **URL** – http://www.ncte.org

Leaders – Kent Williamson, NCTE Executive Director; David Bruce, Commission Director; Mary Christel, Assembly Chair

Description – The NCTE Commission on Media is a deliberative and advisory body which each year identifies and reports to the NCTE Executive Committee on key issues in the teaching of media; reviews what the Council has done concerning media during the year; recommends new projects and persons who might undertake them. The commission monitors current and projected NCTE publications (other than journals), suggests topics for future NCTE publications on media, and performs a similar role of review and recommendation for the NCTE Annual Convention program. Occasionally, the commission undertakes further tasks and projects as approved by the Executive Committee. The NCTE Assembly on Media Arts promotes communication and cooperation among all individuals who have a special interest in media in the English language arts; presents programs and special projects on this subject; encourages the development of research, experimentation, and investigation in the judicious uses of media in the teaching of English; promotes the extensive writing of articles and publications devoted to this subject; and integrates the efforts of those with an interest in this subject.

Membership – The National Council of Teachers of English, with 50,000 individual and institutional members worldwide, is dedicated to improving the teaching and learning of English and the language arts at all levels of education. Members include elementary, middle, and high school teachers; supervisors of English programs; college and university faculty; teacher educators; local and state agency English specialists; and professionals in related fields The members of the NCTE Commission on Media are NCTE members appointed by the director of the group. Membership in the Assembly on Media Arts is open to members and nonmembers of NCTE.

Dues – Membership in NCTE is $40 a year; adding subscriptions to its various journals adds additional fees. Membership in the Assembly on Media Arts is $15 a year.

Meetings – http://www.ncte.org/conventions/ 96th NCTE Annual Convention, November 20–25, 2003, San Francisco, California; 94th NCTE Annual Convention, November 16–21, 2006, Nashville, Tennessee

Publications – NCTE publishes about 20 books a year. Visit http://www.ncte.org/pubs/books/ and http://www.ncte.org/store. NCTEs journals include Language Arts English Journal College English College Composition and Communication English Education Research in the Teaching of English Teaching English in the Two-Year College Voices from the Middle Primary Voices, K-6 Talking Points Classroom Notes Plus English Leadership Quarterly The Council Chronicle (included in NCTE membership) Journal information is available at http://www.ncte.org/pubs/journals/ The Commission on Media doesn't have its own publication. The Assembly on Media Arts publishes Media Matters, a newsletter highlighting issues, viewpoints, materials, and events related to the study of media. Assembly members receive this publication.

Name of Organization or Association – National EBS Association

Acronym – NEBSA

Address:
PO Box 121475

Clermont, FL
34712-1475
US

Phone Number – (407) 401-4630; **Fax Number** – (321) 406-0520

Email Contact – execdirector@nebsa.org; **URL** – http://nebsa.org

Leaders – Lynn Rejniak, Chair, Board of Directors; Don MacCullough, Executive
Director

Description – Established in 1978, NEBSA is a nonprofit, professional organization
of Educational Broadband Service (EBS) licensees, applicants, and others interested
in EBS broadcasting. EBS is a very high frequency television broadcast service that
is used to broadcast distance learning classes, two way internet service, wireless
and data services to schools and other locations where education can take place.
The goals of the association are to gather and exchange information about EBS,
gather data on utilization of EBS, act as a conduit for those seeking EBS information, and assist migration from video broadcast to wireless, broadband Internet
services using EBS channels. The NEBSA represents EBS interests to the FCC,
technical consultants, and equipment manufacturers. The association uses its Web
site and Listserv list to provide information to its members in areas such as technology, programming content, FCC regulations, excess capacity leasing and license and
application data.

Membership – The current membership consists of Educational Institutions and
nonprofit organizations that hold licenses issued by the Federal Communications
Commission for Educational Broadband Service (EBS). We also have members
that have an interest in EBS and members such as manufacturers of EBS related
equipment and Law firms that represent Licensees.

Dues – We have two main types of memberships: Voting memberships for EBS
licensees only, and non-voting memberships for other educational institutions and
sponsors. See the Web site http://www.nebsa.org for details.

Meetings – Annual Member Conference, February/March

Publications – http://www.nebsa.org

Name of Organization or Association – National Endowment for the Humanities

Acronym – NEH

Address:
Division of Public Programs, Media Program, 1100 Pennsylvania Ave., NW,
Room 426
Washington, DC
20506
US

Phone Number – (202)606-8269; **Fax Number** – (202)606-8557

Email Contact – publicpgms@neh.gov; **URL** – http://www.neh.gov

Leaders – Tom Phelps, Acting Director, Division of Public Programs

Description – The NEH is an independent federal grant-making agency that supports research, educational, and public programs grounded in the disciplines of the humanities. The Division of Public Programs Media Program supports film and radio programs in the humanities for public audiences, including children and adults. All programs in the Division of Public Program support various technologies, specifically web sites both as stand alone projects and as extensions of larger projects such as museum exhibitions.

Membership – Nonprofit institutions and organizations including public television and radio stations.

Dues – not applicable

Meetings – not applicable

Publications – Visit the web site (http://www.neh.gov) for application forms and guidelines as well as the Media Log, a cumulative listing of projects funded through the Media Program.

Name of Organization or Association – National Federation of Community Broadcasters

Acronym – NFCB

Address:
1970 Broadway, Ste. 1000
Oakland, CA
94612
US

Phone Number – 510 451-8200; **Fax Number** – 510 451-8208

Email Contact – ginnyz@nfcb.org; **URL** – http://www.nfcb.org.

Leaders – Carol Pierson, President and CEO

Description – NFCB represents non-commercial, community-based radio stations in public policy development at the national level and provides a wide range of practical services, including technical assistance.

Membership – 250. Non-commercial community radio stations, related organizations, and individuals.

Dues – range from $200 to $3,500 for participant and associate members

Meetings – 2002 Charlottesville, VA; 2003 San Francisco; 2004 Albuquerque; 2005 Baltimore; 2006 Portland, OR; 2007 New Orleans

Publications – Public Radio Legal Handbook; AudioCraft; Community Radio News; Let a Thousand Voices Speak: A Guide to Youth in Radio Projects; Guide to Underwriting

Name of Organization or Association – National Film Board of Canada

Acronym – NFBC

Address:
1123 Broadway, STE 307
New York, NY
10010
US

Phone Number – (212)629-8890; **Fax Number** – (212)629-8502

Email Contact – NewYork@nfb.ca; **URL** – www.nfb.ca
Leaders – Dylan McGinty, US Sales Manager; Laure Parsons, US Sales and Marketing Associate

Description – Established in 1939, the NFBCs main objective is to produce and distribute high-quality audiovisual materials for educational, cultural, and social purposes.

Membership – none

Dues – none

Meetings – None

Publications – None

Name of Organization or Association – National Freedom of Information Coalition

Acronym – NFOIC

Address:
133 Neff Annex, University of Missouri
Columbia, MO
65211-0012
US

Phone Number – (573)882-4856; **Fax Number** – (573)884-6204

Email Contact – daviscn@missouri.edu; **URL** – http://www.nfoic.org

Leaders – Dr. Charles N. Davis, Executive Director

Description – The National Freedom of Information Coalition is a national membership organization devoted to protecting the public's right to oversee its government. NFOICs goals include helping start-up FOI organizations; strengthening existing FOI organizations; and developing FOI programs and publications appropriate to the membership.

Membership – The NFOIC offers active memberships to free-standing nonprofit state or regional Freedom of Information Coalitions, academic centers and First Amendment Centers, and associated memberships to individuals and entities supporting NFOICs mission. Membership information is available on the NFOIC Web page. Achieving and maintaining active membership in all 50 states is the primary goal of NFOIC.

Dues – Membership categories and levels of support are described on the NFOIC Web site.

Meetings – The National Freedom of Information Coalition host an annual meeting and a spring conference.

Publications – The FOI Advocate, an electronic newsletter available for free through email subscription. The FOI Report, a periodic White Paper, published electronically.

Name of Organization or Association – National Gallery of Art

Acronym – NGA

Address:
Department of Education Resources, 2000B South Club Drive
Landover, MD
20785
US

Phone Number – (202)842-6273; **Fax Number** – (202)842-6935

Email Contact – EdResources@nga.gov;

URL – http://www.nga.gov/education/classroom/loanfinder/

Leaders – Leo J. Kasun, Education Resources Supervisory Specialist

Description – This department of NGA is responsible for the production and distribution of 120+ educational audiovisual programs, including interactive technologies. Materials available (all loaned free to individuals, schools, colleges and universities, community organizations, and non-commercial television stations) range from videocassettes and color slide programs to CD-ROMs, and DVDs. All videocassette and DVD programs are closed captioned A free catalog of programs is available upon request. All CD-ROMs, DVDs, utilizing digitized images on the gallery's collection are available for long-term loan.

Membership – Our free-loan lending program resembles that of a library and because we are a federally funded institution we have membership system. Last year we lent programs directly to over one million borrowers. Our programs are available to anyone who requests them which ranges from individuals to institutions.
Dues – None

Meetings – None

Publications – Extension Programs Catalogue.

Name of Organization or Association – National PTA

Acronym – National PTA

Address:
541 North Fairbanks Ct, Ste. 1300
Chicago, IL
60611
US

Phone Number – (312)670-6782; **Fax Number** – (312)670-6783

Email Contact – info@pta.org; **URL** – http://www.pta.org

Leaders – Warlene Gary, Chief Executive Officer

Description – Advocates the education, health, safety, and well-being of children and teens. Provides parenting education and leadership training to PTA volunteers. National PTA partners with the National Cable & Telecommunications Association on the "Taking Charge of Your TV" project by training PTA and cable representatives to present media literacy workshops. The workshops teach parents and educators how to evaluate programming so they can make informed decisions about what to allow their children to see. The National PTA in 1997 convinced the television industry to add content information to the TV rating system.

Membership – 6.2 million Membership open to all interested in the health, welfare, and education of children and support the PTA mission – http://www.pta.org/aboutpta/mission_en.asp.

Dues – vary by local unit – national dues portion is $1.75 per member annually.

Meetings – National convention, held annually in June in different regions of the country, is open to PTA members; convention information available on the Website

Publications – Our Children (magazine) plus electronic newsletters and other web-based information for members and general public.

Name of Organization or Association – National Public Broadcasting Archives

Acronym – NPBA

Address:
Hornbake Library, University of Maryland
College Park, MD
20742
US

Phone Number – (301)405-9160; **Fax Number** – (301)314-2634

Email Contact – npba@umd.edu; **URL** – http://www.lib.umd.edu/NPBA

Leaders – Karen King, Acting Curator

Description – NPBA brings together the archival record of the major entities of non-commercial broadcasting in the United States. NPBAs collections include the archives of the Corporation for Public Broadcasting (CPB), the Public Broadcasting Service (PBS), and National Public Radio (NPR). Other organizations represented include the Midwest Program for Airborne Television Instruction (MPATI), the Public Service Satellite Consortium (PSSC), Americas Public Television Stations (APTS), Children's Television Workshop (CTW), and the Joint Council for Educational Telecommunications (JCET). NPBA also makes available the personal papers of many individuals who have made significant contributions to public broadcasting, and its reference library contains basic studies of the broadcasting industry, rare pamphlets, and journals on relevant topics. NPBA also collects and maintains a selected audio and video program record of public broadcastings national production and support centers and of local stations. Oral history tapes and transcripts from the NPR Oral History Project and the Televisionaries Nal History Project are also available at the archives. The archives are open to the public from 9 A.M. to 5 P.M., Monday through Friday. Research in NPBA collections should be arranged by prior appointment. For further information, call (301)405-9988.

Membership – NA

Dues – NA

Meetings – NA

Publications – NA

Name of Organization or Association – National Telemedia Council Inc.

Acronym – NTC

Address:
1922 University Ave.
Madison, WI
53726
USA

Phone Number – (608)218-1182; **Fax Number** – (608)218-1183

Email Contact – NTelemedia@aol.com;

URL – http://www.nationaltelemediacouncil.org, and
www.journalofmedialiteracy.org

Leaders – Karen Ambrosh, President; Marieli Rowe, Executive Director

Description – The NTC is a national, nonprofit professional organization dedi-
cated to promoting media literacy, or critical media viewing and listening skills.
This is done primarily through the Journal of Media Literacy, the publication of the
National Telemedia Council, as well as work with teachers, parents, and caregivers.
NTC activities include publishing The Journal of Media Literacy, the Teacher Idea
Exchange (T.I.E.), the Jessie McCanse Award for individual contribution to media
literacy, assistance to media literacy educators and professionals.

Membership – Member/subscribers to the Journal of Media Literacy, currently
over 500, including individuals, organizations, schools and University libraries
across the Globe including Asia, Australia, Europe, North and South America. Our
membership is open to all those interested in media literacy.

Dues – Individuals: $35, basic; $50, contributing; $100, patron
Organizations/Library: $60 Corporate sponsorship: $500 (Additional Postage
for Overseas)

Meetings – No major meetings scheduled this year

Publications – The Journal of Media Literacy

Name of Organization or Association – Native American Public Telecommunications

Acronym – NAPT

Address:
1800 North 33rd Street
Lincoln, NE
68503
US

Phone Number – (402)472-3522; **Fax Number** – (402)472-8675

Email Contact – rfauver1@unl.edu; **URL** – http://nativetelecom.org

Leaders – Shirley K. Sneve, Executive Director

Description – Native American Public Telecommunications (NAPT) supports the creation, promotion and distribution of Native public media. We accomplish this mission by: • Producing and developing educational telecommunication programs for all media including public television and public radio. • Distributing and encouraging the broadest use of such educational telecommunications programs. • Providing training opportunities to encourage increasing numbers of American Indians and Alaska Natives to produce quality public broadcasting programs. • Promoting increased control and use of information technologies by American Indians and Alaska Natives. • Providing leadership in creating awareness of and developing telecommunications policies favorable to American Indians and Alaska Natives. • Building partnerships to develop and implement telecommunications projects with tribal nations, Indian organizations, and native communities.

Membership – No Membership

Dues – None

Meetings – None

Publications – The Vision Maker (e-newsletter).

Name of Organization or Association – Natural Science Collections Alliance

Acronym – NSC Alliance

Address:
P.O. Box 44095
Washington, DC
20026-4095
US

Phone Number – (202)633-2772; **Fax Number** – (202)633-2821

Email Contact – ddrupa@burkine.com; **URL** – http://www.nscalliance.org

Leaders – Executive Director

Description – Fosters the care, management, and improvement of biological collections and promotes their utilization. Institutional members include free-standing museums, botanical gardens, college and university museums, and public institutions, including state biological surveys and agricultural research centers. The NSC Alliance also represents affiliate societies, and keeps members informed about funding and legislative issues.

Membership – 80 institutions, 30 affiliates, 120 individual and patron members.

Dues – Dues: depend on the size of collections.

Meetings – Annual Meeting (May or June)

Publications – Guidelines for Institutional Policies and Planning in Natural History Collections; Global Genetic Resources; A Guide to Museum Pest Control

Name of Organization or Association – New England School Library Association (formerly New England Educational Media Association)

Acronym – NESLA (formerly NEEMA)

Address:
c/o Merlyn Miller, President Burr & Burton Academy, 57 Seminary Avenue
Manchester, VT
05254
US

Phone Number – 802-362-1775; **Fax Number** – 802-362-0574

Email Contact – mmiller@burrburton.org; **URL** – www.neschoolibraries.org

Leaders – Merlyn Miller, President

Description – An affiliate of AECT, NESLA is a regional professional association dedicated to the improvement of instruction through the effective utilization of school library media services, media, and technology applications. For over 90 years, it has represented school library media professionals through activities and networking efforts to develop and polish the leadership skills, professional representation, and informational awareness of the membership. The Board of Directors consists of representatives from local affiliates within all six of the New England states, as well as professional leaders of the region. An annual leadership conference is offered.

Membership – NESLA focuses on school library media issues among the six New England states, consequently, membership is encouraged for school library media specialists in this region.

Dues – Regular membership $30. Student /retired membership $15.

Meetings – Annual Leadership Conference and Business Meeting

Publications – NESLA Views

Name of Organization or Association – New York Festivals

Acronym – NYF

Address:
260 West 39th Street, 10th Floor
New York, NY
10018
USA

Phone Number – 212-643-4800; **Fax Number** – 212-643-0170

Email Contact – info@newyorkfestivals.com;
URL – http://www.newyorkfestivals.com

Leaders – Alisun Armstrong, Executive Director

Description – New York Festivals (NYF) is an international awards company founded in 1957. Recognizing The World's Best Work^{TM} in advertising, programming, design, and marketing, NYF honors creativity and effectiveness in global communications through six different annual competitions. New York Festivals International Film & Video Awards is one of the oldest extant international festivals in the world. Known best for honoring informational, educational and industrial film production, the New York Festivals Film & Video Awards is entering its 50th year of recognizing The Worlds Best Work^{TM} in categories including Documentaries, Business Theatre, Short and Feature Length Films, Home Video Productions, Distance Learning, Slide Productions, and Multi-Screen Productions. Winners are honored in a black-tie event in Manhattan in January. The 2007 International Film & Video Awards will open for entry on July 5th. The Discount Deadline is August 23rd (enter online by that date and get a 10% discount off the entry total), and the final deadline will be September 22. For more information and fees, plus a full list of categories and the rules and regulations, please visit www.newyorkfestivals.com.

Membership – No membership feature. The competition is open to any non-broadcast media production.

Dues – None

Meetings – None

Publications – Winners are posted on our web site at www.newyorkfestivals.com

Name of Organization or Association – Northwest College and University Council for the Management of Educational Technology

Acronym – NW/MET

Address:
c/o WITS, Willamette University, 900 State St.
Salem, OR
97301
US

Phone Number – (503)370-6650; **Fax Number** – (503)375-5456

Email Contact – mmorandi@willamette.edu; **URL** – http://www.nwmet.org

Leaders – Doug McCartney, Director (effective April 14, 2007); Marti Morandi, Membership Chair.

Description – NW/MET is a group of media professionals responsible for campus-wide media services. Founded in 1976, NW/MET is comprised of members from 2 provinces of Canada and 4 northwestern states.

Membership – The membership of NW/MET is composed of individuals who participate by giving time, energy, and resources to the support and advancement of the organization. Full Membership may be awarded to individuals whose primary professional role involves the facilitation of educational technology, who are employed by an institution of higher education located in the NW/MET membership region, and who submit a membership application in which they list their professional qualifications and responsibilities.

Dues – $35

Meetings – An annual conference and business meeting are held each year, rotating through the region.

Publications – An annual Directory and website.

Name of Organization or Association – Northwest Regional Educational Laboratory

Acronym – NWREL

Address:
101 SW Main St., Suite 500
Portland, OR
97204
US

Phone Number – (503)275-9500; **Fax Number** – (503)275-0448

Email Contact – info@nwrel.org; **URL** – http://www.nwrel.org

Leaders – Dr. Carol Thomas, Executive Director

Description – One of 10 Office of Educational Research and Improvement (OERI) regional educational laboratories, NWREL works with schools and communities to improve educational outcomes for children, youth, and adults. NWREL provides leadership, expertise, and services based on the results of research and development. The specialty area of NWREL is school change processes. It serves Alaska, Idaho, Oregon, Montana, and Washington.

Membership – 856 organizations

Dues – None

Meetings – none

Publications – Northwest Education (quarterly journal)

Name of Organization or Association – OCLC Online Computer Library Center, Inc.

Acronym – OCLC

Address:
6565 Kilgour Place
Dublin, OH
43017-3395
US

Phone Number – (614)764-6000; **Fax Number** – (614)764-6096

Email Contact – oclc@oclc.org; **URL** – http://www.oclc.org

Leaders – Jay Jordan, President and CEO

Description – Founded in 1967, OCLC is a nonprofit, membership, computer library service and research organization dedicated to the public purposes of furthering access to the world's information and reducing information costs. More than 60,000 libraries in 112 countries and territories around the world use OCLC services to locate, acquire, catalog, lend and preserve library materials. Researchers, students, faculty, scholars, professional librarians and other information seekers use OCLC services to obtain bibliographic, abstract and full-text information. OCLC and its member libraries cooperatively produce and maintain WorldCat, the world's largest database for discovery of library materials. OCLC publishes the Dewey Decimal Classification. OCLC Digital Collection and Preservation Services provide digitization and archiving services worldwide. OCLCs NetLibrary provides libraries with eContent solutions that support Web-based research, reference and learning.

Membership – OCLC welcomes information organizations around the world to be a part of our unique cooperative. A variety of participation levels are available to libraries, museums, archives, historical societies, other cultural heritage organizations and professional associations. OCLC membership represents more than 60,000 libraries in 112 countries and territories around the world.

Dues – None

Meetings – OCLC Members Council (3/year) Held in Dublin, Ohio.

Publications – Annual Report (1/year; print and electronic); OCLC Newsletter (4/year; print and electronic); OCLC Abstracts (1/week, electronic only.)

Name of Organization or Association – Online Audiovisual Catalogers

Acronym – OLAC
Address:
None
None, None
None
US

Phone Number – None; **Fax Number** – None

Email Contact – neumeist@buffalo.edu; **URL** – http://www.olacinc.org/

Leaders – None

Description – In 1980, OLAC was founded to establish and maintain a group that could speak for catalogers of audiovisual materials. OLAC provides a means for exchange of information, continuing education, and communication among catalogers of audiovisual materials and with the Library of Congress. While maintaining a voice with the bibliographic utilities that speak for catalogers of audiovisual materials, OLAC works toward common understanding of AV cataloging practices and standards.

Membership – 500

Dues – United States and Canada Personal Memberships One year $20.00 Two years $38.00 Three years $55.00 Institutional Memberships One year $25.00 Two years $48.00 Three years $70.00 Other Countries All Memberships One year $25.00 Two years $48.00 Three years $70.00

Meetings – bi-annual

Publications – OLAC Newsletter

Name of Organization or Association – Ontario Film Association, Inc. (also known as the Association for the Advancement of Visual Media/Lassociation pour lavancement des médias visuels).
Acronym – OLA

Address:
50 Wellington St East Suite 201
Toronto, ON
M5E 1C8
Canada

Phone Number – (416)363-3388; **Fax Number** – 1-800-387-1181

Email Contact – info@accessola.com; **URL** – www.accessola.com

Leaders – Lawrence A. Moore, Executive Director

Description – A membership organization of buyers, and users of media whose objectives are to promote the sharing of ideas and information about visual media through education, publications, and advocacy.

Membership – 112

Dues – $120, personal membership; $215, associate membership.

Meetings – OFA Media Showcase, spring

Publications – Access

Name of Organization or Association – Pacific Film Archive

Acronym – PFA

Address:
University of California, Berkeley Art Museum, 2625 Durant Ave.
Berkeley, CA
94720-2250
US

Phone Number – (510)642-1437 (library); (510)642-1412 (general);
Fax Number – (510)642-4889

Email Contact – NLG@berkeley.edu; **URL** – http://www.bampfa.berkeley.edu

Leaders – Susan Oxtoby, Senior Curator of Film; Nancy Goldman, Head, PFA Library and Film Study Center

Description – Sponsors the exhibition, study, and preservation of classic, international, documentary, animated, and avant-garde films. Provides on-site research screenings of films in its collection of over 7,000 titles. Provides access to its collections of books, periodicals, stills, and posters (all materials are noncirculating). Offers BAM/PFA members and University of California, Berkeley, affiliates reference and research services to locate film and video distributors, credits, stock footage, etc. Library hours are 1 P.M–5 P.M. Monday–Thursday. Research screenings are by appointment only and must be scheduled at least two weeks in advance; other collections are available for consultation on a drop-in basis during Library hours.

Membership – Membership is through our parent organization, the UC Berkeley Art Museum and Pacific Film Archive, and is open to anyone. The BAM/PFA currently has over 3,000 members. Members receive free admission to the Museum; reduced-price tickets to films showing at PFA; access to the PFA Library & Film Study Center; and many other benefits. Applications and more information is available at http://www.bampfa.berkeley.edu/membership_giving/index.html

Dues – $40 indiv. and nonprofit departments of institutions.

Meetings – none

Publications – BAM/PFA Calendar (6/year).

Name of Organization or Association – Pacific Resources for Education and Learning

Acronym – PREL

Address:
900 Fort Street Mall, Suite 1300
Honolulu, HI
96813
US

Phone Number – (808) 441-1300;
Fax Number – (808) 441-1385

Email Contact – askprel@prel.org; **URL** – http://www.prel.org/

Leaders – Thomas W. Barlow, Ed.D., President and Chief Executive Officer

Description – Pacific Resources for Education and Learning (PREL) is an independent, nonprofit 501(c)(3) corporation that serves the educational community in the US-affiliated Pacific islands, the continental United States, and countries throughout the world. PREL bridges the gap between research, theory, and practice in education and works collaboratively to provide services that range from curriculum development to assessment and evaluation. PREL serves the Pacific educational community with quality programs and products developed to promote educational excellence. We work throughout school systems, from classroom to administration, and collaborate routinely with governments, communities, and businesses. Above all, we specialize in multicultural and multilingual environments. From direct instruction to professional development to creation of quality educational materials, PREL is committed to ensuring that all students, regardless of circumstance or geographic location, have an equal opportunity to develop a strong academic foundation. PREL brings together in the Center for Information, Communications, and Technology (CICT) an experienced cadre of specialists in website development and design, educational technology, distance and online learning, multimedia production, interactive software development, writing and editing, graphics, and print production. By combining tested pedagogy with leading edge technology, PREL can create learning materials encompassing a wide variety of subject matter and delivery methods. PREL partners with researchers, schools, evaluators, publishers, and leaders in the learning technology industry to develop state-of-the-art learning tools and technology solutions. There are vast disparities across the Pacific when it comes to school resources, technology access, and bandwidth. PREL's goal is to work effectively in any type of setting in which an application is needed. With routine travel and a staff presence throughout the northern Pacific, PREL has resolved to reach underserved communities, determine their needs, and meet their requirements with the appropriate delivery and dissemination methods. Multimedia, Software, and Website conception, design, and delivery have become critical components of many learning programs. Our projects include development of teacher and student resources and resource kits, learning games, software solutions, and complex interactive database design. Distance Learning Content and Delivery extend educational resources to audiences and individuals outside the classroom setting. Distance options both enhance and exponentially increase learning opportunities. The CICT is a premier provider of distance education, integrating curriculum and technology. High-Quality Publications are a PREL hallmark. PREL produces and distributes numerous high-quality publications for educators, including its research compendium, Research into Practice; Pacific Educator magazine; educational books and videos; and briefs and reports on research findings and current topics of interest.

Membership – PREL serves teachers and departments and ministries of education in American Samoa, Commonwealth of the Northern Mariana Islands, Federated States of Micronesia (Chuuk, Kosrae, Pohnpei, and Yap) Guam, Hawaii, the Republic of the Marshall Islands, and the Republic of Palau. In addition we work with the educational community on the continental United States and countries throughout the world. We are not a membership organization. We are grant funded with grants from the United States Departments of Education, Labor, Health and Human Services, and other federal funding agencies such as the Institute of Museum and Library Services and the National Endowment for the Arts. In addition we have projects in partnership with regional educational institutions. Internationally we have worked with the International Labor Organization and the World Health Organization and are currently working with Save the Children on a US AID project in the Philippines.

Dues – None

Meetings – PREL supports the annual Pacific Educational Conference (PEC), held each July.

Publications – Publications are listed on the PREL website at http://ppo.prel.org/. Most are available in both PDF and HTML format. Some recent publications are described below: Focus on Professional Development, A (Research Based Practices in Early Reading Series). A Focus on Professional Development is the fourth in the Research-Based Practices in Early Reading Series published by the Regional Educational Laboratory (REL) at Pacific Resources for Education and Learning (PREL). Because reading proficiency is fundamental to student achievement across all subjects and grades, the preparation of the teachers and administrators who are responsible for providing early reading instruction is of special importance. This booklet examines what research tells us about professional development and about the role that effective professional development plays in improving both teacher performance and student achievement.

http://www.prel.org/products/re_/prodevelopment.pdf (902 K) Look and See: Using the Visual Environment as Access to Literacy (Research Brief) This paper describes how the visual environment – what we see when we look – can be used to develop both visual and verbal literacy, including aesthetic appreciation, comprehension, and vocabulary. http://www.prel.org/products/re_/look_see.pdf (1 M) Measuring the Effectiveness of Professional Development in Early Literacy: Lessons Learned (Research Brief). This Research Brief focuses on the methodology used to measure professional development (PD) effectiveness. It examines the needs that generated this research, what PREL did to meet those needs, and lessons that have been learned as a result. In particular, it discusses the development of a new instrument designed to measure the quality of PD as it is being delivered. http://www.prel.org/products/re_/effect_of_pd.pdf (730 K) Pacific Early Literacy Resource Kit CD-ROM (Early Literacy Learning Resources) The Pacific Early Literacy Resource Kit was developed from PRELs research-based work performed with early literacy teachers in US-affiliated Pacific islands. The contents of the Resource Kit represent information, products, and processes we found beneficial as we worked to support literacy teachers in their efforts to improve student literacy achievement. http://www.prel.org/toolkit/index.htm Research Into Practice 2006 (PREL Compendium) This 86-page volume of PRELs annual research compendium brings together articles detailing research conducted during 2005 by PREL. The six articles in this issue focus on putting research findings to work to improve education. http://www.prel.org/products/pr_/compendium06/tableofcontents.asp

Name of Organization or Association – Reference and User Services Association, a division of the American Library Association

Acronym – RUSA

Address:
50 E. Huron St.
Chicago, IL
60611
US

Phone Number – (800)545-2433, ext. 4398.; **Fax Number** – Fax (312)280-5273

Email Contact – rusa@ala.org; **URL** – http://rusa.ala.org

Leaders – Barbara A. Macikas, Executive Director
Description – A division of the American Library Association, RUSA is responsible for stimulating and supporting in every type of library the delivery of reference information services to all groups and of general library services and materials to adults.

Membership – 5,200

Dues – Join ALA and RUSA $120; RUSA membership $60 (added to ALA membership); student member $55 ($30 for ALA and $25 for RUSA); retired, support staff or nonsalaried $72 ($42 for ALA and $30 for RUSA)

Meetings – Meetings are held in conjunction with the American Library Association.

Publications – RUSQ (q.), information provided on RUSA website at http://rusa.ala.org, RUSA Update, online membership newsletter, select publications.

Name of Organization or Association – Research for Better Schools, Inc.

Acronym – RBS
Address:
112 North Broad Street
Philadelphia, PA
19102-1510
US

Phone Number – (215)568-6150; **Fax Number** – (215)568-7260

Email Contact – info@rbs.org; **URL** – http://www.rbs.org/

Leaders – Keith M. Kershner, Executive Director

Description – Research for Better Schools is a nonprofit education organization that has been providing services to teachers, administrators, and policymakers since 1966. Our mission is to help students achieve high learning standards by supporting improvement efforts in schools and other education environments. The staff are dedicated to and well experienced in providing the array of services that schools, districts, and states need to help their students reach proficient or higher learning standards: (1) technical assistance in improvement efforts; (2) professional development that is required for the successful implementation of more effective curricula, technologies, or instruction; (3) application of research in the design of specific improvement efforts; (4) evaluation of improvement efforts; (5) curriculum implementation and assessment; and (6) effective communication with all members of the school community. RBS has worked with a wide range of clients over the years, representing all levels of the education system, as well as business and community groups.

Membership – There is no membership in Research for Better Schools.

Dues – None

Meetings – None

Publications – RBS publishes a variety of books and other products designed for educators to use for schools improvement. The catalog for RBS Publications is online (visit our homepage at http://www.rbs.org).

Name of Organization or Association – SERVE Center @ UNCG

Acronym – We no longer use the acronym

Address:
5900 Summit Avenue, Dixon Building
Browns Summit, FL
27214
US

Phone Number – 800-755-3277, 336-315-7457; **Fax Number** – 336-315-7457

Email Contact – info@serve.org; **URL** – http://www.serve.org/

Leaders – Ludy van Broekhuizen, Executive Director

Description – The SERVE Center at the University of North Carolina at Greensboro, under the leadership of Dr. Ludwig David van Broekhuizen, is a university-based education organization with the mission to promote and support the continuous improvement of educational opportunities for all learners in the Southeast. The organizations commitment to continuous improvement is manifest in an applied research-to-practice model that drives all of its work. Building on research, professional wisdom, and craft knowledge, SERVE staff members develop tools, processes, and interventions designed to assist practitioners and policymakers with their work. SERVEs ultimate goal is to raise the level of student achievement in the region. Evaluation of the impact of these activities combined with input from stakeholders expands SERVEs knowledge base and informs future research. This rigorous and practical approach to research and development is supported by an experienced staff strategically located throughout the region. This staff is highly skilled in providing needs assessment services, conducting applied research in schools, and developing processes, products, and programs that support educational improvement and increase student achievement. In the last 3 years, in addition to its basic research and development work with over 170 southeastern schools, SERVE staff provided technical assistance and training to more than 18,000 teachers and administrators across the region. The SERVE Center is governed by a board of directors that includes the governors, chief state school officers, educators, legislators, and private sector leaders from Alabama, Florida, Georgia, Mississippi, North Carolina, and South Carolina. SERVEs operational core is the Regional Educational Laboratory. Funded by the US Department of Educations Institute of Education Sciences, the Regional Educational Laboratory for the Southeast is one of ten Laboratories providing research-based information and services to all 50 states and territories. These Laboratories form a nationwide education knowledge network, building a bank of information and resources shared and disseminated nationally and regionally to improve student achievement. SERVEs National Leadership Area, Expanded Learning Opportunities, focuses on improving student outcomes through the use of exemplary pre–K and extended-day programs.

Membership – None

Dues – none

Meetings – none

Publications – Three titles available in the highlighted products area of website: A Review Of Methods and Instruments Used In State and Local School Readiness Evaluations Abstract: This report provides detailed information about the methods and instruments used to evaluate school readiness initiatives, discusses important considerations in selecting instruments, and provides resources and recommendations that may be helpful to those who are designing and implementing school readiness evaluations. Levers For Change: Southeast Region State Initiatives To Improve High Schools Abstract: This descriptive report aims to stimulate discussion about high school reform among Southeast Region states. The report groups recent state activities in high school reform into six "levers for change." To encourage critical reflection, the report places the reform discussion in the context of an evidence-based decision-making process and provides sample research on reform activities. Evidence-Based Decision making: Assessing Reading Across the Curriculum Intervention Abstract: When selecting reading across the curriculum interventions, educators should consider the extent of the evidence base on intervention effectiveness and the fit with the school or district context, whether they are purchasing a product from vendors or developing it internally. This report provides guidance in the decision making.

Name of Organization or Association – Society for Photographic Education

Acronym – SPE

Address:
126 Peabody Hall, The School of Interdisciplinary Studies, Miami University
Oxford, OH
45056
US

Phone Number – (513) 529-8328;
Fax Number – (513) 529-9301

Email Contact – speoffice@spenational.org; **URL** – www.spenational.org

Leaders – Richard Gray, Chairperson of SPE Board of Directors

Description – An association of college and university teachers of photography, museum photographic curators, writers, publishers and students. Promotes discourse in photography education, culture, and art.

Membership – 1,800 membership dues are for the calendar year, January through December.

Dues – Membership Dues: $90-Regular Membership $50-Student Membership $600-Corporate Member $380-Collector Member (with print) $150-Sustaining Member $65-Senior Member

Meetings – Denver, CO, March 13–16, 2008

Publications – Exposure (Photographic Journal) – bi-annual – Quarterly Newsletter – Membership Directory – Conference Program Guide

Name of Organization or Association – Society of Cable Telecommunications Engineers

Acronym – SCTE

Address:
140 Philips Rd
Exton, PA
19341-1318
US

Phone Number – (610)363-6888; **Fax Number** – (610)363-5898

Email Contact – scte@scte.org; **URL** – http://www.scte.org

Leaders – Mark L. Dzuban, President & CEO

Description – The Society of Cable Telecommunications Engineers (SCTE) is a nonprofit professional association that provides technical leadership for the telecommunications industry and serves its members through professional development, standards, certification and information. SCTE currently has more than 14,000 members from the US and 70 countries worldwide and offers a variety of programs and services for the industry's educational benefit. SCTE has 68 chapters and meeting groups and more than 3,000 employees of the cable telecommunications industry hold SCTE technical certifications. SCTE is an ANSI-accredited standards development organization. Visit SCTE online at www.scte.org.

Membership – SCTE is comprised of a global network of more than 14,000 Broadband engineers, technology experts, industry analysts, technicians, corporate managers and CEOs who work within the Cable Telecommunications industry. SCTE offers industry professionals a multitude of learning opportunities on the latest technological advances, industry news and targeted resources to help keep members better informed, outperform their peers and advance in their careers at a pace that works best for them.

Dues – $68 Individual $350 Expo Partner $34 Full-time Student, Unemployed or Retired (one-year)
Meetings – SCTE Cable-Tec Expo®, Denver, CO, Oct. 28–30, 2009; SCTE Conference on Broadband Learning & Development, Denver, CO, Oct. 27, 2009; SCTE Conference on Emerging Technologies®;

Publications – SCTE Interval SCTE Monthly SCTE NewsBreak Credentials Standards Bulletin

Name of Organization or Association – Society of Photo Technologists

Acronym – SPT

Address:
11112 S. Spotted Rd.
Cheney, WA
99004
US

Phone Number – 800-624-9621 or (509)624-9621;
Fax Number – (509)624-5320

Email Contact – cc5@earthlink.net; **URL** – http://www.spt.info/

Leaders – Chuck Bertone, Executive Director

Description – An organization of photographic equipment repair technicians, which improves and maintains communications between manufacturers and repair shops and technicians. We publish Repair Journals, Newsletters, Parts & Service Directory and Industry Newsletters. We also sponsor SPTNET (a technical email group), Remanufactured parts and residence workshops.

Membership – 1,000 shops and manufactures world wide, eligible people or businesses are any who are involved full or part time in the camera repair field.

Dues – $97.50-$370. Membership depends on the size/volume of the business. Most one man shops are Class A/$170 dues. Those not involved full time in the field is $95.50/Associate Class.

Meetings – SPT Journal; SPT Parts and Services Directory; SPT Newsletter; SPT Manuals – Training and Manufacturer's Tours.

Publications – Journals & Newsletters

Name of Organization or Association – Southwest Educational Development Laboratory

Acronym – SEDL

Address:
211 East Seventh St.
Austin, TX
78701
US

Phone Number – (512) 476-6861; **Fax Number** – (512) 476-2286

Email Contact – info@sedl.org; **URL** – http://www.sedl.org

Leaders – Dr. Wesley A. Hoover, President and CEO

Description– The Southwest Educational Development Laboratory (SEDL) is a private, not-for-profit education research and development corporation based in Austin, Texas. SEDL has worked in schools to investigate the conditions under which teachers can provide student-centered instruction supported by technology, particularly computers alone with other software. From that field-based research with teachers, SEDL has developed a professional development model and modules, which resulted in the production of Active Learning with Technology (ALT) portfolio. ALT is a multimedia training program for teachers to learn how to apply student-centered, problem-based learning theory to their instructional strategies that are supported by technologies. Copies of Active Learning with Technology Portfolio and other products used to integrate technology in the classroom can be viewed and ordered online at http://www.sedl.org/pubs/category_technology.html from SEDLs Office of Institutional Communications. SEDL operates the Southeast Comprehensive Center (SECC), funded by the U.S. Department of Education, which provides high-quality technical assistance in the states of Alabama, Georgia, Louisiana, Mississippi and South Carolina. The goals of the SECC are to build the capacities of states in its region to implement the programs and goals of the No Child Left Behind Act of 2001 (NCLB) and to build states capacity to provide sustained support of high-needs districts and schools. SECC works closely with each state in its region to provide access and use of information, models, and materials that facilitate implementation of and compliance with NCLB. SEDLs Texas Comprehensive Center provides technical assistance and support to the Texas Education Agency to assure Texas has an education system with the capacity and commitment to eliminate achievement gaps and enable all students to achieve at high levels.

Membership – Not applicable.

Dues – Not applicable.

Meetings – Not applicable

Publications – SEDL LETTER and other newsletters and documents are available for free general distribution in print and online. Topic-specific publications related to educational change, education policy, mathematics, language arts, science, and disability research and a publications catalog are available at http://www.sedl.org/pubs on the SEDL Web site.

Name of Organization or Association – Special Libraries Association

Acronym – SLA

Address:
331 South Patrick Street
Alexandria, VA
22314
US

Phone Number – 703-647-4900; **Fax Number** – 703-647-4901

Email Contact – sla@sla.org; **URL** – http://www.sla.org

Leaders – The Honorable Janice R. Lachance, CEO

Description – The Special Libraries Association (SLA) is a nonprofit global organization for innovative information professionals and their strategic partners. SLA serves more than 11,000 members in 75 countries in the information profession, including corporate, academic and government information specialists. SLA promotes and strengthens its members through learning, advocacy, and networking initiatives. For more information, visit us on the Web at www.sla.org.

Membership – 11,500

Dues – Full Membership: USD 160.00 (members earning greater than USD 35,000 in annual salary); USD 99.00 (members earning USD 35,000 or less in annual salary). Student/Retired Membership: USD 35.00

Meetings – 2006 Annual Conference and Exposition: 11–14 June, Baltimore; 2007 Annual Conference and Exposition: 3–6 June, Denver

Publications – Information Outlook (monthly glossy magazine that accepts advertising). SLA Connections (monthly electronic newsletter for members and stakeholders).

Name of Organization or Association – Teachers and Writers Collaborative

Acronym – T&W
Address:

520 Eighth Avenue, Suite 2020
New York, NY
10018
US

Phone Number – (212)691-6590, Toll-free (888)266-5789; **Fax Number** – (212)675-0171

Email Contact – bmorrow@twc.org; **URL** – http://www.twc.org and http://www.writenet.org

Leaders – Amy Swauger, Director

Description – T&W brings the joys and pleasures of reading and writing directly to children. As an advocate for the literary arts and arts education, we support writers and teachers in developing and implementing new teaching strategies; disseminate models for literary arts education to local, national, and international audiences; and showcase both new and established writers via publications and literary events held in our Center for Imaginative Writing. T&W was founded in 1967 by a group of writers and educators who believed that professional writers could make a unique contribution to the teaching of writing and literature. Over the past 40 years, 1,500 T&W writers have taught writing workshops in New York City's public schools. Approximately 700,000 New York City students have participated in our workshops, and we have worked with more than 25,000 teachers. Our wealth of experience, which is reflected in T&W's 80 books about teaching writing, led the National Endowment for the Arts to single out T&W as the arts-in-education group "most familiar with creative writing/literature in primary and secondary schools." The American Book Review has written that T&W "has created a whole new pedagogy in the teaching of English."

Membership – T&W has over 1,000 members across the country. The basic membership is $35; patron membership is $75; and benefactor membership is $150 or more. Members receive a free book or T-shirt; discounts on publications; and a free one-year subscription to Teachers & Writers magazine. (Please see http://www.twc.org/member.htm.)

Dues – T&W is seeking general operating support for all of our programs and program support for specific projects, including: (1) T&W writing residencies in New York City area schools; (2) T&W publications, books and a quarterly magazine, which we distribute across the country; (3) T&W events, including readings for emerging writers and small presses; and (4) T&W's Internet programs for teachers, writers, and students. Grants to T&Ws Endowment support the stability of the organization and help to guarantee the continuation of specific programs.

Meetings – T&W offers year-round public events in our Center for Imaginative Writing in New York City. For a list of events, please see http://www.twc.org/events.htm.

Publications – T&W has published over 80 books on the teaching of imaginative writing, including The T&W Handbook of Poetic Forms; The Dictionary of Wordplay; The Story in History; Personal Fiction Writing; Luna, Luna: Creative Writing from Spanish and Latino Literature; The Nearness of You: Students and Teachers Writing Online. To request a free publications catalog, please send email to info@twc.org or call 888-BOOKS-TW. (Please see http://www.twc.org/pubs)

Name of Organization or Association – The George Lucas Educational Foundation

Acronym – GLEF

Address:
P.O. Box 3494
San Rafael, CA
94912
US

Phone Number – (415)662-1600; **Fax Number** – (415)662-1619

Email Contact – edutopia@glef.org; **URL** – http://edutopia.org

Leaders – Milton Chen, PhD., Executive Director

Description – Mission: The George Lucas Educational Foundation (GLEF) is a nonprofit operating foundation that documents and disseminates models of the most innovative practices in our nation's K-12 schools. We serve this mission through the creation of media – from films, books, and magazine to CD-ROMS and DVDs. GLEF works to provide its products as tools for discussion and action in conferences, workshops, and professional development settings. Audience: A successful educational system requires the collaborative efforts of many different stakeholders. Our audience includes teachers, administrators, school board members, parents, researchers, and business and community leaders who are actively working to improve teaching and learning. Vision: The Edutopian vision is thriving today in our country's best schools: places where students are engaged and achieving at the highest levels, where skillful educators are energized by the excitement of teaching, where technology brings outside resources and expertise into the classroom, and where parents and community members are partners in educating our youth.

Membership – All online content and the Edutopia magazine are offered free of charge to educators.

Dues – Free subscription to Edutopia magazine for those working in education.

Meetings – no public meetings; advisory council meets annually; board of directors meets quarterly

Publications – Edutopia Online: The Foundation's Web site, Edutopia (www.edutopia.org) celebrates the unsung heroes who are making Edutopia a reality. All of GLEF's multimedia content dating back to 1997 is available on its Web site. A special feature, the Video Gallery, is an archive of short documentaries and expert interviews that allow visitors to see these innovations in action and hear about them from teachers and students. Detailed articles, research summaries, and links to hundreds of relevant Web sites, books, organizations, and publications are also available to help schools and communities build on successes in education. Edutopia: Success Stories for Learning in the Digital Age: This book and CD-ROM include numerous stories of innovative educators who are using technology to connect with students, colleagues, the local community, and the world beyond. The CD-ROM contains more than an hour of video footage. Published by Jossey-Bass. Teaching in the Digital Age (TDA) Videocassettes This video series explores elements of successful teaching in the Digital Age. The project grows out of GLEFs belief that an expanded view is needed of all our roles in educating children and supporting teachers. The series explores School Leadership, Emotional Intelligence, Teacher Preparation, and Project-Based Learning and Assessment. Learn & Live This documentary film and 300-page companion resource book showcases innovative schools across the country. The film, hosted by Robin Williams, aired on public television stations nationwide in 1999 and 2000. The Learn & Live CD-ROM includes digital versions of the film and book in a portable, easy-to-use format. Edutopia Magazine A free magazine which shares powerful examples of innovative and exemplary learning and teaching. Edutopia Newsletter This free, semi-annual print newsletter includes school profiles, summaries of recent research, and resources and tips for getting involved in public education. Instructional Modules Free teaching modules developed by education faculty and professional developers. They can be used as extension units in existing courses, or can be used independently in workshops. Includes presenter notes, video segments, discussion questions. Topics include project-based learning, technology integration, and multiple intelligences.

Name of Organization or Association – The NETWORK, Inc.

Acronym – NETWORK

Address:
136 Fenno Drive
Rowley, MA
01969-1004
USA

Phone Number – 800-877-5400, (978)948-7764; **Fax Number** – (978)948-7836

Email Contact – davidc@thenetworkinc.org; **URL** – www.thenetworkinc.org

Leaders – David Crandall, President

Description – A nonprofit research and service organization providing training, research and evaluation, technical assistance, and materials for a fee to schools, educational organizations, and private sector firms with educational interests. The NETWORK has been helping professionals manage and learn about change since 1969. Our Leadership Skills series of computer-based simulations extends the widely used board game versions of Making Change (tm) and Systems Thinking/Systems Changing(tm) with the addition of Improving Student Success: Teachers, Schools and Parents to offer educators a range of proven professional development tools. Available in 2007, Networking for Learning, originally developed for the British Department for Education and Skills, offers schools considering forming or joining a network a risk-free means of exploring the many challenges.

Membership – none required

Dues – no dues, fee for service

Meetings – call

Publications – Making Change: A Simulation Game [board and computer versions]; Systems Thinking/Systems Changing: A Simulation Game [board and computer versions]; Improving Student Success: Teachers, Schools and Parents [computer based simulation]; Systemic Thinking: Solving Complex Problems; Benchmarking: A Guide for Educators; Networking for Learning; Check Yourself into College: A quick and easy guide for high school students.

Name of Organization or Association – University Continuing Education Association

Acronym – UCEA

Address:
One Dupont Cir. NW, Suite 615
Washington, DC
20036
US

Phone Number – (202)659-3130; **Fax Number** – (202)785-0374

Email Contact – kjkohl@ucea.edu; **URL** – http://www.ucea.edu/

Leaders – Kay J. Kohl, Executive Director, kjkohl@ucea.edu

Description – UCEA is an association of public and private higher education institutions concerned with making continuing education available to all population segments and to promoting excellence in continuing higher education. Many institutional members offer university and college courses via electronic instruction.

Membership – 425 institutions, 2,000 professionals.

Dues – vary according to membership category; see: http://www.ucea.edu/membership.htm

Meetings – UCEA has an annual national conference and several professional development seminars throughout the year. See: http://www.ucea.edu/page02.htm

Publications – monthly newsletter; quarterly; occasional papers; scholarly journal, Continuing Higher Education Review; Independent Study Catalog. With Peterson's, The Guide to Distance Learning; Guide to Certificate Programs at American Colleges and Universities; UCEA-ACE/Oryx Continuing Higher Education book series; Lifelong Learning Trends (a statistical factbook on continuing higher education); organizational issues series; membership directory.

Name of Organization or Association – Young Adult Library Services Association

Acronym – YALSA

Address:
50 E. Huron St.
Chicago, IL
60611
US

Phone Number – (312)280-4390; **Fax Number** – (312)280-5276

Email Contact – yalsa@ala.org; **URL** – http://www.ala.org/yalsa

Leaders – Beth Yoke, Executive Director; Judy T. Nelson, President

Description – A division of the American Library Association (ALA), the Young Adult Library Services Association (YALSA) seeks to advocate, promote, and strengthen service to young adults as part of the continuum of total library services. Is responsible within the ALA to evaluate and select books and media and to interpret and make recommendations regarding their use with young adults. Selected List Committees include Best Books for Young Adults, Popular Paperbacks for Young Adults, Quick Picks for Reluctant Young Adult Readers, Outstanding Books for the College Bound, Selected Audiobooks for Young Adults, Great Graphic Novels for Teens and Selected Films for Young Adults. To learn more about our literary awards, such as the Odyssey Award for best audiobook production, and recommended reading, listening and viewing lists go to www.ala.org/yalsa/booklists. YALSA celebrates Teen Tech Week the first full week of March each year. To learn more go to www.ala.org/teentechweek.

Membership – 5,500. YALSA members may be young adult librarians, school librarians, library directors, graduate students, educators, publishers, or anyone for whom library service to young adults is important.

Dues – $50; $20 students; $20 retirees (in addition to ALA membership)

Meetings – 2 ALA conferences yearly, Midwinter (January) and Annual (June); one biennial Young Adult Literature Symposium (beginning in 2008)

Publications – Young Adult Library Services, a quarterly print journal YAttitudes, a quarterly electronic newsletter for members only

There are a total of 91 organizations in the database.

Part V
Graduate Programs

Introduction

Michael Orey and Pamela Fortner

Part 5 includes annotated entries for graduate programs that offer degrees in the fields of learning, design and technology, or library and information science. In an effort to list only active organizations, I deleted all programs that had not updated their information since 2006. Readers are encouraged to contact the institutions that are not listed for investigation and possible inclusion in the 2011 edition.

Information for this part was obtained through e-mail directing each program to an individual web form through which the updated information could be submitted electronically into a database created by Michael Orey. Although the section editors made every effort to contact and follow up with program representatives, responding to the annual request for an update was the responsibility of the program representatives. The editing team would like to thank those respondents who helped assure the currency and accuracy of this part by responding to the request for an update. In this year's edition, I asked for some data on numbers of graduates, number of faculty, and amount of grants and contracts. These data were used as self-report top 20 lists in the preface to this book. Readers should be aware that these data are only as accurate as the person who filled the form for their program.

M. Orey (✉)
Learning, Design, and Technology Program, The University of Georgia, Athens, GA, USA
e-mail: mikeorey@uga.edu

P. Fortner (✉)
Department of Educational Psychology and Instructional Technology, The University of Georgia, Athens, GA, USA
e-mail: phales@uga.edu

M. Orey et al. (eds.), *Educational Media and Technology Yearbook*,
Educational Media and Technology Yearbook 35,
DOI 10.1007/978-1-4419-1516-0_19, © Springer Science+Business Media, LLC 2010

Worldwide List of Graduate Programs in Learning, Design, Technology, Information, or Libraries

Name of Institution – Athabasca University
Name of Department or Program – Centre for Distance Education

Address:
1 University Drive
Athabasca, AB
T9S 3A3
Canada

Phone Number – 17806756406 **Fax Number** – 1-780-675-6170

Email Contact – mohameda@athabascau.ca **URL** – cde.athabascau.ca

Contact Person – Mohamed Ally

Specializations – Doctor of Education in Distance Education. Master of Distance Education. Graduate Diploma in Distance Education. Technology Graduate Diploma in Instructional Design. Graduate Certificate in Instructional Design

Features – Doctor of Education in Distance Education. Master of Distance Education. Graduate Diploma in Distance Education. Technology Graduate Diploma in Instructional Design. Graduate Certificate in Instructional Design

Admission Requirements – Doctorate of Education in Distance Education. Admission requirements for the doctoral program include both academic and experiential elements. * Completion of a master's degree, preferably with a thesis or research project, in a relevant field or area of study (e.g., education or distance education, psychology or educational psychology, instructional technology, adult education, curriculum and instruction) from a recognized university, normally with a GPA of at least 3.7 or 85% (Graduate Grading Policy); * Significant experience in open or distance learning, which demonstrates that the student is capable of study at a distance and of completing high-quality original research with distance supervision only. Master of Distance Education Applicants to the MDE program must hold a baccalaureate degree from a recognized post-secondary education institution. If the potential applicant does not have a degree, but believes his or her education and

M. Orey et al. (eds.), *Educational Media and Technology Yearbook*,
Educational Media and Technology Yearbook 35,
DOI 10.1007/978-1-4419-1516-0_20, © Springer Science+Business Media, LLC 2010

experience is equivalent to an undergraduate degree, then it is the responsibility of the applicant to put forward this position in writing as part of the application process. Graduate Diploma in Distance Education Technology. Applicants to the GDDET program must hold a baccalaureate degree from a recognized post-secondary education institution. If the potential applicant does not have a degree, but believes that his or her education and experience is equivalent to an undergraduate degree, then it is the responsibility of the applicant to put forward this position in writing as part of the application process. Graduate Diploma in Instructional Design. Applicants to the GDID program must hold a baccalaureate degree from a recognized post-secondary education institution. If the potential applicant does not have a degree, but believes that his or her education and experience is equivalent to an undergraduate degree, then it is the responsibility of the applicant to put forward this position in writing as part of the application process. Graduate Certificate in Instructional Design. Applicants to the GCID program must hold a baccalaureate degree from a recognized post-secondary education institution. If the potential applicant does not have a degree, but believes that his or her education and experience is equivalent to an undergraduate degree, then it is the responsibility of the applicant to put forward this position in writing as part of the application process.

Degree Requirements – Doctor of Education in Distance Education. The Doctor of Education in Distance Education program will address the needs of a wide range of practitioners, scholars, and researchers who operate in the distance education arena. The doctorate will provide critical direction as distance education evolves and expands. The primary goal of the doctoral program is to provide students with a complete and rigorous preparation to assume senior responsibilities for planning, teaching, directing, designing, implementing, evaluating, researching, and managing distance education programs. Master of Distance Education. Athabasca University's Master of Distance Education (MDE) program is designed to provide a common base of skills, knowledge, and values regarding distance education and training, independent of any special area of interest. Graduate Diploma in Distance Education Technology. Athabasca University's Graduate Diploma in Distance Education Technology GDDET is a focused, 18-credit (six courses) program designed to provide a solid grounding in the current principles and practices of technology use in distance education and training. The program structure and course content emphasize the concepts and skills required of practitioners who are employed as instructors, teachers, trainers, decision makers, planners, managers, and administrators in distance education or "virtual" programs. The emphasis of the GDDET is on the user of technology for the preparation, delivery, and management of instruction. Graduate Diploma in Instructional Design. The Graduate Diploma in Instructional Design is an 18-credit program comprised of six courses. For those who wish to pursue instructional design as a profession, this diploma program provides more depth and breadth than the certificate. Graduate Certificate in Instructional Design. The Graduate Certificate in Instructional Design is a 9-credit program, comprised of three courses. For those wanting to enhance their instructional design expertise, the certificate program is an expedient way to obtain the appropriate skills and knowledge.

Number of Full-Time Faculty – 11; **Number of Other Faculty** – 15

Degrees awarded in 2007–2008 Academic Year – Master's – 52; **PhD** – 0; **Other** – 12

Grant Monies awarded in 2007–2008 Academic Year – 0

Name of Institution – University of Calgary
Name of Department or Program – Graduate Division of Educational Research

Address:
Education Tower 940, 2500 University Drive NW, University of Calgary,
Calgary, AB
T2N 1N4
Canada

Phone Number – 403-220-5675 **Fax Number** – 403-282-3005

Email Contact – gder@ucalgary.ca
URL – http://wapsrv5.acs.ucalgary.ca/gder/htdocs/

Contact Person – Dr. Michele Jacobsen

Specializations – In a knowledge-based economy, the PhD, EDD, MA, and MEd programs in the Educational Technology specialization in GDER at the University of Calgary have proven valuable to public and private sector researchers, teachers, military/industrial trainers, health educators, managers, and leaders. A spectrum of entrepreneurs and public service experts have successfully completed our programs and are using the skills in higher education and a range of workplaces today. Our graduates have careers as practitioners and scholars in the top government, industry, K-12, and higher education institutions as professors, education and training leaders, teachers, and instructors – worldwide. Your academic and professional career growth is possible through our innovative, student-centered programs and supervision processes in this growing, vibrant area. Degree programs can be completed on campus, in blended formats or completely online.

Features – The Educational Technology Specialization is addressed to at least two audiences: (a) School leaders and teachers who are interested in the application of technology in the classroom or who are interested in technology leadership positions or who are interested in academic careers in higher education; (b) those who are interested in instructional development in settings outside elementary/secondary schools, e.g., instructional developers in colleges, institutes of technology and universities, military/industrial trainers, health educators, and private training consultants. Students in this specialization have the opportunity to investigate a broad spectrum of instructional design and development techniques as they apply to newer technologies and to explore new directions in instructional design and development and evaluation as they emerge in the literature.

Admission Requirements – The Master of Education (MEd) is a course-based professional degree. The MEd program is available in the on-campus and online formats. Admission requirements normally include a completed 4-year bachelor's degree and a 3.0 GPA. The Master of Arts (MA) is a thesis-based degree intended to prepare students for further research. Admission requirements normally include a completed 4-year bachelor's degree and a 3.3 GPA. The Doctor of Education (EdD) is a thesis-based degree intended to prepare scholars for careers in research, teaching, and leadership. The EdD program is available in the online format. Admission requirements normally include a completed master's degree and a 3.5 GPA. The Doctor of Philosophy (PhD) is a thesis-based degree intended to prepare scholars for careers in research and teaching. The PhD program is available in the on-campus format. Admission requirements normally include a completed master's thesis and a 3.5 GPA.

Degree Requirements – Program requirements for the Master of Education (MEd) program are completion of a minimum of six full-course equivalents (12 half-courses). In Educational Technology, master's students complete six half-courses in the specialization, two half-courses in research methodology, and four half-courses in elective areas (can also be in educational technology). Program requirements for the Master of Arts (MA) thesis program include the following: (a) one full-course equivalent (two half-courses) in research methods; (b) a minimum of one full-course equivalent (two half-courses) in the students area of specialization; (c) additional graduate courses or seminars determined by the supervisor in consultation with the student; and (d) a master's thesis and an oral examination on the thesis. Program requirements for the Education Doctorate (EdD) program include the following: (a) a minimum of one and one-half full-course equivalents, including EDER 700 (a full-course equivalent), is required of all doctoral students during their first year of program; (b) additional graduate courses or seminars as determined by the supervisor in consultation with the student (normally, EdD students in Educational Technology complete four half-course equivalents in the specialization); (c) a candidacy examination demonstrating the student's competence to undertake a thesis; (d) a doctoral thesis and an oral examination on the thesis. Program requirements for the on-campus Doctor of Philosophy (PhD) program include: (a) a minimum of one and one-half full-course equivalents, including EDER 700 (a full-course equivalent), is required of all doctoral students during their first year of program (the required half-course is normally a course in research methods suited to the students area of research); (b) Educational Technology: EDER 771 Doctoral Seminar in Educational Technology; (c) additional graduate courses or seminars determined by the supervisor in consultation with the student; (d) a candidacy examination demonstrating the students competence to undertake a thesis; and (e) a doctoral thesis and an oral examination on the thesis.

Number of Full-Time Faculty – 9; **Number of Other Faculty** – 80

Degrees awarded in 2007–2008 Academic Year – Master's – 235; **PhD** – 8; **Other** – 11

Grant Monies awarded in 2007–2008 Academic Year – 20000000

Name of Institution – University of British Columbia
Name of Department or Program – Master of Educational Technology degree program

Address:
1304 – 2125 Main Mall
Vancouver, BC
V6T 1Z4
Canada

Phone Number – 1-888-492-1122 **Fax Number** – 1-604-822-2015

Email Contact – info@met.ubc.ca **URL** – http://met.ubc.ca

Contact Person – David Roy

Specializations – This innovative online program provides an excellent environment in which to learn the techniques of instructional design including the development and management of programs for international and intercultural populations. Attracting students from more than 30 countries, the program provides a unique opportunity to learn and collaborate with professionals and colleagues from around the world. The MET curriculum is designed for K-12 teachers, college and university faculty, course designers, and adult and industry educators.

Features – MET fully online graduate degree. MET Graduate Certificate in Technology-Based Distributed Learning. MET Graduate Certificate in Technology-Based Learning for Schools.

Admission Requirements – Please see website.

Degree Requirements – Master's program: 10 courses. Graduate Certificates: 5 courses

Number of Full-Time Faculty – 9; **Number of Other Faculty** – 8

Degrees awarded in 2007–2008 Academic Year – Master's – 36; **PhD** – 0; **Other** – 0

Grant Monies awarded in 2007–2008 Academic Year – 0

Name of Institution – University of New Brunswick
Name of Department or Program – Faculty of Education

Address:
PO Box 4400
Fredericton, NB
E3B 5A3
Canada

Phone Number – 506-452-6125 **Fax Number** – 506-453-3569

Email Contact – erose@unb.ca **URL** – http://www.unbf.ca/education/

Contact Person – Dr. Ellen Rose

Specializations – Instructional design for e-learning courses are also offered in instructional design theories and processes, cultural studies in instructional design, instructional message design, and needs assessment. In addition, students are expected to take other courses in the Faculty of Education or other applicable areas.

Features – Students can choose the course, project, or thesis stream. UNBs MEd in Instructional Design is very flexible, allowing students to customize their own learning experiences in order to meet their particular learning outcomes. While this is not an online program, several of the instructional design courses, and many other relevant courses in the Faculty of Education, are available online.

Admission Requirements – Applicants must have an undergraduate degree in education or a relevant field, a grade point average of at least 3.0 (B, or its equivalent), and at least 1 year of teaching or related professional experience. Applicants whose first language is not English must submit evidence of their proficiency in the use of the English language. The minimum proficiency levels accepted by the Faculty of Education are scores of 650 on the TOEFL (280 computer-based) and 5.5 on the TWE.

Degree Requirements – Course route: ten 3-credit hour courses. Project route: eight 3-credit hour courses, and one project/report. Thesis route: five 3-credit hour courses and one thesis. Required courses: ED 6221 Instructional Design Theories and ED 6902 Introduction to Research in Education

Number of Full-Time Faculty – 1; **Number of Other Faculty** – 2

Degrees awarded in 2007–2008 Academic Year – Master's – 10; **PhD** – 0; **Other** – 0

Grant Monies awarded in 2007–2008 Academic Year – 0

Name of Institution – Concordia University

Name of Department or Program – Education – MA in Educational Technology, Diploma in Instructional Technology and PhD (Education), Specialization, Educational Technology

Address:
1455 de Maisonneuve Blvd. West
Montreal, QC
H3G 1M8
Canada

Phone Number – (514) 848-2424 x2030 **Fax Number** – (514) 848-4520

Email Contact – anne@education.concordia.ca **URL** – education.concordia.ca

Contact Person – Ms. Anne Brown-MacDougall, Programs Coordinator

Specializations – Concordias Department of Education offers a 30-credit graduate Diploma in Instructional Technology and an MA in Educational Technology, and our PhD in Education has a specialization in the area of Educational Technology as well. Main areas within the programs: Human Performance Technology. Distance Education. Interactive Multi-media Applications. Cybernetics. Administration and Project Management plus many other areas.

Features – Only graduate program in Quebec in this area.

Admission Requirements – For the MA Program: Applicants must have a GPA of 3.0 or higher from a variety of undergraduate disciplines. References, official transcripts, CV, and statement of purpose also required. For the diploma program: Applicants must have a GPA of 2.7 or higher from a variety of undergraduate disciplines. References, official transcripts, CV, and statement of purpose also required. For students for the PhD (Education): Applicants must have a GPA of 3.0 in a master's degree, preferably in the field of educational technology, but related disciplines are also acceptable. References, official transcripts, CV, and statement of purpose.

Degree Requirements – The PhD (Education) is 90-credit program, which includes required courses, tutorials, plus comprehensive examination, dissertation proposal, and dissertation. The MA program is 60-credits, which includes required courses, electives, plus either an internship experience and a report or a small internship, thesis proposal, and thesis. The diploma consists of only30 credits of coursework.

Number of Full-Time Faculty – 9; **Number of Other Faculty** – 40

Degrees awarded in 2007–2008 Academic Year – Master's – 25; **PhD** – 5; **Other** –5

Grant Monies awarded in 2007–2008 Academic Year – 100000

Name of Institution – University of Saskatchewan
Name of Department or Program – Educational Communications and Technology

Address:
28 Campus Drive, College of Education
Saskatoon, SK
S7N 0X1
Canada

Phone Number – 306-966-7558 **Fax Number** – 306-966-7658

Email Contact – richard.schwier@usask.ca **URL** – http://www.edct.ca

Contact Person – Richard A. Schwier

Specializations – We offer a general educational technology degree, but with a particular emphasis on instructional design.

Features – Most of our courses are delivered in flexible formats. Courses can be taken completely online or blended with classroom experiences. A few courses are only offered face-to-face, but an entire program can be taken online.

Admission Requirements – A professional bachelor's degree or the equivalent of a 4-year Bachelor of Arts. Normally, we require a minimum of 1 year of practical experience in education or a related field. An average of 70% in your most recent 60 credit units of university coursework.

Degree Requirements – MEd (non-thesis) students need to undertake 24 credit units of graduate-level coursework and the project seminar (ECMM 992.6) supervised by a faculty member in the program. MEd (thesis) students need to complete 21 units of graduate-level coursework and a thesis supervised by a faculty member in the program and a committee.

Number of Full-Time Faculty – 4; **Number of Other Faculty** – 2

Degrees awarded in 2007–2008 Academic Year – **Masters** – 20; **PhD** – 0; **Other** –0

Grant Monies awarded in 2007–2008 Academic Year – 200000

Name of Institution – The University of Hong Kong
Name of Department or Program – Faculty of Education

Address:
Pokfulam Road
Hong Kong, x
x
China

Phone Number – 852 2241 5856 **Fax Number** – 852 2517 0075

Email Contact – mite@cite.hku.hk **URL** – http://web.edu.hku.hk/programme/mite/

Contact Person – Dr. Daniel Churchill

Specializations – The Master of Science in Information Technology in Education [MSc(ITE)] program offers the following four specialist strands: e-leadership and educational change, e-learning, learning technology design, and library and information studies; *or* choose any of the elective modules to complete the MSc(ITE)

Features – The MSc(ITE) program aims to provide an investigation into Web 2.0, mobile learning, and other emerging learning and teaching technology applications; an opportunity to apply technology in learning and teaching; an opportunity to work in technology-rich learning environment; an exploration of the cultural, administrative, theoretical, and practical implications of technology in education; an introduction to research in technology for education; and an opportunity for those wishing to develop leadership capabilities in the use of technology in education

Admission Requirements – Applicants should normally hold a recognized bachelor's degree or qualifications of equivalent standard. Applicants may be required to sit for a qualifying examination.

Degree Requirements – To complete eight modules in 1-year full-time study or no more than 4 years of part-time studies

Number of Full-Time Faculty – 12; **Number of Other Faculty** – 90

Degrees awarded in 2007–2008 Academic Year – **Master's** – 0; **PhD** – 0; **Other** – 0

Grant Monies awarded in 2007–2008 Academic Year – 0

Name of Institution – Université de Poitiers
Name of Department or Program – Ingénierie des médias pour léducation

Address:
95, avenue du Recteur Pineau
Poitiers, PC
86000
France

Phone Number – +33 5 49 36 62 06 **Fax Number** – +33 5 49 45 32 90

Email Contact – cerisier@univ-poitiers.fr **URL** – ll.univ-poitiers.fr/dime

Contact Person – Jean-François Cerisier

Specializations – EUROMIME: European Master in Media Engineering for Education (Erasmus Mundus master). This master's program trains high-quality specialists in the relatively new discipline of educational technology. Throughout the course, students will be required to develop projects relating to the conception, utilization, and evaluation of various educational media. This work is applicable to the current development of distance teaching/learning. The course unifies several of the leading universities in this sector: the University of Poitiers (France), the National University for Distance Education at Madrid (Spain), and the Lisbon University of Technology (Portugal). For added regional contact, three universities from third countries also participate in this consortium: The National University of Brasil, the Catholic University of Peru, and the University of the Lakes, Chile. The consortium also utilizes many other international links and networks. MIME: national Master in Media Engineering for Education

Admission Requirements – Application and Interview

Degree Requirements – Bachelor's degree

Number of Full-Time Faculty – 25; **Number of Other Faculty** – 25

Degrees awarded in 2007–2008 Academic Year – **Master's** – 23; **PhD** – 0; **Other** – 0

Grant Monies awarded in 2007–2008 Academic Year – 1000000

Name of Institution – Ewha Womans University
Name of Department or Program – Educational Technology Department

Address:
11-1 Daehyun-dong, Seodaemun-ku
Seoul, KO
120-750
Korea

Phone Number – 82-2-3277-2671 **Fax Number** – 82-2-3277-2728

Email Contact – et2670@hanmail.net **URL** – home.ewha.ac.kr/~et

Contact Person – Department Chair, Myunghee Kang

Specializations – Theory and Practice of Instructional Technology e-Leaning Design and Development, Quality Assurance HRD/HPT Program development

Features – Undergraduate Master's Program. PhD Program. Special Master's Program for In-Service Teachers

Admission Requirements – Portfolio, Interview, English Competency

Degree Requirements – 24 credit hours of coursework for master's, 60 credit hours of coursework for PhD, and qualifying exam dissertation

Number of Full-Time Faculty – 8; **Number of Other Faculty** – 2

Degrees awarded in 2007–2008 Academic Year – **Master's** – 6; **PhD** – 4; **Other** –0

Grant Monies awarded in 2007–2008 Academic Year – 2000000

Name of Institution – Andong National University
Name of Department or Program – Department of Educational Technology, College of Education

Address:
388 Songchun-dong
Andong, Kyungbuk
760-749
Korea

Phone Number – +82-54-820-5580, 5585 **Fax Number** – +82-54-820-7653

Email Contact – ycyang@andong.ac.kr
URL – http://edutech.andong.ac.kr/~try/2007-11/main1.html

Contact Person – Dr. Yong-Chil Yang

Specializations – Instruction Systems Design and e-HRD major for Master Degree Educational Technology major for Ph. D

Features – * Only department supported by Ministry of Education in Korea * BA, MA, and PhD programs are offered * Established in 1996 * Inexpensive tuition and living expenses * Small class size

Admission Requirements – Fluent command of English or Korean language

Degree Requirements – BA degree for master's. MA degree in Education for PhD

Number of Full-Time Faculty – 6; **Number of Other Faculty** – 10

Degrees awarded in 2007–2008 Academic Year – **Master's** – 5; **PhD** – 1; **Other** – 3

Grant Monies awarded in 2007–2008 Academic Year – 8000

Name of Institution – Universiti Sains Malaysia
Name of Department or Program – Centre for Instructional Technology and Multimedia

Address:
Centre for Instructional Tech and Multimedia, Universiti Sains Malaysia
Minden, Pg
11800
Malaysia

Phone Number – 604-6533222 **Fax Number** – 604-6576749

Email Contact – Fauzy@usm.my **URL** – http://www.ptpm.usm.my

Contact Person – Assoc. Prof. Wan Mohd. Fauzy Wan Ismail, Director

Specializations– Instructional Design Web/Internet Instruction and Learning Educational Training/Resource Management Instructional Training Technology/Evaluation Instructional System Development Design and Development of Multimedia/Video/Training materials Instructional and Training Technology Constructivism in Instructional Technology E-Learning Systems, Learning Management Systems

Features – Master's in Instructional Technology – entering its third academic year 2004–2005 – Full-time – 1–2 years, Part-time – 2–4 years. Teaching programs – postgraduate programs and research consultancy – services on the application of educational/instructional design technology in teaching and learning. Training and Diffusion, Continuing Education in support of Life Long Learning Academic Support Services – services to support research, teaching, and learning activities and centers within the university

Admission Requirements – Bachelor's and Master's degree from accredited institution or relevant work experience

Degree Requirements – Part-time. Full-time

Number of Full-Time Faculty – None; **Number of Other Faculty** – None

Degrees awarded in 2007–2008 Academic Year – Master's – None; **PhD** – None; **Other** – None

Grant Monies awarded in 2007–2008 Academic Year – None

Name of Institution – Taganrog State Pedagogical Institute
Name of Department or Program – Media Education

Address:
Iniciativnaya, 48
Taganrog, None
347936
Russia

Phone Number – (8634)601753 **Fax Number** – (8634)605397

Email Contact – tgpi@mail.ru **URL** – http://www.tgpi.ttn.ru

Contact Person – Prof. Dr. Alexander Fedorov

Specializations – Media Education, Media Literacy, Media Competence

Admission Requirements – Varies per year, please see http://www.tgpi.ru

Degree Requirements – Admission after high school

Number of Full-Time Faculty – 1; **Number of Other Faculty** – 0

Degrees awarded in 2007–2008 Academic Year – **Master's** – 0; **PhD** – 3; **Other** – 25

Grant Monies awarded in 2007–2008 Academic Year – 100000

Name of Institution – Keimyung University
Name of Department or Program – Department of Education

Address:
2800 Dalgubeldaro
Dalseogu, Daegu
704-701
South Korea

Phone Number – 82-53-580-5962

Email Contact – weom@kmu.ac.kr

Contact Person – Wooyong Eom

Number of Full-Time Faculty – 9; **Number of Other Faculty** – 0

Degrees awarded in 2007–2008 Academic Year – **Masters** – 2; **PhD** – 1; **Other** – 0

Grant Monies awarded in 2007–2008 Academic Year – 0

Name of Institution – University of Balearic Islands
Name of Department or Program – Sciences of Education

Address:
Ctra. Valldemossa km 7,5
Palma de Mallorca, IB
07010
Spain

Phone Number – 34 071173000 **Fax Number** – 34 971173190

Email Contact – jesus.salinas@uib.es **URL** – http://www.uib.es

Contact Person – Dr. Jesus Salinas

Specializations – DoctoradoInteruniversitario de Tecnología Educativa [Interuniversity Doctorate of Educational Technology]. University of Sevilla, University of Murcia, University of Balearic Islands and Rovira i Virgili

Universitity   – Master en Tecnología Educativa. E-learning y gestión del conocimiento. [Master in Educational Technology. E-learning and knowlegde management]. University of Balearic Islands and Universitat Rovira i Virgili. – Especialista Universitario en Tecnología Educativa. Diseño y elaboración de medios didácticos multimedia. [Specialist in Educational Technology. Design and development of didactic multimedia environments]. – "Curso de Dirección y gestión pedagógica de entornos virtuales." [Course of direction and pedagogical management of virtual environments]. University of Balearic Islands, Rovira I Virgili University, University of Sevilla, University Central of Venezuela, University of Panamá, Higher Institute Polytechnic Jose Antonio Echevarria.

Number of Full-Time Faculty – 6; **Number of Other Faculty** – 9

Degrees awarded in 2007–2008 Academic Year – Masters – 12; **PhD** – 6; **Other** – 28

Grant Monies awarded in 2007–2008 Academic Year – 0

Name of Institution – Università della Svizzera italiana
Name of Department or Program – New Media in Education Laboratory & red-ink doctoral school

Address:
via Buffi 13
Lugano, TI
6900
Switzerland

Phone Number – +41586664674
Fax Number – 41586664647

Email Contact – luca.botturi@lu.unisi.ch
URL – www.newmine.org

Contact Person – Lorenzo Cantoni, Prof. & Luca Botturi, PhD

Specializations – None

Features – RED-INK is a doctoral school whose name stands for "Rethinking Education in the Knowledge Society." It strives to understand the complex issues related to the introduction, management, and impact of educational technologies and e-learning in the perspective of the new context of the knowledge society. To this purpose, RED-INK federates three Swiss universities in order to establish an outstanding multidisciplinary research team at national level, with expected international visibility and impact. The RED-INK doctoral school is funded by the pro*doc program of the Swiss National Research Fund, started in 2008, and will award its first doctoral degrees in 2010.

Admission Requirements – Completed master's degree in educational technology or related field

Number of Full-Time Faculty – 3; **Number of Other Faculty** – 0

Degrees awarded in 2007–2008 Academic Year – **Master's** – 0; **PhD** – 0; **Other** – 0
Grant Monies awarded in 2007–2008 Academic Year – 0

Name of Institution – University of Geneva
Name of Department or Program – Master of Science in Learning and Teaching Technologies

Address:
Pont darve 40
Geneva, x
1211
Switzerland

Phone Number – 41 22 379 93 75
Fax Number – 41 22 379 93 79

Email Contact – Mireille.Betrancourt@unige.ch
URL – http://tecfa.unige.ch/maltt

Contact Person – Prof. Dr. Mireille Bétrancourt

Specializations – User-centered design and ergonomy. Design of computer-supported learning technology. Mediated communication and e-learning information and communication technologies. Research methods in educational technologies

Features – Blended education (face-to-face sessions alternately with tutored distance periods) 120 ECTS, 2-year program in French language

Admission Requirements – Applicants should qualify to be admitted in master's program at the University of Geneva. For more information, see http://tecfaetu.unige.ch/maltt/staf.php3?id_article=27

Degree Requirements – Bachelor's degree, Training or experience in training, Education or psychology.

Number of Full-Time Faculty – 4; **Number of Other Faculty** – 1

Degrees awarded in 2007–2008 Academic Year – Master's – 10; PhD – 3; Other – 5

Grant Monies awarded in 2007–2008 Academic Year – 400000

Name of Institution – Utrecht University
Name of Department or Program – Educational Sciences Learning in Interaction

Address:
Heidelberglaan 1
Utrecht, xx
3581RW
The Netherlands

Phone Number – +31302533910 **Fax Number** – +31302534300

Email Contact – t.wubbels@uu.nl
URL – http://www.uu.nl/NL/Informatie/master/edsci/Pages/study.aspx

Contact Person – Theo Wubbels, PhD

Specializations – The 2-year (120 EC) program concentrates on the theory, use, and effects of innovative teaching and learning arrangements aimed at meaningful, enjoyable learning through the application of different theories, paradigms, and media. Research projects use both experimental and design-based approaches and combine qualitative and quantitative analyses of interaction processes and learning products in different teaching and/or learning environments.

Features – The program combines high-level coursework with hands-on research skill and competence development. Students take courses on various theories of learning, instruction, and teaching and are trained in advanced research techniques and statistical methods to study the design and effectiveness of innovative teaching and learning arrangements. Research seminars help students develop their academic skills. Participation in a senior faculty member's research project introduces each student to "hands-on" research. Throughout the program, various e-learning environments are used to support students in their collaborative study assignments and to allow them to experiment with these innovative learning and instruction tools. The program offers a systematic theoretical and empirical analysis of educational phenomena and problems. It emphasizes three goals. Helping students develop: (1) a strong foundation in research and in theories of learning, instruction, and teaching; (2) competence in conducting high-quality educational research; and (3) capacities and skills to apply basic knowledge and specific research methods from various domains to the study of learning in interaction in education. The program concludes with writing a master's thesis in the form of a draft research article for international publication.
Admission Requirements – Applicants should hold a BA or BSc in one of the relevant social or behavioral sciences (such as education, psychology, cognitive science, informatics, and artificial intelligence) or in a domain relevant to teaching in schools

(e.g., math, science, linguistics, and history). It is required of applicants to have successfully completed several undergraduate courses on statistics in order to have a basic knowledge of multivariate analysis at the beginning of their first semester. There is a summer school for students who do not meet this requirement. Students meeting the above criteria who have a GPA of at least 2.85 (Dutch equivalent: 7.0) are encouraged to apply for admission. Students will be selected on the basis of their Grade Point Average (GPA), an essay on their motivation, and their recommendations; in some cases, an intake interview will also be conducted. All courses are taught in English; therefore, all students are required to provide proof of their English language proficiency. Examples of accepted minimum English language test scores: TOEFL paper: 580. TOEFL computer: 237. TOEFL Internet: 93

Degree Requirements – Completion of all courses and thesis

Number of Full-Time Faculty – 12; **Number of Other Faculty** – 7

Degrees awarded in 2007–2008 Academic Year – **Master's** – 110; **PhD** – 5; **Other** – 0

Grant Monies awarded in 2007–2008 Academic Year – 2000000

Name of Institution – Middle East Technical University
Name of Department or Program – Computer Education & Instructional Technology

Address:
Inonu Bulvari
Ankara, Cankaya
06531
Turkey

Phone Number – +90-3122104193 **Fax Number** – +90-3122107986

Email Contact – myozden@metu.edu.tr **URL** – http://www.ceit.metu.edu.tr

Contact Person – M. Yasar Ozden

Specializations – Computer education, instructional technology

Number of Full-Time Faculty – 20; **Number of Other Faculty** – 40

Degrees awarded in 2007–2008 Academic Year – **Masters** – 5; **PhD** – 10; **Other** – 0

Grant Monies awarded in 2007–2008 Academic Year – 0

Name of Institution – Hacettepe University

Name of Department or Program – Computer Education and Instructional Technology

Address:
Faculty of Education, Hacettepe University, Beytepe
Ankara, Turkey
06800
Turkey

Phone Number – +903122977176 **Fax Number** – +903122977176

Email Contact – paskar@hacettepe.edu.tr **URL** – http://www.ebit.hacettepe.edu.tr/

Contact Person – Petek Askar

Specializations – The CEIT department was established in 1998. Innovations and improvements in technology have changed so many things in people's life. There have been huge improvements in terms of diffusion of information. Computers continue to make an ever-increasing impact on all aspects of education from primary school to university and in the growing areas of open and distance learning. In addition, the knowledge and skills related to computers have become essential for everybody in the information age. However, at all levels in society there is a huge need for qualified personnel equipped with the skills that help them to be successful in their personal and professional lives. The department aims to train students (prospective teachers) who would teach computer courses in K-12 institutions. It also provides individuals with professional skills in the development, organization, and application of resources for the solution of instructional problems within schools.

Features – The department has MS and PhD programs. The research areas are learning objects and ontologies, diffusion of innovation, computerized testing, and e-learning environments: design, development, and assessment.

Admission Requirements – BS in education and computer-related fields

Degree Requirements – BS

Number of Full-Time Faculty – 9; **Number of Other Faculty** – 9

Degrees awarded in 2007–2008 Academic Year – Master's – 10; **PhD** – 0; **Other** – 0

Grant Monies awarded in 2007–2008 Academic Year – 0

Name of Institution – University of Manchester
Name of Department or Program – MA: Digital Technologies, Communication and Education

Address:
LTA, School of Education, Ellen Wilkinson Building, Oxford Road
Manchester, UK
M13 9PL
UK

Phone Number – +44 161 275 7843 **Fax Number** – +44 161 275 3484

Email Contact – andrew.whitworth@manchester.ac.uk **URL** – http://www. MAdigitaltechnologies.com

Contact Person – Dr. Andrew Whitworth

Specializations – Educators from any sector are catered for by the program: that is, primary, secondary (K-12), tertiary/higher education, adult education, corporate training, home educators, private tutors, and so on.

Features – The goals of this program are to promote the use of digital technologies, the broadcast media, and/or interpersonal, group, or organizational communication techniques to enhance practice and the professional and academic development of educators in technology-rich environments. There is, therefore, a particular focus on professional development techniques, enquiry-based and problem-based learning, and transformations of practice as well as work with practical EMT techniques (such as web design, Flash, and video production). Students will study the history of educational media and technology and its impact on the organization and management of education as well as on pedagogy. The course is available to study in both face-to-face and distance modes.

Admission Requirements – A first degree to at least a 2:2 (UK degree classification) or equivalent. IELTS score of at least 6.5 and preferably 7.0, or 600 in TOEFL. Teaching experience is desirable, though not mandatory.

Number of Full-Time Faculty – 2; **Number of Other Faculty** – 3

Degrees awarded in 2007–2008 Academic Year – Masters – 20; **PhD** – 0; **Other** –0

Grant Monies awarded in 2007–2008 Academic Year – 0

Name of Institution – Rochester Institute of Technology
Name of Department or Program – None

Address:
1 Lomb Drive
Rochester, NY
14623
USA

Phone Number – 585.475.2893

Email Contact – cjwici@rit.edu

Contact Person – C. J. Wallington

Specializations – Program discontinued c. 2006

Number of Full-Time Faculty – 0; **Number of Other Faculty** – 0

Degrees awarded in 2007–2008 Academic Year – Masters – 0; **PhD** – 0; **Other** – 0

Grant Monies awarded in 2007–2008 Academic Year – 0

Name of Institution – The Ohio State University
Name of Department or Program – Cultural Foundations, Technology, & Qualitative Inquiry

Address:
29 W. Woodruff Dr.
Columbus, OH
43210
USA

Phone Number – (614)688-4007

Email Contact – voithofer.2@osu.edu
URL – http://ehe.osu.edu/epl/academics/cftqi/technology.cfm

Contact Person – Rick Voithofer

Specializations – The Technology area in CFTQI offers both MA and PhD degrees. This interdisciplinary educational technology program focuses on intersections of learning, technology, and culture in formal and informal education and in society at large. Some of the settings addressed in the program include K-12 environments, distance education, e-learning, online education, higher education, urban education, private and non-profit organizations, museums, and community-based organizations and programs. Students in the program are exposed to a variety of technologies and media including educational multimedia, computer-based instruction, pod/video casts, blogs and wikis, educational games, web-based instruction, video, and electronic portfolios. Recent areas of focus studied by faculty and students include: Educational technology, digital divides, and diverse populations Implications of Web 2.0 technologies for education Education and globalization Online educational research Education Policy and Technology Visual Culture and Visual Media Multiliteracies, learning, and technology Games and Simulations Technology, virtuality, and student identities Students in this area integrate theoretical and practical studies of technologies and media through pedagogical, social, cultural, economic, historical and political inquiry and critique, in addition to the

Admission Requirements – Please see: http://ehe.osu.edu/epl/academics/cftqi/downloads/cftqi-checklist.pdf

Degree Requirements – Please see: http://ehe.osu.edu/epl/academics/cftqi/degree-req.cfm

Number of Full-Time Faculty – 4; **Number of Other Faculty** – 2

Degrees awarded in 2007–2008 Academic Year – **Masters** – 10; **PhD** – 5; **Other** –5

Grant Monies awarded in 2007–2008 Academic Year – 1200000

Name of Institution – Widener University
Name of Department or Program – Instructional Technology

Address:
One University Place
Media, PA
19013
USA

Phone Number – 610-499-4256

Email Contact – kabowes@Widener.Edu **URL** – http://www.educator.widener.edu

Contact Person – Dr. Kathleen A. Bowes

Specializations – Instructional Technology, Educational Leadership

Features – Wideners Instructional Technology program has three branches: 1. Masters of Education in Instructional Technology; 2. Instructional Technology Specialist Certification (PA non-teaching certificate); 3. Doctor of School Administration with an Instructional Technology Tract Most courses are hybrids.

Admission Requirements – 3.0 undergraduate, MATs three letters of recommendation, writing sample

Degree Requirements – undergraduate degree

Number of Full-Time Faculty – 1; **Number of Other Faculty** – 4

Degrees awarded in 2007–2008 Academic Year – **Masters** – 0; **PhD** – 0; **Other** –2

Grant Monies awarded in 2007–2008 Academic Year – 150000

Name of Institution – University of Alabama
Name of Department or Program – School of Library and Information Studies

Address:
Box 870252
Tuscaloosa, AL
35487-0252
USA

Phone Number – (205)348-4610 **Fax Number** – (205)348-3746

Email Contact – vwright@bamaed.ua.edu **URL** – http://www.slis.ua.edu

Contact Person – Joan Atkinson, Director; Gordy Coleman, Coordinator of School Media Program

Specializations – M.L.I.S. degrees in a varied program including school, public, academic, and special libraries. PhD in the larger College of Communication and Information Sciences; flexibility in creating individual programs of study. Also a Master of Fine Arts Program in Book Arts (including history of the book).

Features – M.L.I.S. is one of 56 accredited programs in the United States and Canada

Admission Requirements – M.L.I.S.: 3.0 GPA; 50 MAT or 1000 GRE and an acceptable score on Analytical Writing. Doctoral: 3.0 GPA; 60 MAT or 1200 GRE and acceptable score on Analytical Writing.

Degree Requirements – Master's: 36 semester hours. Doctoral: 48–60 semester hours plus 24 h dissertation research.

Number of Full-Time Faculty – 0; **Number of Other Faculty** – 0

Degrees awarded in 2007–2008 Academic Year – **Masters** – 0; **PhD** – 0; **Other** – 0

Grant Monies awarded in 2007–2008 Academic Year – 0

Name of Institution – University of Central Arkansas
Name of Department or Program – Teaching, Learning, and Technology

Address:
201 Donaghey
Conway, AR
72035
USA

Phone Number – (501)450-5463
Fax Number – (501)450-5680

Email Contact – steph@uca.edu **URL** – http://www.coe.uca.edu/

Contact Person – Stephanie Huffman, Program Director of the Library Media and Information Technologies Program

Specializations – MS in Library Media and Information Technologies Tracks: School Library Media and Child and Youth Librarians for Public Libraries.

Features – Specialization in school library media.

Admission Requirements – transcripts, GRE scores, and a copy of the candidates teaching certificate (if enrolled in School Library Media Track).

Degree Requirements – 36 semester hours, practicum (for School Library Media), and a professional portfolio.

Number of Full-Time Faculty – 4; **Number of Other Faculty** – 2

Degrees awarded in 2007–2008 Academic Year – **Masters** – 30; **PhD** – 0; **Other** – 36

Grant Monies awarded in 2007–2008 Academic Year – 0

Name of Institution – Arizona State University; Educational Technology program
Name of Department or Program – Division of Psychology in Education

Address:
Box 870611
Tempe, AZ
85287-0611
USA

Phone Number – (480)965-3384 **Fax Number** – (480)965-0300

Email Contact – dpe@asu.edu **URL** – http://coe.asu.edu/psyched

Contact Person – Dr. Willi Savenye, Associate Professor; Nancy Archer, Admissions Secretary

Specializations – The Educational Technology program at Arizona State University offers an MEd degree and a PhD degree which focus on the design, development, and evaluation of instructional systems and educational technology applications to support learning.

Features – The program offers courses in a variety of areas such as instructional design technology, media development, technology integration, performance improvement, evaluation, and distance education. The doctoral program emphasizes research using educational technology in applied settings.

Admission Requirements – Requirements for admission to the MEd program include a 4-year undergraduate GPA of 3.0 or above and a score of either 500 or above on verbal section of the GRE or a scaled score of 400 on the MAT. A score of 550 or above on the paper-based TOEFL (or 213 on the computer-based test or 80 internet-based test)is also required for students who do not speak English as their first language. Requirements for admission to the PhD program include a 4-year undergraduate GPA of 3.20 or above and a combined score of 1200 or above on the verbal and quantitative sections of the GRE. A score of 600 or above on the paper-based TOEFL (or 250 on the computer-based testor 100 internet-based test)is also required for students who do not speak English as their first language.

Degree Requirements – The MEd degree requires completion of a minimum of 30 credit hours including 18 credit hours of required coursework and a minimum of 12 credit hours of electives. MEd students also must complete an internship and a comprehensive examination. The PhD degree requires a minimum of 84 semester hours beyond the bachelor's degree. At least 54 of these hours must be taken at ASU after admission to the program. PhD students must fulfill a residence requirement and are required to be continuously enrolled in the program. Students also take a comprehensive examination and must satisfy a publication requirement prior to beginning work on their dissertation.

Number of Full-Time Faculty – 5; **Number of Other Faculty** – 5

Degrees awarded in 2007–2008 Academic Year – Masters – 10; **PhD** – 5; **Other** – 0

Grant Monies awarded in 2007–2008 Academic Year – 2000000

Name of Institution – California State University at East Bay
Name of Department or Program – Educational Technology Leadership

Address:
25800 Carlos Bee Blvd.
Hayward, CA
94542
USA

Phone Number – 510-885-2509 **Fax Number** – 510-8854632

Email Contact – bijan.gillani@csueastbay.edu **URL** – http://edtech.csueastbay.edu

Contact Person – Dr. Bijan Gillani

Specializations – Advances in the field of technology and the explosive growth of the Internet in recent years have revolutionized the way instruction is delivered to students. In parallel with these technological advances, the field of Learning Sciences has made phenomenal contributions to how people learn. For the most part, the advances in these two fields (technology and learning sciences) have gone their separate ways. A synergy of these two fields would enable educators and instructional designers to design and develop more effective educational materials to be transmitted over the Internet. To provide a solution for this synergy we the Institute of Learning Sciences and Technology focuses on providing a systematic and more intelligent approach to the design of e-learning environments by applying the research findings in the field of Learning Sciences to the design and development of technological environments.

Features – * How do people learn? What are learning theories? What are the instructional principles that we can derive from learning theories? How can we apply these instructional principles to the design of meaningful learning with existing and emerging technology? How do we make these principles accessible to faculty who wish to use technology more effectively? How do we develop pedagogically sound learning environments that prepare students to pursue meaningful lifework that has local and global contribution?

Admission Requirements – A completed University Graduate Application (Online Only) Two official copies of each transcript (Mail to the Enrollment Office) Statement of residency (Mail to the Department) A Department Application Form (Mail to the Department) Two letter of recommendations (Mail to the Department. GPA 3.0.

Degree Requirements – * Completion of required 24 Units of Core Courses. * Completion of 16 units of Elective Courses. * Completion of Master Degree Project or Thesis Project. * Completion of graduate check list (Online and Forms)

Number of Full-Time Faculty – 3; **Number of Other Faculty** – 3

Degrees awarded in 2007–2008 Academic Year – Masters – 20; **PhD** – 0; **Other** – 20

Grant Monies awarded in 2007–2008 Academic Year – 90

Name of Institution – California State University-San Bernardino
Name of Department or Program – Dept. of Science, Mathematics, and Technology Education

Address:
5500 University Parkway
San Bernardino, CA
92407
USA

Phone Number – (909)880-5290, (909)880-5688
Fax Number – (909)880-7040

Email Contact – aleh@csusb.edu **URL** – http://soe.csusb.edu/etec/index.html

Contact Person – Olga E. Cordero, Administrative Support Coordinator

Specializations – Technology integration, online instruction, instructional design

Features – Preparing educators in K-12, corporate, and higher education

Admission Requirements – Bachelors degree, appropriate work experience, 3.0 GPA, completion of introductory computer course and expository writing course.

Degree Requirements – 48 units including a Master's project (33 units completed in residence); 3.0 GPA; grades of "C" or better in all courses.

Number of Full-Time Faculty – 0; **Number of Other Faculty** – 0

Degrees awarded in 2007–2008 Academic Year – **Masters** – 0; **PhD** – 0; **Other** –0

Grant Monies awarded in 2007–2008 Academic Year – 0

Name of Institution – San Diego State University
Name of Department or Program – Educational Technology

Address:
5500 Campanile Dr.
San Diego, CA
92182-1182
USA

Phone Number – (619)594-6718 **Fax Number** – (619)594-6376

Email Contact – bober@mail.sdsu.edu **URL** – http://edtec.sdsu.edu/

Contact Person – Dr. Marcie Bober, Assoc. Prof., Chair.

Specializations – Certificate in Instructional Technology. Advanced Certificate in Distance Learning, and Software Design. Masters degree in Education with an emphasis in Educational Technology. Doctorate in Education with an emphasis in Educational Technology (a joint program with the University of San Diego).

Features – Focus in design of intervention to improve human performance via strategies that combine theory and practice in relevant, real-world experiences. Offer both campus and online programs.

Admission Requirements – Please refer to SDSU Graduate bulletin at http://libweb.sdsu.edu/bulletin/. Requirements include a minimum score of 950 on the GRE (verbal + quantitative), and 4.5 on the analytical. See our website at http://edtec.sdsu.edu for more information.

Degree Requirements – 36 semester hours for the masters (including 6 prerequisite hours). 15–18 semester hours for the certificates.

Number of Full-Time Faculty -; **Number of Other Faculty** -

Degrees awarded in 2007–2008 Academic Year – **Masters** – 40; **PhD** -; **Other** -

Grant Monies awarded in 2007–2008 Academic Year -

Name of Institution – San Jose State University
Name of Department or Program – Instructional Technology

Address:
One Washington Square
San Jose, CA
95192-0076
USA

Phone Number – (408) 924-3620 **Fax Number** – (408) 924-3713

Email Contact – rbarba@email.sjsu.edu
URL – http://sweeneyhall.sjsu.edu/depts/it

Contact Person – Dr. Robertta Barba, Program Chair

Specializations – Master's degree.

Features – MA in Education with an emphasis on Instructional Technology.

Admission Requirements – Baccalaureate degree from approved university, appropriate work experience, minimum GPA of 2.5, and minimum score of 550 on TOEFL(Test of English as a Foreign Language). 36 semester hours (which includes 6 prerequisite hours).

Degree Requirements – 30 units of approved graduate studies

Number of Full-Time Faculty -; **Number of Other Faculty** -

Degrees awarded in 2007–2008 Academic Year – Masters – 42; **PhD** -; **Other** - **Grant Monies awarded in 2007–2008 Academic Year** -

Name of Institution – University of Southern California, Rossier School of Education
Name of Department or Program – Educational Psychology & Instructional Technology

Address:
3470 Trousdale Parkway
Los Angeles, CA
90089-4036
USA

Phone Number – (213)740-3465
Fax Number – (213)740-2367

Email Contact – rsoemast@usc.edu
URL – http://www.usc.edu/dept/education/academic/masters/index.htm

Contact Person – For Admissions Info (soeinfo@usc.edu), For general program info (rsoemast@usc.edu), For specific program info (rueda@usc.edu)

Specializations – The Educational Psychology/Instructional Technology program focuses on learning and motivation, emphasizing the study of new information and performance technologies used to improve instruction among diverse student populations. To understand human learning, educational psychologists study areas such as: motivation; developmental and individual differences; social, cultural, and group processes; instructional technology; and the evaluation of instruction. Students will be prepared to apply a wide range of computer and telecommunications technologies in achieving educational goals within school, community, corporate and public settings.

Features – Distinctive Features: – Focus on learning and motivation with a strong emphasis on technology and a major concern with urban education settings. – Major objective is to learn how to diagnose and solve learning and motivation problems, especially those characteristic of urban learning settings. – Faculty are well-known in the field and are active researchers. Special emphasis upon instructional design, human performance at work, systems analysis, and computer-based training.

Admission Requirements – Bachelor's degree, 1000 GRE.

Degree Requirements – Program of Study: 28 Units 7 core courses and 2 elective courses. Core Courses: EDPT 576 Technology in Contemporary Education and Training EDPT 550 Statistical Inference EDPT 502 Learning and Individual Differences EDPT 510 Human Learning EDPT 540 Introduction to Educational Measurement and Evaluation EDPT 571 Instructional Design CTSE 593A & B Master's Seminar Electives (2 classes): EDPT 511 Human Motivation in Education EDPT 520 Human Lifespan Development EDPT 570 Language and Cultural Diversity in Learning CTSE 573 Management of Instructional Resources EDPA 671 The Computer and Data Processing Education

Number of Full-Time Faculty -; **Number of Other Faculty** -

Degrees awarded in 2007–2008 Academic Year – Masters – 15; **PhD** -; **Other** -

Grant Monies awarded in 2007–2008 Academic Year -

Name of Institution – Azusa Pacific University
Name of Department or Program – EDUCABS – Advanced Studies

Address:
901 E. Alosta
Azusa, CA
91702
USA

Phone Number – (626)815-5355
Fax Number – (626)815-5416

Email Contact – kbacer@apu.edu
URL – http://www.apu.edu

Contact Person – Kathleen Bacer- Online Master of Arts in Educational Technology

Specializations – Educational Technology, online learning, Infusing technology in teaching/learning environments, digital learning for the twenty-first century learner

Features – 100% Online Master of Arts in Educational Technology program designed for the K-12 educator

Admission Requirements – undergraduate degree from accredited institution with at least 12 units in education, 3.0 GPA

Degree Requirements – 36 unit program

Number of Full-Time Faculty – 2; **Number of Other Faculty** – 8

Degrees awarded in 2007–2008 Academic Year – **Masters** – 90; **PhD** – 0; **Other** – 0

Grant Monies awarded in 2007–2008 Academic Year – 10000

Name of Institution – San Francisco State University
Name of Department or Program – College of Education, Department of Instructional Technology

Address:
1600 Holloway Ave.
San Francisco, CA
94132
USA

Phone Number – (415)338-1509
Fax Number – (415)338-0510

Email Contact – kforeman@sfsu.edu **URL** – www.itec.sfsu.edu

Contact Person – Dr. Kim Foreman, Chair; Anna Kozubek, Office Coord.

Specializations – Masters degree with emphasis on Instructional Multimedia Design, Training and Designing Development, and Instructional Computing. The school also offers an 18-unit Graduate Certificate in Training Systems Development, which can be incorporated into the Master's degree.

Features – This program emphasizes the instructional systems approach, cognitivist principles of learning design, practical design experience, and project-based courses.

Admission Requirements – Bachelors degree, appropriate work experience, 2.5 GPA, purpose statement, 2 letters of recommendation, interview with the department chair.

Degree Requirements – 30 semester hours, field study project, or thesis. Three to nine units of prerequisites, assessed at entrance to the program/

Number of Full-Time Faculty – 3; **Number of Other Faculty** – 9

Degrees awarded in 2007–2008 Academic Year – Masters – 45; **PhD** – 0; **Other** – 0

Grant Monies awarded in 2007–2008 Academic Year – 0

Name of Institution – University of Colorado Denver
Name of Department or Program – School of Education and Human Development

Address:
Campus Box 106, P.O. Box 173364
Denver, CO
80217-3364
USA

Phone Number – (303)315-4963 **Fax Number** – (303)315-6311

Email Contact – brent.wilson@cudenver.edu
URL – http://www.ucdenver.edu/academics/colleges/SchoolOfEducation/Academics/MASTERS/ILT/Pages/eLearning.aspx

Contact Person – Brent Wilson, Program Coordinator, Information and Learning Technologies

Specializations – MA in Information & Learning Technologies; Certificate and MA in eLearning Design and Implementation; EdD in Educational Leadership with concentration in adult education and professional learning

Features – The ILT program focuses on design and use of digital learning resources and social support for online learning. Doctoral students complete 12 semester hours of doctoral labs (small groups collaborating with faculty on difficult problems of practice). Throughout the program, students complete a product portfolio of research, design, teaching, and applied projects. The program is cross-disciplinary, drawing on expertise in technology, adult learning, systemic change, research methods, reflective practice, and cultural studies.

Admission Requirements – MA and PhD: satisfactory GPA, GRE, writing sample, letters of recommendation, transcripts. See website for more detail.

Degree Requirements – MA: 30 semester hours including 27 h of core coursework; professional portfolio; field experience. EdD: 50 semester hours of coursework and labs, plus 20 dissertation hours; portfolio; dissertation.

Number of Full-Time Faculty – 3; **Number of Other Faculty** – 8

Degrees awarded in 2007–2008 Academic Year – **Masters** – 68; **PhD** – 2; **Other** – 0

Grant Monies awarded in 2007–2008 Academic Year – 21500

Name of Institution – University of Northern Colorado
Name of Department or Program – Educational Technology

Address:
College of Education and Behavioral Sciences
Greeley, CO
80639
USA

Phone Number – (970)351-2816 **Fax Number** – (970)351-1622

Email Contact – heng-yu.ku@unco.edu **URL** – http://www.unco.edu/cebs/edtech

Contact Person – Heng-Yu Ku, Associate Professor, Program Coordinator, Educational Technology

Specializations – MA in Educational Technology; MA in School Library Educational; Non-degree endorsement for school library media specialists; PhD in Educational Technology.

Features – Graduates are prepared for careers as instructional technologists, course designers, trainers, instructional developers, media specialists, and human resource managers. Graduates typically follow employment paths into K-12 education, higher education, business, industry, and, occasionally the military.

Admission Requirements – MA: Bachelors degree, 3.0 undergraduate GPA, 3 letters of recommendation, statement of career goals. Endorsement: Same as MA. PhD: 3.2 GPA in last 60 h of coursework, three letters of recommendation, congruency between applicants statement of career goals and program goals, 1000 GRE verbal and quantitative & 3.0 on the written/analytical, interview with faculty.

Degree Requirements – MA-Ed Tech: 30 semester hours (min) MA-School Library Education: 32 semester hours (min) School Library Endorsement(K-12 Added Endorsement): 26 semester hours (min) PhD: 67 semester hours (min)

Number of Full-Time Faculty – 4; **Number of Other Faculty** – 2

Degrees awarded in 2007–2008 Academic Year – Masters – 20; **PhD** – 4; **Other** – 0

Grant Monies awarded in 2007–2008 Academic Year – 0

Name of Institution – Fairfield University
Name of Department or Program – Educational Technology

Address:
N. Benson Road
Fairfield, CT
06824
USA

Phone Number – (203)254-4000 **Fax Number** – (203)254-4047

Email Contact – ihefzallah@mail.fairfield.edu **URL** – http://www.fairfield.edu

Contact Person – Dr. Ibrahim M. Hefzallah, Prof., Chair., Educational Technology Department; Dr. Justin Ahn, Assistant Professor of Educational Technology

Specializations – MA and a certificate of Advanced Studies in Educational Technology in one of five areas of concentrations: Computers-in-Education, Instructional Development, School Media Specialist, Applied Educational Technology in Content Areas, and Television Production; customized course of study also available

Features – emphasis on theory, practice, and new instructional developments in computers in education, multimedia, school/media, and applied technology in education

Admission Requirements – Bachelors degree from accredited institution with 2.67 GPA.

Degree Requirements – 33 credits

Number of Full-Time Faculty – 0; **Number of Other Faculty** – 0
Degrees awarded in 2007–2008 Academic Year – Masters – 12; **PhD** – 0; **Other** – 0

Grant Monies awarded in 2007–2008 Academic Year – 0

Name of Institution – University of Connecticut
Name of Department or Program – Educational Psychology

Address:
249 Glenbrook Rd, Unit-2064
Storrs, CT
06269-2064
USA

Phone Number – (860)486-0182 **Fax Number** – (860)486-0180

Email Contact – myoung@UConn.edu **URL** – http://www.epsy.uconn.edu/

Contact Person – Michael Young, Program Coordinator

Specializations – MA in Educational Technology (portfolio or thesis options), 1-year partially online Masters (summer, fall, spring, summer), Sixth Year certificate in Educational Technology and PhD in Learning Technology

Features – MA can be on-campus or two summers (on campus) and Fall–Spring (online) that can be completed in a year. The PhD emphasis in Learning Technology is a unique program at UConn. It strongly emphasizes Cognitive Science and how technology can be used to enhance the way people think and learn. The Program seeks to provide students with knowledge of theory and applications regarding the use of advanced technology to enhance learning and thinking. Campus facilities include $2 billion twenty-first Century UConn enhancement to campus infrastructure, including a new wing to the Neag School of Education. Faculty research interests include interactive video for anchored instruction and situated learning, telecommunications for cognitive apprenticeship, technology-mediated interactivity for learning by design activities, and in cooperation with the National Research Center for Gifted and Talented, research on the use of technology to enhance cooperative learning and the development of gifted performance in all students.

Admission Requirements – admission to the graduate school at UConn, GRE scores (or other evidence of success at the graduate level). Previous experience in a related area of technology, education, or experience in education or training.

Degree Requirements – completion of plan of study coursework, comprehensive exam (portfolio-based with multiple requirements), and completion of an approved dissertation.

Number of Full-Time Faculty – 0; **Number of Other Faculty** – 0
Degrees awarded in 2007–2008 Academic Year – Masters – 0; PhD – 0; **Other** – 0

Grant Monies awarded in 2007–2008 Academic Year – 0

Name of Institution – George Washington University
Name of Department or Program – School of Education and Human Development

Address:
2134 G Street NW Suite 103
Washington, DC
20052
USA

Phone Number – (202)994-1701 **Fax Number** – (202)994-2145

Email Contact – etladmin~gwu.edu **URL** – http://www.gwu.edu/~etl

Contact Person – Dr. Michael Corry, Educational Technology Leadership Program. Contact student advisors at toll free (866) 498-3382/email etlinfo@gwu.edu.

Specializations – MA in Education and Human Development with a major in Educational Technology Leadership as well as the following Graduate Certificates: Instructional Design, Multimedia Development, Leadership in Educational Technology, E-Learning, Training and Educational Technology, Integrating Technology into Education.

Features – 0

Admission Requirements – application fee, transcripts, GRE or MAT scores (50th percentile), two letters of recommendation from academic professionals, computer access, undergraduate degree with 2.75 GPA. No GRE or MAT is required for entry into the Graduate Certificate programs.

Degree Requirements – MASTERS PROGRAM: 36 credit hours (including 27 required hours and 9 elective credit hours). Required courses include computer application management, media and technology application, software implementation and design, public education policy, and quantitative research methods. GRADUATE CERTIFICATE PROGRAMS: 15 credit hours

Number of Full-Time Faculty – 0; **Number of Other Faculty** – 0

Degrees awarded in 2007–2008 Academic Year – Masters – 0; PhD – 0; Other – 0

Grant Monies awarded in 2007–2008 Academic Year – 0

Name of Institution – Florida Institute of Technology
Name of Department or Program – Science and Mathematics Education Department

Address:
150 University Blvd.
Melbourne, FL
32901-6975
USA

Phone Number – (321)674-8126 **Fax Number** – (321)674-7598

Email Contact – dcook@fit.edu **URL** – http://www.fit.edu/catalog/sci-lib/comp-edu.html#master-info

Contact Person – Dr. David Cook, Department Head.

Specializations – Master's degree options in Computer Education and Instructional Technology; PhD degree in Science Education with options for research in Computer Science, Computer Education and Instructional Technology.

Features – Flexible program depending on student experience.

Admission Requirements – Masters: 3.0 GPA for regular admission PhD: Masters degree and 3.2 GPA

Degree Requirements – Masters: 33 semester hours (15 in computer or and technology education, 9 in education, 9 electives); practicum; no thesis or internship required or 30 semester hrs. for thesis option. PhD: 48 semester hours (12 in computer and technology education, 12 in education, 24 dissertation and research. Also requires 21 graduate hours in computer science/computer information systems 12 of which may be applicable to the required 48 hours.)

Number of Full-Time Faculty – 1; **Number of Other Faculty** – 2

Degrees awarded in 2007–2008 Academic Year – **Masters** – 0; **PhD** – 1; **Other** – 0

Grant Monies awarded in 2007–2008 Academic Year – 0

Name of Institution – Nova Southeastern University – Fischler Graduate School of Education and Human Services
Name of Department or Program – Programs in Instructional Technology and Distance Education (ITDE)

Address:
1750 NE 167th Street
North Miami Beach, FL
33162
USA

Phone Number – 954-262-8572. (800)986-3223, ext. 8572
Fax Number – (954)262-3905

Email Contact – itdeinfo@nova.edu;scisinfo@nova.edu
URL – itde.nova.edu

Contact Person – Marsha L. Burmeister, Recruitment Coordinator & Program Professor ITDE

Specializations – MS and EdD in Instructional Technology and Distance Education.

Features – MS 21 months (MS ITDE program graduates may continue with the EdD program as second-year students) EdD 36 months MS and EdD combined: 4+ years Blended/hybrid delivery model with limited face-to-face and via instruction at-a-distance using Web-based technologies.

Admission Requirements – • Active employment in the field of instructional technology/distance education • Completion of bachelor's degree for MS program (2.5 minimum GPA); master's degree required for admission to EdD program (3.0 minimum GPA). • Miller Analogies Test (MAT) score (test taken within past 5 years) • Submission of application/supplementary materials • Approval of Skills Checklist (application) • Three letters of recommendation • Official copies of transcripts for all graduate work • Resume • Oral interview (via telephone) • Demonstrated potential for successful completion of the program via acceptance of application • Internet Service Provider; Laptop computer

Degree Requirements – 21 months and 30 semester credits. EdD 3 years and 65 semester credits. MS Program: 3 "extended weekends:" One extended weekend in the fall (5 days), one extended weekend in the spring (4 days), one summer instructional session (4–5 days; July), final term online delivery. EdD program: same as above, continues throughout the 3 years (three sessions in first year, two sessions in the second year, and one instructional session in the third year for a total of six (6) face-to-face sessions)

Number of Full-Time Faculty – 0; **Number of Other Faculty** – 0

Degrees awarded in 2007–2008 Academic Year – **Masters** – 100; **PhD** – 0; **Other** – 0

Grant Monies awarded in 2007–2008 Academic Year – 0

Name of Institution – Barry University
Name of Department or Program – Department of Educational Computing and Technology, School of Education

Address:
11300 N.E. Second Ave.
Miami Shores, FL
33161
USA

Phone Number – (305)899-3608 **Fax Number** – (305)899-3718

Email Contact – dlenaghan@bu4090.barry.edu
URL – http://www.barry.edu/ed/programs/masters/ect/default.htm

Contact Person – Donna Lenaghan, Director

Specializations – MS and Ed.S. in Educational Technology Applications and PhD degree in Educational Technology Leadership.

Features – These programs and courses prepares educators to integrate computer/technologies in their disciplines and/or train individuals to use computers/technologies. The focus is on improving the teaching and learning process thought integration of technologies into curricula and learning activities.

Admission Requirements – GRE scores, letters of recommendation, GPA, interview, achievements.

Degree Requirements – MS or Ed. S.: 36 semester credit hours. PhD: 54 credits beyond the Masters including dissertation credits.

Number of Full-Time Faculty – 0; **Number of Other Faculty** – 0

Degrees awarded in 2007–2008 Academic Year – Masters – 75; **PhD** – 0; **Other** – 0

Grant Monies awarded in 2007–2008 Academic Year – 0

Name of Institution – Florida State University
Name of Department or Program – Educational Psychology and Learning Systems

Address:
305 Stone Bldg.
Tallahassee, FL
32306
USA

Phone Number – (850)644-4592 **Fax Number** – (850)644-8776

Email Contact – rreiser@mailer.fsu.edu

URL – http://www.epls.fsu.edu/is/index.htm

Contact Person – Mary Kate McKee, Program Coordinator

Specializations – MS, Ed.S, PhD in Instructional Systems with specializations for persons planning to work in academia, business, industry, government, or military, both in the United States and in International settings.

Features – Core courses include systems and materials development, development of multimedia, project management, psychological foundations, current trends in instructional design, and research and statistics. Internships are recommended.

Admission Requirements – MS: 3.0 GPA in past 2 years of undergraduate program, 1000 GRE (verbal plus quantitative), 550 TOEFL (for international applicants). PhD: 1100 GRE (V+Q), 3.5 GPA in past 2 years; international students, 550 TOEFL.

Degree Requirements – MS: 36 semester hours, 2–4 h internship, comprehensive exam preparation of professional portfolio

Number of Full-Time Faculty – 0; **Number of Other Faculty** – 0

Degrees awarded in 2007–2008 Academic Year – Masters – 0; PhD – 0; Other – 0

Grant Monies awarded in 2007–2008 Academic Year – 0

Name of Institution – University of Central Florida
Name of Department or Program – College of Education – ERTL

Address:
4000 Central Florida Blvd.
Orlando, FL
32816-1250
USA

Phone Number – (407)823-4835 **Fax Number** – (407)823-4880

Email Contact – hirumi@mail.ucf.edu;ggunter@mail.ucf.edu
URL – http://pegasus.cc.ucf.edu/~instsys/
http://pegasus.cc.ucf.edu/~edmedia
http://pegasus.cc.ucf.edu/~edtech.

Contact Person – Gary Orwig, Instructional Systems
Judy Lee, Educational Media
Glenda Gunter, Educational Technology

Specializations – MA in Instructional Technology/Instructional Systems, http://pegasus.cc.ucf.edu/~instsys/; MEd in Instructional Technology/Educational Media – entirely web-based, http://pegasus.cc.ucf.edu/~edmedia/; MA in Instructional Technology/Educational Technology, http://pegasus.cc.ucf.edu/~edtech. PhD and Ed.D. with specialization in Instructional Technology. http://www.graduate.ucf.edu There are approximately 18 Ed.D. students and 22 PhD students in the doctoral programs.

Features – All programs rely heavily on understanding of fundamental competencies as reflected by ASTD, AECT, AASL, and ISTE. There is an emphasis on the practical application of theory through intensive hands-on experiences. Orlando and the surrounding area is home to a plethora of high-tech companies, military training and simulation organizations, and tourist attractions. UCF, established in 1963, now has in excess of 36,000 students, representing more than 90 countries. It has been ranked as one of the leading "most-wired" universities in North America.

Admission Requirements – Interviews (either in person or via email); GRE score of 840 if last 60 h of undergraduate degree is 3.0 or above, 1000 if less; TOEFL of 550 (270 computer-based version) if English is not first language; three letters of recommendation; resume, statement of goals; residency statement, and health record. Financial statement if coming from overseas.

Degree Requirements – MA in Instructional Technology/Instructional Systems, 39–42 semester hours; MEd in Instructional Technology/Educational Media, 39–45 semester hours; MA in Instructional Technology/Educational Technology, 36–45 semester hours. Practicum required in all three programs; thesis, research project, or substitute additional coursework. PhD and Ed.D. require between 58 and 69 h beyond the masters for completion.

Number of Full-Time Faculty – 0; **Number of Other Faculty** – 0

Degrees awarded in 2007–2008 Academic Year – Masters – 65; **PhD** – 0; **Other** – 0

Grant Monies awarded in 2007–2008 Academic Year – 0

Name of Institution – University of South Florida
Name of Department or Program – Instructional Technology Program, Secondary Education Department, College of Education

Address:
4202 E. Fowler Avenue, EDU162,
Tampa, FL
33620-5650
USA

Phone Number – (813)974-3533 **Fax Number** – (813)974-3837

Email Contact – IT@coedu.usf.edu **URL** – http://www.coedu.usf.edu/it

Contact Person – Dr. William Kealy, Graduate Certificates; Dr. Frank Breit, Master's program; Dr. Ann Barron, Education Specialist program; Dr. James White, Doctoral program.

Specializations – Graduate Certificates in Web Design, Instructional Design, Multimedia Design, School Networks, and Distance Education MEd, EdS, and PhD in Curriculum and Instruction with emphasis in Instructional Technology

Features – Many student gain practical experience in the Florida Center for Instructional Technology (FCIT), which provides services to the Department of Education and other grants and contracts; the Virtual Instructional Team for the

Advancement of Learning (VITAL), which provides USF faculty with course development services; and Educational Outreach. The College of Education is one of the largest in the USA in terms of enrollment and facilities. As of Fall 1997, a new, technically state-of-the-art building was put into service. The University of South Florida has been classified by the Carnegie Foundation as a Doctoral/Research University – Extensive.

Admission Requirements – See http://www.coedu.usf.edu/it

Degree Requirements – See http://www.coedu.usf.edu/it

Number of Full-Time Faculty – 0; **Number of Other Faculty** – 0

Degrees awarded in 2007–2008 Academic Year – Masters – 60; PhD – 0; **Other** – 0

Grant Monies awarded in 2007–2008 Academic Year – 0

Name of Institution – Georgia Southern University
Name of Department or Program – College of Education

Address:
Box 8131
Statesboro, GA
30460-8131
USA

Phone Number – (912)478-5307 **Fax Number** – (912)486-7104.

Email Contact – JRepman@georgiasouthern.edu **URL** – http://coe.georgiasouthern.edu/eltr/tech/inst_tech/index.htm

Contact Person – Judi Repman. Professor, Department of Leadership, Technology, and Human Development.

Specializations – Online MEd and GA certification for School Library Media Specialist. An Instructional Technology strand is available in the Ed.S. in Teaching and Learning Program and in the Ed.D. program in Curriculum Studies.

Features – Completely online program. GA Special Technology Certification course available strong emphasis on technology

Admission Requirements – BS (teacher certification NOT required) MAT score of 44 or GRE score of 450 verbal and 450 quantitative for Regular admission. Provisional admission requires lower scores but also requires letters of intent/reference.

Degree Requirements – 36 semester hours, including a varying number of hours of media for individual students.

Number of Full-Time Faculty – 5; **Number of Other Faculty** – 2

Degrees awarded in 2007–2008 Academic Year – Masters – 20; **PhD** – 0; **Other** – 0

Grant Monies awarded in 2007–2008 Academic Year – 8000

Name of Institution – Georgia State University
Name of Department or Program – Middle-Secondary Education and Instructional Technology

Address:
Box 3976
Atlanta, GA
30302-3976
USA

Phone Number – (404)413-8060
Fax Number – (404)413-8063

Email Contact – swharmon@gsu.edu. **URL** – http://edtech.gsu.edu

Contact Person – Dr. Stephen W. Harmon, contact person.

Specializations – MS, EdS, and PhD in Instructional Technology or Library Media

Features – Focus on research and practical application of instructional technology in educational and corporate settings

Admission Requirements – MS: Bachelors degree, 2.5 undergraduate GPA, 800 GRE, 550 TOEFL. Ed.S.: Master's degree, teaching certificate, 3.25 graduate GPA, 48 MAT or 900 GRE. PhD: Master's degree, 3.30 graduate GPA, 53 MAT or 500 verbal plus 500 quantitative GRE or 500 analytical GRE.

Degree Requirements – MS: 36 semester hours, internship, portfolio, comprehensive examination. Ed.S.: 30 sem. hours, internship, and scholarly project. PhD: 66 sem. hours, internship, comprehensive examination, dissertation.

Number of Full-Time Faculty – 6; **Number of Other Faculty** – 4

Degrees awarded in 2007–2008 Academic Year – Masters – 20; **PhD** – 4; **Other** – 2

Grant Monies awarded in 2007–2008 Academic Year – 100000

Name of Institution – University of Georgia
Name of Department or Program – Department of Educational Psychology and Instructional Technology, College of Education

Address:
604 Aderhold Hall
Athens, GA
30602-7144
USA

Phone Number – (706)542-3810 **Fax Number** – (706)542-4032

Email Contact – treeves@uga.edu **URL** – http://www.coe.uga.edu/epit/

Contact Person – Dr. Thomas Reeves, IT Program Leader

Specializations – MEd and EdS in Instructional Technology with two emphasis areas: Instructional Design & Development and School Library Media; PhD for leadership positions as specialists in instructional design and development and university faculty. The program offers advanced study for individuals with previous preparation in instructional media and technology, as well as a preparation for personnel in other professional fields requiring a specialty in instructional systems or instructional technology. Representative career fields for graduates include designing new courses, educational multimedia (especially web-based), tutorial programs, and instructional materials in state and local school systems, higher education, business and industry, research and non-profit settings, and in instructional products development.

Features – Minor areas of study available in a variety of other departments. Personalized programs are planned around a common core of courses and include practical, internships, or clinical experiences. Research activities include grant-related activities and applied projects, as well as dissertation studies.

Admission Requirements – All degrees: application to graduate school, satisfactory GRE score, other criteria as outlined in Graduate School Bulletin and on the program Web site.

Degree Requirements – MEd: 36 semester hours with 3.0 GPA, portfolio with oral exam. EdS: 30 semester hours with 3.0 GPA and project exam. PhD: three full years of study beyond the Master's degree, two consecutive semesters full-time residency, comprehensive exam with oral defense, internship, dissertation with oral defense.

Number of Full-Time Faculty – 12; **Number of Other Faculty** – 2

Degrees awarded in 2007–2008 Academic Year – Masters – 55; **PhD** – 10; **Other** – 0

Grant Monies awarded in 2007–2008 Academic Year – 700000

Name of Institution – University of West Georgia
Name of Department or Program – Department of Media and Instructional Technology

Address:
138 Education Annex
Carrollton, GA
30118
USA

Phone Number – 678-839-6558 or 839-6149 **Fax Number** – 678-839-6153

Email Contact – ebennett@westga.edu **URL** – http://coe.westga.edu/mit
Contact Person – Dr. Elizabeth Bennett, Professor and Chair

Specializations – MEd with specializations in School Library Media and Instructional Technology and Add-On certification in School Library Media for students with Master's degrees in other disciplines. The Department also offers an Ed.S. program in Media with two options, Media Specialist or Instructional Technology. The program strongly emphasizes technology integration in the schools

Features – School library media and certification students complete field experiences as part of each school library media course they take. All courses range from 85 to 100% online.

Admission Requirements – MEd: 800 GRE, 396 MAT, 2.7 undergraduate GPA. Ed.S.: 900 GRE, 400 MAT, and 3.00 graduate GPA.

Degree Requirements – 36 semester hours for MEd 27 semester hours for Ed.S

Number of Full-Time Faculty – 10; **Number of Other Faculty** – 4

Degrees awarded in 2007–2008 Academic Year – **Masters** – 48; **PhD** – 0; **Other** – 41

Grant Monies awarded in 2007–2008 Academic Year – 7000

Name of Institution – Valdosta State University
Name of Department or Program – Curriculum, Leadership, & Technology

Address:
1500 N. Patterson St.
Valdosta, GA
31698
USA

Phone Number – (229)333-5633 **Fax Number** – (229)259-5094

Email Contact – keitjohnson@valdosta.edu

URL – http://www.valdosta.edu/coe/clt/

Contact Person – Keith Johnson

Specializations – MEd in Instructional Technology with two tracks: Library/Media or Technology Applications; Online Ed.S. in Instructional Technology; Ed.D. in Curriculum and Instruction.

Features – The program has a strong emphasis on systematic design and technology in MEd, EdS, and EdD. Strong emphasis on change leadership, reflective practice, applied research in Ed.S and Ed.D.

Admission Requirements – MEd: 2.5 GPA, 800 GRE. Ed.S.: Master's degree, 3 years of experience, 3.0 GPA, 850 GRE, MAT 390 and less than 5 years old. Ed.D.: Masters degree, 3 years of experience, 3.50 GPA, 1000 GRE.
Degree Requirements – MEd: 33 semester hours. Ed.S.: 27 semester hours. Ed.D.: 54 semester hours.

Number of Full-Time Faculty – 20; **Number of Other Faculty** – 10

Degrees awarded in 2007–2008 Academic Year – **Masters** – 14; **PhD** – 0; **Other** – 34

Grant Monies awarded in 2007–2008 Academic Year – 0

Name of Institution – University of Hawaii-Manoa
Name of Department or Program – Department of Educational Technology

Address:
1776 University Ave
Honolulu, HI
96822-2463
USA

Phone Number – (808) 956-7671 **Fax Number** – (808)956-3905

Email Contact – edtech-dept@hawaii.edu **URL** – http://etec.hawaii.edu

Contact Person – Catherine P. Fulford, Phd, Chair

Specializations – MEd in Educational Technology

Features – This nationally accredited program prepares students to create resources for teaching and learning through diverse media as well as integrate technology into educational environments. Educational Technology (ETEC) provides theoretical knowledge and scientific principles that can be applied to problems that arise in a social context; prepares individuals to devise effective messages, teams, materials, devices, techniques, and settings; and, involves the study of theory and practice of design, development, utilization, management, and evaluation of processes and resources for learning. Practitioners in educational technology, whether they are teachers, trainers, developers, administrators, or support personnel, seek innovative and effective ways of organizing the teaching and learning process through the best possible application of technological developments. The program places emphasis on applications of technology in educational settings rather than simple technical skills. Individuals from diverse backgrounds can immediately apply what they learn to their particular context. Upon graduation, these new professionals will have a clearer vision of how they can prepare learners for the future. ETEC graduates are found in many learning environments including K-12 and higher education, government, business, industry, and health occupations.

Admission Requirements – A baccalaureate degree from an accredited institution in any field of study is acceptable to the Department, provided the students undergraduate scholastic record is acceptable to the Graduate Division. A "B" average (i.e., 3.0 on a 4-point scale) in the last 60 semester hours of the undergraduate program is required for regular admission. Students from foreign countries must submit the results of the Test of English as a Foreign Language (TOEFL). The minimum score is 600, representing approximately the 77th percentile rank. Students must submit: an "Intent to Apply for Admission Form," a "Graduate Program Supplemental Information Form" and a "Statement of Objectives Form." These are available on the ETEC website. Three letters of recommendation, to be submitted with the application for admission, should evaluate the applicant's potential in the field of educational technology, not only his or her academic abilities to do graduate work. All applicants should submit a resume, and additional materials, documentation, or samples of work relevant to the evaluation and selection process.

Degree Requirements – The ETEC MEd program requires a minimum of 36 semester credit hours, with seven required and five elective ETEC courses. All required and most elective courses are 3 credits each. Full-time students usually complete their coursework in two academic years. Students attending part-time may take three or more years to finish program requirements. Of the seven (7) required courses, four comprise the core of the Educational Technology program. Students are required to complete the core courses in sequence during the first year. The program is designed as a cohort system in which students admitted at the same time take initial courses together to build a sense of support and professional community. In the final year of the program the students will complete an electronic portfolio and final masters project.

Number of Full-Time Faculty – 7; **Number of Other Faculty** – 7

Degrees awarded in 2007–2008 Academic Year – Masters – 21; **PhD** – 0; **Other** – 0

Grant Monies awarded in 2007–2008 Academic Year – 1097246

Name of Institution – University of Northern Iowa
Name of Department or Program – Educational Technology Program

Address:
618 Schinder Education Center
Cedar Falls, IA
50614-0606
USA

Phone Number – (319)273-3250 **Fax Number** – (319)273-5886

Email Contact – mary.herring@uni.edu **URL** – http://ci.coe.uni.edu/edtech/index.html

Contact Person – Sharon E. Smaldino

Specializations – MA in Curriculum & Instruction: Educational Technology, MA in Performance and Training Technology.

Features – The masters degrees are designed to meet the AECT/ECIT standards and are focused on addressing specific career choices. The Educational Technology masters is designed to prepare educators for a variety of professional positions in educational settings, including: school building level, school district level, vocational-technical school, community college, and university. The Performance and Training Technology masters is designed for persons planning to work in non-school settings. Majors in this area will complete a basic core of coursework applicable to all preparing for work as media specialists, trainers in industry and business, or communications designers. Specific areas of interest will determine the supporting electives. Licensure as a teacher is not required for admission to either masters in Iowa. The bachelors degree may be in any field.

Admission Requirements – Bachelors degree, 3.0 undergraduate GPA, 500 TOEFL

Degree Requirements – 38 semester credits, optional thesis worth 6 credits or alternative research paper of project, comprehensive exam

Number of Full-Time Faculty – 0; **Number of Other Faculty** – 0

Degrees awarded in 2007–2008 Academic Year – Masters – 32; **PhD** – 0; **Other** – 0

Grant Monies awarded in 2007–2008 Academic Year – 0

Name of Institution – Boise State University
Name of Department or Program – Instructional & Performance Technology

Address:
1910 University Drive, ET-327
Boise, Idaho
83725
USA

Phone Number – (208)424-5135;(800)824-7017 ext. 61312 **Fax Number** – (208)426-1970

Email Contact – jfenner@boisestate.edu **URL** – http://ipt.boisestate.edu/

Contact Person – Dr. Don Stepich, IPT Program Chair.; Jo Ann Fenner, IPT Program Developer and distance program contact person.

Specializations – The Master of Science in Instructional & Performance Technology (IPT) degree is intended to prepare students for careers in the areas of instructional technology, performance technology, instructional design, performance improvement, training, education and training management, e-learning, human resources, organizational development, and human performance consulting.

Features – Leading experts in learning styles, evaluation, e-learning, performance improvement and leadership principles serve as adjunct faculty in the program via computer and modem from their various remote locations. For details, visit our faculty web page at http://ipt.boisestate.edu/faculty.htm

Admission Requirements – undergraduate degree with 3.0 GPA, one-to-two page essay describing why you want to pursue this program and how it will contribute to your personal and professional development, and a resume of personal qualifications and work experience. For more information, visit; http://ipt.boisestate.edu/application_admission.htm

Degree Requirements – 36 semester hours in instructional and performance technology and related coursework; and four options for a culminating activity; project, thesis, portfolio or oral comprehensive exam (included in 36 credit hours).

Number of Full-Time Faculty – 0; **Number of Other Faculty** – 0

Degrees awarded in 2007–2008 Academic Year – **Masters** – 45; **PhD** – 0; **Other** – 0

Grant Monies awarded in 2007–2008 Academic Year – 0

Name of Institution – Governors State University
Name of Department or Program – College of Arts and Sciences

Address:
1 University Parkway
University Park, IL
60466
USA

Phone Number – (708)534-4051 **Fax Number** – (708)534-7895
Email Contact – m-lanigan@govst.edu

URL – http://faculty.govst.edu/users/glanigan/homepage.htm

Contact Person – Mary Lanigan, Associate Prof., Human Performance and Training

Specializations – –MA in Communication and Training with HP&T major – Program concentrates on building instructional design skills. Most classes are delivered in a hybrid format of online and face to face. Some classes are almost all online.

Features – Instructional Design overview; front-end analysis including both needs and task; design and delivery using various platforms; evaluation skills and how to predict behavior transfer; various technologies; consulting; project management; systems thinking; principles of message design; and more.

Admission Requirements – Undergraduate degree in any field.

Degree Requirements – 36 credit hours (trimester), All in instructional and performance technology; internship or advanced field project required. Metropolitan Chicago area based

Number of Full-Time Faculty – 1; **Number of Other Faculty** – 3

Degrees awarded in 2007–2008 Academic Year – Masters – 10; **PhD** – 0; **Other** – 0

Grant Monies awarded in 2007–2008 Academic Year – 0

Name of Institution – Southern Illinois University at Carbondale
Name of Department or Program – Department of Curriculum and Instruction

Address:
625 Wham Drive, Mailcode 4610
Carbondale, IL
62901
USA

Phone Number – (618) 4534218 **Fax Number** – (618) 4534244

Email Contact – sashrock@siu.edu. **URL** – http://ci.siu.edu/

Contact Person – Sharon Shrock, Coordinator, Instructional Design/Instructional Technology

Specializations – MS in Curriculum & Instruction with specializations in Instructional Design and Instructional Technology. PhD in Education including specialization in Instructional Technology.

Features – All specializations are oriented to multiple education settings. The ID program emphasizes non-school (primarily corporate) learning environments, human performance technology, and criterion-referenced performance assessment. The IT program includes two mini-tracks: (a) Serious Games and (b) e-Learning.

Admission Requirements – MS: Bachelors degree, 2.7 undergraduate GPA, transcripts. PhD: Masters degree, 3.25 GPA, GRE scores, 3 letters of recommendation, transcripts, writing sample. International students without a degree from a USA institution must submit TOEFL score.

Degree Requirements – MS, 32 credit hours with thesis; 36 credit hours without thesis; PhD, 40 credit hours beyond the master's degree in courses, 24 credit hours for the dissertation.

Number of Full-Time Faculty – 3; **Number of Other Faculty** – 1

Degrees awarded in 2007–2008 Academic Year – **Masters** – 5; **PhD** – 0; **Other** – 0

Grant Monies awarded in 2007–2008 Academic Year – 0

Name of Institution – University of Illinois at Urbana-Champaign
Name of Department or Program – Curriculum, Technology, and Education Reform (CTER) Program, Department of Educational Psychology

Address:
226 Education Bldg.1310 S. 6th St.
Champaign, IL
61820
USA

Phone Number – (217)244-3510 **Fax Number** – (217)244-7620

Email Contact – cter-info-L@listserv.illinois.edu **URL** – http://cter.ed.uiuc.edu

Contact Person – Doe-Hyung Kim, Visiting Project Coordinator, Department of Educational Psychology

Specializations – EdM in Educational Psychology with emphasis in Curriculum, Technology, and Education Reform

Features – This Master of Education program is geared toward teachers and trainers interested in learning more about the integration of computer-based technology in the classroom. This online set of project-based courses offers an opportunity to earn a coherent, high-quality masters degree online, with most interactions through personal computers and Internet connections at home or workplace.

Admission Requirements – Application to the Graduate College, three letters of recommendation, personal statement. For more information go to: http://cterport.ed.uiuc.edu/admissions_folder/application_procedures_html

Degree Requirements – Eight courses (5 requirements + 3 electives) required for EdM.

Number of Full-Time Faculty – 3; **Number of Other Faculty** – 4

Degrees awarded in 2007–2008 Academic Year – Masters – 16; **PhD** – 0; **Other** – 0

Grant Monies awarded in 2007–2008 Academic Year – 0

Name of Institution – Northern Illinois University
Name of Department or Program – Educational Technology, Research and Assessment

Address:
208 Gabel Hall
DeKalb, IL
60115
USA

Phone Number – (815) 753-9339
Fax Number – (815) 753-9388

Email Contact – edtech@niu.edu **URL** – http://www.cedu.niu.edu/etra

Contact Person – Dr. Jeffrey B. Hecht, Department Chair

Specializations – MS Ed. in Instructional Technology with concentrations in Instructional Design, Distance Education, Educational Computing, and Media Administration; Ed.D. in Instructional Technology, emphasizing instructional design and development, computer education, media administration, and preparation for careers in business, industry, and higher education. In addition, Illinois state certification in school library media is offered in conjunction with either degree or alone.

Features – Program is highly individualized. All facilities remodeled and modernized in 2002–2003 featuring five smart classrooms and over 110 student use desktop and laptop computers. Specialized equipment for digital audio and video editing, web site and CD creation, and presentations. All students are encouraged to create portfolios highlighting personal accomplishments and works (required at Masters). Masters program started in 1968, doctorate in 1970.

Admission Requirements – MS Ed.: 2.75 undergraduate GPA, GRE verbal and quantitative scores, two references. Ed.D.: 3.25 MS GPA, writing sample, three references, interview.

Degree Requirements – MS Ed.: 39 h, including 30 in instructional technology; portfolio. Ed.D.: 63 h beyond Master's, including 15 h for dissertation.

Number of Full-Time Faculty – 0; **Number of Other Faculty** – 0

Degrees awarded in 2007–2008 Academic Year – Masters – 0; **PhD** – 0; **Other** – 0

Grant Monies awarded in 2007–2008 Academic Year – 0

Name of Institution – Southern Illinois University Edwardsville
Name of Department or Program – Instructional Technology Program

Address:
School of Education
Edwardsville, IL
62026-1125
USA

Phone Number – (618) 650-3277 **Fax Number** – (618) 650-3808

Email Contact – yliu@siue.edu **URL** – http://www.siue.edu/education/edld/it/index.shtml

Contact Person – Dr. Yuliang Liu, Director, Department of Educational Leadership

Specializations – The Educational Technologies option enables teachers and other school personnel to learn how to plan, implement, and evaluate technology-based instruction and learning activities in p-12 settings. Students pursuing this option will become knowledgeable users of technology as well as designers of curriculum and instruction that effectively utilize and integrate technology to improve student learning. Students interested in leadership roles in educational technology, such as those wishing to become technology coordinators in schools or school districts, can work toward meeting the standards for the Illinois State Board of Education's (ISBE) Technology Specialist endorsement through this program. The Library Information Specialist option enables teachers and other school personnel to learn how to plan, implement, and evaluate library information-based activities in P-12 settings. Students pursuing this option will become knowledgeable users of library information as well as designers of curriculum and instruction that effectively utilize and integrate library information to improve student learning. Students interested in Library Information Specialist endorsement can work towards meeting the standards for the Illinois State Board of Education's Library Information Specialist endorsement through this program. The Instructional Design & Performance Improvement option focuses on skills necessary for careers in the areas of instructional technology, performance technology, instructional design, training, and performance consulting. Emphasis is placed on systematic instructional design and on the use of various media and technologies for learning and instruction. Students in this option may also focus on the design and development of online learning and other performance improvement strategies. The Interactive

Multimedia Technologies option is appropriate for people wishing to pursue the design and development of various interactive multimedia and web-based learning experiences. This option prepares students for careers with publishing and production companies, consulting firms, and other businesses that produce engaging multimedia applications for learning and other opportunities. Coursework focuses on theories and methods for designing compelling user experiences, developing skills with tools for web and other delivery media, and project management strategies.

Features – Several unique features of the program provide students with opportunities for important practical experiences that complement coursework. Juried presentations provide students with an opportunity to share their work with a jury of professors and peers, and defend their work in light of their own goals and the content of their degree program. Design Studios provide students with opportunities to work on real-world projects for a variety of real clients in order to develop skills in collaboration, design, development tools and techniques, and project management.

Admission Requirements – The requirements for admission are a bachelor's degree and a GPA of 3.0 or above during their last 2 years of undergraduate work.

Degree Requirements – 36 semester hours; Thesis or Final Project options.

Number of Full-Time Faculty – 4; **Number of Other Faculty** – 8

Degrees awarded in 2007–2008 Academic Year – Masters – 16; **PhD** – 0; **Other** – 0

Grant Monies awarded in 2007–2008 Academic Year – 0

Name of Institution – Western Illinois University
Name of Department or Program – Instructional Technology and Telecommunications

Address:
37 Harrabin Hall
Macomb, IL
61455
USA

Phone Number – (309)298-1952 **Fax Number** – (309)298-2978

Email Contact – hh-hemphill@wiu.edu **URL** – http://www.wiu.edu/users/miitt/

Contact Person – M.H. Hassan, Chair. Specialization: Master's degree.

Specializations – None

Features – New program approved by Illinois Board of Higher Education in January 1996 with emphases in Instructional Technology, Telecommunications, Interactive Technologies, and Distance Education. Selected courses delivered via satellite TV and compressed video

Admission Requirements – Bachelor's degree 3.0/4.0 GRE score.

Degree Requirements – 32 semester hours, thesis or applied project, or 35 semester hours with portfolio. Certificate Program in Instructional Technology Specialization. Graphic applications, training development, video production. Each track option is made of 5 courses or a total of 15 semester hours.

Number of Full-Time Faculty – 0; **Number of Other Faculty** – 0

Degrees awarded in 2007–2008 Academic Year – **Masters** – 0; **PhD** – 0; **Other** – 0

Grant Monies awarded in 2007–2008 Academic Year – 0

Name of Institution – Indiana State University
Name of Department or Program – Dept. of Curriculum, Instruction, and Media Technology

Address:
None
Terre Haute, IN
47809
USA

Phone Number – (812)237-2937 **Fax Number** – (812)237-4348

Email Contact – espowers@isugw.indstate.edu **URL** – 0

Contact Person – Dr. James E. Thompson, Program Coord.

Specializations – Master's degree in Instructional Technology with education focus or with non-education focus; Specialist Degree program in Instructional Technology; PhD in Curriculum, Instruction with specialization in Media Technology

Features – 0

Admission Requirements – 0

Degree Requirements – Master's: 32 semester hours, including 18 in media; thesis optional; Ed.S.: 60 semester hours beyond bachelor's degree; PhD, approximately 100 h beyond bachelor's degree.

Number of Full-Time Faculty – 0; **Number of Other Faculty** – 0

Degrees awarded in 2007–2008 Academic Year – **Masters** – 0; **PhD** – 0; **Other** – 0

Grant Monies awarded in 2007–2008 Academic Year – 0

Name of Institution – Clarke College
Name of Department or Program – Graduate Studies

Address:
1550 Clarke Drive
Dubuque, IA
52001
USA

Phone Number – (563)588-8180 **Fax Number** – (563)584-8604

Email Contact – llester@clarke.edu **URL** – http://www.clarke.edu

Contact Person – Margaret Lynn Lester

Specializations – M.A.E. (Two tracks: Instructional Leadership & Literacy)

Features – The Instructional Leadership track of this program offers hybrid courses in educational technology. Courses are offered through WEB-ST and face-to-face. Outcomes are aligned with the National Educational Technology Standards for Educators.

Admission Requirements – Completed graduate application, official transcripts, photocopy of all teaching certificates and licenses, 2.75 GPA (4 point scale), two letters of reference, interview, statement of goals, and $25 application fee. (Minimum TOEFL score of 550 if English is not first language.)

Degree Requirements – 9 h in Research Core; 9 h in Instructional Core; and 18 h in Instructional Leadership Track.

Number of Full-Time Faculty -; **Number of Other Faculty** -

Degrees awarded in 2007–2008 Academic Year – **Masters** -; **PhD** -; **Other** -

Grant Monies awarded in 2007–2008 Academic Year -

Name of Institution – Iowa State University
Name of Department or Program – College of Education

Address:
E262 Lagomarcino Hall
Ames, IA

50011
USA

Phone Number – (515)294-7021
Fax Number – (515)294-6260

Email Contact – pkendall@iastate.edu
URL – http://www.educ.iastate.edu/

Contact Person – Niki Davis, Director, Center for Technology in Learning and Teaching

Specializations – MEd, MS, and PhD in Curriculum and Instructional Technology. Features: Prepares candidates as practitioners and researchers in the field of curriculum and instructional technology. All areas of specialization emphasize appropriate and effective applications of technology in teacher education. MEd program also offered at a distance (online and face-to-face learning experiences).

Features – practicum experiences related to professional objectives, supervised study and research projects tied to long-term studies within the program, development and implementation of new techniques, teaching strategies, and operational procedures in instructional resources centers and computer labs, program emphasis on technologies for teachers.

Admission Requirements – Admission Requirements: MEd and MS: Bachelors degree, top half of undergraduate class, official transcripts, three letters, autobiography. PhD: top half of undergraduate class, official transcripts, three letters, autobiography, GRE scores, scholarly writing sample.

Degree Requirements – Degree Requirements: MEd 32 credit hours (7 research, 12 foundations, 13 applications and leadership in instructional technology); and action research project. MS 36 credit hours (16 research, 12 foundations, 8 applications and leadership in instructional technology); and thesis. PhD 78 credit hours (minimum of 12 research, minimum of 15 foundations, additional core credits in conceptual, technical and advanced specialization areas, minimum of 12 dissertation);portfolio, and dissertation.

Number of Full-Time Faculty – 0; **Number of Other Faculty** – 0

Degrees awarded in 2007–2008 Academic Year – **Masters** – 0; **PhD** – 0; **Other** – 0

Grant Monies awarded in 2007–2008 Academic Year – 0

Name of Institution – Emporia State University
Name of Department or Program – School of Library and Information Management

Address:
1200 Commercial, P.O. Box 4025
Emporia, KS
66801
USA

Phone Number – 800/552-4770 **Fax Number** – 620/341-5233

Email Contact – idt@emporia.edu **URL** – http://slim.emporia.edu

Contact Person – Daniel Roland, Director of Communications

Specializations – Masters of Library Science (ALA accredited program); Masters in Legal Information Management – in partnership with the University of Kansas School of Law – 50 semester hours or 15 h certificate. School Library Certification program, which includes 27 h of the M.L.S. program; PhD in Library and Information Management B.S. in Information Resource Studies Information Management Certificate – 18 h of MLS curriculum Library Services Certificates – 6 separate 12-hour programs of undergraduate work available for credit or non-credit. Areas include Information Sources and Services; Collection Management; Technology; Administration; Youth Services; and Generalist.

Features – The Master of Library Science program is also delivered to satellite campus sites in Denver, Salt Lake City, Portland, Oregon. New programs tend to start every 3 years in each location. New programs include Denver – Summer 2004, Portland – Spring 2005, Salt Lake City – Fall 2005.

Admission Requirements – Undergrad GPA of 3.0 or better for masters degrees, 3.5 or better for PhD. GRE score of 1,000 points combined in Verbal and Analytical sections for masters degrees, 1,100 for PhD. GRE can be waived for students already holding a graduate degree in which they earned a 3.75 GPA or better. Admission interview.

Degree Requirements – M.L.S.: 42 semester hours. PhD: total of 55–59 semester hours beyond the masters.

Number of Full-Time Faculty – 0; **Number of Other Faculty** – 0

Degrees awarded in 2007–2008 Academic Year – Masters – 0; **PhD** – 0; **Other** – 0

Grant Monies awarded in 2007–2008 Academic Year – 0

Name of Institution – Kansas State University
Name of Department or Program – Secondary Education

Address:
364 Bluemont Hall
Manhattan, KS

66506
USA

Phone Number – 785-532-5716
Fax Number – (785)532-7304

Email Contact – talab@ksu.edu
URL – http://coe.ksu.edu/ecdol

Contact Person – Dr. Rosemary Talab

Specializations – The Educational Computing, Design, and Online Learning Program has these specializations: I. MS in Curriculum & Instruction with: (1) Educational Computing, Design, and Online Learning; (2) Digital Teaching and Learning II. PhD and Ed.D in Curriculum & Instruction with: in Educational Computing, Design, and Online Learning. III. KSU Graduate School Certificate in Digital Teaching and Learning Masters program started in 1982; doctoral in 1987; Certificate in 1999

Features – All coursework for the Certificate, MA, and PhD can be taken online. ECDOL focuses on research, theory, practice, ethics, and the design of learning environments, with an emphasis on emerging technologies. Coursework includes instructional design, virtual learning environments, digital video, the design and evaluation of e-learning and blended learning coursework, wireless and mobile learning, etc., as classes are offered on a rotating basis. A cohort group is taken each fall for the Professional Seminar 1 and 2 academic year. Personal learning networks are used to enhance student networking and technology skills. At the Certificate and masters level the DTL program offers classroom teachers leadership opportunities as technology facilitators and lead teachers, with coursework available in integrating technology into instruction to improve student achievement through a blend of practical technology skills with research and theory. The masters level ECDOL program is offered to those who have B.A.s in other fields who wish to pursue a specialty in instructional design or prepare for the PhD in ECDOL or who wish to design technology-enhanced, online, and virtual learning environments

Admission Requirements – MS: B average in undergraduate work, one programming language, 590 TOEFL. EdD and PhD: B average in undergraduate and graduate work, one programming language, GRE, three letters of recommendation, experience or course in educational computing.

Degree Requirements – Certificate is 15 h and requires an e-portfolio and technology project DTL is a 15-hour KSU Graduate School Certificate program; e-portfolio and project are required MS: 31 semester hours (minimum of 15 in specialty); thesis, internship, or practicum not required, but all three are possible; e-portfolio and project are required. The PhD degree is 36–42 h, with 30 h of research, for a total of 60 h, minimum. The Ed.D. degree has a focus on assessment with a dissertation that is more classroom-oriented. It, too, is 60 h, but has fewer research hours and a clinical experience which can be conducted at ones school or institution. PhD: 90 semester hours (minimum of 21 h in Educational Computing, Design, and Online Learning or related area approved by committee, 30 h for dissertation research); thesis; internship or practicum not required but available

Number of Full-Time Faculty – 1; **Number of Other Faculty** – 6

Degrees awarded in 2007–2008 Academic Year – Masters – 5; PhD – 3; **Other** – 4

Grant Monies awarded in 2007–2008 Academic Year – 0

Name of Institution – University of Louisville
Name of Department or Program – College of Education and Human Development

Address:
Belknap Campus
Louisville, KY
40292
USA

Phone Number – (502)852-6667 **Fax Number** – (502)852-4563

Email Contact – rod.githens@louisville.edu **URL** – http://www.louisville.edu/edu

Contact Person – Rod Githens

Specializations – MS in Hu man Resource Education PhD in Educational Leadership and Organizational Development

Features – Our program is Relevant, Rigorous, and Conceptually Sound: – Relevant. The program has a strong emphasis on hands-on, applied projects that provide direct application to the field. Our instructors have practitioner experience in the field and many currently work in HR-related positions in Louisville and around the country. – Rigorous. Expect to work hard and complete challenging assignments. Our goal is to help you develop the skills to think unconventionally about conventional problems. – Conceptually Sound. The program is designed around research-based competencies from the American Society for Training and Development, International Society for Performance Improvement, and the Society for Human Resource Management. Faculty members have strong theoretical and conceptual backgrounds that guide both their teaching and their practical approach to the field.

Admission Requirements – 2.75 GPA, 800 GRE, 2 letters of recommendation, goal statement, resume, application fee

Degree Requirements – 30 semester hours, internship/fieldwork

Number of Full-Time Faculty – 7; **Number of Other Faculty** – 14

Degrees awarded in 2007–2008 Academic Year – **Masters** – 25; **PhD** – 5; **Other** – 0

Grant Monies awarded in 2007–2008 Academic Year – 0

Name of Institution – Louisiana State University
Name of Department or Program – School of Library and Information Science

Address:
267 Coates Hall
Baton Rouge, LA
70803
USA

Phone Number – (225)578-3158 **Fax Number** – (225)578-4581

Email Contact – bpaskoff@lsu.edu **URL** – http://slis.lsu.edu

Contact Person – Beth Paskoff, Dean, School of Library and Information Science

Specializations – Archives, academic libraries, information technology, medical libraries, public libraries, special libraries, youth services, Louisiana School Library Certification. Dual degrees are available in Systems Science and in History

Features – Distance education courses available at 7 locations in Louisiana.

Admission Requirements – Bachelors degree, prefer 3.00 GPA GRE scores: prefer 500+ on verbal

Degree Requirements – M.L.I.S.: 40 h, comprehensive exam, completion of degree program in five years

Number of Full-Time Faculty – 11; **Number of Other Faculty** – 0

Degrees awarded in 2007–2008 Academic Year – **Masters** – 60; **PhD** – 0; **Other** – 2

Grant Monies awarded in 2007–2008 Academic Year – 111841

Name of Institution – Boston University
Name of Department or Program – School of Education

Address:
Two Siber Way
Boston, MA
02215-1605
USA

Phone Number – (617)353-3181 **Fax Number** – (617)353-3924

Email Contact – whittier@bu.edu **URL** – http://web.bu.edu/EDUCATION

Contact Person – David B. Whittier, Asst. Professor and Coordinator, Program in Educational Media and Technology.

Specializations – EdM, CAGS (Certificate of Advanced Graduate Study) in Educational Media and Technology; Ed.D. in Curriculum and Teaching, Specializing in Educational Media and Technology; preparation for Massachusetts public school License as Instructional Technology Specialist

Features – The Masters Program prepares graduates for professional careers as educators, instructional designers, developers of educational materials, and managers of the human and technology-based resources necessary to support education and training with technology. Graduates are employed in pK-12 schools, higher education, industry, medicine, public health, government, publishing, and a range of services such as finance and insurance. Students come to the program from many different backgrounds and with a wide range of professional goals. The doctoral program sets the study of Educational Media & Technology within the context of education and educational research in general, and curriculum and teaching in particular. In addition to advanced work in the field of Educational Media and Technology, students examine and conduct research and study the history of educational thought and practice. Graduates make careers in education as professors and researchers, technology directors and managers, and as developers of technology-based materials and systems. Graduates who work in both educational and non-educational organizations are often responsible for managing the human and technological resources required to create learning experiences that include the development and delivery of technology-based resources and distance education.

Admission Requirements – All degree programs require either the GRE or MAT test score completed within past 5 years and recommendations. Specific programs also include: EdM: undergraduate degree and GPA. For CAGS, in addition to above, an earned Ed.M is required. For Ed.D. 3 letters of recommendation, test scores, transcripts, earned masters degree, and two writing samples: a statement of goals and qualifications and an analytical essay are required. Contact Graduate Admissions office.

Degree Requirements – EdM: 36 credit hours (including 26 h from required core curriculum, 10 from electives). CAGs: 32 credits beyond EdM, one of which must be a curriculum and teaching course and a comprehensive exam. EdD: 60 credit hours of courses selected from Educational Media and Technology, curriculum and teaching, and educational thought and practice with comprehensive exams; coursework and apprenticeship in research; dissertation

Number of Full-Time Faculty – 1; **Number of Other Faculty** – 10

Degrees awarded in 2007–2008 Academic Year – Masters – 12; **PhD** – 1; **Other** – 0

Grant Monies awarded in 2007–2008 Academic Year – 30000

Name of Institution – Fitchburg State College
Name of Department or Program – Division of Graduate and Continuing Education

Address:
160 Pearl Street
Fitchburg, MA
01420
USA

Phone Number – (978) 665-3544 **Fax Number** – (978) 665-3055

Email Contact – rhowe@fsc.edu **URL** – http://www.fsc.edu

Contact Person – Dr. Randy Howe, Chair

Specializations – MS in Applied Communication with specializations in Applied Communication and Library Media. MEd in Educational Leadership and Management with specialization in Technology Leadership.

Features – Collaborating with professionals working in the field both for organizations and as independent producers, Fitchburg offers unique MS and MEd programs. The objectives are to develop in candidates the knowledge and skills for the effective implementation of communication within business, industry, government, not-for-profit agencies, health services, and education.

Admission Requirements – MAT or GRE scores, official transcript(s) of a baccalaureate degree, 2 or more years of experience in communications or media or education, three letters of recommendation.

Degree Requirements – 39 semester credit hours.

Number of Full-Time Faculty – 5; **Number of Other Faculty** – 7

Degrees awarded in 2007–2008 Academic Year – Masters – 10; **PhD** – 0; **Other** – 0

Grant Monies awarded in 2007–2008 Academic Year – 0

Name of Institution – Lesley University
Name of Department or Program – Technology In Education

Address:
29 Everett St.
Cambridge, MA
02138-2790
USA

Phone Number – (617)349-8419
Fax Number – (617)349-8169

Email Contact – gblakesl@lesley.edu
URL – http://www.lesley.edu/soe/111tech.html

Contact Person – Dr. George Blakeslee, Division Director

Specializations – MEd in Technology in Education CAGS/Ed.S. in Technology in Education PhD in Educational Studies with specialization in Technology in Education

Features – MEd program is offered off-campus at 70+ sites in 21 states; contact 617-349-8311 for information. The degree is also offered completely online. Contact Maureen Yoder, myoder@lesley.edu, or (617)348-8421 for information. Or check our website: URL above.

Admission Requirements – Completed bachelors Teaching certificate

Degree Requirements – MEd: 33 semester hours in technology, integrative final project in lieu of thesis, no internship or practicum. C.A.G.S.: 36 semester hours. PhD requirements available on request.

Number of Full-Time Faculty -; **Number of Other Faculty** -

Degrees awarded in 2007–2008 Academic Year – **Masters** -; **PhD** -; **Other** -

Grant Monies awarded in 2007–2008 Academic Year -

Name of Institution – Harvard University
Name of Department or Program – Graduate School of Education

Address:
Appian Way
Cambridge, MA
02138
USA

Phone Number – (617)495-3543
Fax Number – (617)495-9268

Email Contact – pakir@gse.harvard.edu **URL** – http://www.gse.harvard.edu/tie

Contact Person – Joseph Blatt, Director, Technology, Innovation, and Education Program; Irene Pak, Program Coordinator, Technology, Innovation, and Education Program

Specializations – The Technology, Innovation, and Education Program (TIE) at Harvard prepares students to contribute to the thoughtful design, implementation, and assessment of educational media and technology initiatives. Graduates of the program fill leadership positions in a wide range of fields, including design and production, policy development and analysis, technology integration and administration, research and evaluation, and teaching with new technologies. Some distinctive features of studying educational technology in TIE include: * Focus on learning and teaching: Our approach puts learning and teaching at the center, with technology as the means, not the mission. Our courses examine cutting-edge technologies that bridge distance and time, the research behind them and the design that goes into them – but we always center on the cognitive, affective, and social dimensions of learning, not on hardware or fashion. * A world-class faculty: Our faculty combines internationally recognized researchers with leading professionals in design and evaluation. We are all committed teachers and learners, dedicated to supporting you as a student and helping you craft a course of study that meets your goals. * A curriculum that builds leaders: Our curriculum bridges three broad strands of design, implementation, and research. Design courses apply learning principles to creating software, networks, digital video and television, handheld applications, and multi-user virtual environments. Implementation courses focus on using new technologies to bring about transformative changes in educational practice. Courses on research emphasize formulating evaluation designs that are both rigorous and practical. To deepen connections between theory and practice, TIE students often undertake an internship in one of the many research projects, educational technology firms, or media production organizations in the Boston area. * A diverse community of learners: Our community includes students of all ages, from all parts of the globe, with varied professional backgrounds and experience in technology. The upshot is that students have endless opportunities to learn from one another, exchanging insights about the potential role for learning technologies in different settings and cultures. More information about the program, our faculty, and the student experience, is available on our Web site, http://www.gse.harvard.edu/tie.

Features – Courses in design, technology policy and leadership, research and evaluation, leading to the EdM degree in Technology, Innovation, and Education. The program offers access to other courses throughout Harvard University, and at MIT, as well as many internship opportunities in the Greater Boston media and technology community.

Admission Requirements – GRE scores, 600 TOEFL, academic transcripts, 3 letters of recommendation, and a statement of purpose. Students interested in further information about the TIE Program should visit our Web site, http://www.gse.harvard.edu/tie, which includes a link to the Harvard Graduate School of Education online application.

Degree Requirements – 32 semester credits

Number of Full-Time Faculty – 5; **Number of Other Faculty** – 6

Degrees awarded in 2007–2008 Academic Year – Masters – 40; **PhD** – 0; **Other** – 0

Grant Monies awarded in 2007–2008 Academic Year – 3000000

Name of Institution – Simmons College

Address:
300 The Fenway
Boston, MA
02115-5898
USA

Phone Number – (617)521-2800 **Fax Number** – (617)521-3192

Email Contact – michele.cloonan@simmons.edu
URL – http://www.simmons.edu/gslis/

Contact Person – Michèle V. Cloonan

Specializations – MS Dual degrees: M.L.S./MA in Education (for School Library Media Specialists); M.L.S./MA in History (Archives Management Program). A Doctor of Arts in Administration is also offered.

Features – The program prepares individuals for a variety of careers, media technology emphasis being only one. There are special programs for School Library Media Specialist and Archives Management with strengths in Information Science/Systems, Media Management.

Admission Requirements – B.A. or B.S. degree with 3.0 GPA, statement, three letters of reference.

Degree Requirements – 36 semester hours.

Number of Full-Time Faculty – 0; **Number of Other Faculty** – 0

Degrees awarded in 2007–2008 Academic Year – Masters – 0; **PhD** – 0; **Other** – 0

Grant Monies awarded in 2007–2008 Academic Year – 0

Name of Institution – McDaniel College (formerly Western Maryland College)
Name of Department or Program – Graduate and Professional Studies

Address:
2 College Hill
Westminster, MD
21157
USA

Phone Number – (410)857-2507 **Fax Number** – (410)857-2515

Email Contact – rkerby@mcdaniel.edu **URL** – http://www.mcdaniel.edu

Contact Person – Dr. Ramona N. Kerby, Coordinator, School Library Media Program, Department of Education

Specializations – MS in Education with an emphasis in School Library Media

Features – School librarianship

Admission Requirements – 3.0 Undergraduate GPA, 3 reference checklist forms from principal and other school personnel, acceptable application essay, acceptable Praxis test scores

Degree Requirements – 37 credit hours, including professional digital portfolio.

Number of Full-Time Faculty – 1; **Number of Other Faculty** – 5

Degrees awarded in 2007–2008 Academic Year – **Masters** – 18; **PhD** – 0; **Other** – 0

Grant Monies awarded in 2007–2008 Academic Year – 0

Name of Institution – Towson University
Name of Department or Program – College of Education

Address:
Hawkins Hall
Towson, MD
21252
USA

Phone Number – (410)704-4226
Fax Number – (410)704-4227

Email Contact – jkenton@towson.edu
URL – http://wwwnew.towson.edu/coe/rset/insttech/

Contact Person – Dr. Jeffrey M. Kenton, Assistant Professor. Department: Educational Technology and Literacy

Specializations – MS degrees in Instructional Development, and Educational Technology (Contact, Jeff Kenton, kkenton@towosn.edu)and School Library Media

(Contact, David Robinson: derobins@towson.edu). Ed. D. degrees in Instructional Technology (Contact, William Sadera, bsadera@towson.edu).

Features – Excellent labs. Strong practical hands-on classes. Focus of MS program-Students produce useful multimedia projects for use in their teaching and training. Many group activities within courses. School library media degree confers with Maryland State Department of Education certification as a Prek-12 Library Media Specialist. Innovative Ed. D. program with online hybrid courses and strong mix of theory and practical discussions.

Admission Requirements – Bachelor's degree from accredited institution with 3.0 GPA. (Conditional admission granted for many applicants with a GPA over 2.75).

Degree Requirements – MS degree is 36 graduate semester hours without thesis. Ed. D. is 63 h beyond the MS degree.

Number of Full-Time Faculty – 17; **Number of Other Faculty** – 5

Degrees awarded in 2007–2008 Academic Year – Masters – 157; **PhD** – 0; **Other** – 4

Grant Monies awarded in 2007–2008 Academic Year – 0

Name of Institution – University of Maryland Baltimore County (UMBC). **Name of Department or Program** – Department of Education

Address:
1000 Hilltop Circle
Baltimore, MD
21250
USA

Phone Number – (410)455-2310
Fax Number – (410)455-3986

Email Contact – gregw@umbc.edu
URL – http://www.research.umbc.edu/~eholly/ceduc/isd/

Contact Person – Greg Williams, Ed.D, Program Director

Specializations – MA degrees in School Instructional Systems, Post-Baccalaureate Teacher Certification, Training in Business and Industry, Experienced Teacher – Advanced Degree, ESOL/Bilingual

Features – Programs are configured with evening courses to accommodate students who are changing careers. Maryland teacher certification is earned two thirds of the way through the postbaccalaureate program.

Admission Requirements – 3.0 undergraduate GPA, GRE scores

Degree Requirements – 36 semester hours (including 18 in systems development for each program); internship.

Number of Full-Time Faculty – 0; **Number of Other Faculty** – 0

Degrees awarded in 2007–2008 Academic Year – Masters – 75; PhD – 0; **Other** – 0

Grant Monies awarded in 2007–2008 Academic Year – 0

Name of Institution – Eastern Michigan University
Name of Department or Program – Teacher Education

Address:
313 John W. Porter Building
Ypsilanti, MI
48197
USA

Phone Number – (734)487-3260
Fax Number – (734)487-2101

Email Contact – ncopeland@emich.edu **URL** – http://www.emich.edu

Contact Person – Toni Stokes Jones, PhD – Assistant Professor/Graduate Coordinator

Specializations – MA in Educational Psychology with concentration in Educational Technology. The mission of this program is to prepare professionals who are capable of facilitating student learning in a variety of settings. The program is designed to provide students with both the knowledge base and the application skills that are required to use technology effectively in education. Focusing on the design, development, utilization, management and evaluation of instructional systems moves us toward achieving this mission. Students who complete the educational technology concentration will be able to: (a) provide a rationale for using technology in the educational process; (b) identify contributions of major leaders in the field of educational media technology and instructional theory, and the impact that each leader has had on the field; (c) assess current trends in the area of educational media technology and relate the trends to past events and future implications; (d) integrate technology into instructional programs; (e) teach the operation and various uses of educational technology in instruction; (f) act as consultants/facilitators in educational media technology; (g) design and develop instructional products to meet specified needs; and (h) evaluate the effectiveness of instructional materials and systems.

Features – Courses in our 30 credit hour Educational Media & Technology (EDMT) program include technology and the reflective teacher, technology and student-centered learning, technology-enhanced learning environments, issues and emerging technologies, instructional design, internet for educators, advanced technologies, psychology of the adult learning, principles of classroom learning, curriculum foundations, research seminar and seminar in educational technology. Effective Spring 2003, all of the EDMT courses will be taught online. In some EDMT courses, students may be asked to come to campus only 3 times during the semester. Students who do not want to receive a masters degree can apply for admission to our 18 credit hour Educational Media and Technology certificate. The EDMT courses for the certificate are also offered online.

Admission Requirements – Individuals seeking admission to this program must: 1-Comply with the Graduates School admission requirements. 2-Score 550 or better on the TOEFL and 5 or better on TWE, if a non-native speaker of English. 4-Have a 2.75 undergraduate grade point average, or a 3.30 grade point average in 12 h or more of work in a masters program. 5-Solicit three letters of reference. 6-Submit a statement of professional goals.

Degree Requirements – In order to graduate, each student is expected to: 1-Complete all work on an approved program of study. (30 semester hours) 2-Maintain a "B" (3.0 GPA) average or better on coursework taken within the program. 3-Get a recommendation from the faculty adviser. 4-Fill out an application for graduation and obtain the advisers recommendation. 5-Meet all other requirements for a masters degree adopted by the Graduate School of Eastern Michigan University. 5-Complete a culminating experience (research, instructional development or evaluation project) as determined by the student and faculty adviser.

Number of Full-Time Faculty – 0; **Number of Other Faculty** – 0

Degrees awarded in 2007–2008 Academic Year – **Masters** – 10; **PhD** – 0; **Other** – 0

Grant Monies awarded in 2007–2008 Academic Year – 0

Name of Institution – Michigan State University
Name of Department or Program – College of Education

Address:
509D Erickson Hall
East Lansing, MI
48824
USA

Phone Number – 517-432-7195
Fax Number – 517-353-6393

Email Contact – msumaet@msu.edu **URL** – http://edutech.msu.edu

Contact Person – Leigh Wolf

Specializations – MA in Educational Technology with Learning, Design and Technology specialization.

Features – Extensive opportunities to work with faculty in designing online courses and online learning environments.

Admission Requirements – Please visit: http://edutech.msu.edu/apply_masters.html

Degree Requirements – 30 semester hours, Web-based portfolio.

Number of Full-Time Faculty – 6; **Number of Other Faculty** – 6

Degrees awarded in 2007–2008 Academic Year – **Masters** – 30; **PhD** – 0; **Other** – 0

Grant Monies awarded in 2007–2008 Academic Year – 0

Name of Institution – Wayne State University
Name of Department or Program – Instructional Technology

Address:
381 Education
Detroit, MI
48202
USA

Phone Number – (313)577-1728
Fax Number – (313)577-1693

Email Contact – tspannaus@wayne.edu
URL – http://www.coe.wayne.edu/InstructionalTechnology

Contact Person – Timothy W. Spannaus, PhD, Program Coordinator, Instructional Technology Programs, Division of Administrative and Organizational Studies, College of Education.

Specializations – MEd degrees in Instructional Design, Performance Improvement and Training, K-12 Technology Integration, and Interactive Technologies. Ed.D. and PhD programs to prepare individuals for leadership in academic, business, industry, health care, and the K-12 school setting as professor, researcher, instructional design and development specialists; media or learning resources managers or consultants; specialists in instructional video; and computer-assisted instruction and multimedia specialists. The school also offers a 6-year specialist degree program in Instructional Technology. The IT program offers certificates in Online Learning, Educational Technology, and University Teaching.

Features – Guided experiences in instructional design and development activities in business and industry are available.

Admission Requirements – PhD: Masters degree, 3.5 GPA, GRE, strong academic recommendations, interview.

Degree Requirements – MEd: 36 semester hours, including required project; internship recommended.

Number of Full-Time Faculty – 6; **Number of Other Faculty** – 10

Degrees awarded in 2007–2008 Academic Year – Masters – 48; **PhD** – 11; **Other** – 8

Grant Monies awarded in 2007–2008 Academic Year – 0

Name of Institution – Walden University

Address:
155 5th Avenue South
Minneapolis, MN
55401
USA

Phone Number – (800)444-6795

Email Contact – info@waldenu.edu.
URL – http://www.waldenu.edu; http://www.waldenu.edu/ecti/ecti.html.

Contact Person – Dr. Gwen Hillesheim, Chair

Specializations – MS in Educational Change and Technology Innovation. PhD in Education in Learning and Teaching with specialization in Educational Technology. In 1998 a specialization in Distance Learning will be added. In addition, there is a generalist PhD in Education in which students may choose and design their own areas of specialization.

Features – delivered primarily online.

Admission Requirements – accredited Bachelor's. PhD: accredited Master's, goal statement, letters of recommendation

Degree Requirements – Master's: 45 credit curriculum, 2 brief residencies, Master's project.

Number of Full-Time Faculty – 0; **Number of Other Faculty** – 0

Degrees awarded in 2007–2008 Academic Year – Masters – 0; **PhD** – 0; **Other** – 0

Grant Monies awarded in 2007–2008 Academic Year – 0

Name of Institution – Northwest Missouri State University
Name of Department or Program – Department of Computer Science/Information Systems

Address:
800 University Ave.
Maryville, MO
64468
USA

Phone Number – (660)562-1600. **Fax Number** – 660-562-1963

Email Contact – nzeliff@nwmissouri.edu **URL** – http://www.nwmissouri.edu/csis

Contact Person – Dr. Nancy Zeliff

Specializations – MS Ed. in Instructional Technology. Certificate Program in Instructional Technology.

Features – These degrees are designed for industry trainers and computer educators at the elementary, middle school, high school, and junior college level.

Admission Requirements – 3.0 undergraduate GPA, 700 GRE (V+Q).
Degree Requirements – 32 semester hours of graduate courses in computer science, education and instructional technology courses. Fifteen hours of computer education and instructional technology courses for the Certificate.

Number of Full-Time Faculty – 5; **Number of Other Faculty** – 7

Degrees awarded in 2007–2008 Academic Year – Masters – 10; PhD – 0; **Other** – 0

Grant Monies awarded in 2007–2008 Academic Year – 0

Name of Institution – St. Cloud State University
Name of Department or Program – College of Education

Address:
720 Fourth Avenue South
St. Cloud, MN
56301-4498
USA

Phone Number – (308)255-206
2 **Fax Number** – (308)255-4778

Email Contact – cim@stcloudstate.edu
URL – http://www.stcloudstate.edu/cim

Contact Person – Merton E. Thompson Coordinator, Center for Information Media.

Specializations – Undergraduate major and minor in Information Media. Undergraduate certificate in Instructional Technology. Masters degrees in Information Technologies, Educational Media, and Instructional Design & Training. Graduate certificates in Instructional Technology, Design for E-learning, and School Library Media.

Features – Most courses are available online as well as face to face.

Admission Requirements – acceptance to Graduate School, written and oral preliminary examination

Degree Requirements – Master's: 42 semester credits with thesis; 39 semester credits with starred paper or portfolio; 200-hour practicum is required for library media licensure. Coursework for licensure may be applied to Educational Media Master's program.

Number of Full-Time Faculty – 5; **Number of Other Faculty** – 21

Degrees awarded in 2007–2008 Academic Year – **Masters** – 15; **PhD** – 0; **Other** – 0

Grant Monies awarded in 2007–2008 Academic Year – 0

Name of Institution – University of Missouri-Columbia
Name of Department or Program – School of Information Science & Learning Technologies

Address:
303 Townsend Hall
Columbia, MO
65211
USA

Phone Number – (573)882-4546 **Fax Number** – (573)884-2917

Email Contact – wedmanj@missouri.edu **URL** – http://sislt.missouri.edu

Contact Person – John Wedman

Specializations – The Educational Technology program takes a theory-based approach to designing, developing, implementing, and researching computer-mediated environments to support human activity. We seek individuals who are committed to life-long learning and who aspire to use advanced technology to improve human learning and performance. Graduates of the program will find opportunities to use their knowledge and competencies as classroom teachers, media specialists, district technology specialists and coordinators, designers and developers of technology-based learning and information systems, training specialists for businesses, medical settings, and public institutions, as well as other creative positions. The curriculum at the Masters and Specialist levels has two focus areas: Technology in Schools and Learning Systems Design and Development; with coursework tailored to each focus area. For information regarding our PhD, see http://sislt.missouri.edu/phd

Features – Both focus areas are available online via the Internet or on the MU campus. The Technology in Schools focus area is based on the ISTE competencies and culminates in an online portfolio based on these competencies. Several courses are augmented by technical resources developed at MU, including a technology integration knowledge repository and online collaboration tools. The Learning Systems Design and Development focus area links to business, military, and government contexts. This focus area offers a challenging balance of design and development coursework, in addition to coursework dealing with needs assessment and evaluation. For information regarding our PhD, see http://sislt.missouri.edu/phd

Admission Requirements – Master: Bachelors degree, GRE (V>500; A>500; W>3.5) EdS: Masters degree, GRE (V>500; A>500; W>3.5) PhD: 3.5 graduate GPA, 1GRE (V>500; A>500; W>3.5) See website for details

Degree Requirements – Masters and EdS: Minimum of 30 graduate credit hours required for the degree; 15 h of upper-division coursework. Maximum of 6 h of transfer credit. PhD. See website for details
Number of Full-Time Faculty – 10; **Number of Other Faculty** – 2

Degrees awarded in 2007–2008 Academic Year – Masters – 47; PhD – 6; Other – 5

Grant Monies awarded in 2007–2008 Academic Year – 800000

Name of Institution – The University of Southern Mississippi
Name of Department or Program – Instructional Technology and Design

Address:
118 College Drive #5036
Hattiesburg, MS
39406-0001
USA

Phone Number – 601-266-4446 **Fax Number** – 601-266-5957

Email Contact – Taralynn.Hartsell@usm.edu **URL** – http://dragon.ep.usm.edu/~it

Contact Person – Dr. Taralynn Hartsell

Specializations – The University of Southern Mississippi's Department of Technology Education has two graduate programs relating to Instructional Technology and Design. The Masters of Science in Instructional Technology is a

33–36 h program, and the PhD of Instructional Technology and Design is a 60–75 h program.

Features – The Masters of Science concentrates more on the technology application and integration aspect that helps students learn both hands-on application of technology, as well as theoretical and historical aspects related to the field of study. A majority of the coursework in the program can be completed online (about 70%), and the remaining coursework are hybrid or blended in nature (about 60% online and 40% traditional). The PhD program is a new advanced study program for those wishing to pursue their education in the application of technology and design, research, and leadership (begins in Fall 2009). The PhD program also has two emphasis areas that meets students needs: instructional technology or instructional design. A majority of the coursework in the program can be completed online (between 60 and 80% depending upon emphasis area selected), and the remaining coursework are hybrid or blended in form (about 60% online and 40% traditional).

Admission Requirements – Please review the IT Web site for more information on the application procedures for each program: http://dragon.ep.usm.edu/~it. The GRE is mandatory for graduate programs.

Degree Requirements – Please review the IT Web site for more information on degree requirements for each program: http://dragon.ep.usm.edu/~it

Number of Full-Time Faculty – 3; **Number of Other Faculty** – 2
Degrees awarded in 2007–2008 Academic Year – Masters – 5; PhD – 0; **Other** – 0

Grant Monies awarded in 2007–2008 Academic Year – 0

Name of Institution – University of Montana
Name of Department or Program – School of Education

Address:
32 Campus Drive
Missoula, MT
59812
USA

Phone Number – (406)243-2563 **Fax Number** – (406)243-4908

Email Contact – sally.brewer@mso.umt.edu **URL** – http://www.umt.edu

Contact Person – Dr. Sally Brewer, Associate Professor of Library/Media

Specializations – MEd and Specialist degrees; K-12 School Library Media specialization with Library Media endorsement Not represented in the rest of this is that we also have a Masters in Curricular Studies with an option in Instructional Design for Technology. Dr. Martin Horejsi is the coordinator of this program. His phone is

406.243.5785. His email is martin.horejsi@umontana.edu This program is 37 credits and can be taken totally online. There are three full-time faculty members in this program.

Features – Combined online program with University of Montana-Western in Dillon, MT. 25 credits.

Admission Requirements – (both degrees): GRE, letters of recommendation, 2.75 GPA

Degree Requirements – MEd: 37 semester credit hours (18 overlap with library media endorsement). Specialist: 28 semester hours (18 overlap).

Number of Full-Time Faculty – 3; **Number of Other Faculty** – 1

Degrees awarded in 2007–2008 Academic Year – **Masters** – 2; **PhD** – 0; **Other** – 19

Grant Monies awarded in 2007–2008 Academic Year – 0

Name of Institution – East Carolina University
Name of Department or Program – Department of Mathematics, Science, and Instructional Technology Education

Address:
MSITE Department, Mail Stop 566 East Carolina University
Greenville, NC
27858-4353
USA

Phone Number – (252)328-9353
Fax Number – (252)328-4368

Email Contact – browncar@mail.ecu.edu **URL** – http://www.ecu.edu/educ/msite/it/maed/index.cfm

Contact Person – Dr. Carol Brown, MAEd Program Coordinator

Specializations – Master of Arts in Education (North Carolina Instructional Technology Specialist licensure); Master of Science in Instructional Technology; Certificate in Distance Education; Certificate in Virtual Reality in Education and Training; Certificate in Performance Improvement; Certificate for Special Endorsement in Computer Education.

Features – MA Ed. graduates are eligible for North Carolina Instructional Technology certification; Cert. for Special Endorsement in Computer Education for North Carolina Licensure as Technology Facilitator. ALL programs available 100% online. The program is housed in the Department of Mathematics, Science, and Instructional Technology Education. An important mission for this program is the emphasis on STEM in K12 schools including support of math and science teachers who are teacher leaders in their school systems.

Admission Requirements – Bachelor's degree; Admission to East Carolina University Graduate School. GRE [or Millers Analogy Test], references, and writing sample.

Degree Requirements – MA Ed.: 39 semester hours;

Number of Full-Time Faculty – 7; **Number of Other Faculty** – 2

Degrees awarded in 2007–2008 Academic Year – Masters – 48; **PhD** – 0; **Other** – 0

Grant Monies awarded in 2007–2008 Academic Year – 0

Name of Institution – North Carolina State University
Name of Department or Program – Department of Curriculum and Instruction

Address:
P.O. Box 7801
Raleigh, NC
27695-7801
USA

Phone Number – (919) 515-6229 **Fax Number** – (919) 515-6978

Email Contact – kevin_oliver@ncsu.edu **URL** – http://ced.ncsu.edu/ci/it/index.php

Contact Person – Dr. Kevin Oliver, Assistant Professor

Specializations – Certificate in E-Learning. MEd and MS in Instructional Technology. PhD in Curriculum and Instruction with focus on Instructional Technology.

Features – Fully online E-Learning Certificate and Masters programs with flexibility for residents near the Raleigh-Durham area to take some on-campus courses if they wish. Doctoral program is not online. A limited number of assistantships are available for students who live near Raleigh, go to school full-time (9 h/semester), and can work on campus 20 h/week. Pays $12–15 k per semester with health benefits and tuition remission.

Admission Requirements – Master's: undergraduate degree from an accredited institution, 3.0 GPA in major or in latest graduate degree program; transcripts; GRE or MAT scores; 3 references; goal statement. PhD: undergraduate degree from accredited institution, 3.0 GPA in major or latest graduate program; transcripts;

recent GRE scores, writing sample, three references, vita, research and professional goals statement (see http://ced.ncsu.edu/ci/admissions.php).

Degree Requirements – Masters: 36 semester hours, internship, thesis optional (note, the number of hours required for the Masters may reduce from 36 to 30 in Fall 2009). PhD: 72 h beyond Bachelors (minimum 33 in Curriculum and Instruction core, 27 in Research). Up to 12 h of graduate-level transfer credits may be applied to any Masters or PhD program. The transfer credits should be in Instructional Technology or similar to another required course in a program area.

Number of Full-Time Faculty – 3; **Number of Other Faculty** – 3

Degrees awarded in 2007–2008 Academic Year – **Masters** – 2; **PhD** – 1; **Other** – 0

Grant Monies awarded in 2007–2008 Academic Year – 300000

Name of Institution – University of North Carolina
Name of Department or Program – School of Information and Library Science

Address:
100 Manning Hall, CB#3360
Chapel Hill, NC
27599-3360
USA

Phone Number – (919)843-5276 **Fax Number** – (919)962-8071

Email Contact – smhughes@email.unc.edu **URL** – http://www.ils.unc.edu/

Contact Person – Sandra Hughes-Hassell, Associate Professor, Coordinator, School Media Program

Specializations – Master of Science Degree in Library Science (M.S.L.S.) with specialization in school library media. Post-Masters certification program

Features – Rigorous academic program plus field experience requirement; excellent placement record.

Admission Requirements – Competitive admission based on all three GRE components (quantitative, qualitative, analytical), undergraduate GPA (plus graduate work if any), letters of recommendation, and student statement of career interest and school choice.

Degree Requirements – 48 semester hours, field experience, comprehensive exam, Master's paper

Number of Full-Time Faculty – 26; **Number of Other Faculty** – 6

Degrees awarded in 2007–2008 Academic Year – Masters – 115; PhD – 3; Other – 22

Grant Monies awarded in 2007–2008 Academic Year – 11502614

Name of Institution – University of Nebraska at Kearney
Name of Department or Program – Teacher Education

Address:
905 West 25th Street
Kearney, NE
68849-5540
USA

Phone Number – (308)865-8833 **Fax Number** – (308)865-8097

Email Contact – fredricksons@unk.edu
URL – http://www.unk.edu/departments/pte

Contact Person – Dr. Scott Fredrickson, Professor and Chair of the Instructional Technology Graduate Program

Specializations – MS Ed. in Instructional Technology, MS Ed in Library Media.

Features – Two main emphasis areas – Instructional Technology and Library Media; Additionally – Assistive Technology

Admission Requirements – MS GRE (or electronic portfolio meeting dept. requirements), acceptance into graduate school, approval of Instructional Technology Committee

Degree Requirements – MS: 36 credit hours, Instructional technology project or field study.

Number of Full-Time Faculty – 3; **Number of Other Faculty** – 23

Degrees awarded in 2007–2008 Academic Year – Masters – 35; PhD – 0; Other – 0

Grant Monies awarded in 2007–2008 Academic Year – 0

Name of Institution – University of Nebraska-Omaha
Name of Department or Program – Department of Teacher Education

Address:
College of Education, Kayser Hall 514G
Omaha, NE

68182
USA

Phone Number – (402)554-2119 **Fax Number** – (402)554-2125

Email Contact – rpasco@unomaha.edu **URL** – http://www.unomaha.edu/libraryed/

Contact Person – Dr. R. J. Pasco

Specializations – School Library Media Endorsement (undergraduate and Graduate) MS in Secondary and Elementary Education, MA in Secondary and Elementary Education, both with School Library Media concentration MS in Reading with School Library Media concentration Masters in Library Science Program (Cooperative program with University of Missouri at Columbia)

Features – Web-assisted format (combination of online and on-campus) for both undergraduate and graduate programs. School Library programs nationally recognized by AASL Public, Academic and Special Libraries programs Cooperative UNO/University of Missouri MLS program is ALA accredited

Admission Requirements – As per University of Nebraska at Omaha undergraduate and graduate requirements

Degree Requirements – School Library Media Endorsement (Undergraduate and Graduate) – 33 h MS in Secondary and Elementary Education, MA in Secondary and Elementary Education, both with School Library Media concentration – 36 h MS in Reading with School Library Media concentration – 36 h Masters in Library Science Program (Cooperative program with University of Missouri at Columbia) – 42 h

Number of Full-Time Faculty – 1; **Number of Other Faculty** – 10

Degrees awarded in 2007–2008 Academic Year – **Masters** – 33; **PhD** – 0; **Other** – 0

Grant Monies awarded in 2007–2008 Academic Year – 10000

Name of Institution – New York Institute of Technology
Name of Department or Program – Dept. of Instructional Technology

Address:
Tower House
Old Westbury, NY
11568
USA

Phone Number – (516)686-7777 **Fax Number** – (516)686-7655

Email Contact – smcphers@nyit.edu **URL** – http://www.nyit.edu.

Contact Person – Davenport Plumer, Chair, Departments of Instructional Technology and Elementary Education – pre. Service & in-service

Specializations – MS in Instructional Technology; MS in Elementary Education; Specialist Certificates in Computers in Education, Distance Learning, and Multimedia (not degrees, but are earned after the first 18 credits of the Master's degree).

Features – computer integration in virtually all courses; online courses; evening, weekend, and summer courses.

Admission Requirements – Bachelors degree from accredited college with 3.0 cumulative average

Degree Requirements – 36 credits with 3.0 GPA for MS, 18 credits with 3.0 GPA for certificates.

Number of Full-Time Faculty – 0; **Number of Other Faculty** – 0

Degrees awarded in 2007–2008 Academic Year – **Masters** – 0; **PhD** – 0; **Other** – 0

Grant Monies awarded in 2007–2008 Academic Year – 0

Name of Institution – Rutgers-The State University of New Jersey
Name of Department or Program – School of Communication, Information and Library Studies

Address:
4 Huntington Street New Brunswick NJ USA
New Brunswick, NJ
08901-1071
USA

Phone Number – (732)932-7500 Ext 8955 **Fax Number** – (732)932-2644

Email Contact – rtodd@scils.rutgers.edu **URL** – http://www.scils.rutgers.edu/
Contact Person – Dr. Ross J Todd, Director, Master of Library and Information Science, Department of Library and Information Studies, School of Communication, Information and Library Studies. (732)932-7500 Ext 8955. Fax (732)932-2644. Dr. Michael Lesk, Chair.

Specializations – The Master of Library and Information Science (M.L.I.S.) program provides professional education for a wide variety of service and management careers in libraries, information agencies, the information industry, and in business, industry, government, research, and similar environments where information is a vital resource. Specializations include: school library media; services for children and youth; digital libraries; information retrieval/information systems; knowledge management (http://www.scils.rutgers.edu/programs/lis/Curriculum.jsp)

Features – The M.L.I.S. program, available both on campus and online, is organized around six themes in the field of library and information science: human-information interaction; information access; information and society; information systems; management; and organization of information. Six lead courses, one in each area, form the foundation of the curriculum and offer general knowledge of the major principles and issues of the field. Two or more central courses in each theme offer basic understanding and competencies in important components of the field. Specialization courses in each theme allow students to develop expertise in preparation for specific career objectives. All students on campus in the New Brunswick M.L.I.S. program work with an advisor to plan a course of study appropriate for their interests and career objectives.

Admission Requirements – A bachelors degree or its equivalent from a recognized institution of higher education with a B average or better; GRE scores; Personal statement which presents a view of the library and information science profession and applicants aspirations and goals in the library and information science professions; 3 Letters of recommendation which focus on the applicants academic capacity to undertake a rigorous program of graduate study.

Degree Requirements – A minimum of thirty-six credits, or twelve courses, is required to earn the M.L.I.S. degree. All students are required to enroll in two non-credit classes, 501–Introduction to Library and Information Professions in their first semester, and 502–Colloquium in a later semester. There are no language requirements for the M.L.I.S. degree, and there is no thesis or comprehensive examination.

Number of Full-Time Faculty -; **Number of Other Faculty** -

Degrees awarded in 2007–2008 Academic Year – Masters -; PhD -; Other -

Grant Monies awarded in 2007–2008 Academic Year -

Name of Institution – Appalachian State University
Name of Department or Program – Department of Curriculum and Instruction

Address:
College of Education
Boone, NC
28608
USA

Phone Number – 828-262-2277 **Fax Number** – 828-262-2686

Email Contact – muffoletto@appstate.edu;riedlre@appstate.edu
URL – http://edtech.ced.appstate.edu

Contact Person – Robert Muffoletto

Specializations – MA in Educational Media and Technology with three areas of concentration: Computers, Media Literacy, and Media Production. A plan of study in Internet distance teaching is offered online. Two certificate programs: (1) Distance Learning -Internet delivered; (2) Media Literacy

Features – Business, university, community college, and public school partnership offers unusual opportunities for learning. The programs are focused on developing learning environments over instructional environments.

Admission Requirements – Undergraduate degree

Degree Requirements – 36 graduate semester hours We also have certificates in (1) Distance Learning and (2) Media Literacy

Number of Full-Time Faculty – 0; **Number of Other Faculty** – 0

Degrees awarded in 2007–2008 Academic Year – Masters – 5; **PhD** – 0; **Other** – 0

Grant Monies awarded in 2007–2008 Academic Year – 0

Name of Institution – Buffalo State College
Name of Department or Program – Computer Information Systems Department

Address:
1300 Elmwood Avenue, Chase Hall 201
Buffalo, NY
14222-1095
USA

Phone Number – (716) 878-5528 **Fax Number** – (716) 878-6677

Email Contact – gareause@buffalostate.edu
URL – http://www.buffalostate.edu/cis/x471.xml

Contact Person – Dr. Stephen E. Gareau, Program Coordinator

Specializations – MS in Education in Educational Technology

Features – This program is designed for K-12 and higher education educators, as well as trainers from business and industry, who wish to develop and expand their knowledge and skills in the development and application of various educational technologies. A wide range of media and tools are covered in the program, including text, graphics, audio, video, animation, models, simulations, games, and Web tools.

Admission Requirements – Bachelor's degree from accredited institution, undergraduate 3.0 GPA, 3 letters of recommendation, one letter from applicant.

Degree Requirements – 36 semester hours. See http://www. buffalostate.edu/cis/x471.xml for full details.

Number of Full-Time Faculty – 3; **Number of Other Faculty** – 2

Degrees awarded in 2007–2008 Academic Year – **Masters** – 50; **PhD** – 0; **Other** – 0

Grant Monies awarded in 2007–2008 Academic Year – 25000

Name of Institution – Fordham University
Name of Department or Program – MA Program in Public Communications in the Department of Communication and Media Studies

Address:
Rose Hill Campus, 441 E. Fordham Rd.
Bronx, NY
10458
USA

Phone Number – (718)817-4860 **Fax Number** – (718)817-4868

Email Contact – andersen@fordham.edu **URL** – http://www.fordham.edu

Contact Person – James VanOosting, Department Chair, Robin Andersen, Director of Graduate Studies

Specializations – MA in Public Communications

Features – Internship or thesis option; full-time students can complete program in twelve months.

Admission Requirements – 3.0 undergraduate GPA.

Degree Requirements – 10 courses plus internship or thesis.

Number of Full-Time Faculty – 12; **Number of Other Faculty** – 4

Degrees awarded in 2007–2008 Academic Year – **Masters** – 20; **PhD** – 0; **Other** – 0

Grant Monies awarded in 2007–2008 Academic Year – 80000

Name of Institution – Ithaca College
Name of Department or Program – School of Communications

Address:
Park Hall
Ithaca, NY
14850
USA

Phone Number – (607)274-1025 **Fax Number** – (607)274-7076

Email Contact – hkalman@ithaca.edu
URL – http://www.ithaca.edu/gps/gradprograms/comm/

Contact Person – Howard K. Kalman, Associate Professor, Chair, Graduate Program in Communications; Roy H. Park, School of Communications.

Specializations – MS in Communications. Students in this program find employment in such areas as instructional design/training, web development, corporate/community/public relations and marketing, and employee communication. The program can be tailored to individual career goals.

Features – Program is interdisciplinary, incorporating organizational communication, instructional design, management, and technology.

Admission Requirements – 3.0 GPA, recommendations, statement of purpose, resume, application forms and transcripts, TOEFL 550 (or 213 computer-scored; 80 on the iBT version) where applicable.

Degree Requirements – 36 semester hours including capstone seminar.

Number of Full-Time Faculty – 6; **Number of Other Faculty** – 0

Degrees awarded in 2007–2008 Academic Year – Masters – 15; **PhD** – 0; **Other** – 0

Grant Monies awarded in 2007–2008 Academic Year – 0

Name of Institution – State University College of Arts and Science at Potsdam.
Name of Department or Program – Information and Communication Technology

Address:
392 Dunn Hall
Potsdam, NY
13676
USA

Phone Number – (315)267-2670
Fax Number – (315)267-2987

Email Contact – betrusak@potsdam.edu **URL** – http://www.potsdam.edu/ict

Contact Person – Dr. Anthony Betrus, Chair, Information and Communications Technology

Specializations – MS in Education in Instructional Technology with concentrations in: Educational Technology Specialist, Organizational Performance and Leadership Technology, Technology Educator, and Information Technology Production.

Features – A progressive, forward looking program with a balance of theoretical and hands-on practical coursework.

Admission Requirements – 1. Submission of an official transcript of an earned baccalaureate degree from an accredited institution. 2. A minimum GPA of 2.75 (4.0 scale) in the most recent 60 credit hours of coursework. 3. Submission of the Application for Graduate Study (w/$50 nonrefundable fee). 4. For students seeking the Educational Technology Specialist Certification, a valid NYS Teaching Certificate is required.

Degree Requirements – 36 semester hours, including internship or practicum; culminating project required

Number of Full-Time Faculty – 4; **Number of Other Faculty** – 5

Degrees awarded in 2007–2008 Academic Year – Masters – 32; **PhD** – 0; **Other** – 0

Grant Monies awarded in 2007–2008 Academic Year – 0

Name of Institution – Wright State University

Name of Department or Program – College of Education and Human Services, Dept. of Educational Leadership

Address:
421 Allyn Hall, 3640 Colonel Glenn Highway
Dayton, OH
45435
USA

Phone Number – (937)775-2509 or (937)775-4148 **Fax Number** – (937)775-2405

Email Contact – susan.berg@wright.edu **URL** – http://www.ed.wright.edu

Contact Person – Dr. Susan Berg, Library Media Program Advisor

Specializations – MEd or MA in Computer/Technology or Library Media

Features – Ohio licensure available in Multi-age library media (ages 3–21) Computer/technology endorsement Above licensure only available on a graduate basis. Multi-age library media licensure available in two tracks: initial (no previous teaching license) and advanced (with current teaching license in another field). The computer/technology endorsement must be added to a current teaching license.

Admission Requirements – Completed application with nonrefundable application fee, Bachelor's degree from accredited institution, official transcripts, 2.7 overall GPA for regular status (conditional acceptance possible), statement of purpose, satisfactory scores on MAT or GRE.

Degree Requirements – MEd requires a comprehensive portfolio; MA requires a 6-hour thesis

Number of Full-Time Faculty – 3; **Number of Other Faculty** – 5

Degrees awarded in 2007–2008 Academic Year – **Masters** – 10; **PhD** – 0; **Other** – 0

Grant Monies awarded in 2007–2008 Academic Year – 0

Name of Institution – Kent State University
Name of Department or Program – Instructional Technology

Address:
405 White Hall
Kent, OH
44242
USA

Phone Number – (330) 672-2294
Fax Number – (330) 672-2512

Email Contact – dtiene@kent.edu **URL** – http://www.ehhs.kent.edu/itec/

Contact Person – Dr. Drew Tiene, Coordinator, Instructional Technology Program

Specializations – MEd or MA in Instructional Technology, and licensure programs in Computing/Technology and Library/Media; PhD in Educational Psychology with specialization in Instructional Technology.

Features – Programs are planned with advisors to prepare students for careers in elementary, secondary, or higher education, business, industry, government agencies, or health facilities. Students may take advantage of independent research, individual study, practical, and internships. Most courses and programs can be taken online.

Admission Requirements – Master's: Bachelors degree with 3.00 undergraduate GPA

Degree Requirements – Master's: 37–42 semester hours; portfolio Doctoral: 45 post-masters semester hours; comprehensive exam; dissertation

Number of Full-Time Faculty – 4; **Number of Other Faculty** – 0

Degrees awarded in 2007–2008 Academic Year – Masters – 20; **PhD** – 3; **Other** – 0

Grant Monies awarded in 2007–2008 Academic Year – 0

Name of Institution – Ohio University

Name of Department or Program – Educational Studies

Address:
313D McCracken Hall
Athens, OH
45701-2979
USA

Phone Number – (740)593-4561 **Fax Number** – (740)593-0477

Email Contact – franklit@ohio.edu
URL – http://www.ohio.edu/education/dept/es/it/index.cfm

Contact Person – Teresa Franklin, Instructional Technology Program Coordinator

Specializations – MEd in Computer Education and Technology. PhD in Curriculum and Instruction with a specialization in Instructional Technology also available; call for details (740-593-4561) or visit the website: http://www.ohio.edu/education/dept/es/it/index.cfm

Features – Masters program is a blended online delivery.

Admission Requirements – Bachelors degree, 3.0 undergraduate GPA, 35 MAT, 500 GRE (verbal), 400 GRE (quantitative), 550 TOEFL, three letters of recommendation, Paper describing future goals and career expectations from completing a degree in our program.

Degree Requirements – Masters – 54 qtr. credits, electronic portfolio or optional thesis worth 2–10 credits or alternative seminar research paper. Students may earn two graduate degrees simultaneously in education and in any other field. PhD – 109 h with 15 h being dissertation work

Number of Full-Time Faculty – 3; **Number of Other Faculty** – 1

Degrees awarded in 2007–2008 Academic Year – Masters – 18; **PhD** – 4; **Other** – 0

Grant Monies awarded in 2007–2008 Academic Year – 500000

Name of Institution – University of Cincinnati

Name of Department or Program – College of Education

Address:
401 Teachers College, ML002
Cincinnati, OH
45221-0002
USA

Phone Number – (513)556-3579 **Fax Number** – (513)556-1001

Email Contact – richard.kretschmer@uc.edu **URL** – http://www.uc.edu/

Contact Person – Richard Kretschmer

Specializations – MEd or EdD in Curriculum and Instruction with an emphasis on Instructional Design and Technology; Educational Technology degree programs for current professional, technical, critical, and personal knowledge.

Features – Contact division for features

Admission Requirements – Bachelor's degree from accredited institution, 2.8 undergraduate GPA; GRE 1500 or better

Degree Requirements – 54 qtr. hours, written exam, thesis or research project. (12–15 credit hours college core; 12–15 C&I; 18–27 credit hours specialization; 3–6 credit hours thesis or project).
Number of Full-Time Faculty -; **Number of Other Faculty** -

Degrees awarded in 2007–2008 Academic Year – Masters -; **PhD** -; **Other** -

Grant Monies awarded in 2007–2008 Academic Year -

Name of Institution – University of Toledo
Name of Department or Program – Curriculum & Instruction

Address:
2801 W. Bancroft Street, Mail Stop 924
Toledo, OH
43606
USA

Phone Number – (419)530-7979 **Fax Number** – (419)530-2466

Email Contact – Berhane.Teclehaimanot@utoledo.edu
URL – http://tipt3.utoledo.edu
Contact Person – Berhane Teclehaimanot, PhD

Specializations – Technology Using Educator/Technology Coordinator, Instructional Designer, and Performance Technologist

Features – Graduate students may concentrate in one of the three primary "roles," or may choose a blended program of study. Program was completely redesigned in 2004.

Admission Requirements – Master's: 3.0 undergrad. GPA, GRE (if undergrad. GPA < 2.7), recommendations; Doctorate: Master's degree, GRE, TOEFL (as necessary), recommendations, entrance writing samples, and interview.

Degree Requirements – Computer Technology Endorsement: 36 semester hours; Master's: 30 semester hours, culminating project; Doctorate: 60 sem. hours (after Ms), major exams, dissertation.

Number of Full-Time Faculty – 0; **Number of Other Faculty** – 0

Degrees awarded in 2007–2008 Academic Year – Masters – 0; PhD – 0; Other – 0

Grant Monies awarded in 2007–2008 Academic Year – 0

Name of Institution – The University of Oklahoma
Name of Department or Program – Instructional Psychology and Technology, Department of Educational Psychology

Address:
321 Collings Hall
Norman, OK
73019
USA

Phone Number – (405)325-5974 **Fax Number** – (405)325-6655

Email Contact – bradshaw@ou.edu
URL – http://www.ou.edu/education/edpsy/iptwww/

Contact Person – Dr. Amy Bradshaw, Program Coordinator

Specializations – Master's degree with emphases in Instructional Design & Technology (includes instructional design and interactive learning technologies), and Instructional Psychology & Technology (includes instructional psychology & technology, teaching & assessment, teaching & learning, and integrating technology in teaching). Doctoral degree in Instructional Psychology and Technology.

Features – Strong interweaving of principles of instructional psychology with instructional design and development. Application of IP&T in K-12, vocational education, higher education, business and industry, and governmental agencies.

Admission Requirements – Master's: acceptance by IPT program and Graduate College based on minimum 3.00 GPA for last 60 h of undergraduate work or last 12 h of graduate work; written statement that indicates goals and interests compatible with program goals. Doctoral: minimum 3.25 GPA, GRE scores, written statement that indicates goals and interests compatible with program goals, writing sample, and letters of recommendation.

Degree Requirements – Master's: 36 h coursework with 3.0 GPA; successful completion of thesis or comprehensive exam. Doctorate: see program description from institution or http://education.ou.edu/ipt/

Number of Full-Time Faculty – 11; **Number of Other Faculty** – 0
Degrees awarded in 2007–2008 Academic Year – **Masters** – 10; **PhD** – 1; **Other** – 0

Grant Monies awarded in 2007–2008 Academic Year – 0

Name of Institution – Bloomsburg University
Name of Department or Program – Instructional Technology & Institute for Interactive Technologies

Address:
2221 McCormick Bldg.
Bloomsburg, PA
17815
USA

Phone Number – (717)389-48875 **Fax Number** – (717)389-4943

Email Contact – tphillip@bloomu.edu **URL** – http://iit.bloomu.edu

Contact Person – Dr. Timothy L. Phillips, contact person

Specializations – MS in Instructional Technology – Corporate Concentration MS in Instructional Technology – Instructional Technology Specialist Concentration (education MS Instructional Technology – Instructional Game and Interactive Environments Concentration (currently under development) eLearning Developer Certificate
Features – MS in Instructional Technology with emphasis on preparing for careers as Instructional Technologist in corporate, government, healthcare, higher education and K-12 educational settings. The program is highly applied and provides opportunities for students to work on real-world projects as part of their coursework. Our program offers a corporate concentration and an Instructional Technology Specialist Concentration for educators. The program offers a complete masters degree online as well as on campus. Graduate assistantships are available for full-time students. The program is closely associated with the nationally known Institute for Interactive Technologies.

Admission Requirements – Bachelors degree

Degree Requirements – 33 semester credits (27 credits + 6 credit thesis, or 30 credits + three credit internship).

Number of Full-Time Faculty – 5; **Number of Other Faculty** – 3

Degrees awarded in 2007–2008 Academic Year – Masters – 40; **PhD** – 0; **Other** – 5

Grant Monies awarded in 2007–2008 Academic Year – 500000

Name of Institution – Drexel University
Name of Department or Program – College of Information Science and Technology
Address:
3141 Chestnut Street
Philadelphia, PA
19104-2875
USA

Phone Number – (215) 895-2474 **Fax Number** – (215) 895-2494

Email Contact – info@ischool.drexel.edu **URL** – http://www.ischool.drexel.edu

Contact Person – David E. Fenske, Dean

Specializations – MS Master of Science (Library and Information Science; M.S.I.S. Master of Science in Information Systems; M.S.S.E. Master of Science in Software Engineering; PhD

Features – On campus and online degree programs for MS, M.S.I.S., and M.S.S.E.

Admission Requirements – GRE scores; applicants with a minimum 3.2 GPA in last half of undergraduate credits may be eligible for admission without GRE scores.

Degree Requirements – 15 courses

Number of Full-Time Faculty -; **Number of Other Faculty** -
Degrees awarded in 2007–2008 Academic Year – Masters -; **PhD** -; **Other** -

Grant Monies awarded in 2007–2008 Academic Year -

Name of Institution – Lehigh University
Name of Department or Program – Teaching, Learning, and Technology

Address:
111 Research Drive
Bethlehem, PA
18015
USA

Phone Number – (610)758-3249 **Fax Number** – (610)758-6223

Email Contact – TLTProgram@Lehigh.edu

URL – http://www.lehigh.edu/collegeofeducation/degree_programs/ed_technology/ index.htm

Contact Person – MJ Bishop, Teaching, Learning, and Technology Program Coordinator

Specializations – MS in Instructional Technology: Emphasizes implementation, integration, and evaluation of technology in school settings. The degree is well suited to both classroom teachers and technology specialists. Graduate certificate in Technology Use in the Schools: This twelve-credit grad certificate focuses on integrating technology into daily practice in the schools. PhD in Learning Sciences and Technology: Emphasizes cognitive processes and their implications for the design, implementation, and evaluation of technology-based teaching and learning products in a variety of settings. Involves university-wide coursework in departments in all four colleges of the university.

Features – High level of integration with teacher education and certification, leading to a practical and quickly applicable program of study. Our Integrated Professional Development School approach offers further opportunities to get into the schools and work on solving meaningful teaching and learning problems, not just "tech support." Both masters and doctoral students collaborate with faculty on projects and studies (including national presentation and publication).

Admission Requirements – MS (competitive): 3.0 undergraduate GPA or 3.0 graduate GPA, GREs recommended, transcripts, at least 2 letters of recommendation, statement of personal and professional goals, application fee. Application deadlines: July 15 for fall admission, Dec 1 for spring admission, Apr 30 for summer admission. PhD (highly competitive): 3.5 graduate GPA, GREs required. Copy of two extended pieces of writing (or publications); statement of future professional goals; statement of why Lehigh best place to meet those goals; identification of which presentations, publications, or research by Lehigh faculty attracted applicant to Lehigh. Application deadline: February 1 (admission only once per year from competitive pool)

Degree Requirements – MS: 30 credits; thesis option. PhD: 72 credits past bachelors or 48 credits past masters (including dissertation). Qualifying Research Project (publication quality) + Comprehensive Exams (written and oral) + dissertation.

Number of Full-Time Faculty – 2; **Number of Other Faculty** – 7

Degrees awarded in 2007–2008 Academic Year – **Masters** – 10; **PhD** – 1; **Other** – 2

Grant Monies awarded in 2007–2008 Academic Year – 500000

Name of Institution – Pennsylvania State University
Name of Department or Program – Instructional Systems

Address:
314 Keller Bldg.
University Park, PA
16802
USA

Phone Number – (814)865-0473
Fax Number – (814)865-0128

Email Contact – nxc1@psu.edu
URL – http://www.ed.psu.edu/insys/

Contact Person – Priya Sharma, Associate Professor of Education, Professor in Charge of Instructional Systems

Specializations – M.Ed., MS, D.Ed, and PhD in Instructional Systems. Current teaching emphases are on Learning Technology Design, Educational Systems Design, Learning Sciences, and Corporate Training. Research interests include multimedia, visual learning, educational reform, emerging technologies, constructivist learning, open-ended learning environments, scaffolding, technology integration in classrooms, technology in higher education, change and diffusion of innovations.

Features – A common thread throughout all programs is that candidates have basic competencies in the understanding of human learning; instructional design, development, and evaluation; and research procedures. Practical experience is available in mediated independent learning, research, instructional development, computer-based education, and dissemination projects. Exceptional opportunities for collaboration with faculty (30%+ of publications and presentations are collaborative between faculty and students).

Admission Requirements – D.Ed., PhD: GRE (including written GRE), TOEFL, transcript, three letters of recommendation, writing sample, vita or resume, and letter of application detailing rationale for interest in the degree, match with interests of faculty.

Degree Requirements – MEd: 33 semester hours; MS: 36 h, including either a thesis or project paper; doctoral: candidacy exam, courses, residency, comprehensives, dissertation

Number of Full-Time Faculty – 7; **Number of Other Faculty** – 5

Degrees awarded in 2007–2008 Academic Year – Masters – 28; **PhD** – 10; **Other** – 0

Grant Monies awarded in 2007–2008 Academic Year – 373028

Name of Institution – The University of Rhode Island
Name of Department or Program – Graduate School of Library and Information Studies

Address:
Rodman Hall, 94 W. Alumni Ave.
Kingston, RI
02881-0815
USA

Phone Number – (401)874-2947 **Fax Number** – (401)874-4964

Email Contact – geaton@mail.uri.edu **URL** – http://www.uri.edu/artsci/lsc

Contact Person – E. Gale Eaton, Director

Specializations – M.L.I.S. degree with specialties in School Library Media Services, Information Literacy Instruction, Youth Services Librarianship, Public Librarianship, Academic Librarianship, and Special Library Services.
Features – Fifteen-credit Post-Baccalaureate Certificate in Information Literacy Instruction

Admission Requirements – undergraduate GPA of 3.0, score in 50th percentile or higher on SAT or MAT, statement of purpose, current resume, letters of reference

Degree Requirements – 42 semester-credit program offered in Rhode Island and regionally in Worcester, MA and Durham, NH

Number of Full-Time Faculty – 7; **Number of Other Faculty** – 36

Degrees awarded in 2007–2008 Academic Year – **Masters** – 68; **PhD** – 0; **Other** – 0

Grant Monies awarded in 2007–2008 Academic Year – 0

Name of Institution – University of South Carolina Aiken and University of South Carolina Columbia
Name of Department or Program – Aiken: School of Education; Columbia: Department of Educational Psychology

Address:
471 University Parkway
Aiken, SC
29801
USA

Phone Number – 803.641.3489 **Fax Number** – 803.641.3720

Email Contact – smyth@usca.edu **URL** – http://edtech.usca.edu

Contact Person – Dr. Thomas Smyth, Professor, Program Director

Specializations – Master of Education in Educational Technology (A Joint Program of The University of South Carolina Aiken and Columbia)

Features – The Masters Degree in Educational Technology is designed to provide advanced professional studies in graduate-level coursework to develop capabilities essential to the effective design, evaluation, and delivery of technology-based instruction and training (e.g., software development, multimedia development, assistive technology modifications, web-based development, and distance learning). The program is intended (1) to prepare educators to assume leadership roles in the integration of educational technology into the school curriculum, and (2) to provide graduate-level instructional opportunities for several populations (e.g., classroom teachers, corporate trainers, educational software developers) that need to acquire both technological competencies and understanding of sound instructional design principles and techniques. The program is offered entirely online as high-quality, interactive, web-based courses. There are occasional optional meetings on the Columbia or Aiken campuses.

Admission Requirements – Application to the Educational Technology Program can be made after completion of at least the bachelor's degree from a college or university accredited by a regional accrediting agency. The standard for admission will be based on a total profile for the applicant. The successful applicant should have an undergraduate grade point average of at least 3.0, a score of 45 on the Miller's Analogies Test or scores of 450 on both the verbal and quantitative portions of the Graduate Record Exam, a well-written letter of intent that matches the objectives of the program and includes a description of previous technology experience, and positive letters of recommendation from individuals who know the professional characteristics of the applicant. Any exceptions for students failing to meet these standards shall be referred to the Admissions Committee for review and final decision.

Degree Requirements – 36 semester hours, including instructional theory, computer design, and integrated media

Number of Full-Time Faculty – 3; **Number of Other Faculty** – 3

Degrees awarded in 2007–2008 Academic Year – Masters – 8; **PhD** – 0; **Other** – 0

Grant Monies awarded in 2007–2008 Academic Year – 0

Name of Institution – Dakota State University
Name of Department or Program – Educational Technology

Address:
820 North Washington Ave.
Madison, SD
57042
USA

Phone Number – 1-888-DSU-9988 **Fax Number** – (605) 256-5093

Email Contact – mark.hawkes@dsu.edu
URL – http://www.dsu.edu/mset/index.aspx

Contact Person – Mark Hawkes

Specializations – The MSET program offers two specializations: Distance Education and Technology Systems. These specializations are indicated on the official transcript. You can also get a K-12 Educational Technology Endorsement. Students who wish to choose one of these specializations or the technology endorsement must take designated electives as follows: K-12 Educational Technology Endorsement Individuals who hold or are eligible for teaching certification may earn the K-12 Educational Technology Endorsement by completing specified courses within the MSET program. These courses include:

Features – The Master of Science in Educational Technology (MSET) is an instructional technology program designed to meet the rapidly increasing demand for educators who are trained to integrate computer technologies into the curriculum and instruction. As computers and technology have become a significant part of the teaching and learning process, addressing the information needs of teachers has become the key to integrating technology into the classroom and increasing student learning. The primary emphasis of the masters program is to prepare educators who can create learning environments that integrate computers into the teaching and learning process. The MSET degree is an advanced degree designed to equip educators to be: leaders in educational technology current in teaching and learning processes and practices current in research technologies and designs knowledgeable of technologies and programming skills knowledgeable of current, technology-based educational tools and products. Specifically by the end of the program MSET students will understand the capabilities of the computer and its impact upon education. They will be proficient in a programming language and in the use and application of computer software and will be able to demonstrate proficiency in using computers and related technologies to improve their own and their students learning needs. The program integrates a highly technological environment with a project-based curriculum. Its focus is supported by an institutionally systemic belief that there is a substantial role for technology in teaching and learning in all educational environments.

Admission Requirements – Baccalaureate degree from an institution of higher education with full regional accreditation for that degree. Satisfactory scores on the GRE. The test must have been taken within the past 5 years. The test can be waived if one of the following conditions is met: A cumulative grade point average of 3.25 or higher on a 4.0 scale for a baccalaureate degree from a regionally accredited college or university in the US Official admission into and demonstrated success in a regionally accredited graduate program in the US Demonstrated success is defined as grades of A or B in at least 12 h of graduate work. OR Graduation from a regionally accredited college/university in the US at least 15 years ago or more. Other factors (such as student maturity, references, or special expertise) also may be used to determine admission to the program. Also see program specific admission requirements for additional requirements. Minimum undergraduate grade point average of 2.70 on a 4.0 scale (or equivalent on an alternative grading system). Demonstrated basic knowledge of computers and their applications for educational purposes. Basic knowledge can be demonstrated in one of the following ways: Technology endorsement from an accredited university; or In-service position as full or part-time technology coordinator in a public school. A personal statement of technological competency. The statement should not exceed 2 pages and should be accompanied by supporting documentation or electronic references, e.g., URL.

Degree Requirements – The program requires a total of 36 credits beyond the baccalaureate degree. All students must take the following: 15 h of required common courses (shared between DSU and USD); 10 h of required DSU courses; and 11 h of electives. It is possible to specialize in either Distance Education or Technology Systems by selecting the designated electives for that specialization. You can also get a K-12 Educational Technology Endorsement. It is also possible to select the thesis option from among the electives. MSET courses are offered using a variety of delivery methods. Certain courses require a limited hands-on campus residency. At this time, one required course and one elective course has a campus requirement. These courses are offered in summer and the residency requirement is limited to one week per course.

Number of Full-Time Faculty – 6; **Number of Other Faculty** – 2

Degrees awarded in 2007–2008 Academic Year – Masters – 36; **PhD** – 0; **Other** – 0

Grant Monies awarded in 2007–2008 Academic Year – 0

Name of Institution – Texas A&M University
Name of Department or Program – Educational Technology Program, Dept. of Educational psychology

Address:
College of Education & Human Development
College Station, TX
77843-4225
USA

Phone Number – (979)845-7276 **Fax Number** – (979)862-1256

Email Contact – zellner@tamu.edu **URL** – http://educ.coe.tamu.edu/~edtc

Contact Person – Ronald D. Zellner, Assoc. Prof., Coordinator Program information/Carol Wagner for admissions materials

Specializations – MEd in Educational Technology; EDCI PhD program with specializations in Educational Technology and in Distance Education; PhD in Educational Psychology Foundations: Learning & Technology. The purpose of the Educational Technology Program is to prepare educators with the competencies required to improve the quality and effectiveness of instructional programs at all levels. A major emphasis is placed on multimedia instructional materials development and techniques for effective distance education and communication. Teacher preparation with a focus on field-based instruction and school to university collaboration is also a major component. The program goal is to prepare graduates with a wide range of skills to work as professionals and leaders in a variety of settings, including education, business, industry, and the military.

Features – Program facilities include laboratories for teaching, resource development, and production. Computer, video, and multimedia development are supported in a number of facilities. The college and university also maintain facilities for distance education materials development and fully equipped classrooms for course delivery to nearby collaborative school districts and sites throughout the state.

Admission Requirements – MEd: Bachelors degree, (range of scores, no specific cut-offs) 400 GRE Verbal, 550 (213 computer version) TOEFL; PhD: 3.0 GPA, 450 GRE Verbal. Composite score from GRE verbal & Quantitative and GPA, letters of recommendation, general background, and student goal statement.

Degree Requirements – MEd: 39 semester credits, oral exam; PhD: coursework varies with student goals -degree is a PhD in Educational Psychology Foundations with specialization in educational technology.

Number of Full-Time Faculty – 0; **Number of Other Faculty** – 0

Degrees awarded in 2007–2008 Academic Year – **Masters** – 0; **PhD** – 0; **Other** – 0

Grant Monies awarded in 2007–2008 Academic Year – 0

Name of Institution – The University of Texas at Austin
Name of Department or Program – Curriculum and Instruction

Address:
406 Sanchez Building
Austin, TX
78712-1294
USA

Phone Number – (512)471-5211 **Fax Number** – (512)471-8460

Email Contact – Mliu@mail.utexas.edu

URL – http://www.edb.utexas.edu/education/departments/ci/programs/it/

Contact Person – Min Liu, Ed.D., Professor and IT Program Area Coordinator/Graduate Advisor

Specializations – The Instructional Technology Program at the University of Texas at Austin is a graduate program and offers degrees at the master and doctoral levels. This comprehensive program prepares professionals for various positions in education and industry. Masters degrees (MA and MEd) in Instructional Technology (IT) provide students with knowledge and skills of cutting-edge new media technologies, learning theories, instructional systems design, human-computer interaction, and evaluation. They prepare students to be practitioners in various educational settings, such as K-12, higher education, and training in business and industry. The doctoral program (PhD) in Instructional Technology is comprehensive and research-oriented, providing knowledge and skills in areas such as instructional systems design, learning and instructional theories, design and development of learning environments using cutting-edge new media technologies. Graduates assume academic, administrative, and other leadership positions such as instructional evaluators, managers of instructional systems, and professors and researchers of instructional design and performance technology.

Features – The program is interdisciplinary in nature, although certain competencies are required of all students. Programs of study and dissertation research are based on individual needs and career goals. Learning resources include state-of-art labs in the Learning Technology Center in the College of Education, and university-wide computer labs. Students can take courses offered by other departments and colleges as relevant to their interests. Students, applying to the program, have diverse backgrounds and pursue careers of their interests. The program caters students with both K-12 as well as corporate backgrounds.

Admission Requirements – Instructional Technology program considers only applications for Fall admission, with the deadline of December 15. November 15 – Deadline for consideration of financial award Admission decisions are rendered based on consideration of the entire applicant file, including GPA, test scores, references, experience, and stated goals. No single component carries any more significance than another. However, priority may be given to applicants who meet the following preferred criteria: GPA 3.0 or above GRE 1100 or above (verbal + quantitative, with at least 400 verbal) TOEFL 213 or above (computer)/550 or above (paper-based)/79 or 80 (Internet-based) TOEFL

Degree Requirements – see http://www.edb.utexas.edu/education/departments/ci/programs/it/studentinfo/cstudents/grad/degrees/ for details

Number of Full-Time Faculty – 4; **Number of Other Faculty** – 40

Degrees awarded in 2007–2008 Academic Year – Masters – 4; PhD – 4; **Other** – 0

Grant Monies awarded in 2007–2008 Academic Year – 0

Name of Institution – East Tennessee State University
Name of Department or Program – College of Education, Dept. of Curriculum and Instruction

Address:
Box 70684
Johnson City, TN
37614-0684
USA

Phone Number – (423)439-7843 **Fax Number** – (423)439-8362

Email Contact – danielsh@etsu.edu **URL** – http://www.etsu.edu/coe/cuai/emet-ma.asp
Contact Person – Harold Lee Daniels

Specializations – (1) MEd in School Library Media (2) MEd in Educational Technology (3) School Library media specialist add on for those with current teaching license and a masters degree. (4) MEd in Classroom Technology for those with teaching license.

Features – Two(MAC &PC)dedicated computer labs (45+ computers) Online and evening course offerings for part-time, commuter, and employed students. Student pricing/campus licensing on popular software (MS, Adobe, Macromedia, etc.) Off site cohort programs for classroom teachers Extensive software library (900 + titles) with review/checkout privileges

Admission Requirements – Bachelor's degree from accredited institution, transcripts, personal essay; in some cases, GRE and/or interview

Degree Requirements – 36 semester hours, including 12 h in common core of instructional technology and media, 18 professional content hours and 5 credit hour practicum (200 field experience hours)

Number of Full-Time Faculty – 4; **Number of Other Faculty** – 4

Degrees awarded in 2007–2008 Academic Year – Masters – 18; PhD – 0; Other – 2

Grant Monies awarded in 2007–2008 Academic Year – 32000

Name of Institution – University of Tennessee-Knoxville
Name of Department or Program – Instructional Technology and Educational Studies, College of Education

Address:
A535 Claxton Addition
Knoxville, TN

37996-3456
USA

Phone Number – 865-974-5037 **Fax Number** -.

Email Contact – ecounts1@utk.edu **URL** – http://ites.tennessee.edu/

Contact Person – Jay Pfaffman

Specializations – MS EdS and PhD in Ed. Concentrations in Curriculum/Evaluation/Research and Instructional Technology; MS and PhD in Ed. Concentration in Cultural Studies in Education

Features – coursework in media production and management, advanced software production, utilization, research, theory, instructional computing, and instructional development.
Admission Requirements – See Graduate Catalog for current program requirements.

Degree Requirements – See Graduate Catalog for current program requirements.
Number of Full-Time Faculty – 0; **Number of Other Faculty** – 0

Degrees awarded in 2007–2008 Academic Year – **Masters** – 0; **PhD** – 0; **Other** – 0

Grant Monies awarded in 2007–2008 Academic Year – 0

Name of Institution – Texas Tech University
Name of Department or Program – Instructional Technology

Address:
Box 41071, TTU
Lubbock, TX
79409
USA

Phone Number – (806)742-1998, ext. 433
Fax Number – (806)742-2179

Email Contact – Steven.Crooks@ttu.edu **URL** – http://www.educ.ttu.edu/edit

Contact Person – Dr. Steven Crooks, Program Coordinator, Instructional Technology

Specializations – MEd in Instructional Technology; completely online MEd in Instructional Technology; EdD in Instructional Technology

Features – Program is NCATE accredited and follows ISTE and AECT guidelines.

Admission Requirements – Holistic evaluation based on GRE scores (Doctorate only), GPA, student goals and writing samples

Degree Requirements – MEd: 39 h (30 h in educational technology, 6 h in education, 3 h electives). EdD: 93 h (60 h in educational technology, 21 h in education or resource area, 12 h dissertation.

Number of Full-Time Faculty – 4; **Number of Other Faculty** – 2

Degrees awarded in 2007–2008 Academic Year – **Masters** – 11; **PhD** – 10; **Other** – 0

Grant Monies awarded in 2007–2008 Academic Year – 6000000

Name of Institution – University of Houston
Name of Department or Program – Curriculum & Instruction

Address:
256 Farish
Houston, TX
77204-5027
USA

Phone Number – 713-743-4975 **Fax Number** – 713-743-4990

Email Contact – brobin@uh.edu **URL** – http://www.it.coe.uh.edu/

Contact Person – Bernard Robin

Specializations – Instructional design Urban community partnerships enhanced by technology Integration of technology in teacher education Visual representation of information Linking instructional technology with content area instruction Educational uses of digital media (including digital photography, digital video and digital storytelling) Collaborative Design of Multimedia Uses of instructional technology in health science education

Features – The IT Program at the University of Houston can be distinguished from other IT programs at other institutions through our unique philosophy based on a strong commitment to the broad representations of community, the individual, and the collaboration that strengthens the two. We broadly perceive community to include our college, the university, and the local Houston environment. The community is a rich context and resource from which we can solicit authentic learning tasks and clients, and to which we can contribute new perspectives and meaningful products. Our students graduate with real-world experience that can only be gained by experience with extended and coordinated community-based projects, not by contrived course requirements. Our program actively seeks outside funding to promote and continue such authentic projects because we so strongly believe it is the best context in which our students can develop expertise in the field. We recognize that each student brings to our program a range of formal training, career experience, and future goals. Thus, no longer can we be satisfied with presenting a single, static curriculum and still effectively prepare students for a competitive marketplace. Our beliefs have led us to develop a program that recognizes and celebrates student individuality and diversity. Students work with advisors to develop a degree plan that begins from their existing knowledge and strives toward intended career goals. We aim to teach not specific software or hardware operations, but instead focus on transferable technical skills couched in solid problem-solving experiences, theoretical discussions, and a team-oriented atmosphere. Students work throughout the program to critically evaluate their own work for the purpose of compiling a performance portfolio that will accurately and comprehensively portray their individual abilities to themselves, faculty, and future employers. Completing our philosophical foundation is a continuous goal of collaboration. Our faculty operates from a broad collaborative understanding that recognizes how everyone involved in any process brings unique and valuable experiences and perspectives. Within the IT program, faculty, staff, and students rely on each other to contribute relevant expertise. Faculty members regularly seek collaboration with other faculty in the College of Education, especially those involved with teacher education, as well as with faculty in other schools across campus. Collaboration is a focus that has been infused through the design of our courses and our relationships with students.

Admission Requirements – Admission information for graduate programs: http://www.it.coe.uh.edu/ Masters program: 3.0 grade point average (GPA) for unconditional admission or a 2.6 GPA or above for conditional admission over the last 60 h of coursework attempted Graduate Record Exam: The GRE must have been taken within 5 years of the date of application for admission to any Graduate program in the College of Education. Doctoral program: Each applicant must normally have earned a masters degree or have completed 36 semester hours of appropriate graduate work with a minimum GPA of 3.0 (A = 4.0). Graduate Record Exam: The GRE must have been taken within 5 years of the date of application for admission to any Graduate program in the College of Education.

Degree Requirements – Masters: Students with backgrounds in educational technology can complete the Masters program with 36 h of coursework. For the typical student, the MEd in Instructional Technology consists of 9 semester hours of core courses required by the College of Education, and an additional 18 hour core in Instructional Technology as well as 9 h that are determined by the students career goals (K-12, higher education, business and industry). Students take a written comprehensive examination over the program, coursework, and experiences. Doctoral: The minimum hours required in the doctoral program is 66. More details about the courses and requirements can be found online at: http://coe.uh.edu/IT/doctorate.cfm

Number of Full-Time Faculty – 6; **Number of Other Faculty** – 0

Degrees awarded in 2007–2008 Academic Year – Masters – 15; **PhD** – 10; **Other** – 0

Grant Monies awarded in 2007–2008 Academic Year – 2000000

Name of Institution – University of North Texas
Name of Department or Program – Technology & Cognition (College of Education)

Address:
Box 311337
Denton, TX
76203-1337
USA

Phone Number – (940)565-2057 **Fax Number** – (940)565-2185

Email Contact – iyoung@unt.edu **URL** – http://www.cecs.unt.edu
Contact Person – Dr. Mark Mortensen & Mrs. Donna Walton, Computer Education and Cognitive Systems. Dr. Jon Young, Chair, Department of Technology and Cognition.

Specializations – MS in Computer Education and Cognitive Systems – two emphasis areas: Instructional Systems Technology & Teaching & Learning with Technology. PhD in Educational Computing. See www.cecs.unt.edu.

Features – Unique applications of theory through research and practice in curriculum integration of technology, digital media production, and web development. See www.cecs.unt.edu.

Admission Requirements – Toulouse Graduate School Requirements, 18 h in education, acceptable GRE: 405 V,489 A, 3 Analytical Writing for MS degree. Increased requirements for PhD program.

Degree Requirements – 36 semester hours (12 hour core, 12 hour program course requirement based on MS track, 12 hour electives. see www.cecs.unt.edu.

Number of Full-Time Faculty – 0; **Number of Other Faculty** – 0

Degrees awarded in 2007–2008 Academic Year – Masters – 0; **PhD** – 0; **Other** – 0

Grant Monies awarded in 2007–2008 Academic Year – 0

Name of Institution – Brigham Young University
Name of Department or Program – Department of Instructional Psychology and Technology

Address:
150 MCKB, BYU
Provo, UT
84602
USA

Phone Number – (801)422-5097 **Fax Number** – (801)422-0314

Email Contact – andy-gibbons@byu.edu **URL** – http://www.byu.edu/ipt

Contact Person – Russell Osguthorpe, Prof., Chair.

Specializations – MS degrees in Instructional Design, Research and Evaluation, and Multimedia Production. PhD degrees in Instructional Design, and Research and Evaluation

Features – Course offerings include principles of learning, instructional design, assessing learning outcomes, evaluation in education, empirical inquiry in education, project management, quantitative reasoning, microcomputer materials production, multimedia production, naturalistic inquiry, and more. Students participate in internships and projects related to development, evaluation, measurement, and research.

Admission Requirements – both degrees: transcript, 3 letters of recommendation, letter of intent, GRE scores. Apply by Feb 1. Students agree to live by the BYU Honor Code as a condition for admission

Degree Requirements – Master's: 38 semester hours, including prerequisite (3 h), core courses (14 h), specialization (12 h), internship (3 h), thesis or project (6 h) with oral defense. PhD: 94 semester hours beyond the Bachelor's degree, including: prerequisite and skill requirements (21 h), core course (16 h), specialization (18 h), internship (12 h), projects (9 h), and dissertation (18 h). The dissertation must be orally defended. Also, at least two consecutive 6-hour semesters must be completed in residence.

Number of Full-Time Faculty – 0; **Number of Other Faculty** – 0

Degrees awarded in 2007–2008 Academic Year – Masters – 18; **PhD** – 0; **Other** – 0

Grant Monies awarded in 2007–2008 Academic Year – 0

Name of Institution – Utah State University
Name of Department or Program – Department of Instructional Technology & Learning Sciences, Emma Eccles Jones College of Education and Human Services

Address:
2830 Old Main Hill

Logan, UT
84322-2830
USA

Phone Number – (435)797-2694 **Fax Number** – (435)797-2693

Email Contact – mimi.recker@usu.edu **URL** – http://itls.usu.edu

Contact Person – Dr. Mimi Recker, Prof., Chair.

Specializations – MS and MEd with concentrations in the areas of Instructional Technology, Learning Sciences, Multimedia, Educational Technology, and Information Technology/School Library Media Administration. PhD in Instructional Technology & Learning Sciences is offered for individuals seeking to become professionally involved in instructional/learning sciences research and development in higher education, corporate education, public schools, community colleges, and government.

Features – MEd programs in Instructional Technology/School Library Media Administration and Educational Technology are also available completely online. The doctoral program is built on a strong Master's and Specialists program in Instructional Technology. All doctoral students complete a core with the remainder of the course selection individualized, based upon career goals.

Admission Requirements – MS and Ed.S.: 3.0 GPA, a verbal and quantitative score at the 40th percentile on the GRE or 43 MAT, three written recommendations. PhD: relevant Master's degree, 3.0 GPA, verbal and quantitative score at the 40th percentile on the GRE, three written recommendations, essay on research interests.

Degree Requirements – MS: 39 sem. hours; thesis or project option. Ed.S.: 30 sem. hours if MS is in the field, 40 h if not. PhD: 60 total hours, dissertation, 3-sem. residency, and comprehensive examination.

Number of Full-Time Faculty – 10; **Number of Other Faculty** – 1

Degrees awarded in 2007–2008 Academic Year – Masters – 48; **PhD** – 9; **Other** – 0

Grant Monies awarded in 2007–2008 Academic Year – 500000

Name of Institution – George Mason University
Name of Department or Program – Instructional Technology Programs

Address:
Mail Stop 5D6, 4400 University Dr.
Fairfax, VA
22030-4444
USA

Phone Number – (703)993-3798 **Fax Number** – (703)993-2722

Email Contact – kclark6@gmu.edu **URL** – http://it.gse.gmu.edu/

Contact Person – Dr. Kevin Clark, Coordinator of Instructional Technology Academic Programs

Specializations – Phd specializations in Instructional Design & Development Integration of Technology in Schools Assistive Technology Masters Degrees Curriculum and Instruction with emphasis in Instructional Technology Track I – Instructional Design & Development Track II – Integration of Technology in Schools Track III- Assistive Technology Graduate Certificates eLearning Integration of Technology in Schools Assistive Technology

Features – The Instructional Technology program promotes the theory-based design of learning opportunities that maximize the teaching and learning process using a range of technology applications. Program efforts span a range of audiences, meeting the needs of diverse learners – school-aged, adult learners, and learners with disabilities – in public and private settings. Within this framework, the program emphasizes research, reflection, collaboration, leadership, and implementation and delivery models. The Instructional Technology (IT) program provides professionals with the specialized knowledge and skills needed to apply today's computer and telecommunications technologies to educational goals within school, community and corporate settings. The IT program serves professional educators as well as those involved in instructional design, development and training in government and private sectors. Master degrees and certificates can be earned in each of three program tracks. Refer to the IT website (http://it.gse.gmu.edu/) for detailed information on admissions, · Track 1 – Instructional Design and Development (IDD) – Students are prepared to craft effective solutions within public, private and educational contexts to instructional challenges by using the latest information technologies in the design and development of instructional materials. · Track II – Integration of Technology in Schools (ITS) – Students are prepared to effectively integrate technology in the K-12 learning environment. Graduates frequently become the local expert and change agent for technology in schools. · Track III – Assistive/Special Education Technology (A/SET) – Graduates will use technology to assist individuals to function more effectively in school, home, work and community environments. Graduates are prepared to incorporate technology into the roles of educators, related service providers, Assistive Technology consultants, hardware/software designers and school based technology coordinators.

Admission Requirements – Teaching or training experience, undergrad GPA of 3.0,TOEFL of 575(written)/230(computer), three letters of recommendation, goal statement.

Degree Requirements – MEd in Curriculum and Instruction: 30 h; practicum, internship, or project. MEd in Special Education: 30 h. PhD: 56–62 h beyond Master's degree for either specialization. Certificate programs: 12–15 h

Number of Full-Time Faculty – 7; **Number of Other Faculty** – 5

Degrees awarded in 2007–2008 Academic Year – **Masters** – 130; **PhD** – 15; **Other** – 0

Grant Monies awarded in 2007–2008 Academic Year – 2500000

Name of Institution – Virginia Tech
Name of Department or Program – College of Liberal Arts and Human Sciences

Address:
112 War Memorial Hall
Blacksburg, VA
24061-0341
USA

Phone Number – (540)231-5587
Fax Number – (540)231-9075

Email Contact – jburton@vt.edu
URL – http://www.soe.vt.edu/idt/

Contact Person – John Burton, Program Area Leader, Instructional Design & Technology, Department of Learning Sciences & Technologies

Specializations – MA, EdS, EdD, and PhD in Instructional Design and Technology. Graduates of our Masters and Educational Specialist programs find themselves applying their expertise in a variety of rewarding, professional venues; for example, as instructional designers, trainers, or performance consultants in industrial settings and as teachers or technology coordinators in preK-12. Graduates of our Doctoral program typically assume exciting roles as faculty in higher education, advancing research in the field and preparing the next generation of instructional technologists for the profession.

Features – Areas of emphasis are Instructional Design, Distance Education, and Multimedia Development. Facilities include two computer labs, extensive digital video and audio equipment, distance education classroom, and computer graphics production areas.

Admission Requirements – Ed.D. and PhD: 3.3 GPA from Masters degree, GRE scores, writing sample, three letters of recommendation, transcripts. MA.: 3.0 GPA Undergraduate.

Degree Requirements – PhD: 96 h above B.S., 2-year residency, 12 h research classes, 30 h dissertation; Ed.D.: 90 h above B.S., 1-year residency, 12 h research classes; MA.: 30 h above B.S.

Number of Full-Time Faculty – 6; **Number of Other Faculty** – 2

Degrees awarded in 2007–2008 Academic Year – Masters – 15; **PhD** – 6; **Other** – 2

Grant Monies awarded in 2007–2008 Academic Year – 1

Name of Institution – University of Virginia
Name of Department or Program – Department of Leadership, Foundations, and Policy, Curry School of Education

Address:
Ruffner Hall
Charlottesville, VA
22903
USA

Phone Number – (434)924-7471 **Fax Number** – (434)924-0747

Email Contact – jbb2 s@virginia.edu
URL – http://curry.edschool.virginia.edu/curry/dept/edlf/instrtech/

Contact Person – John B. Bunch, Assoc. Prof., Coordinator, Instructional Technology Program, Department of Leadership, Foundations and Policy Studies.

Specializations – MEd, EdS, EdD, and PhD degrees with focal areas in Media Production, Interactive Multimedia, e-Learning/Distance learning and K-12 Educational Technologies

Features – The IT program is situated in a major research university with linkages to multiple disciplines. Graduate Students have the opportunity to work with faculty across the Curry School and the University.

Admission Requirements – undergraduate degree from accredited institution in any field, undergraduate GPA 3.0,1000 GRE (V+Q), 600 TOEFL. Financial aid application deadline is March 1st of each year for the fall semester for both Master's and doctoral degrees; admission is rolling.

Degree Requirements – MEd: 36 semester hours, comprehensive examination. Ed.S.: 60 semester hours beyond undergraduate degree. Ed.D.: 54 semester hours, dissertation, at least one conference presentation or juried publication, comprehensive examination, residency; PhD: same as Ed.S. with the addition of 18 semester hours. For specific degree requirements, see Web site, write to the address above, or refer to the UVA

Number of Full-Time Faculty – 0; **Number of Other Faculty** – 0

Degrees awarded in 2007–2008 Academic Year – Masters – 0; **PhD** – 0; **Other** – 0

Grant Monies awarded in 2007–2008 Academic Year – 0

Name of Institution – University of Washington
Name of Department or Program – College of Education

Address:
115 Miller Hall, Box 353600
Seattle, WA
98195-3600
USA

Phone Number – (206)543-1847 **Fax Number** – (206)543-1237

Email Contact – billwinn@u.washington.edu
URL – http://www.educ.washington.edu/COE/c-and-i/c_and_i_med_ed_tech.htm

Contact Person – William Winn, Prof. of Education

Specializations – MEd, EdD, and PhD for individuals in business, industry, higher education, public schools, and organizations concerned with education or communication (broadly defined)

Features – Emphasis on design of materials and programs to encourage learning and development in school and non-school settings; research and related activity in such areas as interactive instruction, web-based learning, virtual environments, use of video as a tool for design and development. Close collaboration with program in Cognitive Studies.

Admission Requirements – MEd: goal statement (2–3 pp.), writing sample, 1000 GRE (verbal plus quantitative), undergraduate GPA indicating potential to successfully accomplish graduate work. Doctoral: GRE scores, letters of reference, transcripts, personal statement, Master's degree or equivalent in field appropriate to the specialization with 3.5 GPA, 2 years of successful professional experience and/or experience related to program goals desirable.

Degree Requirements – MEd: 45 qtr. hours (including 24 in technology); thesis or project recommended, exam optional. Ed.D.: see http://www.educ.washington.edu/COEWebSite/programs/ci/EdD.html PhD: http://www.educ.washington.edu/COEWebSite/students/prospective/phdDescrip.html

Number of Full-Time Faculty – None; **Number of Other Faculty** – None

Degrees awarded in 2007–2008 Academic Year – Masters – 5; **PhD** -; **Other** -

Grant Monies awarded in 2007–2008 Academic Year -

Name of Institution – Western Washington University

Address:
MS 9087
Bellingham, WA

98225-9087
USA

Phone Number – 360)650-3387 **Fax Number** – (360)650-6526

Email Contact – Tony.Jongejan@wwu.edu
URL – http://www.wce.wwu.edu/depts/IT

Contact Person – Tony Jongejan

Specializations – MEd with emphasis in Instructional Technology in Adult Education, Special Education, Elementary Education, and Secondary Education

Admission Requirements – 3.0 GPA in last 45 qtr. credit hours, GRE or MAT scores, three letters of recommendation, and, in some cases, 3 years of teaching experience

Degree Requirements – 48–52 qtr. hours (24–28 h in instructional technology; 24 h in education-related courses, thesis required; internship and practicum possible).

Number of Full-Time Faculty – 0; **Number of Other Faculty** – 0

Degrees awarded in 2007–2008 Academic Year – **Masters** – 0; **PhD** – 0; **Other** – 0

Grant Monies awarded in 2007–2008 Academic Year – 0

Name of Institution – University of Alaska Southeast
Name of Department or Program – Educational Technology Program

Address:
11120 Glacier Hwy, HA1
Juneau, AK
99801
USA

Phone Number – 907-796-6050 **Fax Number** – 907-796-6059

Email Contact – marsha.gladhart@uas.alaska.edu
URL – http://uas.alaska.edu/education/experienced

Contact Person – Marsha Gladhart

Specializations – Educational Technology

Features – * distance program * standards-based learning * integration of the most current technologies * collaboration with other teachers * instructors with k-12 teaching experience * focus on improving student learning * use of technology as a tool to assist learning

Admission Requirements – # A completed graduate application and $60 process-ing fee. # Official academic transcript indicating baccalaureate degree and a GPA of 3.0 # Two (2) general recommendations written by former or current profes-sors, employers, or supervisors who are familiar with your work and performance. Each recommendation must be submitted using the Letter of Recommendation for Graduate Programs form. # A recommendation documenting your ability to meet the educational technology standards required for entry to the program. This rec-ommendation should be completed by an administrator, supervisor, or technology leader. # Statement of Professional Objectives. # A copy of a current teaching or administrative certificate.

Degree Requirements – Official academic transcript indicating baccalaureate degree and a GPA of 3.0

Number of Full-Time Faculty – 2; **Number of Other Faculty** – 5

Degrees awarded in 2007–2008 Academic Year – Masters – 11; **PhD** – 0; **Other** – 0

Grant Monies awarded in 2007–2008 Academic Year – 0

Name of Institution – University of South Alabama
Name of Department or Program – Department of Behavioral Studies and Educational Technology, College of Education

Address:
University Commons 3700
Mobile, AL
36688
USA

Phone Number – (251)380-2861 **Fax Number** – (251)380-2713

Email Contact – jdempsey@usouthal.edu
URL – http://www.southalabama.edu/coe/bset/

Contact Person – Daniel W. Surry, IDD Program Coordinator; Mary Ann Robinson, Ed Media Program Coordinator

Specializations – MS and PhD in Instructional Design and Development. MEd in Educational Media (Ed Media). Online master's degrees in ED Media and IDD are available for qualified students. For information about online masters degree programs, http://usaonline.southalabama.edu

Features – The IDD masters and doctoral programs emphasize extensive education and training in the instructional design process, human performance technology and multimedia – and online-based training. The IDD doctoral program has an addi-tional emphasis in research design and statistical analysis. The Ed Media masters program prepares students in planning, designing, and administering library/media centers at most levels of education, including higher education.

Admission Requirements – For the ED Media & IDD Masters: undergraduate degree in appropriate academic field from an accredited university or college; admission to Graduate School; satisfactory score on the GRE. ED Media students must have completed requirements for a certificate at the baccalaureate or masters level in a teaching field. For IDD PhD: Masters degree, all undergraduate & graduate transcripts, 3 letters of recommendations, written statement of purpose for pursuing PhD in IDD, satisfactory score on GRE.

Degree Requirements – Ed Media masters: satisfactorily complete program requirements (minimum 33 semester hours), 3.0 or better GPA, satisfactory score on comprehensive exam. IDD masters: satisfactorily complete program requirements (minimum 40 semester hours), 3.0 or better GPA; satisfactory complete comprehensive exam. PhD: satisfactory complete program requirements (minimum 82 semester hours of approved graduate course), 1-year residency, satisfactory score on examinations (research & statistical exam and comprehensive exam), approved dissertation completed. Any additional requirements will be determined by students doctoral advisory committee.

Number of Full-Time Faculty – 0; **Number of Other Faculty** – 0

Degrees awarded in 2007–2008 Academic Year – **Masters** – 0; **PhD** – 0; **Other** – 0

Grant Monies awarded in 2007–2008 Academic Year – 0

Name of Institution – University of Arkansas
Name of Department or Program – Educational Technology

Address:
255 Graduate Education Building
Fayetteville, AR
72701
USA

Phone Number – 479-575-5111 **Fax Number** – 479-575-2493

Email Contact – cmurphy@uark.edu **URL** – http://etec.uark.edu

Contact Person – Dr. Cheryl Murphy

Specializations – The program prepares students for a variety of work environments by offering core courses that are applicable to a multitude of professional venues. The program also allows for specific emphasis area studies via open-ended assignments and course electives that include courses particularly relevant to business/industry or K-12 environments. The primary focus of the program is on the processes involved in instructional design, training and development, media production, teacher education, and utilization of instructional technologies. Because technology is continually changing, we emphasize acquisition of a process over the creation of a product. Although we teach skills necessary in making Educational Technology products, technology changes rapidly; therefore, a primary emphasis on making technological products would lead to the acquisition of skills that are quickly outdated. However, learning the principles and mental tools critical to producing successful training and education will endure long after "new" technologies have become obsolete. That is why our ETEC program focuses on the processes as opposed to specific technologies.

Features – The Educational Technology Program is a 33-hour non-thesis online masters program that prepares students for professional positions as educational technologists of education, business, government, and the health professions. Because the program is offered online, there are no on-campus requirements for the completion of this degree.

Admission Requirements – The Educational Technology online masters program is an open enrollment program and admits students in the fall, spring, and summer. Applications and all accompanying documents should be submitted within three months of the desired starting semester to ensure adequate processing time. Applicants for the MEd degree must have met all requirements of Graduate School admission, completed a bachelors degree and earned a 3.0 GPA in all undergraduate coursework or obtain an acceptable score on the Graduate Record Examinations or Miller Analogies Test. A Graduate School application, ETEC Program Application, writing sample, autobiographical sketch, and letters of recommendation are required for admission consideration.

Degree Requirements – In addition to general admission requirements, students must complete a minimum of 33 h to include 18 semester hours of educational technology courses; six semester hours of educational technology electives; and nine semester hours from the College of Education and Health Professions common core. Additionally, a Culminating Student Portfolio must be successfully completed during the last 3 h of coursework. There are no on-campus requirements for the completion of this degree, although approved courses that meet the college core requirements may be taken on campus if desired.

Number of Full-Time Faculty – 1; **Number of Other Faculty** – 3

Degrees awarded in 2007–2008 Academic Year – **Masters** – 8; **PhD** – 0; **Other** – 0

Grant Monies awarded in 2007–2008 Academic Year – 0

Name of Institution – University of Arkansas at Little Rock
Name of Department or Program – Learning Systems Technology

Address:
2801 S. University
Little Rock, AR
72204
USA

Phone Number – 501-569-3269
Fax Number – (501) 569-3547

Email Contact – dsspillers@ualr.edu
URL – http://ualr.edu/med/LSTE/

Contact Person – David S. Spillers

Specializations – The Learning Systems Technology master's degree prepares you for the design, production, and application of these new methods, including creating and designing the following learning products: * documents and electronic displays * interactive tutorials for web-based delivery * instructional blogs * useful web pages * complete instructional packages using digital images and film clips * courses using a variety of online course management systems * learning resource centers

Features – This program is offered entirely online.

Admission Requirements – Admission to the LSTE master's program requires: * a baccalaureate degree from a regionally accredited institution with substantially the same undergraduate programs as the University of Arkansas at Little Rock * a 3.0 GPA on the last 60 h (including postbaccalaureate hours or a 2.7 GPA on all undergraduate hours taken for the baccalaureate degree) * successful application to the UALR graduate school * academic evaluation by the LSTE program coordinator After you have completed your online application to the Graduate School, your folder with all of your transcripts will be sent to the program coordinator for evaluation. The program coordinator will then send you a letter with your status in the process. Once you get your letter of acceptance you will be able to start the program in any semester: Fall, Spring, or Summer. If you have any questions, please contact the program coordinator.

Degree Requirements – The 36 graduate credit hours include: * 9 Educational Foundations hours * 18 Learning Technologies hours * up to 3 elective courses (Foundations, English writing, Learning Technologies or other content area approved by the adviser) or a 3 to 6 hour field experience No more than 6 h of workshop credit will be accepted in the program. No more than 6 h earned within the past 3 years of transfer credit will be accepted in the program.

Number of Full-Time Faculty – 1; **Number of Other Faculty** – 5

Degrees awarded in 2007–2008 Academic Year – Masters – 7; PhD – 0; **Other** – 0

Grant Monies awarded in 2007–2008 Academic Year – 0

Name of Institution – California State Polytechnic University
Name of Department or Program – Educational Multimedia

Address:
3801 West Temple Ave
Pomona, CA
91768
USA

Phone Number – 909-869-2255 **Fax Number** – 909-869-5206

Email Contact – slotfipour@csupomona.edu
URL – www.ceis.csupomona.edu/emm

Contact Person – Dr. Shahnaz Lotfipour

Specializations – Production of educational multimedia software (from audio, to video, animation, web programming, graphics, etc) for educational settings and corporate raining environments using the sound instructional principles.

Features – Hands-on training, project-based, online and hybrid courses where appropriate, internship possibilities

Admission Requirements – Undergraduate GPA of 3.0, three strong letters of recommendations, Satisfying graduate writing test

Degree Requirements – BA or BS

Number of Full-Time Faculty – 2; **Number of Other Faculty** – 5

Degrees awarded in 2007–2008 Academic Year – **Masters** – 20; **PhD** – 2; **Other** – 0

Grant Monies awarded in 2007–2008 Academic Year – 0

Name of Institution – California State University Monterey Bay (CSUMB)
Name of Department or Program – Interdisciplinary Master in Instructional Science and Technology (MIST)

Address:
100 Campus Center
Seaside, CA
93955
USA

Phone Number – 831-582-3621 **Fax Number** – 831-582-4484

Email Contact – mist@csumb.edu **URL** – http://itcd.csumb.edu/mist

Contact Person – Eric Tao, PhD

Features – Interdisciplinary collaboration that integrates instructional science and information technology is the hallmark of the IST graduate program and a CSUMB core value. Recognizing that the use of technology is critical to the design, development, and delivery of instruction in the twenty-first century, IST integrates modern learning technology and pedagogy to create educational experiences adequate for the contemporary world. This technology infusion models best practices to learners. Rather than setting aside one course that deals solely with ethics and social responsibility, our curriculum integrates ethical reflection and practice throughout the program. All required courses incorporate the basic concepts and concerns of ethics into their design, development, and delivery. Multiculturalism and globalism are infused into the IST curriculum, including discussion of diversity in the conduct of instructional design and diversity in the understanding of ethics. Applied learning is critical to the IST program, and we use an integrated pedagogy that builds on each semesters outcome.

Admission Requirements – 1. Complete and submit an application form at CSUMENTOR.org and $55.00 application fee payable to CSUMB. A. Select Summer 2009 as the application term. B. On line 10a, insert "INTD" as the objective, "49993" as the program code, and indicate "IDMA/IST" as the emphasis. On line 10b, enter "5" signifying that the degree is a Master of Arts degree. 2. Submit all required supporting documents. All supporting documents should be submitted to: School of Information Technology and Communication Design Attention: IDMA/IST Program, Building 18, Room 150 100 Campus Center Seaside, CA 93955 A. Submit two (2) official copies of each of the following: (1) Transcripts of all college coursework taken * Have two (2) official transcripts from all colleges and universities you have attended mailed directly to the IDMA/IST Program at the address listed above. (We recommend that you request that an additional copy be mailed directly to you at home and that you leave that envelope unopened until you have confirmation that we have received our copies.) * A GPA of 3.0 is expected for the most recent 60 units of college-level work attempted. GPA between 2.5 and 3.0 may be considered with substantial alternative demonstration of ability to succeed in the program. (2) Test scores (TOEFL, GRE, etc.), (if applicable) * We recommend that you take the GRE test to improve your competitive standing but it is not required. CSUMBs school code for ETS is 1945. * For those students required to demonstrate English proficiency: the IDMA/IST program requires a TOEFL score of 575 for admission. Selected applicants with TOEFL scores between 525 and 574 and applicants demonstrating English proficiency with test scores other than TOEFL must pass a writing workshop offered by ITCD before the first day of classes as a condition of admission. Applicants with TOEFL scores below 525 will not be considered. * CSUMB minimum requirements for English proficiency for applicants with degrees from foreign universities are listed on the Admissions & Recruitment website at: http://ar.csumb.edu/site/x5362.xml#requirements (3) Foreign Credential Evaluation (if applicable) * All transcripts from schools outside the United States must be sent, at the applicants expense, to a foreign credential evaluation service. A detailed "course-by-course" report is required for all programs. Three credential evaluation services accepted by CSU Monterey Bay are: 1. World Education Services WES http://www.wes.org/ 2. American Association of Collegiate Registrars and Admissions Offices AACRAO http://www.aacrao.org/credential/ 3. International Education Research Foundation IERF http://www.ierf.org/ * CSUMB minimum requirements for foreign credential evaluation for applicants with degrees from foreign universities are listed on the Admissions & Recruitment website at: http://ar.csumb.edu/site/x5362.xml#requirements B. Submit an original "Statement of Purpose" (one copy is sufficient). * Include a 1,000–2,000 word Statement of Purpose (statement of educational and professional goals) that demonstrates your writing ability. C. Submit two (2) or three (3) letters of reference (one copy of each is sufficient). * Include two or three letters of recommendation from individuals familiar with your professional and academic work. D. Technology Screening Assessment * Upon receipt of your application, we will email you a technology screening assessment that you must complete and submit prior to your document deadline. The results of the technology assessment will be considered in the selection process

Degree Requirements – Outcomes, Courses, and Assessment The Interdisciplinary Master of Arts with Instructional Science and Technology Emphasis (IST) degree requires 24 semester hours of core courses, four semester hours of an elective, and four semester hours for the culminating Capstone experience or thesis. [Learn more at CSUMB.EDU/capstone]. As the title signifies, the core courses are a cluster of instructional design, instructional systems and best educational practices that represent the core of the collaborative program. By guiding you toward the Learning Outcomes (LOs) listed below, these courses provide you with the skills necessary to become an effective instructional designer and e-learning developer in today's high-tech, global marketplace. Given the complexities that emanate from strong and growing global forces and conflicting values, we discuss international and ethical issues in all courses. The IST program consists of four terms that must be taken sequentially covering the following courses and outcomes. Term I Courses: IST 522 Instructional Design IST 524 Instructional Technology Outcomes: LO 1 Learning Theories LO 2 Instructional Design Students generate a detailed instructional design document that applies learning theories appropriate to the target audience. Students are encouraged to incorporate projects from their current employment into the class assignments. Term II Courses: IST 520 Learning Theory IST 526 Interactive Multimedia for Instruction Outcomes: LO 3 Instructional Technology LO 4 Interactive Multimedia Students use the design document generated in the previous term to collaboratively construct a functioning learning module using interactive multimedia software, information technology, and media. Term III Courses: IST 622 Assessment and Evaluation IST 624 Research Methods for Instructional Sciences Outcomes: LO 5 Assessment and Evaluation LO 6 Research Methods Students apply the learning objectives produced in the previous term and develop an assessment and research plan that uses academic research methods to evaluate the efficacy of their learning objectives. Term IV Courses: IST 630 Graduate Capstone in Instructional Sciences and Technology Minimum of four elective upper-division or graduate-level credits, approved by program coordinator and faculty advisor, related to the field of instructional science and technology. For example: CST 336, CST 451, CST 610, CST 655, CST 551, CST 404, CST 424, etc. Outcomes: LO 7 Breadth of Knowledge LO 8 Instructional Sciences and Technology Capstone Project or Thesis Students finish a Capstone project or thesis that connects with their career as the culminating experience.

Number of Full-Time Faculty – 10; **Number of Other Faculty** – 12

Degrees awarded in 2007–2008 Academic Year – Masters – 30; PhD – 0; **Other** – 50

Grant Monies awarded in 2007–2008 Academic Year – 1000000

Name of Institution – California State University, Fresno
Name of Department or Program – Certificate of Advanced Study in Educational Technology

Address:
None
Fresno, CA
93740
USA

Phone Number – 559-278-7395 **Fax Number** – 559-278-7395

Email Contact – royb@csufresno.edu
URL – http://education.csufresno.edu/departments/ci/ci_aset.htm

Contact Person – Roy M. Bohlin

Specializations – None

Features – None

Admission Requirements – None

Degree Requirements – Bachelors degree

Number of Full-Time Faculty – 3; **Number of Other Faculty** – 2

Degrees awarded in 2007–2008 Academic Year – Masters – 0; PhD – 0; **Other** – 0

Grant Monies awarded in 2007–2008 Academic Year – 0

Name of Institution – Regis University
Name of Department or Program – School of Education and Counseling

Address:
3333 Regis Boulevard
Denver, CO
80221
USA

Phone Number – 800-388-2366 **Fax Number** – 303-964-5053

Email Contact – chruskoc@regis.edu **URL** – www.regis.edu

Contact Person – Dr. Carole Hruskocy

Specializations – Instructional Technology Curriculum, Instruction, and Assessment Professional Leadership Adult Learning, Training, and Development Self-Designed Reading Space Studies

Features – The majority of our programs are offered in the online format.

Admission Requirements – Essay Letters of Recommendation Minimum GPA of 2.75

Number of Full-Time Faculty – 15; **Number of Other Faculty** – 150

Degrees awarded in 2007–2008 Academic Year – **Masters** – 200; **PhD** – 0; **Other** – 0

Grant Monies awarded in 2007–2008 Academic Year – 0

Name of Institution – University of Bridgeport
Name of Department or Program – Instructional Technology

Address:
126 Park Avenue
Bridgeport, CT
06604
USA

Phone Number – 2035764217 **Fax Number** – 2035764633

Email Contact – jcole@bridgeport.edu **URL** – http://www.bridgeport.edu/imsit
Contact Person – Jerald D. Cole

Specializations – Masters and Professional Diploma (sixth year) Instructional Technology Tracks: 1. Teacher 2. Trainer 3. Developer 4. Technology Education 5. Technology Leadership

Features – 1. Open Source Curriculum and Software Model. 2. Cross Platform Mobil Tablet Computing Initiative. 3. Social Constructionist Pedagogy. 4. Hybrid and online courses. 5. Cohort-based. 6. Tuition-free internships for Teacher track.

Admission Requirements – Online Application Essay on experience and objectives for study Two letters of reference Praxis 1 for teacher track TOEFL for non-native English speakers Transcripts Phone interview

Degree Requirements – 4 core courses, 2 distribution requirements, 1 research, 1 practicum, 4 electives

Number of Full-Time Faculty – 11; **Number of Other Faculty** – 14

Degrees awarded in 2007–2008 Academic Year – **Masters** – 294; **PhD** – 6; **Other** – 117

Grant Monies awarded in 2007–2008 Academic Year – 2000000

Name of Institution – University of Florida
Name of Department or Program – School of Teaching and Learning

Address:
2403 Norman Hall
Gainesville, FL
32611-7048
USA

Phone Number – 352-392-9191 X261 **Fax Number** – 352-392-9193

Email Contact – kdawson@coe.ufl.edu
URL – http://www.coe.ufl.edu/school/edtech/index.htm (Hybrid programs); http://www.coe.ufl.edu/online/edtech/index.html (Online programs)

Contact Person – Kara Dawson

Specializations – Hybrid Program: Educational technology students may earn MEd, Ed.S., Ed.D. or PhD degrees and have an opportunity to specialize in one of two tracks: (1) Teaching and teacher education or (2) Design and Production of educational materials. many students merge these tracks. Teacher education students and students in other degree programs may also elect to specialize in Educational Technology. Online Programs: We offer a online Masters, Ed.S. and Ed.D. degrees in "Teaching, learning & facilitating change with educational technology" http://www.coe.ufl.edu/online/edtech/index.html
Features – Students take core courses listed on our Educational Technology website and then select an area of specialization. Opportunities to collaborative research, write and design with faculty members. Strong community of graduate students.

Admission Requirements – Please see the Educational Technology website for the most up-to-date information.

Degree Requirements – Please see the Educational Technology website for the most up-to-date information. Program and college requirements must be met but there is considerable flexibility for doctoral students to plan an appropriate program with their advisors.

Number of Full-Time Faculty – 5; **Number of Other Faculty** – 3

Degrees awarded in 2007–2008 Academic Year – Masters – 20; **PhD** – 5; **Other** – 15

Grant Monies awarded in 2007–2008 Academic Year – 1000000

Name of Institution – University of West Florida
Name of Department or Program – Instructional and Performance Technology

Address:
11000 University Parkway
Pensacola, FL
32514
USA

Phone Number – 850-474-2300
Fax Number – 850-474-2804

Email Contact – krasmuss@uwf.edu
URL – http://uwf.edu/ect/graduate.cfm#IPT

Contact Person – Karen Rasmussen

Specializations – MEd, Instructional Technology: Curriculum and Technology Telecommunications and Distance Learning Technology Leadership Human Performance Technology M.S.A., H.P.T.: Human Performance Technology Ed.S., Instructional Technology Performance Technology Distance Learning Ed.D., Curriculum and Instruction, Instructional Technology Specialization: Performance Technology Distance Learning

Features – Fully online programs Small classes Recognized nationally as a "Best Buy" in Online Degree Programs in Human Performance Technology based on quality and affordability.

Admission Requirements – GRE or MAT Score Official Transcripts Letter of Intent See Department Website for additional information.

Degree Requirements – M.Ed., 36 credit hours M.S.A., 33 credit hours Ed.S., 36 credit hours Ed.D., 66 credit hours
Number of Full-Time Faculty – 3; **Number of Other Faculty** – 1

Degrees awarded in 2007–2008 Academic Year – Masters – 25; **PhD** – 0; **Other** – 22

Grant Monies awarded in 2007–2008 Academic Year – 350700

Name of Institution – Indiana University
Name of Department or Program – School of Education

Address:
W. W. Wright Education Bldg., Rm. 2276, 201 N. Rose Ave.
Bloomington, IN
47405-1006
USA

Phone Number – (812)856-8451
Fax Number – (812)856-8239

Email Contact – istdept@indiana.edu
URL – http://education.indiana.edu/~ist/

Contact Person – Elizabeth Boling, Chair, Department of Instructional Systems Technology

Specializations – MS and Ed.S. degrees designed for individuals seeking to be practitioners in the field of Instructional Technology. MS degree also offered in web-based format with instructional product and portfolio requirements. Offers PhD degree with heavy research emphasis via faculty-mentored research groups and student dossiers for assessing research, teaching and service.

Features – Requires computer skills as a prerequisite and makes technology utilization an integral part of the curriculum; eliminates separation of various media formats; and establishes a series of courses of increasing complexity integrating production and development. The latest in technical capabilities have been incorporated, including teaching, computer, and laptop-ready laboratories, a multimedia laboratory, and video and audio production studios. PhD students participate in faculty-mentored research groups throughout their program. Students construct dossiers with evidence of research, teaching and service that are evaluated by faculty on three occasions during the program.

Admission Requirements – MS: Bachelor's degree from an accredited institution, 1350 GRE (3 tests required)or 900 plus 3.5 analytical writing (new format), 2.75 undergraduate GPA. Ed.S. and PhD: 1650 GRE (3 tests required)or 1100 plus 4.5 analytical writing (new format), 3.5 graduate GPA.

Degree Requirements – MS: 36 credit hours (including 15 credits in required courses); colloquia; an instructional product; and 9 credits in outside electives, and portfolio. Ed.S.: 65 h, capstone project with written report and a portfolio. PhD: 90 h, dossier reviews, and thesis
Number of Full-Time Faculty – 11; **Number of Other Faculty** – 4

Degrees awarded in 2007–2008 Academic Year – **Masters** – 20; **PhD** – 16; **Other** – 0

Grant Monies awarded in 2007–2008 Academic Year – 1450000

Name of Institution – Purdue University

Name of Department or Program – College of Education, Department of Curriculum and Instruction

Address:
100 N. University St.
West Lafayette, IN
47907-2098
USA

Phone Number – (765)494-5669 **Fax Number** – (765)496-1622

Email Contact – edtech@soe.purdue.edu **URL** – http://www.edci.purdue.edu/et/

Contact Person – Dr. Tim Newby, Prof. of Educational Technology.

Specializations – Master's degree and PhD in Educational Technology. Master's program started in 1982; PhD in 1985

Features – Vision Statement The Educational Technology Program at Purdue University nurtures graduates who are effective designers of learning experiences and environments that incorporate technology to engage learners and improve learning.

Admission Requirements – Master's and PhD: 3.0 GPA, three letters of recommendation, statement of personal goals. A score of 550 (paper-based) or 213 (computer-based) or above on the Test of English as a Foreign Language (TOEFL) for individuals whose first language is not English. PhD Additional Requirement: 1000 GRE (V+Q); Verbal score of at least 500 preferred.

Degree Requirements – Masters: minimum of 32 semester hours (17 in educational technology, 6–9 in research, development, and exit requirements, 6–9 electives); thesis optional. PhD: 60 semester hours beyond the Masters degree (15–18 in educational technology, 27–30 in education and supporting areas; 15 dissertation research hours)

Number of Full-Time Faculty – 0; **Number of Other Faculty** – 0

Degrees awarded in 2007–2008 Academic Year – **Masters** – 3; **PhD** – 0; **Other** – 0

Grant Monies awarded in 2007–2008 Academic Year – 0

Name of Institution – Purdue University Calumet

Name of Department or Program – Instructional Technology

Address:
2200 169th Street
Hammond, IN

46323
USA

Phone Number – 219-989-2692
Fax Number – 219-983215

Email Contact – buckenme@calumet.purdue.edu
URL – http://www.calumet.purdue.edu/education/grad/it.html

Contact Person – Janet Buckenmeyer

Specializations – Instructional Technology and Instructional Design

Features – The Instructional Technology program at Purdue University Calumet is a practitioner-based program. Students entering the program may be teachers but do not need a teaching license to enroll. The program does not lead to licensure.

Admission Requirements – 3.0 GPA; Three (3) letters of recommendation; Essay; Two (2) official copies of all transcripts; Interview

Number of Full-Time Faculty – 3; **Number of Other Faculty** – 1

Degrees awarded in 2007–2008 Academic Year – Masters – 10; PhD – 0; **Other** – 0

Grant Monies awarded in 2007–2008 Academic Year – 125000

Name of Institution – Emporia State University
Name of Department or Program – Instructional Design and Technology

Address:
1200 Commercial St. – Campus Box 4037
Emporia, KS
66801
USA

Phone Number – 620-341-5829 **Fax Number** – 620-341-5785

Email Contact – mchildre@emporia.edu **URL** – http://idt.emporia.edu

Contact Person – Dr. Marcus D. Childress, Chair

Specializations – Distance learning, online learning, corporate education, P-12 technology integration

Features – All program courses are available online. Emporia State University's IDT department has the largest graduate instructional technology program in the state and is the only program in Kansas that grants a Master of Science Degree in Instructional Design and Technology. ESUs Instructional Design and Technology program prepares individuals for leadership in the design, development, and integration of technology and online learning into teaching and private sector training. Forms and application materials available at the website, http://idt.emporia.edu

Admission Requirements – Graduate application, official transcripts, GPA of 2.75 or more based on a 4-point scale in the last 60 semester hours of undergraduate study, resume, two current recommendations, writing competency. The program admits on a rolling basis. The departmental admission committee reviews and decides on applications as they are received, until there are no remaining openings.

Degree Requirements – 36 semester hours: 21 cr. core, 6 cr. research, 9 cr. electives.

Number of Full-Time Faculty – 6; **Number of Other Faculty** – 2

Degrees awarded in 2007–2008 Academic Year – Masters – 38; **PhD** – 0; **Other** – 0

Grant Monies awarded in 2007–2008 Academic Year – 0

Name of Institution – Pittsburgh State University
Name of Department or Program – Masters Degree in Educational Technology

Address:
1701 S. Broadway
Pittsburgh, KS
66762
USA

Phone Number – 620 235 4484

Email Contact – jstidham@pittstate.edu **URL** – http://www.pittstate.edu

Contact Person – Dr. Sue Stidham

Specializations – Library Media licensure

Number of Full-Time Faculty – 3; **Number of Other Faculty** – 0

Degrees awarded in 2007–2008 Academic Year – Masters – 0; **PhD** – 0; **Other** – 0

Grant Monies awarded in 2007–2008 Academic Year – 0

Name of Institution – Morehead State University
Name of Department or Program – Educational Technology Program

Address:
Ginger Hall
Morehead, KY
40351
USA

Phone Number – 606-783-2040

Email Contact – c.miller@morehead-st.edu
URL – www.moreheadstate.edu/education

Contact Person – Christopher T. Miller

Specializations – Focus on technology integration and instructional design.

Features – Fully online

Admission Requirements – Standard or Provisional Teaching Certificate, a statement of eligibility for teaching, or documentation stating role of educational support. Those students seeking to develop expertise in the area of educational support will be able to obtain the Master's Degree, but it cannot be used for initial teacher certification. Minimum composite GRE score of 750 on the verbal and quantitative section. Demonstration of basic writing proficiency by scoring at least 2.5 on the analytic writing subtest of the GRE. Minimum 2.75 undergraduate GPA

Degree Requirements – Satisfy general degree requirements. Students are required to apply for the exit exam at least two weeks prior to the exam date and must have advisor permission to take the exam. Additional written and/or oral examinations may be required as part of the comprehensive examination. The student must submit a professional portfolio demonstrating work completed within the program. The student must apply for graduation in the Graduate Office, 701 Ginger Hall. Maintain a 3.0 GPA in all courses taken after completing the Bachelor's degree. Must be unconditionally admitted. If a student has not been unconditionally admitted after completing twelve graduate hours, he/she will not be allowed to register for additional hours.

Number of Full-Time Faculty – 2;
Number of Other Faculty – 0

Degrees awarded in 2007–2008 Academic Year – Masters – 6; PhD – 0; Other – 0

Grant Monies awarded in 2007–2008 Academic Year – 0

Name of Institution – University of Massachusetts, Amherst
Name of Department or Program – Learning, Media and Technology Masters Program/Math Science and Learning Technology Doctoral Program

Address:
813 N. Pleasant St.
Amherst, MA
01003
USA

Phone Number – 413-545-0246 **Fax Number** – 413-545-2879

Email Contact – fsullivan@educ.umass.edu
URL – http://www.umass.edu/education/academics/tecs/ed_tech.shtml

Contact Person – Florence R. Sullivan

Specializations – The Master of Education concentration in Learning, Media and Technology prepares students to understand, critique and improve technology- and media-based learning and teaching. The program is structured such that students construct solid knowledge of theories of learning and instruction, as well as theories of the design and use of educational technologies and media. Just as importantly, we offer a number of courses and research experiences through which students develop facility with applied aspects of technology-centered educational practices (e.g., authoring software systems, utilizing tools such as Director and Flash). By encountering multiple opportunities for the analysis, design and testing of educational technology/media, students develop a principled approach to technology- and media-based instruction and learning. The overall mission of the Mathematics, Science and Learning Technologies doctoral program of study is to use new research findings to improve the learning and teaching of mathematics and science–from pre-school to higher education, in schools and in nonformal settings–by preparing professional mathematics/science educators, scholars, and researchers.

Features – In the masters program, we consider media and technology both as tools in learning and teaching specific disciplines (e.g., mathematics and science) and as objects of study in and of themselves. With regard to the former, and in line with the affiliated faculty's expertise, students explore the educational uses of a variety of technological forms (e.g., robotics systems for learning engineering, physics, programming, and the arts) and computer-based environments (e.g., software systems for learning scientific image processing). As for the latter, students actively engage in designing and using various learning technologies and media, including Web-based environments, computer-mediated communications systems, computer-based virtual worlds, and new media for new literacies. The features of the doctoral program of study are: * provide an interconnected locus of intellectual activity for graduate students and faculty; * increase equity (in gender, ethnicity, and opportunities) in recruitment, admission, and retention of students and faculty and pursue issues of equity in science education; * teach relevant courses, seminars, and independent studies in mathematics and science education; * conduct pertinent research studies in mathematics and science learning, teaching, curriculum development, and assessment; * build a base of scholarship, disseminate new knowledge, and apply it actively in education; * provide apprenticeship opportunities for graduate students; * understand and support effective practice in mathematics and science education; * coordinate outreach efforts with K-12 schools and related projects; * collaborate with faculty in the Department, School, and University as well as in the wider profession throughout the Commonwealth of Massachusetts, nationally, and internationally.

Admission Requirements – For the masters program – GPA of 2.75 or higher, TESOL test score of 80 points or higher, excellent letters of recommendation, clear statement of purpose. For the doctoral program – earned masters degree in math, natural sciences, learning technology or education, GPA of 2.75 or higher, TESOL test score of 80 points or higher, excellent letters of recommendation, clear statement of purpose.

Degree Requirements – Masters degree – 33 credit hours and thesis. Doctoral degree – 36 credit hours beyond the masters degree, 18 dissertation credit hours, successful completion of comprehensive exams, successful completion of doctoral dissertation.

Number of Full-Time Faculty – 7; **Number of Other Faculty** – 1

Degrees awarded in 2007–2008 Academic Year – Masters – 5; PhD – 2; **Other** – 0

Grant Monies awarded in 2007–2008 Academic Year – 1000000

Name of Institution – Oakland University
Name of Department or Program – Master of Training and Development Program

Address:
2200 North Squirrel Road
Rochester, MI
48309-4494
USA

Phone Number – 248 370-4171 **Fax Number** – 248 370-4095

Email Contact – ouhrdmtd@gmail.com **URL** – www2.oakland.edu/sehs/hrd/

Contact Person – Dr. Chaunda L. Scott – Graduate Coordinator

Specializations – The Master of Training and Development Program at Oakland University provides a unique blend of knowledge and skills in all aspects of training and development. Students can choose between two area of emphasis: * Instructional Design and Technology * Organizational Development and Leadership

Features – The Master of Training and Development Program develops practitioners with the knowledge and skills required to enhance individual performance.

Graduates of the program will be able to lead interventions associated with diagnosing performance problems and opportunities. Graduates will also be able to design and implement individual and organizational solutions and evaluate results. All courses are taught by outstanding faculty who have diverse backgrounds and experience in business and academia. The Master of Training and Development Program and be completed in two and one-half years. Graduates of the program will be qualified to work as human resource development professionals including directors of training centers, organizational development consultants, instructional designers and performance technologists.

Admission Requirements – Official transcripts for undergraduate and graduate coursework showing a bachelors degree from a regionally accredited institution and a cumulative GPA of 3.0 or higher. A formal statement, between 100 and 1500 words, highlighting work and life experience – preferably 1 year or longer that have led to desire to pursue the Master of Training and Development Degree. Three letters of recommendations to attest to the quality and scope of the applicant's academic and professional ability and an interview will be required.

Degree Requirements – The completion of 36 credits approved credits with an overall GPA of 3.0 or better and a grade of 2.8 or above in each additional course. The completion of five core courses is also required; HRD 530 Instructional Design, HRD 506 Theoretical Foundations of Training and Development, HRD 507 Needs Assessment, HRD 605 Program Evaluation and HRD 611 Program Administration

Number of Full-Time Faculty – 7; **Number of Other Faculty** – 4

Degrees awarded in 2007–2008 Academic Year – Masters – 15; **PhD** – 0; **Other** – 0

Grant Monies awarded in 2007–2008 Academic Year – 0

Name of Institution – University of Michigan
Name of Department or Program – Department of Educational Studies

Address:
610 East University
Ann Arbor, MI
48109-1259
USA

Phone Number – (734) 763-7500
Fax Number – (734) 615-1290

Email Contact – fishman@umich.edu
URL – http://www.soe.umich.edu/learningtechnologies/

Contact Person – Barry J. Fishman

Specializations – M.A., MS, PhD in Learning Technologies

Features – The Learning Technologies Program at the University of Michigan integrates the study of technology with a focus in a substantive content area. A unique aspect of the program is that your learning and research will engage you in real-world educational contexts. You will find that understanding issues related to a specific content area provides an essential context for meaningful research in learning. Your understanding of technology, school contexts, and a content area will place you among the leaders who design and conduct research on advanced technological systems that change education and schooling. The Doctoral specialization in Learning Technologies must be taken in conjunction with a substantive concentration designed in consultation with your advisor. Current active concentrations include: Science, Literacy, Culture and Gender, Teacher Education, Design and Human-Computer Interaction, Policy, and Social Studies. Other areas are possible. The Master's Degree in Learning Technologies at the University of Michigan prepares professionals for leadership roles in the design, development, implementation, and research of powerful technologies to enhance learning. Our approach to design links current knowledge and research about how people learn with technological tools that enable new means of organizing and evaluating learning environments. Course and project work reflects the latest knowledge and practice in learning, teaching, and technology. Core courses prepare students to use current understandings about learning theory, design principles, research methodologies, and evaluation strategies in educational settings ranging from classrooms to web-based and distributed learning environments. Faculty work with students to shape programs that meet individual interests. Practical experience is offered through internships with area educational institutions.

Admission Requirements – GRE, B.A. for M.A., MS, or PhD; TOEFL for students from countries where English is not the primary language

Degree Requirements – M.A. and MS: 30 h beyond B.A. PhD: 60 h beyond B.A. or 30 h beyond Masters plus research paper/qualifying examination, and dissertation.

Number of Full-Time Faculty – 3;
Number of Other Faculty – 5

Degrees awarded in 2007–2008 Academic Year – Masters – 4; PhD – 1; **Other** – 0

Grant Monies awarded in 2007–2008 Academic Year – 0

Name of Institution – Bemidji State University
Name of Department or Program – Professional Education

Address:
1500 Birchmont Drive NE
Bemidji, MN
56601
USA

Phone Number – 218-755-3734

Email Contact – solson@bemidjistate.edu **URL** – http://www.bemidjistate.edu

Contact Person – Shari Olson

Number of Full-Time Faculty – 0; **Number of Other Faculty** – 0
Degrees awarded in 2007–2008 Academic Year – Masters – 0; **PhD** – 0;
Other – 0

Grant Monies awarded in 2007–2008 Academic Year – 0

Name of Institution – University of Missouri – Columbia
Name of Department or Program – School of Information Science and Learning
Technologies

Address:
303 Townsend Hall
Columbia, MO
65211
USA

Phone Number – 573-882-4546 **Fax Number** – 573-884-2917

Email Contact – sislt@missouri.edu **URL** – www.coe.missouri.edu/~sislt

Contact Person – John Wedman

Specializations – The Educational Technology emphasis area prepares educators
and technologists for excellence and leadership in the design, development, and
implementation of technology in education, training, and performance support.
The program offers three focus areas: Technology In Schools Networked Learning
Systems Training Design and Development Each focus area has its own set of
competencies, coursework, and processes.

Features – All three focus areas are available online via the Internet or on the MU
campus. The Technology in Schools focus area is based on the ISTE competencies
and culminates in an online portfolio based on these competencies. Several courses
are augmented by technical resources developed at MU, including a technology
integration knowledge repository and online collaboration tools. The Networked
Learning Systems focus area offers a truly challenging and innovative set of technical learning experiences. Students have opportunities to work on large-scale

software development projects, acquiring valuable experience and broadening their skill-set. The Digital Media ZONE supports anytime/anywhere technical skill development. The Training and Development focus area links to business, military, and government contexts. The curriculum is offered by faculty with extensive experience in these contexts and is grounded in the problems and processes of today's workplace. EdS and PhD programs are also available.

Admission Requirements – Bachelors degree with 3.0 in last 60 credit hours of coursework. GRE (V>500; A>500; W>3.5) TOEFL of 540 (207 computer-based test) (if native language is not English) Letters of reference

Degree Requirements – Masters: 30–34 credit hours; 15 h at 400 level. Specific course requirements vary by focus area.

Number of Full-Time Faculty – 0; **Number of Other Faculty** – 0

Degrees awarded in 2007–2008 Academic Year – **Masters** – 72; **PhD** – 0; **Other** – 0

Grant Monies awarded in 2007–2008 Academic Year – 0

Name of Institution – University of Missouri-Kansas City
Name of Department or Program – Curriculum and Instructional Leadership

Address:
4100 Oak Street
Kansas City, MO
64101
USA

Phone Number – 314.210.6996
Fax Number – 816.235.5270

Email Contact – russelldl@umkc.edu
URL – http://r.web.umkc.edu/russelldl/

Contact Person – Donna Russell

Specializations – 3D Virtual Learning Environments

Number of Full-Time Faculty – 30;
Number of Other Faculty – 15

Degrees awarded in 2007–2008 Academic Year – **Masters** – 60; **PhD** – 3; **Other** – 0

Grant Monies awarded in 2007–2008 Academic Year – 700000

Name of Institution – East Carolina University
Name of Department or Program – Mathematics, Science, and Instructional Technology Education

Address:
342 Flanagan
Greenville, NC
27858
USA

Phone Number – 252-328-9353 **Fax Number** – 252-328-9371

Email Contact – sugarw@coe.ecu.edu **URL** – http://www.ecu.edu/educ/msite/it/

Contact Person – William Sugar

Specializations – MS in Instructional Technology MAEd in Instructional Technology (see corresponding Educational Media & Technology Yearbook entry) Certificates in Computer-based Instruction, Distance Learning and Administration; Performance Improvement and Virtual Reality
Features – All required and elective courses are offered online. Courses include innovative approaches to online instruction.

Admission Requirements – MAT or GRE exam score

Degree Requirements – Bachelors degree

Number of Full-Time Faculty – 7; **Number of Other Faculty** – 3

Degrees awarded in 2007–2008 Academic Year – Masters – 9; **PhD** – 0; **Other** – 0

Grant Monies awarded in 2007–2008 Academic Year – 0

Name of Institution – University of North Carolina at Wilmington
Name of Department or Program – Master of Science in Instructional Technology–Department of Instructional Technology, Foundations and Secondary Education

Address:
601 South College Rd.
Wilmington, NC
28403
USA

Phone Number – 910-962-4183 **Fax Number** – 910-962-3609

Email Contact – moallemm@uncw.edu **URL** – http://www.uncw.edu/ed/mit

Contact Person – Mahnaz Moallem

Specializations – The Master of Science degree in Instructional Technology (MIT) program provides advanced professional training for teachers and school technology coordinators; business and industry personnel such as executives, trainers, and human resource development employees; persons in the health care field; and community college instructors. The program focuses on the theory and practice of design and development, utilization, management, and evaluation of processes and resources for learning. It emphasizes product development and utilization of advanced technology and provides applied training in the total design, development, implementation, and evaluation of educational and training programs.

Features – As an exciting and innovative program, MIT provides students the opportunity to gain skills and knowledge from educational and applied psychology, instructional systems design, computer science, systems theory, and communication theory, allowing for considerable flexibility to tailor individual needs across other academic disciplines. Students from diverse fields can plan programs which are consistent with their long-range academic and professional goals. MIT courses are offered both on campus and online, allowing professionals to earn their degrees and/or certificates by taking MIT on-campus courses, or MIT online courses, or a combination of both types. In addition, the MIT program is directed toward preparing students to function in a variety of roles to be performed in a broad range of settings, including business and industry, human services, health institutions, higher education, government, military, and public and private K-12 education.

Admission Requirements – Students desiring admission into the graduate program in instructional technology must present the following: A bachelor's degree from an accredited college or university or its equivalent from a foreign institution of higher education based on a four-year program. A strong academic record (an average GPA of 3.0 or better is expected) in the basic courses required in the area of the proposed graduate study. Academic potential as indicated by satisfactory performance on standardized test scores (e.g., Miller Analogy Test or Graduate Record Examination). The MAT or GRE must have been taken within the past 5 years. Three recommendations from individuals who are in a position to evaluate the students professional competence as well as potential for graduate study. A statement of career goals and degree objectives. A letter describing educational and professional experiences, their reasons for pursuing graduate study, and the contributions that the student hopes to make after completing the degree. North Carolina essential and advanced technology competencies. Individuals who fall below a specified criterion may be admitted if other factors indicate potential for success. Individuals with identified deficiencies may be accepted provisionally with specified plans and goals for the remediation of those deficiencies. Such remediation may include a requirement of additional hours beyond those normally required for the degree.

Number of Full-Time Faculty – 5; **Number of Other Faculty** – 5

Degrees awarded in 2007–2008 Academic Year – Masters – 10; **PhD –** 0; **Other –** 0
Grant Monies awarded in 2007–2008 Academic Year – 0

Name of Institution – University of North Dakota
Name of Department or Program – Instructional Design & Technology

Address:
231 Centennial Drive, Stop 7189
Grand Forks, ND
58202
USA

Phone Number – 701-777-3574 **Fax Number –** 701-777-3246

Email Contact – richard.vaneck@und.edu **URL –** idt.und.edu

Contact Person – Richard Van Eck

Specializations – Serious Games, Game-Based Learning K-12 Technology Integration Human Performance Technology eLearning

Features – Online Hybrid with synchronous and asynchronous learning Masters and Certificates fully available at a distance. Three graduate certificates (K-12 Technology Integration; Corporate Training & Performance; eLearning) MS and M.Ed. PhD Interdisciplinary studies

Admission Requirements – See idt.und.edu

Degree Requirements – See idt.und.edu

Number of Full-Time Faculty – 3; **Number of Other Faculty –** 1

Degrees awarded in 2007–2008 Academic Year – Masters – 3; **PhD –** 0; **Other –** 2

Grant Monies awarded in 2007–2008 Academic Year – 50000

Name of Institution – Valley City State University
Name of Department or Program – School of Education and Graduate Studies

Address:
101 College St
Valley City, ND
58072
USA

Phone Number – 701-845-7303 **Fax Number –** 701-845-7300
Email Contact – terry.corwin@vcsu.edu **URL –** www.vcsu.edu/graduate

Contact Person – Terry Corwin

Specializations – The Master of Education program has three concentrations that focus on technology and the learner Teaching and Technology concentration Technology Education concentration Library and Information Technologies

Features – This is a completely online program which focuses on how technology can be used in a school setting to enhance student learning.

Admission Requirements – 1. Bachelorette degree with a 3.0 undergraduate GPA or a test is required. 2. Three letters of recommendation 3. Written goals statement

Degree Requirements – Completion of 32–37 credits depending on concentration. Action Research proposal and report. Final portfolio demonstrating program core values.

Number of Full-Time Faculty – 12; **Number of Other Faculty** – 8

Degrees awarded in 2007–2008 Academic Year – **Masters** – 13; **PhD** – 0; **Other** – 168

Grant Monies awarded in 2007–2008 Academic Year – 450000

Name of Institution – Montclair State University
Name of Department or Program – Department of Curriculum & Teaching

Address:
1 College Avenue
Montclair, NJ
07043
USA

Phone Number – (973)655-5187 **Fax Number** – (973)655-7084

Email Contact – dominev@mail.montclair.edu **URL** – http://cehs.montclair.edu

Contact Person – Dr. Vanessa Domine, Professor of Educational Technology

Specializations – MSU offers 1) an M.Ed. degree program in Educational Technology (EDTC); 2) a post-bac certification program for Associate School Library Media Specialists (ALMS); and 3) an advanced certification program for School Library Media Specialists (SLMS).

Features – All three programs draw from the same pool of educational technology courses and can be completed together in a carefully assembled program of approximately 46 graduate credits. Three areas comprise coursework: Philosophical foundations, Pedagogical design and integration, and Practical design and application. In the M.Ed. program, students can choose to emphasize in one of three areas: (A) Administration, Policy and Leadership; (B) Organizational Planning and Development; and (C) Curriculum and Technology Integration.

Admission Requirements – Students can apply in person or online to the Graduate School (http://www.montclair.edu/graduate). The M.Ed. program requires submission of GRE scores, letters of recommendation, and a project sample. The ALMS program requires a bachelor's degree and standard NJ teaching license. The SLMS program requires a master's degree, a standard NJ teaching license, and at least 1 year of successful teaching as an associate school library media specialist.

Degree Requirements – The MEd program requires 33 credits of coursework and field experience. The ALMS program requires 18–21 credits of coursework and field experience. The SLMS program requires 36 credits of coursework and field experience.

Number of Full-Time Faculty -; **Number of Other Faculty** -

Degrees awarded in 2007–2008 Academic Year – Masters -; **PhD** -; **Other** -

Grant Monies awarded in 2007–2008 Academic Year -

Name of Institution – New York University
Name of Department or Program – Educational Communication and Technology Program, Steinhardt School of Education

Address:
239 Greene St., Suite 300
New York, NY
10003
USA

Phone Number – (212)998-5520 **Fax Number** – (212)995-4041

Email Contact – jan.plass@nyu.edu
URL – http://www.nyu.edu/education/alt/ectprogram

Contact Person – Francine Shuchat-Shaw, Assoc. Prof. (MA Advisor), Dir.; W. Michael Reed, Prof., (Doctoral Advisor)

Specializations – MA, EdD, and PhD in Education – for the preparation of individuals as instructional media designers, developers, media producers, and/or researchers in education, business and industry, health and medicine, community services, government, museums and other cultural institutions; and to teach or become involved in administration in educational communications and instructional technology programs in higher education, including instructional television, micro-computers, multimedia, Internet and telecommunications. The program also offers a post-MA 30-point Certificate of Advanced Study in Education.

Features – Emphasizes theoretical foundations, especially a cognitive science perspective of learning and instruction, and their implications for designing media-based learning environments and materials. All efforts focus on video, multimedia, instructional television, web-based technology and telecommunications; participation in special research and production projects and field internships. CREATE – Consortium for Research and Evaluation of Advanced Technologies in Education – uses an apprenticeship model to provide doctoral students and advanced MA students with research opportunities in collaboration with faculty.

Admission Requirements – MA: 3.0 undergraduate GPA, responses to essay questions, interview related to academic and professional goals. PhD: 3.0 GPA, 1000 GRE, responses to essay questions, interview related to academic or professional preparation and career goals. For international students, 600 TOEFL and TWE.

Degree Requirements – MA: 36 semester hours including specialization, elective courses, thesis, English essay examination. PhD: 57 semester hours beyond MA, including specialization, foundations, research, content seminar, and elective coursework; candidacy papers; dissertation; English essay examination.

Number of Full-Time Faculty – 0; **Number of Other Faculty** – 0

Degrees awarded in 2007–2008 Academic Year – **Master's** – 0; **PhD** – 0; **Other** – 0

Grant Monies awarded in 2007–2008 Academic Year – 0

Name of Institution – Syracuse University
Name of Department or Program – Instructional Design, Development, and Evaluation Program, School of Education

Address:
330 Huntington Hall
Syracuse, NY
13244-2340
USA

Phone Number – (315)443-3703 **Fax Number** – (315)443-1218

Email Contact – nlsmith@syr.edu
URL – http://soeweb.syr.edu/academics/grad/instructional_design_dev_eval/

Contact Person – Nick Smith, Professor and Department Chair

Specializations – Certificates in Educational Technology and Adult Lifelong Learning, MS, CAS, and PhD degree programs in Instructional Design, Educational Evaluation, Human Issues in Instructional Development, Technology Integration, and Educational Research and Theory (learning theory, application of theory, and educational media research). Graduates are prepared to serve as curriculum developers, instructional designers, program and project evaluators, researchers, resource center administrators, technology coordinators, distance learning design and delivery specialists, trainers and training managers, and higher education faculty.

Features – The courses and programs are typically project centered. Collaborative project experience, fieldwork, and internships are emphasized throughout. There are special issue seminars, as well as student- and faculty-initiated mini-courses, seminars and guest lecturers, faculty-student formulation of department policies, and multiple international perspectives. International collaborations are an ongoing feature of the program. The graduate student population is highly diverse.

Admission Requirements – Certificates and MS: undergraduate transcripts, recommendations, personal statement, interview recommended; TOEFL for international applicants; GRE recommended. Certificate of Advanced Study: Relevant master's degree from accredited institution or equivalent, GRE scores, recommendations, personal statement, TOEFL for international applicants; interview recommended. Doctoral: Relevant master's degree from accredited institution or equivalent, GRE scores, recommendations, personal statement, TOEFL for international applicants; interview strongly encouraged.

Degree Requirements – Certificates: 15 and 24 semester hours. MS: 36 semester hours, portfolio required. CAS: 60 semester hours, exam and project required. PhD: 90 semester hours, research apprenticeship, portfolio, qualifying exams, and dissertation required.

Number of Full-Time Faculty – 4; **Number of Other Faculty** – 5

Degrees awarded in 2007–2008 Academic Year – Master's – 10; **PhD** – 3; **Other** – 1

Grant Monies awarded in 2007–2008 Academic Year – 35800

Name of Institution – East Stroudsburg University
Name of Department or Program – Instructional Technology, Media Communication and Technology Department

Address:
200 Prospect Street
East Stroudsburg, PA
18301
USA

Phone Number – 470 422 3621 **Fax Number** – (570) 422-3876

Email Contact – bsockman@po-box.esu.edu **URL** – www.esu.edu/gradmcom

Contact Person – Beth Rajan Sockman

Specializations – The graduate programs are designed to develop the technology literacy of educators, prepare specialists to work in K-12 schools, school districts, or instructional technology personnel in education, business, or industry. Students can obtain a Master's of Education degree in Instructional Technology and/or a Pennsylvania Instructional Technologist Specialist Certificate.

Features – The program provides students with an opportunity to take courses from ESU and Kutztown University. Students who successfully complete the program become proficient in using technology in teaching. Students can choose courses that explore the following areas: * Desktop publishing * Interactive web design (Including Web 2.0 applications) * Graphics * Video * New and emerging technologies * Instructional design * Learning theories * Research in Instructional Technology.

Admission Requirements – For MEd degree: * Two letters of recommendation * Portfolio or interview (Interview is granted after the application is received) * For full admission a minimum overall undergraduate 2.5 QPA * Rolling deadline. For certification: * Contact the graduate coordinator for additional admission information to comply with Pennsylvania Department of Education requirements. * Minimum overall undergraduate QPA 3.0 (Pennsylvania Act 354) * If not 3.0 QPA, then completion of nine credits of Media Communication and Technology Department courses with prior written approval of department faculty adviser * Two letters of recommendation * Rolling deadline.

Degree Requirements – Total = 33 credits * Take courses and learn – take 30 credits of courses for the master's and learn based on your needs. You will learn to use and implement technologies outside average persons experience. * Create, submit, and present your portfolio – this is the time to display your learning in a professional manner. In the portfolio you articulate your goals and may identify learning goals for your internship. Click here for the Portfolio Guidelines. * Complete an internship – you complete a 90-h internship that extends your knowledge base – 3 credits. * Complete portfolio and graduate.
Number of Full-Time Faculty – 7; **Number of Other Faculty** – 3

Degrees awarded in 2007–2008 Academic Year – **Master's** – 6; **PhD** – 0; **Other** – 0

Grant Monies awarded in 2007–2008 Academic Year – 3400

Name of Institution – Penn State Great Valley School of Graduate Professional Studies
Name of Department or Program – Education Division/Instructional Systems Program

Address:
30 E. Swedesfordd Road

Malvern, PA
19355
USA

Phone Number – 610-725-5250 **Fax Number** – 610-725-5232

Email Contact – ydl1@psu.edu **URL** – http://www.sgps.psu.edu

Contact Person – Doris Lee

Specializations – Instructional Systems/Designs

Admission Requirements – Online application, MAT/GRE scores, two letters of recommendations,

Degree Requirements – 36 cr.

Number of Full-Time Faculty – 10; **Number of Other Faculty** – 15

Degrees awarded in 2007–2008 Academic Year – **Master's** – 45; **PhD** – 0; **Other** – 0

Grant Monies awarded in 2007–2008 Academic Year – 0

Name of Institution – Temple University
Name of Department or Program – Department of Psychological Studies in Education

Address:
1301 Cecil B. Moore Avenue
Philadelphia, PA
19122
USA

Phone Number – (215) 204-4497 **Fax Number** – (215) 204-6013

Email Contact – susan.miller@temple.edu
URL – http://www.temple.edu/education/

Contact Person – Susan Miller, PhD

Specializations – Instructional and Learning Technology (ILT) is a new masters program within the Educational Psychology Program in the Department of Psychological Studies in Education. As such, ILT is designed to address conceptual as well as technical issues in using technology for teaching and learning. Program areas include (a)instructional theory and design issues, (b) application of technology, and (c) management issues.
Features – Instructional Theory and Design topics includes psychology of the learner, cognitive processes, instructional theories, human development, and individual differences, as well as psychological and educational characteristics of

technology resources and identification of strengths and weaknesses of instructional technology resources. The Application of Technology area focuses on clarification of instructional objectives; identification of resources to facilitate learning, operation, and application of current and emergent technologies; facility using graphic design, multimedia, video, and distributed learning resources; WWW; and print publishing. Management and Consultation is structured around defining instructional needs; monitoring progress; evaluating outcomes; designing technology delivery systems; preparing policy statements, budgets, and facility design criteria; managing skill assessment and training, understanding legal and ethical issues, and managing and maintaining facilities.

Admission Requirements – Bachelor's degree from an accredited institution, GRE (MAT)scores, three letters of recommendation, transcripts from each institution of higher learning attended(undergraduate and graduate), goal statement

Degree Requirements – Coursework (33 h: five core courses, three technology electives, three cognate area courses). Practicum in student's area of interest. Comprehensive Exam Portfolio of Certification Competencies (for students interested in PA Department of Education Certification as Instructional Technology Specialist).

Number of Full-Time Faculty -; **Number of Other Faculty** -

Degrees awarded in 2007–2008 Academic Year – **Master's** -; **PhD** -; **Other** -

Grant Monies awarded in 2007–2008 Academic Year -

Name of Institution – University of Memphis
Name of Department or Program – Instruction and Curriculum Leadership/Instructional Design & Technology

Address:
406 Ball Hall
Memphis, TN
38152
USA

Phone Number – 901-678-2365
Fax Number – 901-678-3881

Email Contact – dlowther@memphis.edu **URL** – http://idt.memphis.edu

Contact Person – Dr. Richard Van Eck

Specializations – Instructional Design, Web-based instruction, Computer-based instruction, Digital Video, K-12 NTeQ technology integration model, Instructional Games, Pedagogical Agents

Features – The Advanced Instructional Media (AIM) lab, staffed and run by IDT faculty and students, serves as an R&D space for coursework and research involving technologies such as digital media, WBT/CBT (Dreamweaver, Flash, Authorware, WebCT, DV cameras, DV editing, DVD authoring, etc.), pedagogical agents, gaming and simulation. The AIM lab and IDT program are connected to the Center for Multimedia Arts in the FedEx Institute of Technology. The AIM Lab brings in outside contract work from corporate partners to provide real-world experience to students. We have also partnered with the Institute for Intelligent Systems and the Tutoring Research Group (www.autotutor.org) to work on intelligent agent development and research.

Admission Requirements – Minimum standards that identify a pool of master's-level applicants from which each department selects students to be admitted: An official transcript showing a bachelor's degree awarded by an accredited college or university with a minimum GPA of 2.0 on a 4.0 scale, competitive MAT or GRE scores, GRE writing test, two letters of recommendation, graduate school, and departmental application. Doctoral students must also be interviewed by at least two members of the program.

Degree Requirements – MS: 36 h, internship, master's project or thesis, 3.0 GPA. EdD: 54 h, 45 in major, 9 in research; residency project; comprehensive exams; dissertation.

Number of Full-Time Faculty – 0; **Number of Other Faculty** – 0

Degrees awarded in 2007–2008 Academic Year – **Master's** – 0; **PhD** – 0; **Other** – 0

Grant Monies awarded in 2007–2008 Academic Year – 0

Name of Institution – Texas A&M University-Commerce
Name of Department or Program – Department of Educational Leadership

Address:
PO Box 3011
Commerce, TX
75429-3011
USA

Phone Number – (903)886-5607 **Fax Number** – (903)886-5507

Email Contact – Sue_Espinoza@tamu-commerce.edu **URL** – http://www.tamu-commerce.edu/

Contact Person – Dr. Sue Espinoza, Professor, Program Coordinator

Specializations – MS or MEd degrees in Educational Technology Leadership and in Educational Technology-Library Science Certification programs – School Librarian, and Technology Applications, both approved by the Texas State Board for Educator Certification.

Features – Programs may be completed totally online, although some courses may also be offered in web-enhanced formats, and one or more electives may be offered only face-to-face.

Admission Requirements – Apply to the Graduate School at Texas A&M University-Commerce. For school library certification, must also apply to the professional certification program.

Degree Requirements – 36 h for each master's degree; each program contains core courses, and specialization area courses are selected in consultation with an advisor, who is assigned when each student is admitted to the program.

Number of Full-Time Faculty – 3; **Number of Other Faculty** – 6

Degrees awarded in 2007–2008 Academic Year – **Master's** – 19; **PhD** – 0; **Other** – 0

Grant Monies awarded in 2007–2008 Academic Year – 0

Name of Institution – Old Dominion University
Name of Department or Program – Instructional Design and Technology

Address:
Education 228
Norfolk, VA
23529
USA

Phone Number – 757-683-6275 **Fax Number** – 757-683-5862

Email Contact – gmorriso@odu.edu **URL** – http://education.odu.edu/eci/idt/

Contact Person – Gary R. Morrison

Specializations – Our faculty engages students in a rigorous course of study tailored to meet individual educational and career interests. Research opportunities and coursework ensures that all students receive a solid foundation in Instructional Design, Instructional Design Theory, Human Performance Technology, Gaming and Simulation, Distance Education, Evaluation & Assessment, Trends and Issues in Instructional Technology, Quantitative and Qualitative Research.

Features – All of our courses are offered via distance using a hybrid format. A reduced tuition rate is available for students living outside of Virginia who are accepted into the program.

Admission Requirements – MS degree: GRE scores or MAT scores; transcripts for undergraduate and graduate courses PhD: GRE scores, transcripts for under-graduate and graduate courses, letters of recommendation, and an essay describing professional goals.

Degree Requirements – MS program is 30–36 h PhD program is a post-master's degree consisting of 60 h

Number of Full-Time Faculty – 5; **Number of Other Faculty** – 0

Degrees awarded in 2007–2008 Academic Year – **Master's** – 0; **PhD** – 0; **Other** – 0

Grant Monies awarded in 2007–2008 Academic Year – 0

Name of Institution – Concordia University Wisconsin
Name of Department or Program – Educational Technology

Address:
12800 N Lakeshore Drive
Mequon, WI
53092
USA

Phone Number – 262-243-4595 **Fax Number** – 262-243-3595

Email Contact – bernard.bull@cuw.edu **URL** – http://www.cuw.edu/go/edtech

Contact Person – Dr. Bernard Bull

Specializations – Digital culture, designing digital age learning experiences, and social/spiritual/ethical implications of technology.

Features – Courses are available via e-learning or face-to-face. Some courses are also offered at off-campus sites throughout Wisconsin. In addition, we run special thematic cohorts where a group of students work through the program together over an 18–24-month period, all agreeing to focus their thesis or culminating project on the cohort theme (e.g., new literacies, bridging the digital divide, global education, and discipleship in the digital age).

Admission Requirements – To be considered for admission, a student must have a bachelor's degree from an accredited college or university and have a minimum GPA of 3.00 in the undergraduate program.

Degree Requirements – The following courses are required for anyone desiring an MS in Education – Educational Technology (33 credits): EDG 670/970 – Integrating Technology in the Classroom (3) EDG 589/889 – Applying Technology in the Content Areas (3) EDG 608/908 – Critical Issues in Educational Technology (3) EDG 507/807 – Instructional Design (3) EDG 528/828 – Learning, Theory, and

Design (3) EDG 515 – Educational Research Methods (3) EDG 627, 628, 629 – Portfolio I, II, and III (0) EDG 595/895 – Capstone Project (3) OR EDG 590/890 – Thesis Completion Seminar (3) Electives (12 credits)
Number of Full-Time Faculty – 3; **Number of Other Faculty** – 5

Degrees awarded in 2007–2008 Academic Year – Master's – 0; **PhD** – 0; **Other** – 0

Grant Monies awarded in 2007–2008 Academic Year – 0

Name of Institution – University of Wisconsin-Madison
Name of Department or Program – Curriculum and Instruction, School of Education
Address:
225 North Mills Street
Madison, WI
53706
USA

Phone Number – 608) 263-4670 **Fax Number** – (608) 263-9992

Email Contact – streibel@education.wisc.edu
URL – http://www.education.wisc.edu/ci/

Contact Person – Michael J. Streibel

Specializations – MS and PhD degree programs to prepare Educational Technology faculty and professionals. Ongoing research includes: studying the impact of contemporary gaming practices on learning, schooling, and society; understanding ways in which online play spaces align (or fail to align) with practices valued outside the game (i.e., informal scientific reasoning, collaborative problem-solving, and media literacy); interrogating the implementation of technology-rich innovations in local and international schools as well as the role of culture in the design of instruction; and using photography as a research method in education.

Features – Educational Technology courses are processed through social, cultural, historical, and design-based frames of reference. Current curriculum emphasizes new media theories, critical cultural and visual culture theories, and constructivist theories of instructional design and development. Many courses are offered in the evening.

Admission Requirements – Master's and PhD: previous experience in Instructional Technology preferred, previous teaching experience, 3.0 GPA on last 60 undergraduate credits, acceptable scores on GRE, and 3.0 GPA on all graduate work.

Degree Requirements – MS: 24 credits plus thesis and exam (an additional 12 credits of Educational Foundations if no previous educational background); PhD:

1 year of residency beyond the bachelor's, major, minor, and research requirements, preliminary exam, dissertation, and oral exam.

Number of Full-Time Faculty – 4; **Number of Other Faculty** – 0

Degrees awarded in 2007–2008 Academic Year – **Master's** – 1; **PhD** – 1; **Other** – 0

Grant Monies awarded in 2007–2008 Academic Year – 1000000

There are a total of 159 graduate programs in the database.

Part VI
Mediagraphy: Print and Nonprint Resources

Introduction

Jinn-Wei Tsao

Contents

This resource lists journals and other resources of interest to practitioners, researchers, students, and others concerned with educational technology and educational media. The primary goal of this part is to list current publications in the field. The majority of materials cited here were published in 2008 or mid-2009. Media-related journals include those listed in past issues of EMTY, as well as new entries in the field. A thorough list of journals in the educational technology field has been updated for the 2009 edition using *Ulrich's Periodical Index Online* and journal websites. This chapter is not intended to serve as a specific resource location tool, although it may be used for that purpose in the absence of database access. Rather, readers are encouraged to peruse the categories of interest in this chapter to gain an idea of recent developments within the field. For archival purposes, this chapter serves as a snapshot of the field of instructional technology publications in 2008. Readers must bear in mind that technological developments occur well in advance of publication and should take that fact into consideration when judging the timeliness of resources listed in this chapter.

Selection

Items were selected for the mediagraphy in several ways. The EBSCO Host Databases were used to locate most of the journal citations. Others were taken from the journal listings of large publishing companies. Items were chosen for this list when they met one or more of the following criteria: reputable publisher, broad circulation, coverage by indexing services, peer review, and coverage of a gap in

J.-W. Tsao (✉)
Learning, Design, and Technology Program, The University of Georgia, Athens, GA, USA
e-mail: miketsao@uga.edu

M. Orey et al. (eds.), *Educational Media and Technology Yearbook*,
Educational Media and Technology Yearbook 35,
DOI 10.1007/978-1-4419-1516-0_21, © Springer Science+Business Media, LLC 2010

the literature. The author chose items on subjects that seem to reflect the instructional technology field as it is today. Because of the increasing tendency for media producers to package their products in more than one format and for single titles to contain mixed media, titles are no longer separated by media type. The author makes no claims as to the comprehensiveness of this list. It is, instead, intended to be representative.

Obtaining Resources

Media-Related Periodicals

The author has attempted to provide various ways to obtain the resources listed in this mediagraphy, including telephone and fax numbers, Web and postal addresses, as well as e-mail contacts. Prices are also included for individual and institutional subscriptions. The information presented reflects the most current information available at the time of publication.

ERIC Documents

As of December 31, 2003, ERIC was no longer funded. However, ERIC documents can still be read and copied from their microfiche form at any library holding an ERIC microfiche collection. The identification number beginning with ED (for example, ED 332 677) locates the document in the collection. Document delivery services and copies of most ERIC documents continue to be available from the ERIC Document Reproduction Service. Prices charged depend on format chosen (microfiche or paper copy), length of the document, and method of shipping. Online orders, fax orders, and expedited delivery are available.

To find the closest library with an ERIC microfiche collection, contact: ACCESS ERIC, 1600 Research Blvd, Rockville, METHOD 20850-3172; (800) LET-ERIC (538-3742); e-mail: acceric@inet.ed.gov.

To order ERIC documents, contact:

ERIC Document Reproduction Services (EDRS),
7420 Fullerton Rd, Suite 110, Springfield, VA 22153-2852;
(800) 433-ERIC (433-3742); (703) 440-1400;
fax: (703) 440-1408;
e-mail: service@edrs.com.

Journal Articles

Photocopies of journal articles can be obtained in one of the following ways: (1) from a library subscribing to the title, (2) through interlibrary loan, (3) through the purchase of a back issue from the journal publisher, or (4) from an article reprint service such as UMI.

UMI Information Store, 500 Sansome St, Suite 400
San Francisco, CA 94111
(800) 248-0360 (toll-free in United States and Canada), (415) 433-5500 (outside
  United States and Canada)
E-mail: orders@infostore.com.

  Journal articles can also be obtained through the Institute for Scientific Information (ISI).

ISI Document Solution
P.O. Box 7649
Philadelphia, PA 19104-3389
(215) 386-4399
Fax: (215) 222-0840 or (215) 386-4343
E-mail: ids@isinet.com.

Arrangement

Mediagraphy entries are classified according to major subject emphasis under the following headings:

- Artificial Intelligence, Robotics, and Electronic Performance Support Systems
- Computer-Assisted Instruction
- Distance Education
- Educational Research
- Educational Technology
- Information Science and Technology
- Instructional Design and Development
- Learning Sciences
- Libraries and Media Centers
- Media Technologies
- Professional Development
- Simulation, Gaming, and Virtual Reality
- Special Education and Disabilities
- Telecommunications and Networking

Mediagraphy

Artificial Intelligence, Robotics, and Electronic Performance Support Systems

Artificial Intelligence Review. Springer Science+Business Media, 333 Meadowlands Pkwy, Secaucus, NJ 07094. www.springer.com/journal/10462, tel: 800-777-4643, fax: 201-348-4505, journals-ny@springer.com [8/year; $824 inst (print + online), $988.80 inst (print + E-access, content through 1997)]. Publishes commentary on issues and development in artificial intelligence foundations and current research.

AI Magazine. Association for the Advancement of Artificial Intelligence, 445 Burgess Dr, Suite 100, Menlo Park, CA 94025. www.aaai.org/Magazine/magazine.php, tel: 650-328-3123, fax: 650-321-4457, info08@aaai.org [4/year; $50 student, $120 indiv, $245 inst]. Proclaimed "journal of record for the AI community," this magazine provides full-length articles on research and new literature, but is written to allow access to those reading outside their area of expertise.

International Journal of Robotics Research. Sage Publications, 2455 Teller Rd, Thousand Oaks, CA 91320. ijr.sagepub.com, tel: 800-818-7243, fax: 800-583-2665, journals@sagepub.com [12/year; $198 indiv (print), $1598 inst (online), $1740 inst (print), $1775 inst (print + online)]. Interdisciplinary approach to the study of robotics for researchers, scientists, and students. The first scholarly publication on robotics research.

Journal of Intelligent and Robotic Systems. Springer Science+Business Media, 333 Meadowlands Pkwy, Secaucus, NJ 07094. www.springer.com/journal/10846, tel: 800-777-4643, fax: 201-348-4505, journals-ny@springer.com [12/year; $1,791 inst (print + online), $2,149.20 inst (print + E-access, content through 1997)]. Main objective is to provide a forum for the fruitful interaction of ideas and techniques that combine systems and control science with artificial intelligence and other related computer science concepts. It bridges the gap between theory and practice.

M. Orey et al. (eds.), *Educational Media and Technology Yearbook*,
Educational Media and Technology Yearbook 35,
DOI 10.1007/978-1-4419-1516-0_22, © Springer Science+Business Media, LLC 2010

Journal of Interactive Learning Research. Association for the Advancement of Computing in Education, P.O. Box 1545, Chesapeake, VA 23327-1545. www.aace.org/pubs/jilr, tel: 757-366-5606, fax: 703-997-8760, info@aace.org [4/year; $35 AACE student members, $115 AACE members (discount available for ordering multiple AACE journals), $185 inst]. Publishes articles on how intelligent computer technologies can be used in education to enhance learning and teaching. Reports on research and developments, integration, and applications of artificial intelligence in education.

Knowledge-Based Systems. Elsevier, Inc., Customer Service Dept, 11830 Westline Industrial Drive, St. Louis, MO 63146. www.elsevier. com/locate/knosys, tel: 877-839-7126, fax: 314-523-5153, journalcustomerservice-usa@elsevier.com [8/year; $194 indiv, $1,268 inst]. Interdisciplinary applications-oriented journal on fifth-generation computing, expert systems, and knowledge-based methods in system design.

Minds and Machines. Springer Science+Business Media, 333 Meadowlands Pkwy, Secaucus, NJ 07094. www.springer.com/journal/11023, tel: 800-777-4643, fax: 201-348-4505, journals-ny@springer.com [4/year; $720 inst (print + online), $864 inst (print + E-access, content through 1997)]. Discusses issues concerning machines and mentality, artificial intelligence, epistemology, simulation, and modeling.

Computer-Assisted Instruction

AACE Journal. Association for the Advancement of Computing in Education, P.O. Box 1545, Chesapeake, VA 23327-1545. www.aace.org/pubs/aacej, tel: 757-366-5606, fax: 703-997-8760, info@aace.org [4/year; $35 for AACE student members, $115 AACE members (discount available for ordering multiple AACE journals), $185 inst]. Publishes articles dealing with issues in instructional technology.

CALICO Journal. Computer Assisted Language Instruction Consortium, 214 Centennial Hall, Texas State Univ, San Marcos, TX 78666. calico.org, tel: 512-245-1417, fax: 512-245-9089, info@calico.org [3/year; $65 indiv, $50 K-12 or community college teacher, $40 students or senior citizen, $105 inst]. Provides information on the applications of technology in teaching and learning languages.

Children's Technology Review. Active Learning Associates, 120 Main St, Flemington, NJ 08822. www.childrenstechnology.com, tel: 800-993-9499, fax: 908-284-0405, lisa@childrenssoftware.com [12/year; $64 (online), $108 (print + online)]. Provides reviews and other information about software to help parents and educators more effectively use computers with children.

Computers and Composition. Elsevier, Inc., Customer Service Dept, 11830 Westline Industrial Drive, St. Louis, MO 63146. www.elsevier.com/locate/compcom, tel: 877-839-7126, fax: 314-523-5153, journal customerservice-usa@elsevier.com [4/year; $72 indiv, $377 inst]. International journal for teachers of writing that focuses on the use of computers in writing instruction and related research.

Computers & Education. Elsevier, Inc., Customer Service Dept, 11830 Westline Industrial Drive, St. Louis, MO 63146. www.elsevier.com/locate/compedu, tel: 877-839-7126, fax: 314-523-5153, journalcustomerservice-usa@elsevier.com [8/year; $356 indiv, $1,867 inst]. Presents technical papers covering a broad range of subjects for users of analog, digital, and hybrid computers in all aspects of higher education.

Computers in Education Journal. American Society for Engineering Education, Computers in Education Division, Port Royal Square, P.O. Box 68, Port Royal, VA 22535. www.asee.org/about/publications/divisions/coed.cfm, tel: 804-742-5611, fax: 804-742-5030, ed-pub@crosslink.net [4/year; $20 student, $69 indiv, inst prices vary]. Covers transactions, scholarly research papers, application notes, and teaching methods.

Computers in Human Behavior. Elsevier, Inc., Customer Service Dept, 11830 Westline Industrial Drive, St. Louis, MO 63146. www.elsevier.com/locate/comphumbeh, tel: 877-839-7126, fax: 314-523-5153, journalcustomerservice-usa@elsevier.com [6/year; $279 indiv, $1,462 inst]. Scholarly journal dedicated to examining the use of computers from a psychological perspective.

Computers in the Schools. Taylor & Francis Group, Customer Service Dept, 325 Chestnut Street, Suite 800, Philadelphia, PA 19106. www.tandf.co.uk/journals/titles/07380569, tel: 800-354-1420, fax: 215-625-2940, subscriptions@tandf.co.uk [4/year; $120 indiv, $637 inst (online), $671 inst (print + online)]. Features articles that combine theory and practical applications of small computers in schools for educators and school administrators.

Converge. e.Republic, Inc., 100 Blue Ravine Rd, Folsom, CA 95630. www.convergemag.com, tel: 800-940-6039 ext. 1460, fax: 916-932-1470, subscriptions@convergemag.com [4/year; free]. Explores the revolution of technology in education.

Dr. Dobb's Journal. CMP Media, P.O. Box 1126, Skokie, IL 60076. www.ddj.com, tel: 888-847-6188, fax: 902-563-4807, drdobbsjournal@halldata.com [12/year; free to qualified applicants]. Articles on the latest in operating systems, programming languages, algorithms, hardware design and architecture, data structures, and telecommunications; in-depth hardware and software reviews.

eWEEK. Ziff Davis Media Inc., 28 E 28th St, New York, NY 10016-7930. www.eweek.com, tel: 888-663-8438, fax: 847-564-9453, eweek@ziffdavis.com [36/year; $195 (print), $125 (online), free to qualified applicants]. Provides current information on the IBM PC, including hardware, software, industry news, business strategies, and reviews of hardware and software.

Information Technology in Childhood Education Annual. Association for the Advancement of Computing in Education, P.O. Box 1545, Chesapeake, VA 23327-1545. www.aace.org/pubs/itce, tel: 757-366-5606, fax: 703-997-8760, info@aace.org [1/year; $115 indiv, $185 inst]. Scholarly trade publication reporting on research and investigations into the applications of instructional technology.

Instructor. Scholastic Inc., P.O. Box 420235, Palm Coast, FL 32142-0235. teacher.scholastic.com/products/instructor, tel: 866-436-2455, fax: 212-343-4799, instructor@emailcustomerservice.com [8/year; $8 (8 issues), $14.95 (16 issues)]. Features articles on applications and advances of technology in education for K-12 and college educators and administrators.

Interactive Learning Environments. Taylor & Francis Group, Customer Services Dept, 325 Chestnut St, Suite 800, Philadelphia, PA 19106. www. tandf.co.uk/journals/titles/10494820, tel: 800-354-1420, fax: 215-625-2940, subscriptions@tandf.co.uk [4/year; $169 indiv, $501 inst (online), $527 inst (print + online)]. Explores the implications of the Internet and multimedia presentation software in education and training environments.

Journal of Computer Assisted Learning. John Wiley & Sons, Inc., Journal Customer Services, 350 Main St, Malden, MA 02148. www. blackwellpublishing.com/journals/JCA, tel: 800-835-6770, fax: 781-388-8232, cs-agency@wiley.com [6/year; $203 individual (print + online), $1,178 inst (print/online), $1,296 inst (print + online)]. Articles and research on the use of computer-assisted learning.

Journal of Educational Computing Research. Baywood Publishing Co., Inc., 26 Austin Ave, Box 337, Amityville, NY 11701-0337. www.baywood. com/journals/previewjournals.asp?id=0735-6331, tel: 800-638-7819, fax: 631-691-1770, info@baywood.com [8/year; $209 indiv (online), $220 indiv (print + online), $507 inst (online), $534 inst (print + online)]. Presents original research papers, critical analyses, reports on research in progress, design and development studies, article reviews, and grant award listings.

Journal of Educational Multimedia and Hypermedia. Association for the Advancement of Computing in Education, P.O. Box 1545, Chesapeake, VA 23327-1545. www.aace.org/pubs/jemh, tel: 757-366-5606, fax: 703-997-8760, info@aace.org [4/year; $35 AACE student members, $115 AACE members (discount available for ordering multiple AACE journals), $185 inst]. A multidisciplinary information source presenting research about and applications for multimedia and hypermedia tools.

Journal of Research on Technology in Education. International Society for Technology in Education, 180 West 8th Ave., Suite 300, Eugene, OR 97401-2916. www.iste.org/jrte, tel: 800-336-5191, fax: 541-302-3778, iste@iste.org [4/year; $155]. Contains articles reporting on the latest research findings related to classroom and administrative uses of technology, including system and project evaluations.

Language Resources and Evaluation. Springer Science+Business Media, 333 Meadowlands Pkwy, Secaucus, NJ 07094. www.springer.com/journal/10579, tel: 800-777-4643, fax: 201-348-4505, journals-ny@springer.com [4/year; $708 inst (print + online), $849.60 inst (print + E-access, content through 1997)]. Contains papers on computer-aided studies, applications, automation, and computer-assisted instruction.

Learning and Leading with Technology. International Society for Technology in Education, 180 West 8th Ave., Suite 300, Eugene, OR 97401-2916. www.iste.org/LL, tel: 800-336-5191, fax: 541-302-3778, iste@iste.org [8/year; $100]. Focuses on the use of technology, coordination, and leadership; written by educators for educators. Appropriate for classroom teachers, lab teachers, technology coordinators, and teacher educators.

MacWorld. Mac Publishing, Macworld Subscription Services, P.O. Box 37781, Boone, IA 50037. www.macworld.com/magazine, tel: 800-288-6848, fax: 515-432-6994, subhelp@macworld.com [12/year; $19.97]. Describes hardware, software, tutorials, and applications for users of the Macintosh microcomputer.

OnCUE. Computer-Using Educators, Inc., 877 Ygnacio Valley Road, Suite 104, Walnut Creek, CA 94596. www.cue.org/oncue, tel: 925-478-3460, fax: 925-934-6799, cueinc@cue.org [4/year; free to CUE members, not sold separately]. Contains articles, news items, and trade advertisements addressing computer-based education.

PC Magazine. Ziff Davis Media Inc., 28 E 28th St, New York, NY 10016-7930. www.pcmag.com, tel: 212-503-3500, fax: 212-503-4399, pcmag@ziffdavis.com [12/year; $9.97]. Comparative reviews of computer hardware and general business software programs.

Social Science Computer Review. Sage Publications, 2455 Teller Rd, Thousand Oaks, CA 91320. ssc.sagepub.com, tel: 800-818-7243, fax: 800-583-2665, journals@sagepub.com [4/year; $118 indiv (print), $581 inst (online), $632 inst (print), $645 inst (print + online)]. Interdisciplinary peer-reviewed scholarly publication covering social science research and instructional applications in computing and telecommunications; also covers societal impacts of information technology.

Wireless Networks. Springer Science+Business Media, 333 Meadowlands Pkwy, Secaucus, NJ 07094. www.springer.com/journal/11276, tel: 800-777-4643, fax: 201-348-4505, journals-ny@springer.com [8/year; $728 inst (print + online), $873.60 inst (print + E-access, content through 1997)]. Devoted to the technological innovations that result from the mobility allowed by wireless technology.

Distance Education

American Journal of Distance Education. Taylor & Francis Group, Customer Services Dept, 325 Chestnut St, Suite 800, Philadelphia, PA 19106. www.tandf.co.uk/journals/titles/08923647, tel: 800-354-1420, fax: 215-625-2940, subscriptions@tandf.co.uk [4/year; $68 indiv, $249 inst (online), $262 inst (print + online)]. Created to disseminate information and act as a forum for criticism and debate about research on and practice of systems, management, and administration of distance education.

Journal of Distance Education. Canadian Network for Innovation in Education, BCIT Learning & Teaching Centre, British Columbia Institute of Technology, 3700 Willingdon Ave, Burnaby, BC, V5G 3H2, Canada. www.jofde.ca, tel: 604-454-2280, fax: 604-431-7267, journalofde@gmail.com [at least 2/year; $40 (print), free online]. Aims to promote and encourage scholarly work of empirical and theoretical nature relating to distance education in Canada and throughout the world.

Journal of Library & Information Services in Distance Learning. Taylor & Francis Group, Customer Service Dept, 325 Chestnut Street, Suite 800, Philadelphia, PA 19106. www.tandf.co.uk/journals/titles/1533290X, tel: 800-354-1420, fax: 215-625-2940, subscriptions@tandf.co.uk [4/year; $72 indiv, $150 inst (online), $190 inst (print + online)]. Contains peer-reviewed articles, essays, narratives, current events, and letters from distance learning and information science experts.

Journal of Research on Technology in Education. International Society for Technology in Education, 180 West 8th Ave., Suite 300, Eugene, OR 97401-2916. www.iste.org/jrte, tel: 800-336-5191, fax: 541-302-3778, iste@iste.org [4/year; $155]. Contains articles reporting on the latest research findings related to classroom and administrative uses of technology, including system and project evaluations.

Open Learning. Taylor & Francis Group, Customer Services Dept, 325 Chestnut St, Suite 800, Philadelphia, PA 19106. www.tandf.co.uk/journals/titles/02680513, tel: 800-354-1420, fax: 215-625-2940, subscriptions@tandf.co.uk [3/year; $104 indiv, $313 inst (online), $329 inst (print + online)]. Academic, scholarly publication on aspects of open and distance learning anywhere in the world. Includes issues for debate and research notes.

Educational Research

American Educational Research Journal. Sage Publications, 2455 Teller Rd, Thousand Oaks, CA 91320. aer.sagepub.com, tel: 800-818-7243, fax: 800-583-2665, journals@sagepub.com [4/year; $52 indiv (print + online), $278 inst (online), $303 inst (print), $309 inst (print + online)]. Reports original research, both empirical and theoretical, and brief synopses of research.

Educational Research. Taylor & Francis Group, Customer Services Dept, 325 Chestnut St, Suite 800, Philadelphia, PA 19106. www.tandf.co.uk/journals/titles/00131881, tel: 800-354-1420, fax: 215-625-2940, subscriptions@tandf.co.uk [4/year; $176 indiv, $494 inst (online), $520 inst (print + online)]. Reports on current educational research, evaluation, and applications.

Educational Researcher. Sage Publications, 2455 Teller Rd, Thousand Oaks, CA 91320. edr.sagepub.com, tel: 800-818-7243, fax: 800-583-2665, journals@sagepub.com [9/year; $52 indiv (print + online), $298 inst (online), $324 inst (print), $331 inst (print + online)]. Contains news and features of general significance in educational research.

Journal of Interactive Learning Research. Association for the Advancement of Computing in Education, P.O. Box 1545, Chesapeake, VA 23327-1545. www.aace.org/pubs/jilr, tel: 757-366-5606, fax: 703-997-8760, info@aace.org [4/year; $35 AACE student members, $115 AACE members (discount available for ordering multiple AACE journals), $185 inst]. Publishes articles on how intelligent computer technologies can be used in education to enhance learning and teaching. Reports on research and developments, integration, and applications of artificial intelligence in education.

Learning Technology. IEEE Computer Society, Technical Committee on Learning Technology. lttf.ieee.org/learn_tech, tel: (+30) 210-4142766, fax: (+30) 210-4142767, sampson@unipi.gr [4/year; free]. Online publication that reports developments, projects, conferences, and findings of the Learning Technology Task Force.

Meridian. North Carolina State University, College of Education, Poe Hall, Box 7801, Raleigh, NC 27695-7801. www.ncsu.edu/meridian, meridian_mail@ncsu.edu [2/year; free]. Online journal dedicated to research in middle school educational technology use.

Research in Science & Technological Education. Taylor & Francis Group, Customer Services Dept, 325 Chestnut St, Suite 800, Philadelphia, PA 19106. www.tandf.co.uk/journals/titles/02635143, tel: 800-354-1420, fax: 215-625-2940, subscriptions@tandf.co.uk [3/year; $333 indiv, $1,608 inst (online), $1,693 inst (print + online)]. Publication of original research in the science and technological fields. Includes articles on psychological, sociological, economic, and organizational aspects of technological education.

Educational Technology

Appropriate Technology. Research Information Ltd., Grenville Court, Britwell Rd, Burnham, Bucks, SL1 8DF, United Kingdom. www. researchinformation.co.uk/apte.php, tel: +44 (0) 1628 600499, fax: +44 (0) 1628 600488, info@researchinformation.co.uk [4/year; $315]. Articles on less technologically advanced, but more environmentally sustainable, solutions to problems in developing countries.

British Journal of Educational Technology. John Wiley & Sons, Inc., Journal Customer Services, 350 Main St, Malden, MA 02148. www. blackwellpublishing.com/journals/BJET, tel: 800-835-6770, fax: 781-388-8232, cs-agency@wiley.com [6/year; $194 indiv (print + online), $1,121 inst (print/online), $1,234 inst (print + online)]. Published by the National Council for Educational Technology, this journal includes articles on education and training, especially theory, applications, and development of educational technology and communications.

Canadian Journal of Learning and Technology. Canadian Network for Innovation in Education (CNIE), 260 Dalhousie St., Suite 204, Ottawa, ON, K1N 7E4, Canada. www.cjlt.ca, tel: 613-241-0018, fax: 613-241-0019, cjlt@ucalgary.ca [3/year; free]. Concerned with all aspects of educational systems and technology.

Educational Technology. Educational Technology Publications, Inc., 700 Palisade Ave, P.O. Box 1564, Englewood Cliffs, NJ 07632-0564. www.bookstoread.com/etp, tel: 800-952-2665, fax: 201-871-4009, edtecpubs@aol.com [6/year; $199]. Covers telecommunications, computer-aided instruction, information retrieval, educational television, and electronic media in the classroom.

Educational Technology Abstracts. Taylor & Francis Group, Customer Services Dept, 325 Chestnut St, Suite 800, Philadelphia, PA 19106. www. tandf.co.uk/journals/titles/02663368, tel: 800-354-1420, fax: 215-625-2940, subscriptions@tandf.co.uk [1/year; $600 indiv, $1,541 inst (online), $1,622 inst (print + online)]. An international publication of abstracts of recently published material in the field of educational and training technology.

Educational Technology Research & Development. Springer Science+Business Media, 333 Meadowlands Pkwy, Secaucus, NJ 07094. www.springer.com/journal/11423, tel: 800-777-4643, fax: 201-348-4505, journals-ny@springer.com [6/year; $320 inst (print + online), $384 inst (print + E-access, content through 1997)]. Focuses on research, instructional development, and applied theory in the field of educational technology.

International Journal of Technology and Design Education. Springer Science+Business Media, 333 Meadowlands Pkwy, Secaucus, NJ 07094. www.springer.com/journal/10798, tel: 800-777-4643, fax: 201-348-4505, journals-ny@springer.com [4/year; $376 inst (print + online), $451.20 inst (print + E-access, content through 1997)]. Publishes research reports and scholarly writing about aspects of technology and design education.

Journal of Computing in Higher Education. Springer Science+Business Media, 333 Meadowlands Pkwy, Secaucus, NJ 07094. www.springer.com/journal/12528, tel: 800-777-4643, fax: 201-348-4505, journals-ny@springer.com [3/year; $130 inst (print + online), $156 inst (print + E-access, content through 1997)]. Publishes scholarly essays, case studies, and research that discuss instructional technologies.

Journal of Educational Technology Systems. Baywood Publishing Co., Inc., 26 Austin Ave, Box 337, Amityville, NY 11701-0337. www.baywood. com/journals/previewjournals.asp?id=0047-2395, tel: 800-638-7819, fax: 631-691-1770, info@baywood.com [4/year; $345 inst (online), $364 (print + online)]. Deals with systems in which technology and education interface; designed to inform educators who are interested in making optimum use of technology.

Journal of Interactive Media in Education. Open University, Knowledge Media Institute, Milton Keynes MK7 6AA United Kingdom. www-jime.open.ac.uk, tel: +44 (0) 1908 653800, fax: +44 (0) 1908 653169, jime@open.ac.uk [irregular; free]. A multidisciplinary forum for debate and idea sharing concerning the practical aspects of interactive media and instructional technology.

Journal of Science Education and Technology. Springer Science+Business Media, 333 Meadowlands Pkwy, Secaucus, NJ 07094. www. springer.com/journal/10956, tel: 800-777-4643, fax: 201-348-4505, journals-ny@springer.com [6/year; $969 inst (print + online), $1,162.80 inst (print + E-access, content through 1997)]. Publishes studies aimed at improving science education at all levels in the United States.

MultiMedia & Internet@Schools. Information Today, Inc., 143 Old Marlton Pike, Medford, NJ 08055-8750. www.mmischools.com, tel: 609-654-6266, fax: 609-654-4309, custserv@infotoday.com [6/year; $19.95]. Reviews and evaluates hardware and software. Presents information pertaining to basic troubleshooting skills.

Science Communication. Sage Publications, 2455 Teller Rd, Thousand Oaks, CA 91320. scx.sagepub.com, tel: 800-818-7243, fax: 800-583-2665, journals@sagepub.com [4/year; $153 indiv (print), $683 inst (online), $744 inst (print), $759 inst (online + print)]. An international, interdisciplinary journal examining the nature of expertise and the translation of knowledge into practice and policy.

Social Science Computer Review. Sage Publications, 2455 Teller Rd, Thousand Oaks, CA 91320. ssc.sagepub.com, tel: 800-818-7243, fax: 800-583-2665, journals@sagepub.com [4/year; $118 indiv (print), $581 inst (online), $632 inst (print), $645 inst (online + print)]. Interdisciplinary peer-reviewed scholarly publication covering social science research and instructional applications in computing and telecommunications; also covers societal impacts of information technology.

TechTrends. Springer Science+Business Media, 333 Meadowlands Pkwy, Secaucus, NJ 07094. www.springer.com/journal/11528, tel: 800-777-4643, fax: 201-348-4505, journals-ny@springer.com [6/year; $114 inst (print + online), $136.80 inst (print + E-access, content through 1997)]. Targeted at leaders in education and training; features authoritative, practical articles about technology and its integration into the learning environment.

T.H.E. Journal. 1105 Media, P.O. Box 2170, Skokie, IL 60076. www.thejournal. com, tel: 866-293-3194, fax: 847-763-9564, THEJournal@1105service.com [12/year; $29, free to those in K-12, free online]. For educators of all levels; focuses on a specific topic for each issue, as well as technological innovations as they apply to education.

Information Science and Technology

Canadian Journal of Information and Library Science. University of Toronto Press, Journals Division, 5201 Dufferin St, Toronto, ON, M3H 5T8, Canada. www.utpjournals.com/cjils/cjils.html, tel: 416-667-7777, fax: 800-221-9985, journals@utpress.utoronto.ca [4/year; $75 indiv, $109 inst]. Published by the Canadian Association for Information Science to contribute to the advancement of library and information science in Canada.

EContent. Information Today, Inc., 143 Old Marlton Pike, Medford, NJ 08055-8750. www.econtentmag.com, tel: 609-654-6266, fax: 609-654-4309, custserv@infotoday.com [10/year; $119]. Features articles on topics of interest to online database users; includes database search aids.

Information Processing & Management. Elsevier, Inc., Customer Service Dept, 11830 Westline Industrial Drive, St. Louis, MO 63146. www. elsevier.com/locate/infoproman, tel: 877-839-7126, fax: 314-523-5153, journalcustomerservice-usa@elsevier.com [6/year; $325 indiv, $1,887 inst]. International journal covering data processing, database building, and retrieval.

Information Services & Use. IOS Press, Nieuwe Hemweg 6B, 1013 BG Amsterdam, The Netherlands. www.iospress.nl/html/01675265.php, tel: +31 20 688 3355, fax: +31 20 687 0039, info@iospress.nl [4/year; $135 indiv (online), $530 inst (online), $585 inst (print + online)]. An international journal for those in the information management field. Includes online and offline systems, library automation, micrographics, videotex, and telecommunications.

The Information Society. Taylor & Francis Group, Customer Services Dept, 325 Chestnut St, Suite 800, Philadelphia, PA 19106. www.tandf.co.uk/journals/titles/01972243, tel: 800-354-1420, fax: 215-625-2940, subscriptions@tandf.co.uk [5/year; $165 indiv, $427 inst (online), $449 inst (print + online)]. Provides a forum for discussion of the world of information, including transborder data flow, regulatory issues, and the impact of the information industry.

Information Technology and Libraries. American Library Association, Subscriptions, 50 E Huron St, Chicago, IL 60611-2795. www.lita.org/ala/mgrps/divs/lita/ital/italinformation.cfm, tel: 800-545-2433, fax: 312-944-2641, membership@ala.org [4/year; $65]. Articles on library automation, communication technology, cable systems, computerized information processing, and video technologies.

Information Today. Information Today, Inc., 143 Old Marlton Pike, Medford, NJ 08055-8750. www.infotoday.com/it, tel: 609-654-6266, fax: 609-654-4309, custserv@infotoday.com [11/year; $84.95]. Newspaper for users and producers of electronic information services. Includes articles and news about the industry, calendar of events, and product information.

Information Technology Management. IGI Global, 701 E Chocolate Ave, Suite 200, Hershey, PA 17033-1240. www.igi-pub.com/journals/details.asp?id=200, tel: 866-342-6657, fax: 717-533-8661, cust@igi-global.com [2/year; $70 indiv, $90 inst]. Designed for library information specialists, this bi-annual newsletter presents current issues and trends in information technology presented by and for specialists in the field.

Internet Reference Service Quarterly. Taylor & Francis Group, Customer Services Dept, 325 Chestnut St, Suite 800, Philadelphia, PA 19106. www.tandf.co.uk/journals/WIRS, tel: 800-354-1420, fax: 215-625-2940, subscriptions@tandf.co.uk [4/year; $81 indiv, $199 inst (online), $209 inst (print + online)]. Discusses multidisciplinary aspects of incorporating the Internet as a tool for reference service.

Journal of Access Services. Taylor & Francis Group, Customer Services Dept, 325 Chestnut St, Suite 800, Philadelphia, PA 19106. http://www.tandf.co.uk/journals/WJAS, tel: 800-354-1420, fax: 215-625-2940, subscriptions@tandf.co.uk [4/year; $76 indiv, $199 inst (online), $209 inst (print + online)]. Explores topics and issues surrounding the organization, administration, and development of information technology on access services and resources.

Journal of the American Society for Information Science and Technology. John Wiley & Sons, Inc., Journal Customer Services, 350 Main St, Malden, MA 02148. www3.interscience.wiley.com/journal/117946195/grouphome/home.html, tel: 800-835-6770, fax: 781-388-8232, cs-agency@wiley.com [12/year; $2,199 inst (print), $2,419 inst (print + online)]. Provides an overall forum for new research in information transfer and communication processes, with particular attention paid to the context of recorded knowledge.

Journal of Database Management. IGI Global, 701 E Chocolate Ave, Suite 200, Hershey, PA 17033-1240. www.idea-group.com/journals/details.asp?id=198, tel: 866-342-6657, fax: 717-533-8661, cust@igi-global.com [4/year; $1,125 inst (online), $750 inst (print), $1,500 inst (print + online)]. Provides state-of-the-art research to those who design, develop, and administer DBMS-based information systems.

Journal of Documentation. Emerald Group Publishing Limited, One Mifflin Place Suite 400 Harvard Square, Cambridge, MA 02138. www.emeraldinsight.com/jd.htm, tel: 888-622-0075, fax: 617-354-6875, america@emeraldinsight.com [6/year; $1,019]. Focuses on theories, concepts, models, frameworks, and philosophies in the information sciences.

Journal of Library Metadata. Taylor & Francis Group, Customer Services Dept, 325 Chestnut St, Suite 800, Philadelphia, PA 19106. www.tandf.co.uk/journals/titles/19386389, tel: 800-354-1420, fax: 215-625-2940, subscriptions@tandf.co.uk [4/year; $79 indiv, $236 inst (online), $248 inst (print + online)]. A forum for the latest research, innovations, news, and expert views about all aspects of metadata applications and information retrieval in libraries.

Resource Sharing & Information Networks. Taylor & Francis Group, Customer Services Dept, 325 Chestnut St, Suite 800, Philadelphia, PA 19106. www.tandf.co.uk/journals/WRSI, tel: 800-354-1420, fax: 215-625-2940, subscriptions@tandf.co.uk [4/year; $74 indiv, $290 inst (online), $330 inst (print + online)]. A forum for ideas on the basic theoretical and practical problems faced by planners, practitioners, and users of network services.

Instructional Design and Development

Human–Computer Interaction. Taylor & Francis Group, Customer Services Dept, 325 Chestnut St, Suite 800, Philadelphia, PA 19106. www. tandf.co.uk/journals/titles/07370024, tel: 800-354-1420, fax: 215-625-2940, subscriptions@tandf.co.uk [4/year; $73 indiv, $626 inst (online), $659 institution (print + online)]. A journal of theoretical, empirical, and methodological issues of user science and of system design.

Instructional Science. Springer Science+Business Media, 333 Meadowlands Pkwy, Secaucus, NJ 07094. www.springer.com/journal/11251, tel: 800-777-4643, fax: 201-348-4505, journals-ny@springer.com [6/year; $696 inst (print + online), $835.20 inst (print + E-access, content through 1997)]. Promotes a deeper understanding of the nature, theory, and practice of the instructional process and the learning resulting from this process.

International Journal of Human–Computer Interaction. Taylor & Francis Group, Customer Services Dept, 325 Chestnut St, Suite 800, Philadelphia, PA 19106. www.tandf.co.uk/journals/titles/10447318, tel: 800-354-1420, fax: 215-625-2940, subscriptions@tandf.co.uk [6/year; $117 indiv, $951 inst (online), $1,001 inst (print + online)]. Addresses the cognitive, social, health, and ergonomic aspects of work with computers. It also emphasizes both the human and computer science aspects of the effective design and use of computer interactive systems.

Journal of Educational Technology Systems. Baywood Publishing Co., Inc., 26 Austin Ave, Box 337, Amityville, NY 11701-0337. www.baywood.com/journals/previewjournals.asp?id=0047-2395, tel: 800-638-7819, fax: 631-691-1770, info@baywood.com [4/year; $345 inst (online), $364 inst (print + online)]. Deals with systems in which technology and education interface; designed to inform educators who are interested in making optimum use of technology.

Journal of Instructional Delivery Systems. Learning Technology Institute, 50 Culpeper St, Warrenton, VA 20186. www.salt.org/salt.asp?ss=l&pn=jids, tel: 540-347-0055, fax: 540-349-3169, info@lti.org [4/year; $45 indiv, $40 lib]. Devoted to the issues, problems, and applications of instructional delivery systems in education, training, and job performance.

Journal of Interactive Instruction Development. Learning Technology Institute, 50 Culpeper St, Warrenton, VA 20186. www.salt.org/salt.asp?ss=l&pn=jiid, tel: 540-347-0055, fax: 540-349-3169, jiid@lti.org [4/year; $45 indiv, $40 lib]. A showcase of successful programs that will heighten awareness of innovative, creative, and effective approaches to courseware development for interactive technology.

Journal of Technical Writing and Communication. Baywood Publishing Co., Inc., 26 Austin Ave, Box 337, Amityville, NY 11701-0337. www. baywood.com/journals/previewjournals.asp?id=0047-2816, tel: 800-638-7819, fax: 631-691-1770, info@baywood.com [4/year; $97 indiv (online), $102 indiv (print + online), $345 inst (online), $364 inst (print + online)]. Essays on oral and written communication, for purposes ranging from pure research to needs of business and industry.

Journal of Visual Literacy. International Visual Literacy Association, Dr. Constance L. Cassity, IVLA Executive Treasurer, Northeastern State University, 3100 E New Orleans St, Broken Arrow, OK 74014. plato.ou.edu/~jvl, tel: 918-449-6511, cassityc@nsuok.edu [2/year; $30 student, $60 indiv]. Explores empirical, theoretical, practical, and applied aspects of visual literacy and communication.

Performance Improvement. John Wiley & Sons, Inc., Journal Customer Services, 350 Main St, Malden, MA 02148. www3.interscience. wiley.com/journal/117946259/grouphome/home.html, tel: 800-835-6770, fax: 781-388-8232, cs-agency@wiley.com [10/year; $75 indiv, $299 inst]. Promotes performance science and technology. Contains articles, research, and case studies relating to improving human performance.

Performance Improvement Quarterly. John Wiley & Sons, Inc., Journal Customer Services, 350 Main St, Malden, MA 02148. www3.interscience. wiley.com/journal/117865970/home, tel: 800-835-6770, fax: 781-388-8232, cs-agency@wiley.com [4/year; $60 indiv, $150 inst]. Presents the cutting edge in research and theory in performance technology.

Training. Nielsen Business Media, Customer Service, PO Box 3601, Northbrook, IL 60065-3601. www.trainingmag.com, tel: 800-697-8859, fax: 847-291-4816, ninc@omeda.com [12/year; $79]. Covers all aspects of training, management, and organizational development, motivation, and performance improvement.

Learning Sciences

International Journal of Computer-Supported Collaborative Learning. Springer Science+Business Media, 333 Meadowlands Pkwy, Secaucus, NJ 07094. www.springer.com/journal/11412, tel: 800-777-4643, fax: 201-348-4505, journals-ny@springer.com [6/year; $385 inst (print + online), $462 inst (print + E-access, content through 1997)]. Promotes a deeper understanding of the nature, theory, and practice of the uses of computer-supported collaborative learning.

Journal of the Learning Sciences. Taylor & Francis Group, Customer Services Dept, 325 Chestnut St, Suite 800, Philadelphia, PA 19106.

www.tandf.co.uk/journals/titles/10508406, tel: 800-354-1420, fax: 215-625-2940, subscriptions@tandf.co.uk [4/year; $68 indiv, $653 inst (online), $687 inst (print + online)]. Provides a forum for the discussion of research on education and learning, with emphasis on the idea of changing one's understanding of learning and the practice of education.

Libraries and Media Centers

Collection Building. Emerald Group Publishing Limited, One Mifflin Place Suite 400 Harvard Square, Cambridge, MA 02138. www.emeraldinsight.com/cb.htm, tel: 888-622-0075, fax: 617-354-6875, america@emeraldinsight.com [4/year; $1,639]. Provides well-researched and authoritative information on collection, maintenance, and development for librarians in all sectors.

Computers in Libraries. Information Today, Inc., 143 Old Marlton Pike, Medford, NJ 08055-8750. www.infotoday.com/cilmag/default.shtml, tel: 609-654-6266, fax: 609-654-4309, custserv@infotoday.com [10/year; $99.95]. Covers practical applications of microcomputers to library situations and recent news items.

The Electronic Library. Emerald Group Publishing Limited, One Mifflin Place Suite 400 Harvard Square, Cambridge, MA 02138. info.emeraldinsight.com/products/journals/journals.htm?id=el, tel: 888-622-0075, fax: 617-354-6875, america@emeraldinsight.com [6/year; $739]. International journal for minicomputer, microcomputer, and software applications in libraries; independently assesses current and forthcoming information technologies.

Government Information Quarterly. Elsevier, Inc., Customer Service Dept, 11830 Westline Industrial Drive, St. Louis, MO 63146. www.elsevier.com/locate/govinf, tel: 877-839-7126, fax: 314-523-5153, journalcustomerservice-usa@elsevier.com [4/year; $172 indiv, $556 inst]. International journal of resources, services, policies, and practices.

Information Outlook. Special Libraries Association, Information Outlook Subscriptions, 331 S Patrick St, Alexandria, VA 22314-3501. www.sla.org/io, tel: 703-647-4900, fax: 703-647-4901, shales@sla.org [12/year; $160]. Discusses administration, organization, and operations. Includes reports on research, technology, and professional standards.

The Journal of Academic Librarianship. Elsevier, Inc., Customer Service Dept, 11830 Westline Industrial Drive, St. Louis, MO 63146. www.elsevier.com/locate/jacalib, tel: 877-839-7126, fax: 314-523-5153, journalcustomerservice-usa@elsevier.com [6/year; $123 indiv, $338 inst]. Results of significant research, issues, and problems facing academic libraries, book reviews, and innovations in academic libraries.

Journal of Librarianship and Information Science. Sage Publications, 2455 Teller Rd, Thousand Oaks, CA 91320. lis.sagepub.com, tel: 800-818-7243, fax: 800-583-2665, journals@sagepub.com [4/year; $93 indiv (print), $576 inst (online), $627 inst (print), $640 inst (print + online)]. Deals with all aspects of library and information work in the United Kingdom and reviews literature from international sources.

Journal of Library Administration. Taylor & Francis Group, Customer Services Dept, 325 Chestnut St, Suite 800, Philadelphia, PA 19106. www. haworthpress.com/web/JLA, tel: 800-354-1420, fax: 215-625-2940, subscriptions@tandf.co.uk [8/year; $202 indiv, $737 inst (online), $776 inst (print + online)]. Provides information on all aspects of effective library management, with emphasis on practical applications.

Library & Information Science Research. Elsevier, Inc., Customer Service Dept, 11830 Westline Industrial Drive, St. Louis, MO 63146. www. elsevier.com/locate/lisres, tel: 877-839-7126, fax: 314-523-5153, journalcustomerservice-usa@elsevier.com [4/year; $145 indiv, $422 inst]. Research articles, dissertation reviews, and book reviews on issues concerning information resources management.

Library Hi Tech. Emerald Group Publishing Limited, One Mifflin Place Suite 400 Harvard Square, Cambridge, MA 02138. www. emeraldinsight.com/lht.htm, tel: 888-622-0075, fax: 617-354-6875, america@emeraldinsight.com [4/year; $469]. Concentrates on reporting on the selection, installation, maintenance, and integration of systems and hardware.

Library Hi Tech News. Emerald Group Publishing Limited, One Mifflin Place Suite 400 Harvard Square, Cambridge, MA 02138. www.emeraldinsight.com/lhtn.htm, tel: 888-622-0075, fax: 617-354-6875, america@emeraldinsight.com [10/year; $599]. Supplements Library Hi Tech and updates many of the issues addressed in depth in the journal; keeps the reader fully informed of the latest developments in library automation, new products, network news, new software and hardware, and people in technology.

Library Journal. Reed Business Information, 360 Park Avenue South, New York, NY 10010. www.libraryjournal.com, tel: 800-588-1030, fax: 712-733-8019, LJLcustserv@cds-global.com [23/year; $157.99]. A professional periodical for librarians, with current issues and news, professional reading, a lengthy book review section, and classified advertisements.

Library Media Connection. Linworth Publishing, Inc., P.O. Box 204, Vandalia, OH 45377. www.linworth.com/lmc, tel: 800-607-4410, fax: 937-890-0221, linworth@linworthpublishing.com [7/year; $69]. Journal for junior and senior high school librarians; provides articles, tips, and ideas for day-to-day school library management, as well as reviews of audiovisuals and software, all written by school librarians.

The Library Quarterly. University of Chicago Press, Journals Division, Journals Division, P.O. Box 37005, Chicago, IL 60637. www.journals.uchicago.edu/LQ, tel: 877-705-1878, fax: 877-705-1879, subscriptions@press.uchicago.edu [$26 students (online), $45 indiv (print), $44 indiv (online), $49 indiv (print + online), inst prices vary]. Scholarly articles of interest to librarians.

Library Collections & Technical Services. American Library Association, Subscriptions, 50 E Huron St, Chicago, IL 60611-2795. www.ala.org/ala/ alcts/alcts.cfm, tel: 800-545-2433, fax: 312-944-2641, membership@ala.org [4/year; $75]. Scholarly papers on bibliographic access and control, preservation, conservation, and reproduction of library materials.

Library Trends. Johns Hopkins University Press, P.O. Box 19966, Baltimore, MD 21211-0966. www.press.jhu.edu/journals/library_trends, tel: 800-548-1784, fax: 410-516-3866, jrnlcirc@press.jhu.edu [4/year; $80 indiv (print/online), $135 inst (print)]. Each issue is concerned with one aspect of library and information science, analyzing current thought and practice and examining ideas that hold the greatest potential for the field.

Public Libraries. American Library Association, Subscriptions, 50 E Huron St, Chicago, IL 60611-2795. www.ala.org/ala/mgrps/divs/pla/ plapublications/publiclibraries/index.cfm, tel: 800-545-2433, fax: 312-944-2641, membership@ala.org [6/year; $50]. News and articles of interest to public librarians.

Public Library Quarterly. Taylor & Francis Group, Customer Services Dept, 325 Chestnut St, Suite 800, Philadelphia, PA 19106. www.tandf.co.uk/journals/WPLQ, tel: 800-354-1420, fax: 215-625-2940, subscriptions@tandf.co.uk [4/year; $109 indiv, $340 inst (online), $358 inst (print + online)]. Addresses the major administrative challenges and opportunities that face the nation's public libraries.

Reference and User Services Quarterly. American Library Association, Subscriptions, 50 E Huron St, Chicago, IL 60611-2795. rusq.org, tel: 800-545-2433, fax: 312-944-2641, membership@ala.org [4/year; $33 student, $65 indiv]. Disseminates information of interest to reference librarians, bibliographers, adult services librarians, those in collection development and selection, and others interested in public services.

The Reference Librarian. Taylor & Francis Group, Customer Services Dept, 325 Chestnut St, Suite 800, Philadelphia, PA 19106. www.tandf.co.uk/journals/WREF, tel: 800-354-1420, fax: 215-625-2940, subscriptions@tandf.co.uk [4/year; $240 indiv, $982 inst (online), $1,034 inst (print + online)]. Each issue focuses on a topic of current concern, interest, or practical value to reference librarians.

Reference Services Review. Emerald Group Publishing Limited, One Mifflin Place Suite 400 Harvard Square, Cambridge, MA 02138. www. emeraldinsight.com/rsr.htm, tel: 888-622-0075, fax: 617-354-6875, america@emeraldinsight.com [4/year; $499]. Dedicated to the enrichment of reference knowledge and the advancement of reference services. It prepares its readers to understand and embrace current and emerging technologies affecting reference functions and information needs of library users.

School Library Journal. Reed Business Information, 360 Park Avenue South, New York, NY 10010. www.slj.com, tel: 800-595-1066, fax: 712-733-8019, sljcustserv@cds-global.com [15/year; $136.99]. For school and youth service librarians. Reviews about 4,000 children's books and 1,000 educational media titles annually.

School Library Media Activities Monthly. Libraries Unlimited, Inc., P.O. Box 1911, Santa Barbara, CA 93116-1911. www.schoollibrarymedia.com, tel: 800-368-6868 ext. 550, fax: 805-270-3858, dlevitov@abc-clio.com [10/year; $55]. A vehicle for distributing ideas for teaching library media skills and for the development and implementation of library media skills programs.

School Library Media Research. American Library Association and American Association of School Librarians, Subscriptions, 50 E Huron St, Chicago, IL 60611-2795. www.ala.org/ala/aasl/aaslpubsandjournals/slmrb/schoollibrary.cfm, tel: 800-545-2433, fax: 312-944-2641, membership@ala.org [annual compilation; free online]. For library media specialists, district supervisors, and others concerned with the selection and purchase of print and nonprint media and with the development of programs and services for preschool through high school libraries.

Teacher Librarian. The Scarecrow Press, Inc., 4501 Forbes Blvd, Suite 200, Lanham, MD 20706. www.teacherlibrarian.com, tel: 800-462-6420, fax: 800-338-4550, admin@teacherlibrarian.com [5/year; $56 prepaid, $61 billed]. "The journal for school library professionals"; previously known as Emergency Librarian. Articles, review columns, and critical analyses of management and programming issues.

Media Technologies

Broadcasting & Cable. Reed Business Information, 360 Park Avenue South, New York, NY 10010. www.broadcastingcable.com, tel: 800-554-5729, fax: 712-733-8019, bcbcustserv@cdsfulfillment.com [47/year; $214.99]. All-inclusive newsweekly for radio, television, cable, and allied business.

Communication Abstracts. Sage Publications, 2455 Teller Rd, Thousand Oaks, CA 91320. www.sagepub.com/journalsProdDesc.nav?prodId=Journal200918, tel: 800-818-7243, fax: 800-583-2665, journals@sagepub.com [6/year; $343 indiv (print), $1,682 inst (print)]. Abstracts communication-related articles, reports, and books. Cumulated annually.

Educational Media International. Taylor & Francis Group, Customer Services Dept, 325 Chestnut St, Suite 800, Philadelphia, PA 19106. www.tandf.co.uk/journals/titles/09523987, tel: 800-354-1420, fax: 215-625-2940, subscriptions@tandf.co.uk [4/year; $129 indiv, $483 inst (online), $508 inst (print + online)]. The official journal of the International Council for Educational Media.

Historical Journal of Film, Radio and Television. Taylor & Francis Group, Customer Services Dept, 325 Chestnut St, Suite 800, Philadelphia, PA 19106. www.tandf.co.uk/journals/titles/01439685, tel: 800-354-1420, fax: 215-625-2940, subscriptions@tandf.co.uk [4/year; $379 indiv, $1,035 inst (online), $1,089 inst (print + online)]. Articles by international experts in the field, news and notices, and book reviews concerning the impact of mass communications on political and social history of the 20th century.

International Journal of Instructional Media. Westwood Press, Inc., 118 5 Mile River Rd, Darien, CT 06820-6237. www.adprima.com/ijim.htm, tel: 203-656-8680, fax: 212-353-8291, PLSleeman@aol.com [4/year; $181.20]. Focuses on quality research on ongoing programs in instructional media for education, distance learning, computer technology, instructional media and technology, telecommunications, interactive video, management, media research and evaluation, and utilization.

Journal of Educational Multimedia and Hypermedia. Association for the Advancement of Computing in Education, P.O. Box 1545, Chesapeake, VA 23327-1545. www.aace.org/pubs/jemh, tel: 757-366-5606, fax: 703-997-8760, info@aace.org [4/year; $35 for AACE student members, $115 AACE members (discount available for ordering multiple AACE journals), $185 inst]. A multidisciplinary information source presenting research about and applications for multimedia and hypermedia tools.

Journal of Popular Film and Television. Heldref Publications, 1319 18th St NW, Washington, DC 20036-1802. http://www.heldref.org/pubs/jpft/about.html, tel: 866-802-7059, fax: 205-995-1588, heldref@subscriptionoffice.com [4/year; $58 indiv (online), $61 (print + online), $139 inst (print/online), $167 (print + online)]. Articles on film and television, book reviews, and theory. Dedicated to popular film and television in the broadest sense. Concentrates on commercial cinema and television, film and television theory or criticism, filmographies, and bibliographies. Edited at the College of Arts and Sciences of Northern Michigan University and the Department of Popular Culture, Bowling Green State University.

Learning, Media & Technology. Taylor & Francis Group, Customer Services Dept, 325 Chestnut St, Suite 800, Philadelphia, PA 19106. www.tandf.co.uk/journals/titles/17439884, tel: 800-354-1420, fax: 215-625-2940, subscriptions@tandf.co.uk [4/year; $424 indiv, $1,509 inst (online), $1,588 inst (print + online)]. This journal of the Educational Television Association serves as an international forum for discussions and reports on developments in the field of television and related media in teaching, learning, and training.

Media & Methods. American Society of Educators, 1429 Walnut St, Philadelphia, PA 19102. www.media-methods.com, tel: 215-563-6005, fax: 215-587-9706, info@media-methods.com [5/year; $35]. The only magazine published for the elementary school library media and technology specialist. A forum for K-12 educators who use technology as an educational resource, this journal includes information on what works and what does not, new product reviews, tips and pointers, and emerging technologies.

Multichannel News. Reed Business Information, 360 Park Avenue South, New York, NY 10010. www.multichannel.com, tel: 888-343-5563, fax: 712-733-8019, mulcustserv@cdsfulfillment.com [51/year; $169.99]. A newsmagazine for the cable television industry. Covers programming, marketing, advertising, business, and other topics.

MultiMedia & Internet@Schools. Information Today, Inc., 143 Old Marlton Pike, Medford, NJ 08055-8750. www.mmischools.com, tel: 609-654-6266, fax: 609-654-4309, custserv@infotoday.com [6/year; $19.95]. Reviews and evaluates hardware and software. Presents information pertaining to basic troubleshooting skills

Multimedia Systems. Springer Science+Business Media, 333 Meadowlands Pkwy, Secaucus, NJ 07094. www.springer.com/journal/00530, tel: 800-777-4643, fax: 201-348-4505, journals-ny@springer.com [6/year; $622 inst (print + online), $746.40 inst (print + E-access, content through 1997)]. Publishes original research articles and serves as a forum for stimulating and disseminating innovative research ideas, emerging technologies, state-of-the-art methods and tools in all aspects of multimedia computing, communication, storage, and applications among researchers, engineers, and practitioners.

Telematics and Informatics. Elsevier, Inc., Customer Service Dept, 11830 Westline Industrial Drive, St. Louis, MO 63146. www.elsevier.com/locate/tele, tel: 877-839-7126, fax: 314-523-5153, journalcustomerservice-usa@elsevier.com [4/year; $136 indiv, $1,227 inst]. Publishes research and review articles in applied telecommunications and information sciences in business, industry, government, and educational establishments. Focuses on important current technologies, including microelectronics, computer graphics, speech synthesis and voice recognition, database management, data encryption, satellite television, artificial intelligence, and the ongoing computer revolution.

Professional Development

Journal of Computing in Teacher Education. International Society for Technology in Education, Special Interest Group for Teacher Educators, 180 West 8th Ave., Suite 300, Eugene, OR 97401. www.iste.org/jcte, tel: 800-336-5191, fax: 541-302-3778, iste@iste.org [4/year; $122]. Contains refereed articles on preservice and inservice training, research in computer education and certification issues, and reviews of training materials and texts.

Journal of Technology and Teacher Education. Association for the Advancement of Computing in Education, P.O. Box 1545, Chesapeake, VA 23327-1545. www.aace.org/pubs/jtate, tel: 757-366-5606, fax: 703-997-8760, info@aace.org [4/year; $35 AACE student members, $115 AACE members (discount available for ordering multiple AACE journals), $185 inst]. Serves as an international forum to report research and applications of technology in preservice, inservice, and graduate teacher education.

Simulation, Gaming, and Virtual Reality

Simulation & Gaming. Sage Publications, 2455 Teller Rd, Thousand Oaks, CA 91320. sag.sagepub.com, tel: 800-818-7243, fax: 800-583-2665, journals@sagepub.com [4/year; $135 indiv (print), $905 inst (online), $985 inst (print), $1,005 inst (print + online)]. An international journal of theory, design, and research focusing on issues in simulation, gaming, modeling, role-playing, and experiential learning.

Special Education and Disabilities

Journal of Special Education Technology. Council for Exceptional Children, Technology and Media Division, 1110 N. Glebe Road, Arlington, VA 22201-5704. www.tamcec.org/jset/index.htm, tel: 405-325-1533, fax: 405-325-7661, jset@ou.edu [4/year; $69 indiv, $149 inst]. Provides information, research, and reports of innovative practices regarding the application of educational technology toward the education of exceptional children.

Telecommunications and Networking

Canadian Journal of Learning and Technology. Canadian Network for Innovation in Education (CNIE), 260 Dalhousie St., Suite 204, Ottawa, ON, K1N 7E4, Canada. www.cjlt.ca, tel: 613-241-0018, fax: 613-241-0019, cjlt@ucalgary.ca [3/year; free]. Concerned with all aspects of educational systems and technology.

Computer Communications. Elsevier, Inc., Customer Service Dept, 11830 Westline Industrial Drive, St. Louis, MO 63146. www.elsevier.com/locate/comcom, tel: 877-839-7126, fax: 314-523-5153, journalcustomerservice-usa@elsevier.com [18/year; $2,009 inst]. Focuses on networking and distributed computing techniques, communications hardware and software, and standardization.

EDUCAUSE Review. EDUCAUSE, 4772 Walnut St, Suite 206, Boulder, CO 80301-2536. www.educause.edu/er, tel: 303-449-4430, fax: 303-440-0461, ersubs@educause.edu [6/year; $30]. Features articles on current issues and applications of computing and communications technology in higher education. Reports on EDUCAUSE consortium activities.

International Journal on E-Learning. Association for the Advancement of Computing in Education, P.O. Box 1545, Chesapeake, VA 23327-1545. www.aace.org/pubs/ijel, tel: 757-366-5606, fax: 703-997-8760, info@aace.org [4/year; $35 AACE student members, $115 AACE members (discount available for ordering multiple AACE journals), $185 inst]. Reports on current theory, research, development, and practice of telecommunications in education at all levels.

The Internet and Higher Education. Elsevier, Inc., Customer Service Dept, 11830 Westline Industrial Drive, St. Louis, MO 63146. www.elsevier.com/locate/iheduc, tel: 877-839-7126, fax: 314-523-5153, journalcustomerservice-usa@elsevier.com [4/year; $70 indiv, $366 inst]. Designed to reach faculty, staff, and administrators responsible for enhancing instructional practices and productivity via the use of information technology and the Internet in their institutions.

Internet Reference Services Quarterly. Taylor & Francis Group, Customer Services Dept, 325 Chestnut St, Suite 800, Philadelphia, PA 19106. www.tandf.co.uk/journals/titles/10875301, tel: 800-354-1420, fax: 215-625-2940, subscriptions@tandf.co.uk [4/year; $81 indiv, $199 inst (online), $209 inst (print + online)]. Describes innovative information practice, technologies, and practice. For librarians of all kinds.

Internet Research. Emerald Group Publishing Limited, One Mifflin Place Suite 400 Harvard Square, Cambridge, MA 02138. www.emeraldinsight.com/intr.htm, tel: 888-622-0075, fax: 617-354-6875, america@emeraldinsight.com [5/year; $2,929]. A cross-disciplinary journal presenting research findings related to electronic networks, analyses of policy issues related to networking, and descriptions of current and potential applications of electronic networking for communication, computation, and provision of information services.

Online. Information Today, Inc., 143 Old Marlton Pike, Medford, NJ 08055-8750. www.infotoday.com/online, tel: 609-654-6266, fax: 609-654-4309, custserv@infotoday.com [6/year; $124.95]. For online information system users. Articles cover a variety of online applications for general and business use.

Index

M. Orey et al. (eds.), *Educational Media and Technology Yearbook*,
Educational Media and Technology Yearbook 35,
DOI 10.1007/978-1-4419-1516-0, © Springer Science+Business Media, LLC 2010

CPSIA information can be obtained at www.ICGtesting.com

233580LV00003B/56/P

9 781441 915023